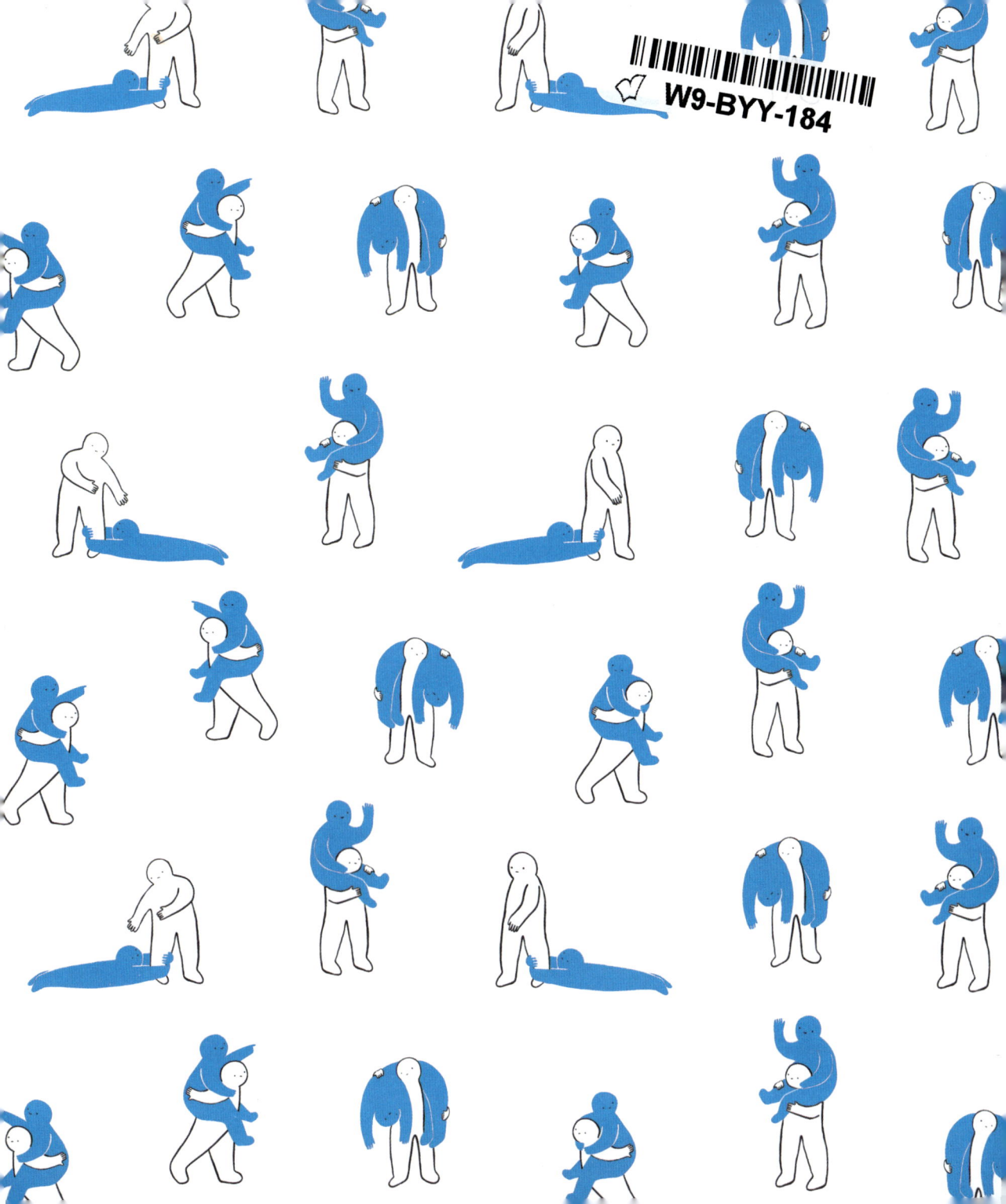

W9-BYY-184

THIS BOOK IS FOR YOU

(I HOPE YOU FIND IT MILDLY UPLIFTING)

BY WORRY LINES

TEN SPEED PRESS
CALIFORNIA | NEW YORK

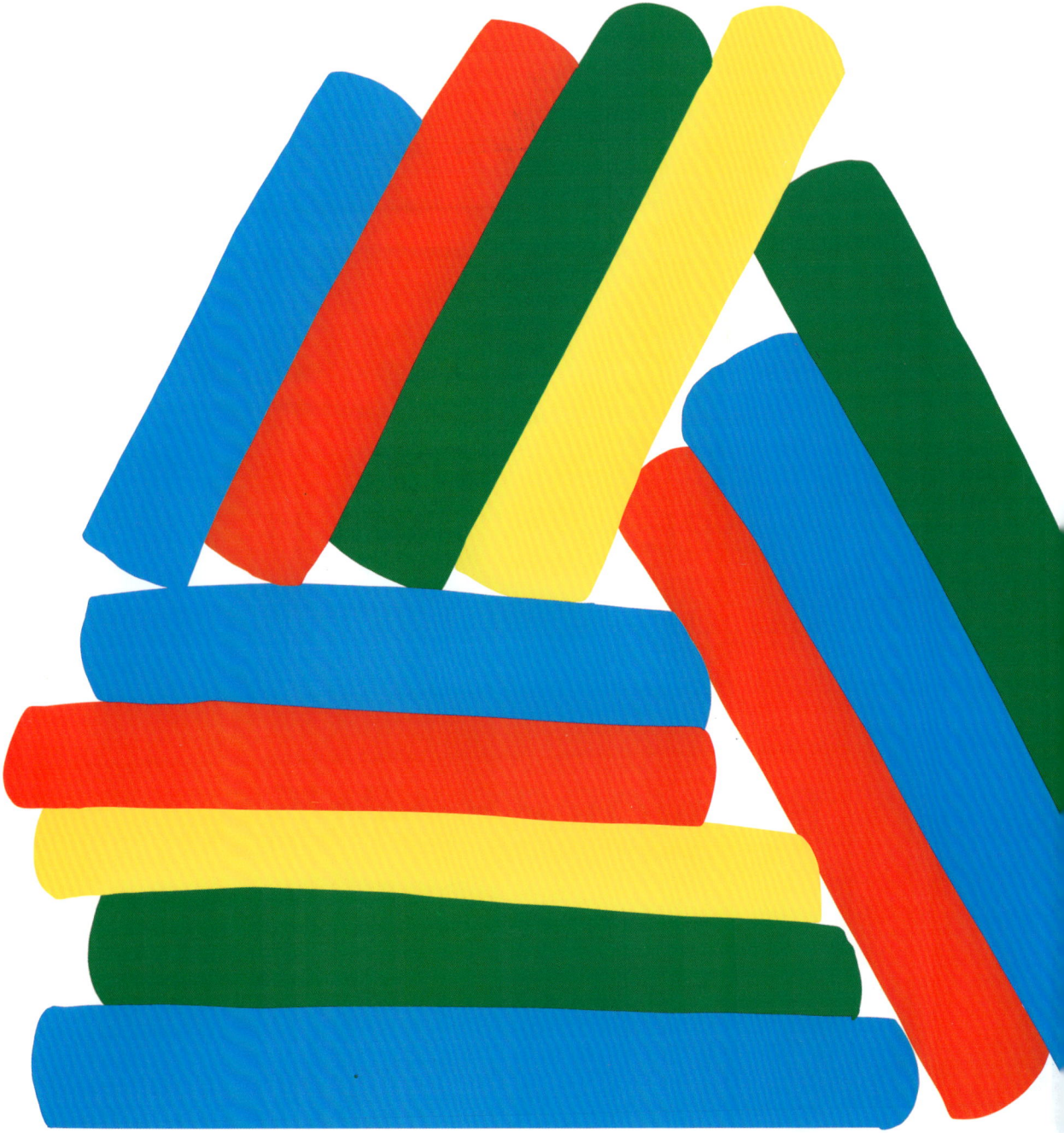

CONTENTS

A NOTE FROM THE AUTHOR 8

DEDICATION IDEAS 31

DRAWINGS ABOUT THOUGHTS 53

DRAWINGS ABOUT FEELINGS 75

DRAWINGS ABOUT WORRY 93

DRAWINGS ABOUT EMPATHY 137

DRAWINGS ABOUT LOVE 163

DRAWINGS ABOUT HOPE 181

THIS IS ME

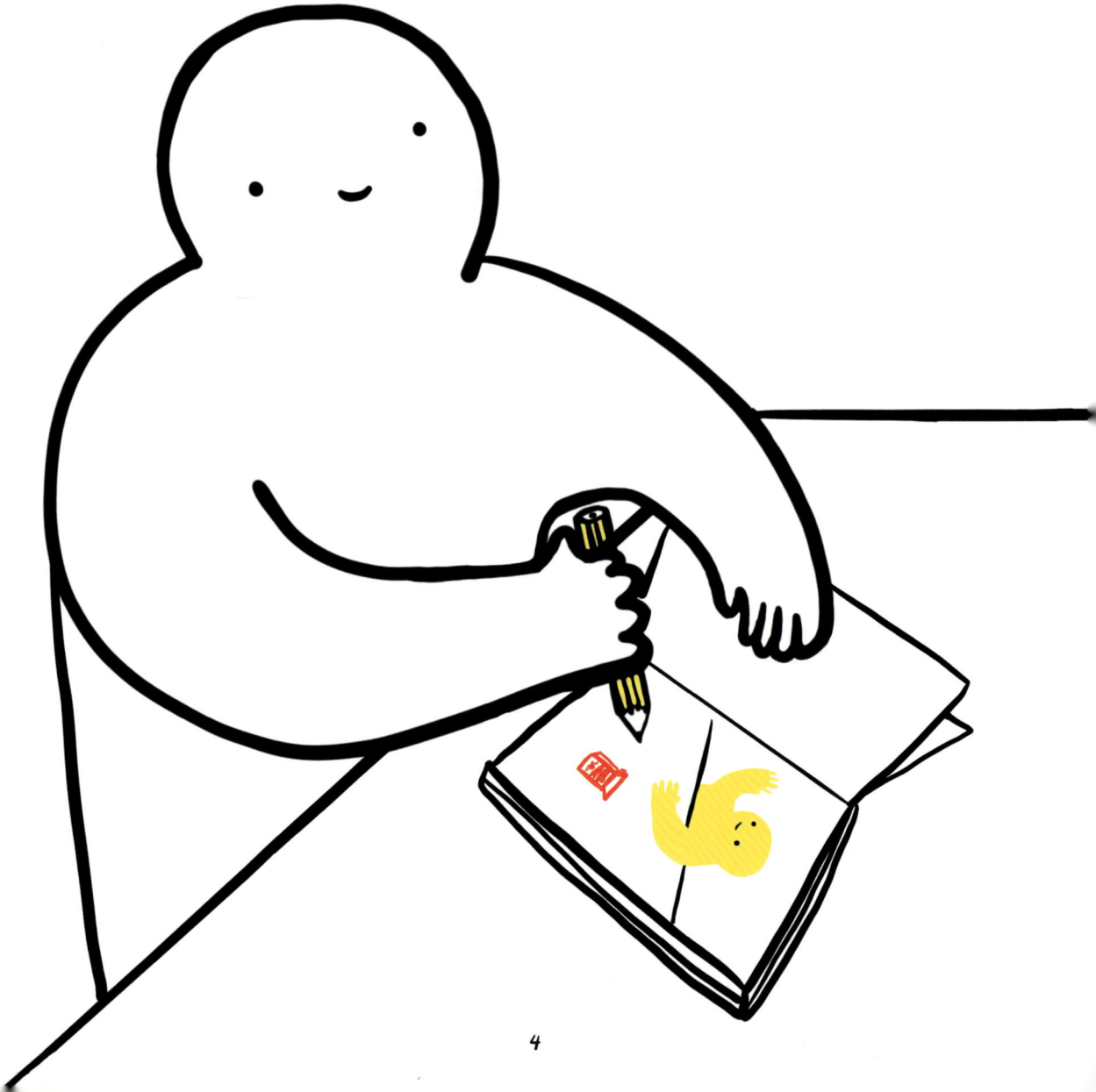

THIS IS HOPE

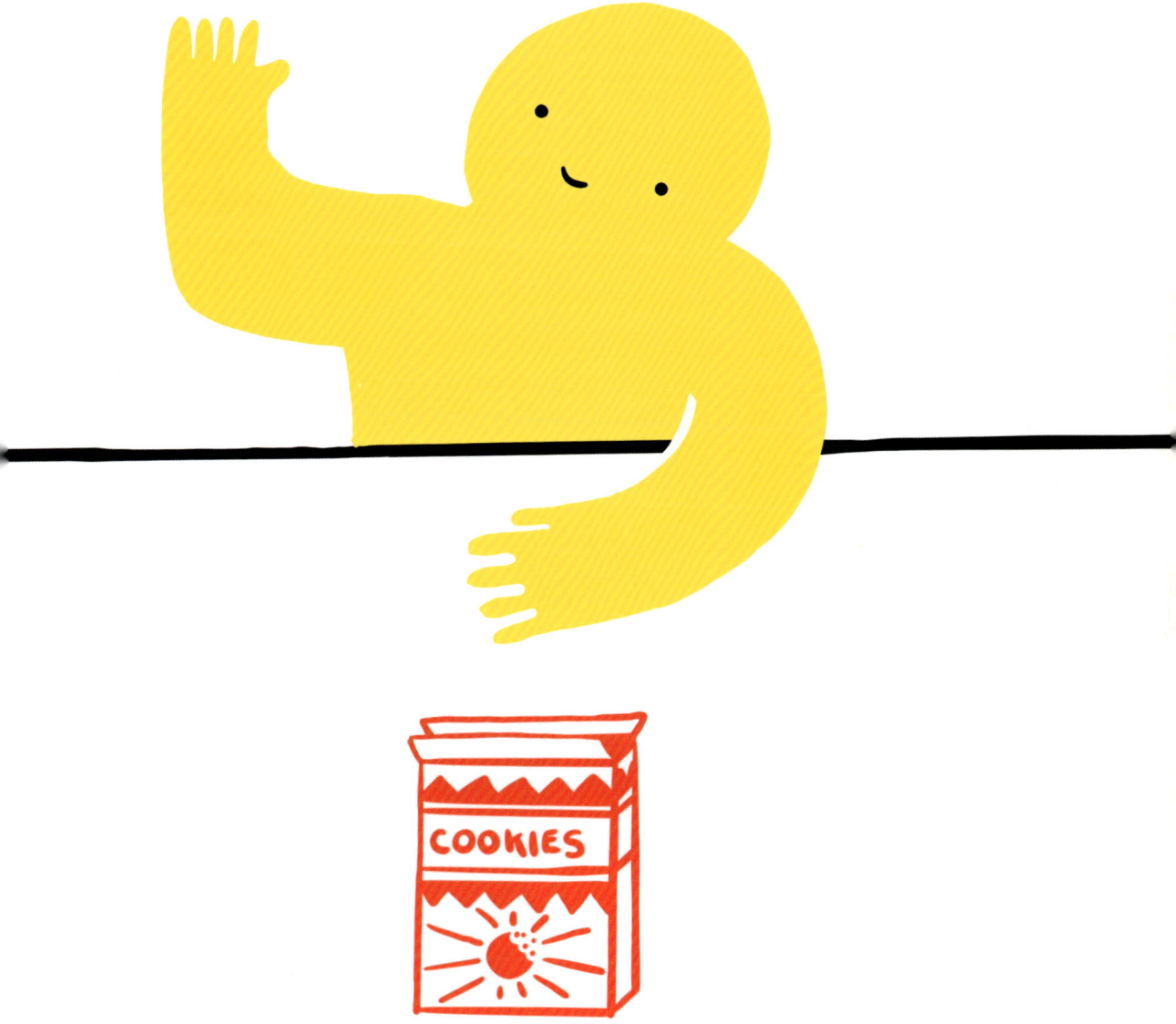

THIS IS WORRY

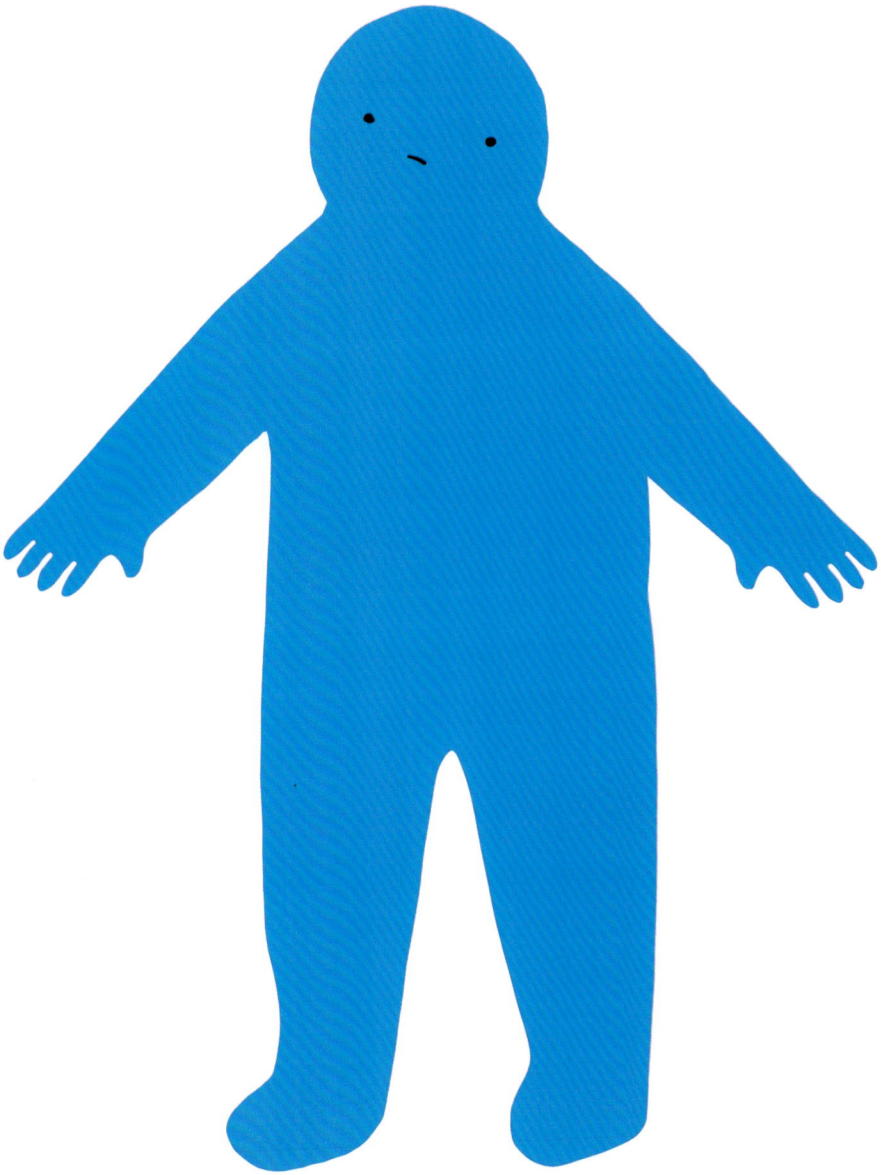

THIS BOOK IS FOR YOU

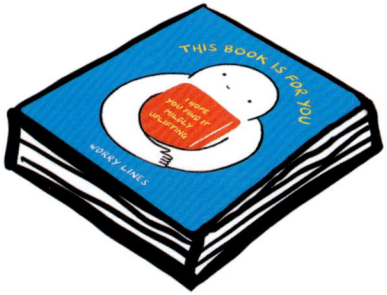

A NOTE FROM THE AUTHOR

WHEN THE GOOD PEOPLE AT TEN SPEED PRESS AGREED TO PUBLISH THIS BOOK - A COLLECTION OF MY MOST POPULAR DRAWINGS ABOUT THOUGHTS, FEELINGS, WORRY, AND EMPATHY FRAMED BY A HOPEFUL NARRATIVE - I WAS THRILLED. I'D ALWAYS WANTED TO MAKE A LONG-FORM PROJECT AND THIS SEEMED LIKE THE PERFECT OPPORTUNITY TO MAKE SOMETHING THAT COULDN'T EXIST ON THE INTERNET - SOMETHING THAT ONLY MADE SENSE AS A BOOK. I WAS EXCITED TO GET DRAWING.

BUT ALMOST BEFORE I HAD TIME TO REGISTER THE EXCITEMENT, I WAS OVERCOME BY ANOTHER FAMILIAR EMOTION: WORRY.

I'VE LIVED WITH WORRY MY WHOLE LIFE. IT HAS BEEN BOTH A CONSTANT COMPANION AND A SOURCE OF COMPLETE CREATIVE PARALYSIS. I KNEW THAT IF I ALLOWED MYSELF TO WORRY NOW, ABOUT THIS BOOK, THEN THIS BOOK WOULD NOT GET MADE. I KNEW THAT IF I LET IT, WORRY WOULD SOON DOMINATE THE WHOLE PROJECT AND I COULD RUN THE RISK OF JEOPARDIZING NOT ONLY THE BOOK, BUT MY OWN MENTAL HEALTH AS WELL.

AND SO I DECIDED, FOR THE FIRST TIME IN MY LIFE, THAT I WAS

ANXIETY PROJECT OF A MY SO MUCH TO ME.

HAVING MY OWN ANXIETY NOT LOST ON ME SO I MADE THAT WORRY WAS IN THE MAKING OF THIS BOOK.

THAT DECISION INTO A REAL CHALLENGE. WELL, READER, - WORRY LINES

NOT GOING TO LET TAKE CONTROL THAT MEANT

THE IRONY OF GET IN THE WAY ABOUT ANXIETY WAS (OR MY THERAPIST), THE DECISION NOT INVITED TO PARTICIPATE BOOK.

NOW, ACTUALLY PUTTING PRACTICE WAS OF COURSE DID I SUCCEED? LET'S FIND OUT.

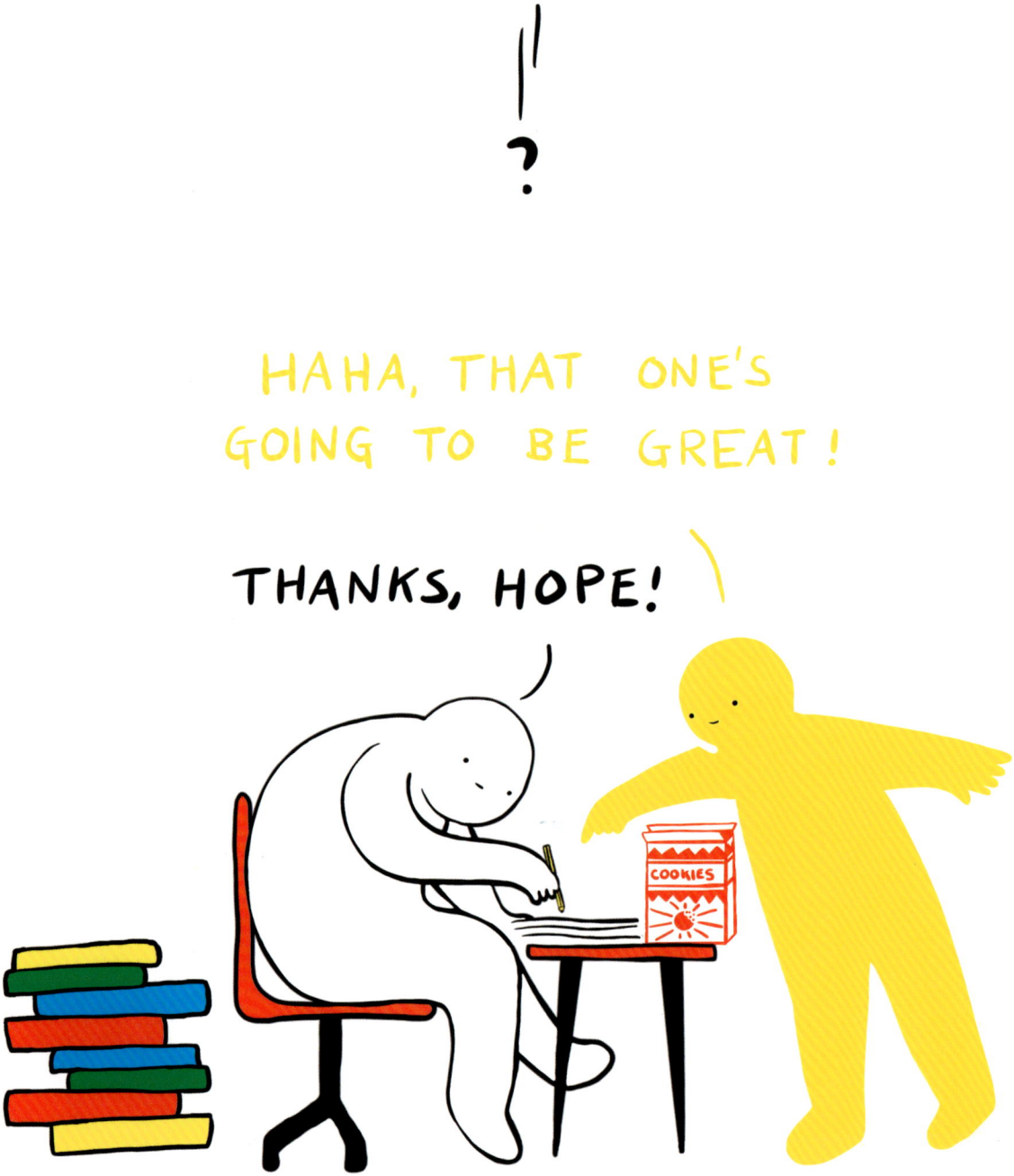
!?
HAHA, THAT ONE'S GOING TO BE GREAT!
THANKS, HOPE!
COOKIES

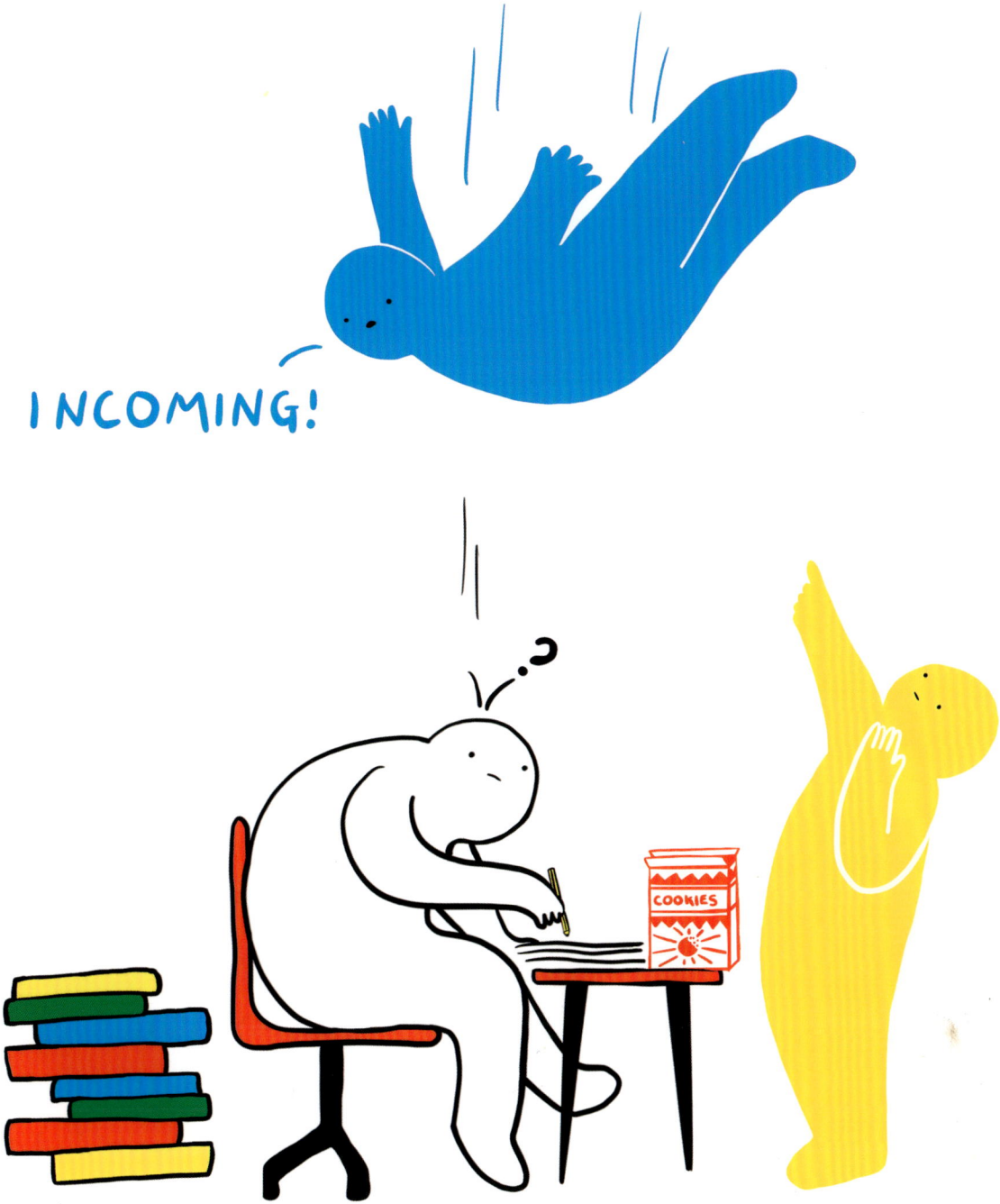
INCOMING!
COOKIES

Cookies
To Do

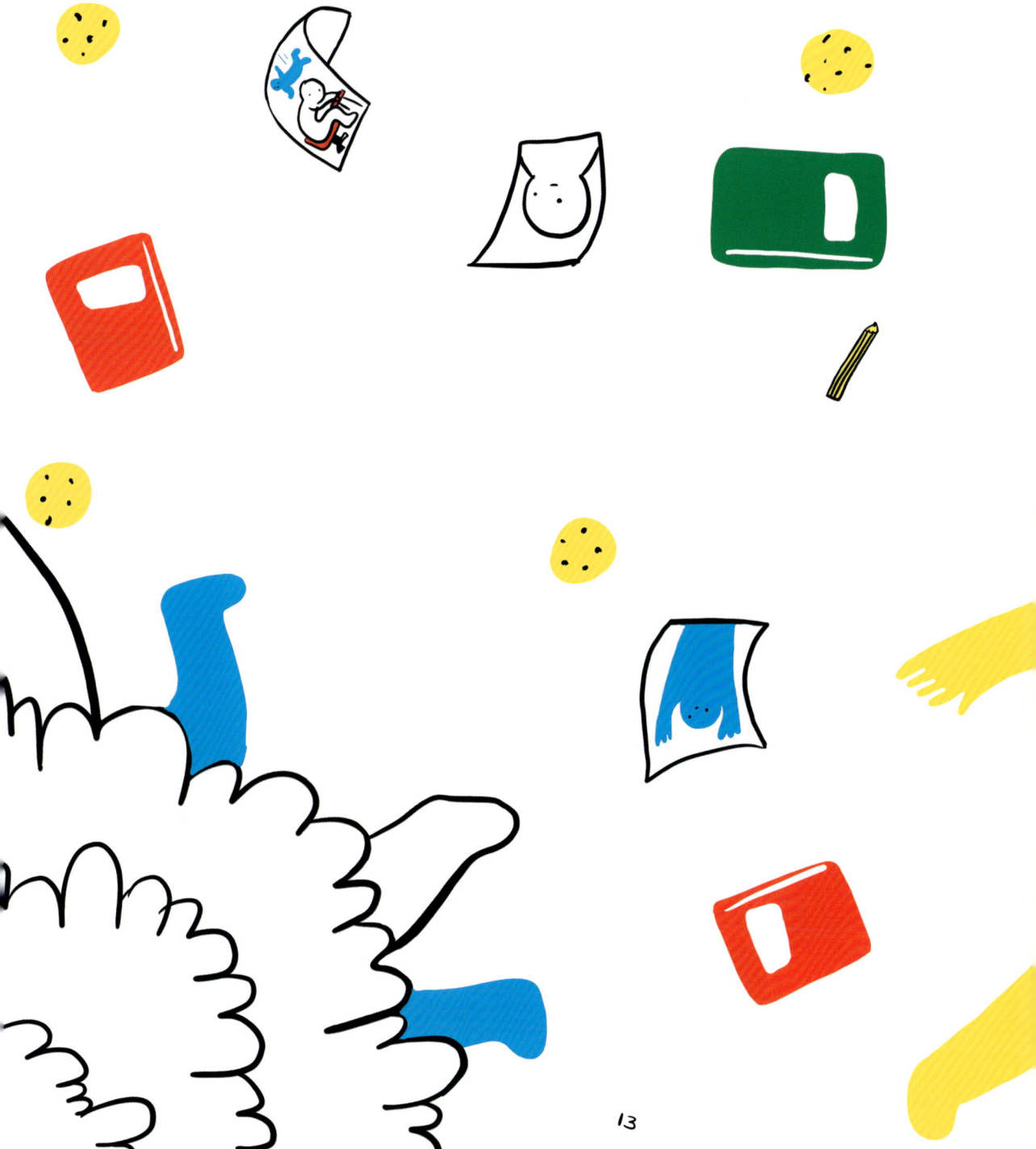

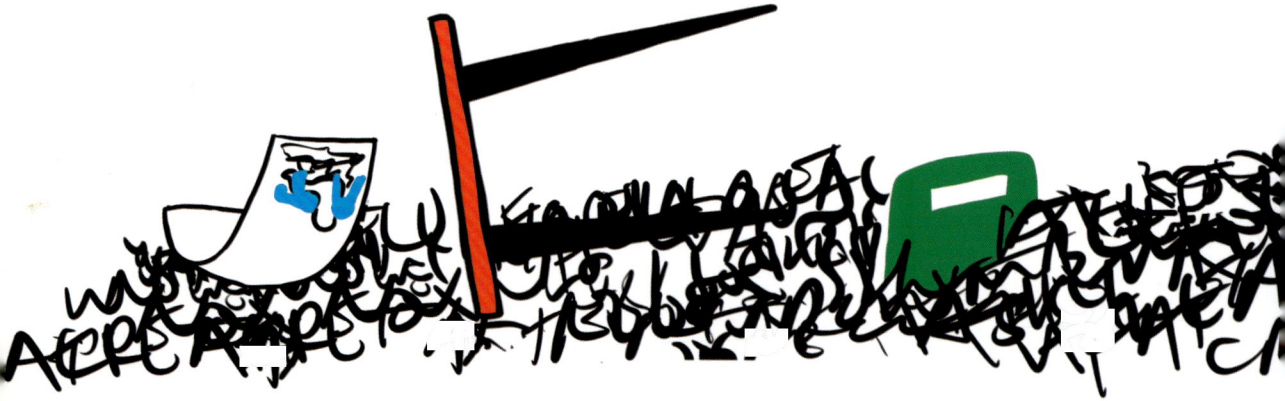

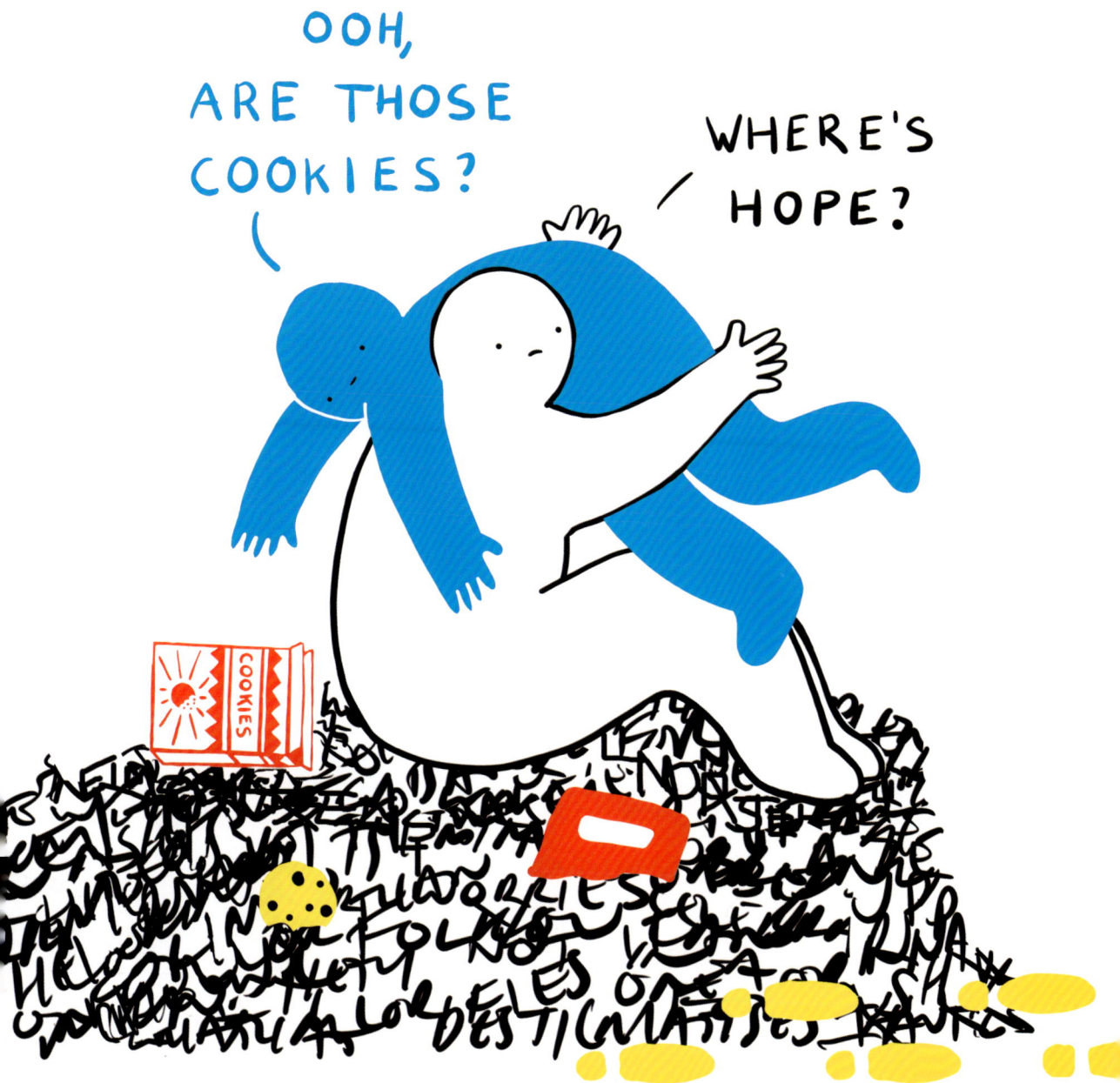
OOH, ARE THOSE COOKIES?
WHERE'S HOPE?
COOKIES

WORRY, THIS ISN'T GOOD.
HOW AM I GOING TO FINISH
MY BOOK WITHOUT HOPE?

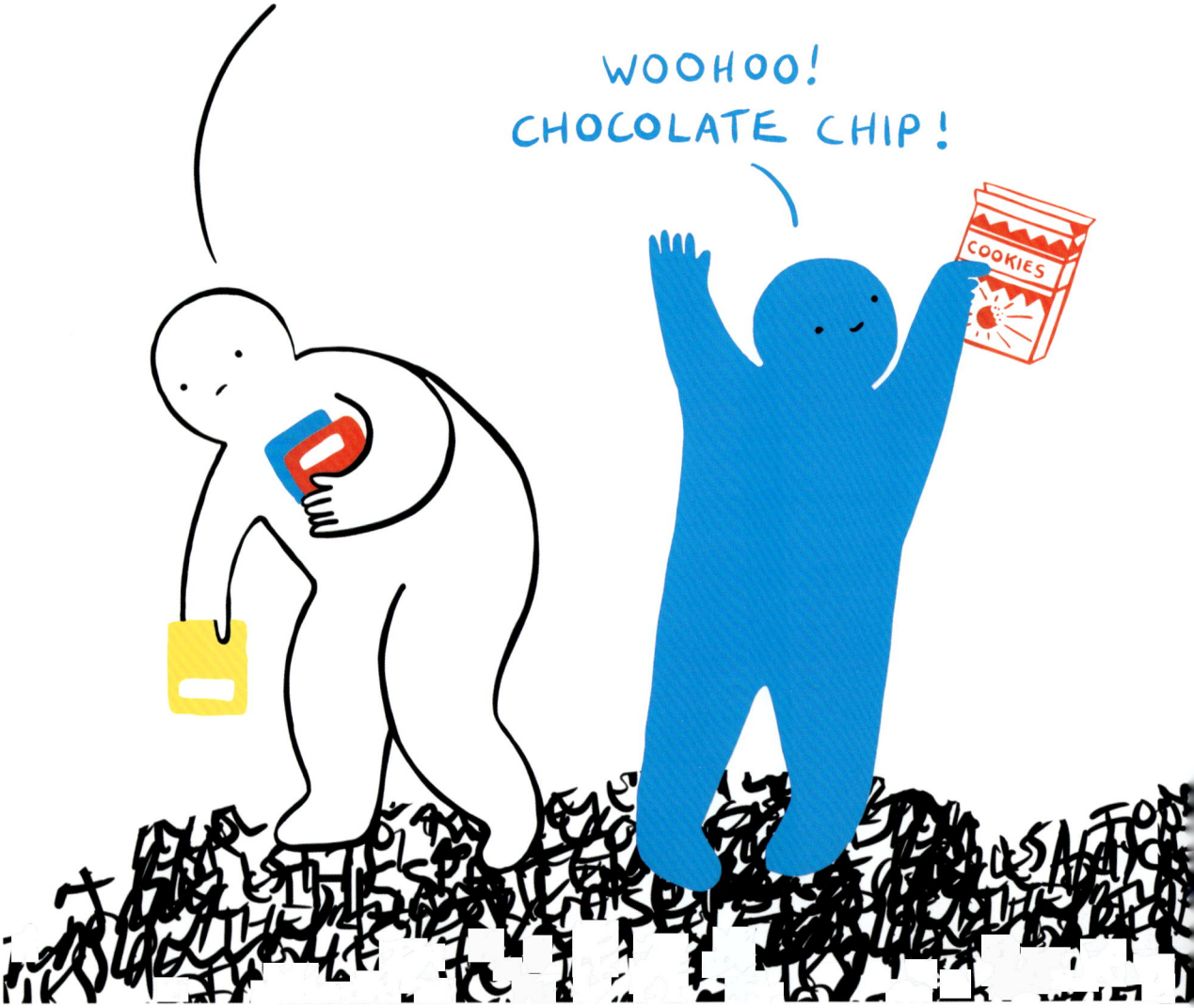

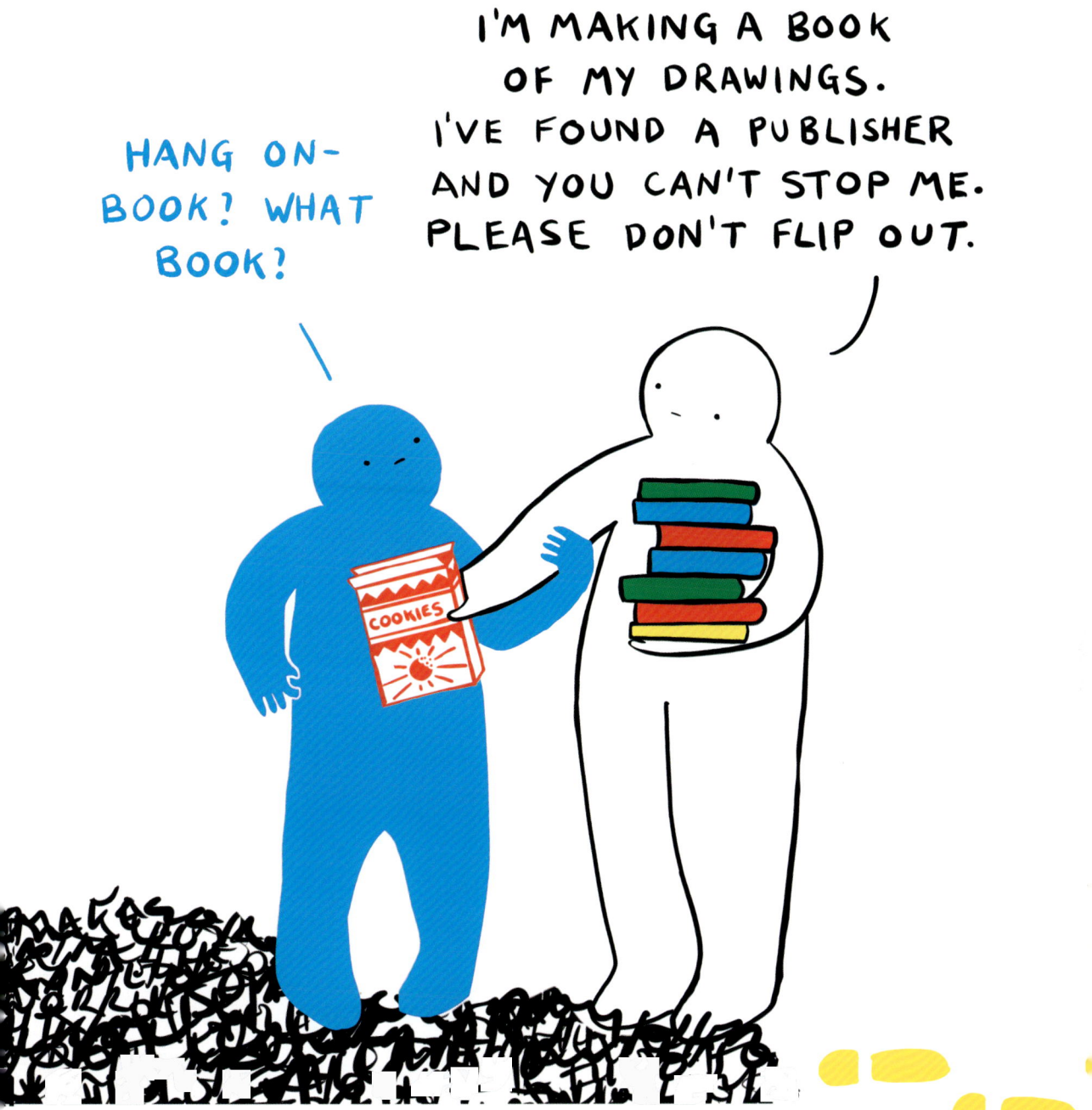
I'M MAKING A BOOK OF MY DRAWINGS. I'VE FOUND A PUBLISHER AND YOU CAN'T STOP ME. PLEASE DON'T FLIP OUT.
HANG ON- BOOK? WHAT BOOK?
COOKIES

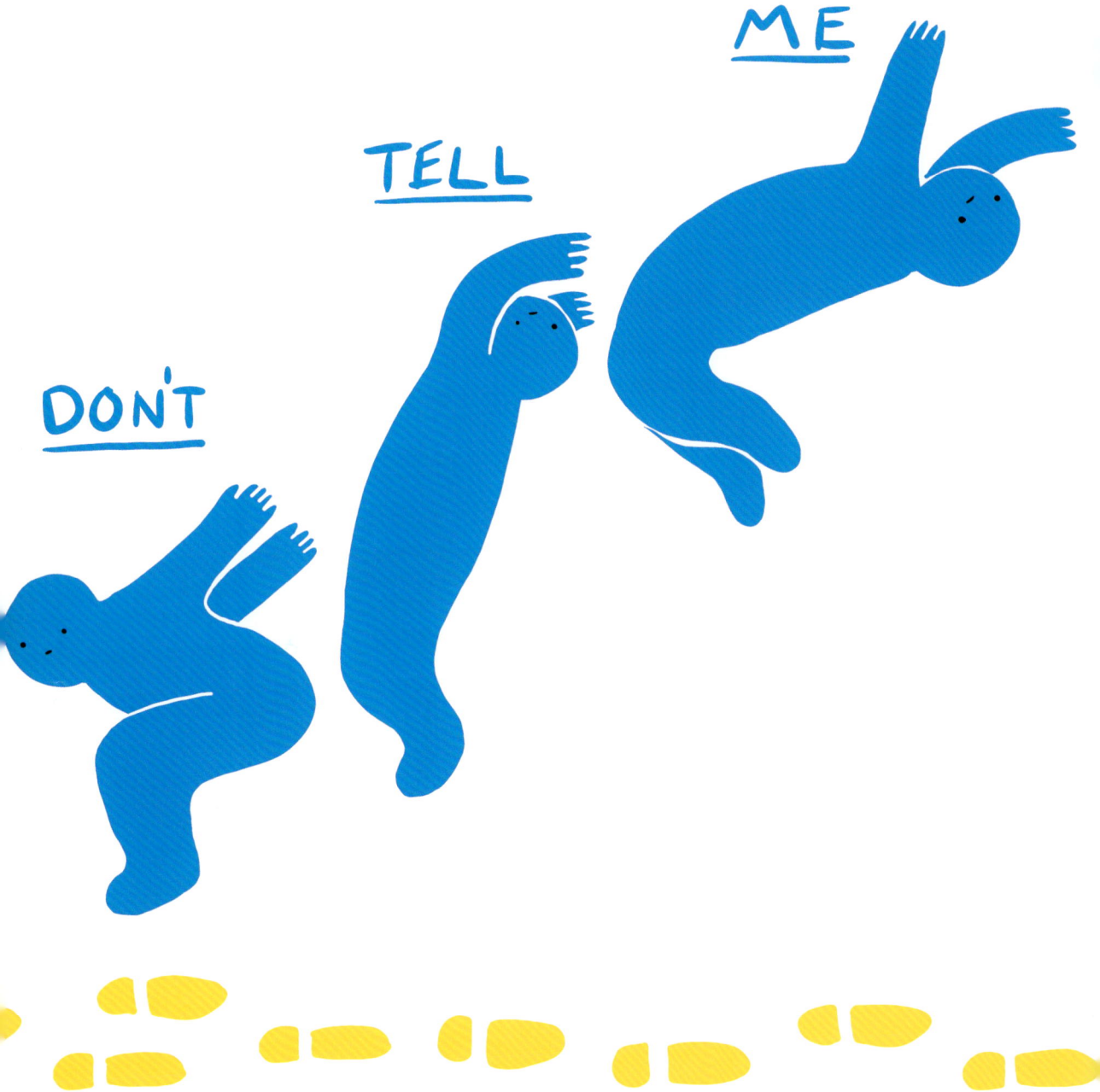
DON'T
TELL
ME

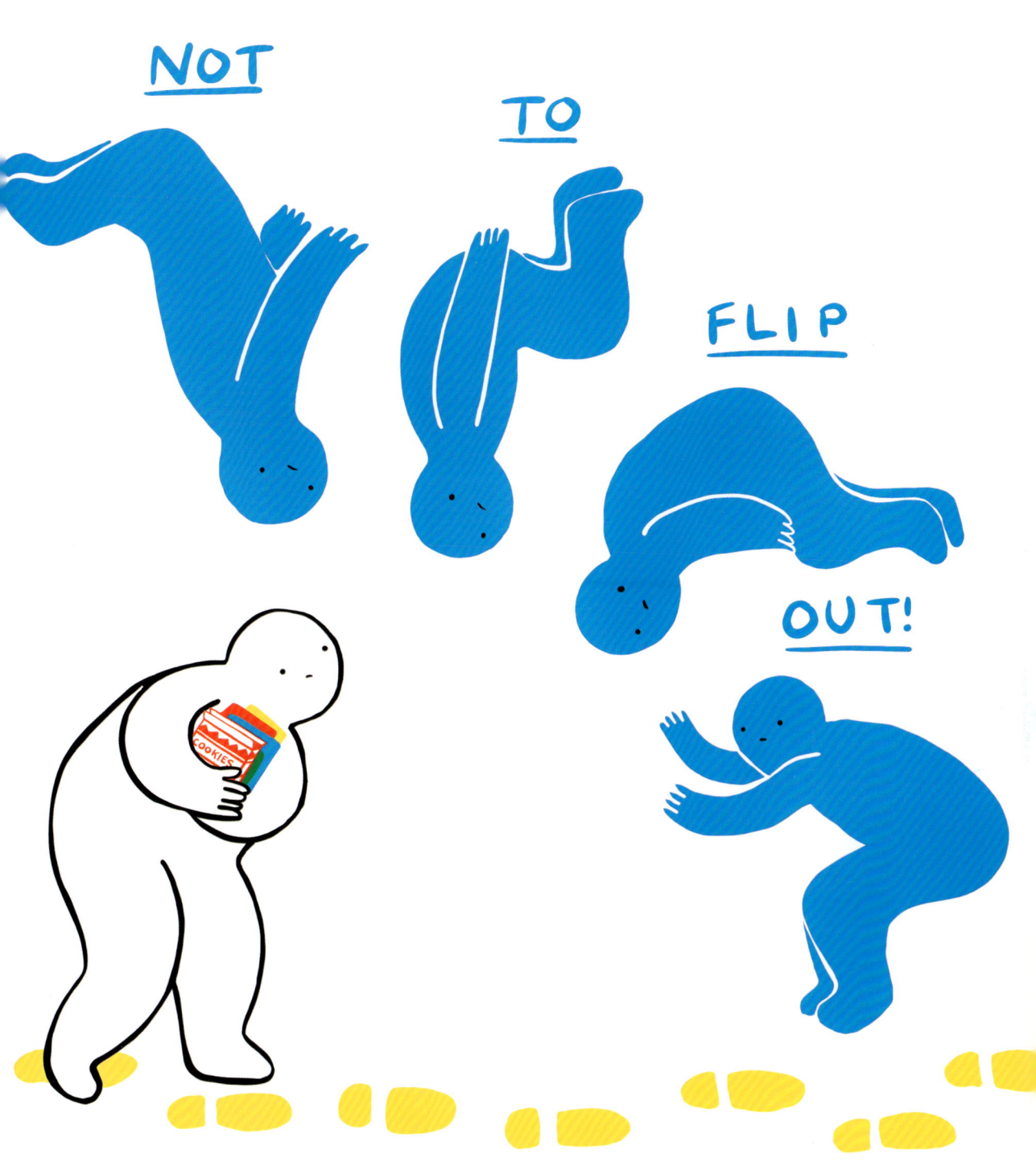
NOT
TO
FLIP
OUT!
COOKIES

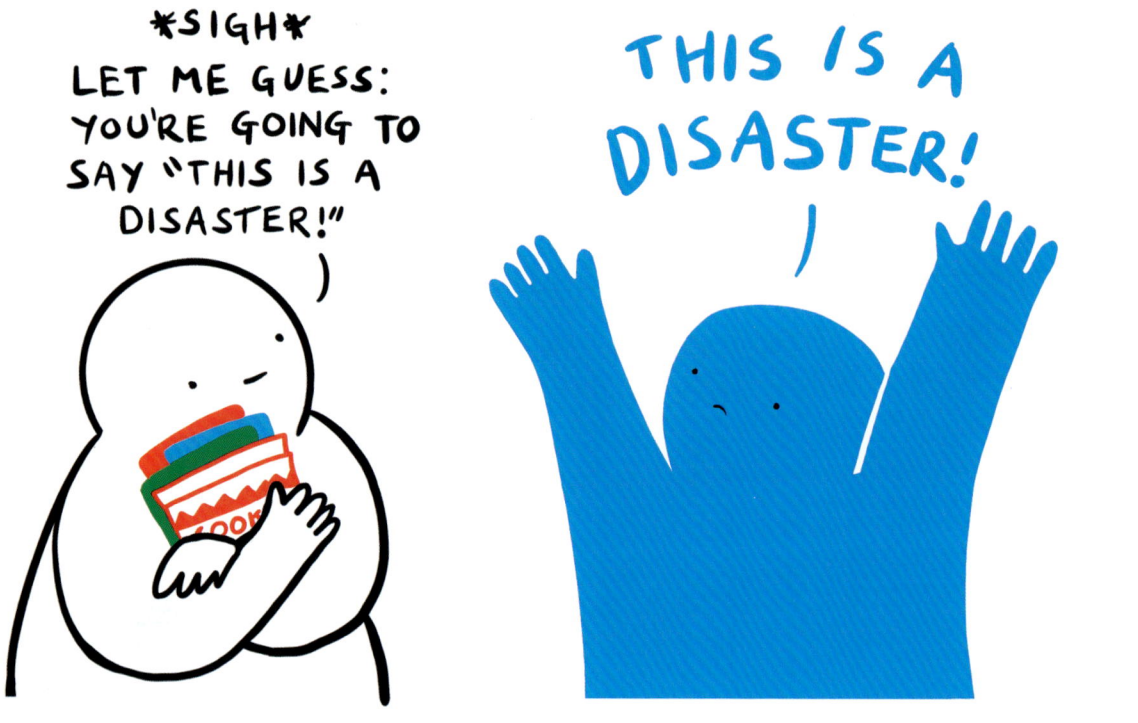
SIGH
LET ME GUESS: YOU'RE GOING TO SAY "THIS IS A DISASTER!"
THIS IS A DISASTER!

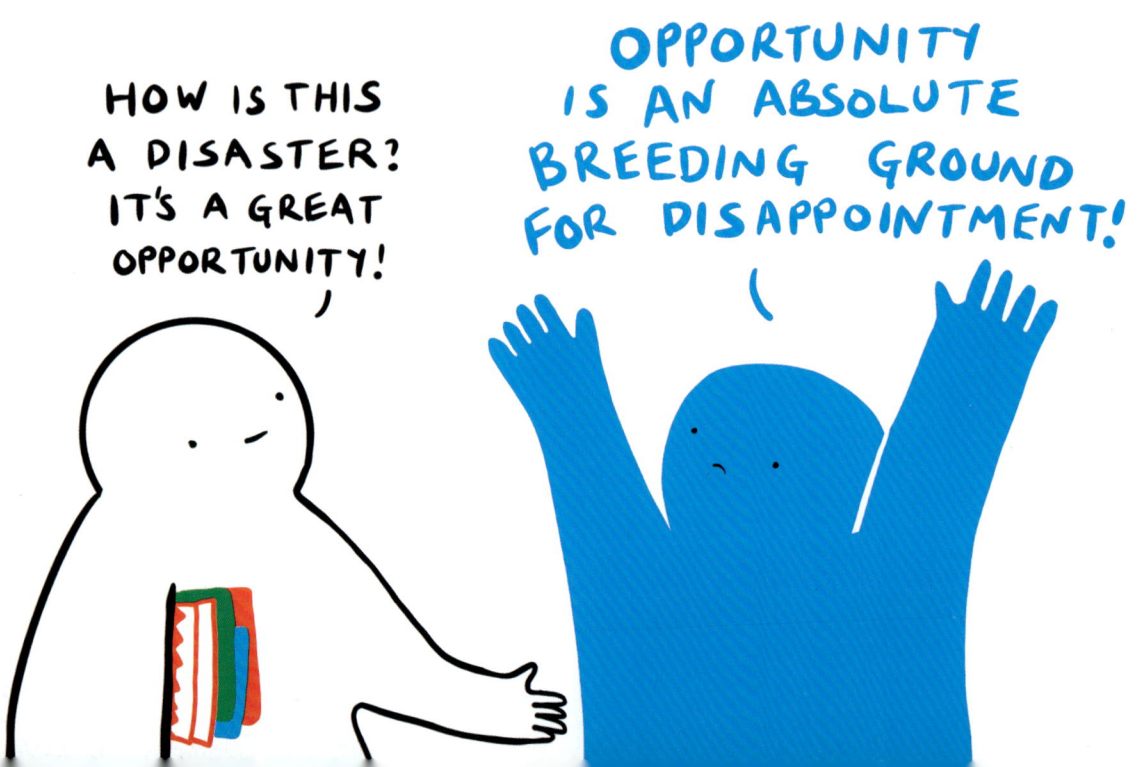
HOW IS THIS A DISASTER? IT'S A GREAT OPPORTUNITY!
OPPORTUNITY IS AN ABSOLUTE BREEDING GROUND FOR DISAPPOINTMENT!

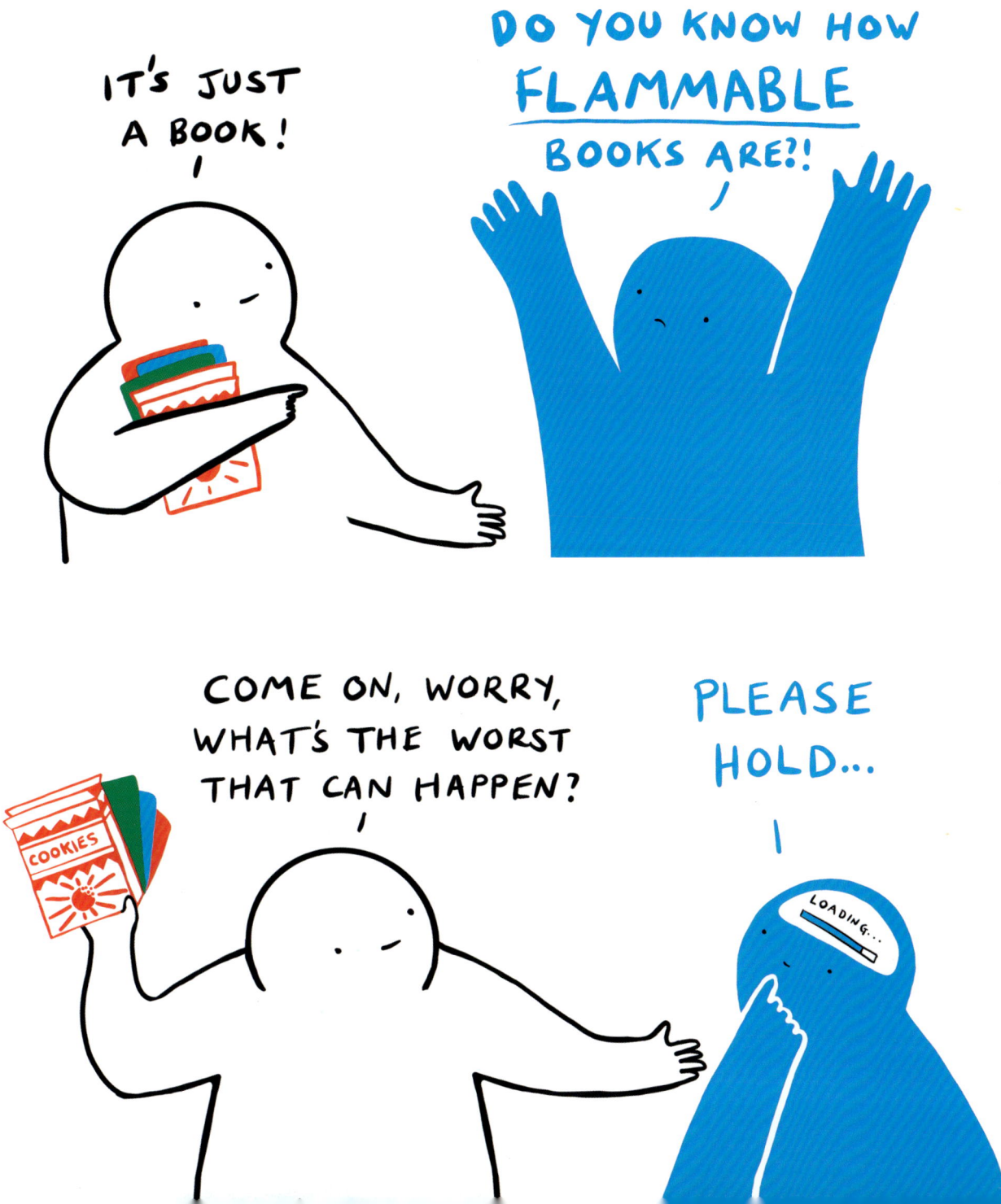
IT'S JUST A BOOK!
DO YOU KNOW HOW FLAMMABLE BOOKS ARE?!
COOKIES
COME ON, WORRY, WHAT'S THE WORST THAT CAN HAPPEN?
PLEASE HOLD...
LOADING...

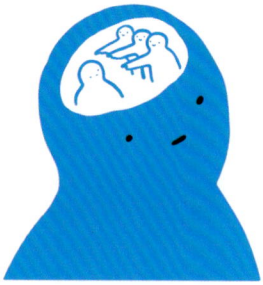

PUBLIC HUMILIATION?

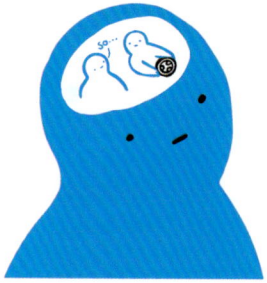

HAVING TO MAKE SMALL TALK WITH A TAXI DRIVER?

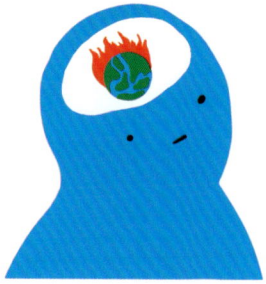

COMPLETE ECOLOGICAL COLLAPSE?

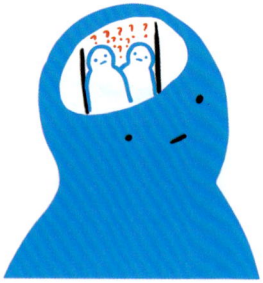

GETTING STUCK IN AN ELEVATOR WITH YOUR THERAPIST?

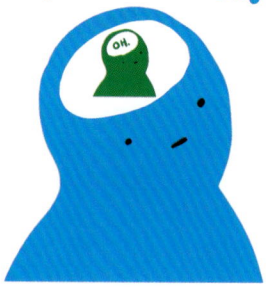

REALIZING YOU AREN'T WHO YOU THOUGHT YOU WERE?

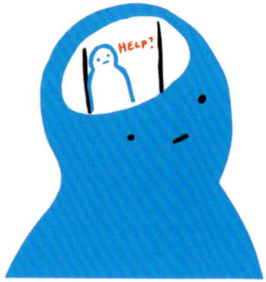

GETTING STUCK IN AN ELEVATOR WITHOUT YOUR THERAPIST?

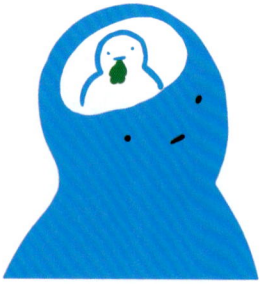

HAVING SALAD STUCK IN YOUR TEETH AT A FUNERAL?

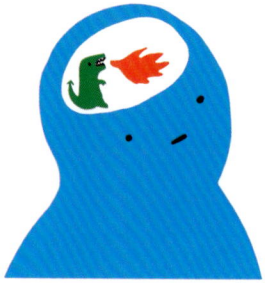

ROASTED BY A DRAGON?

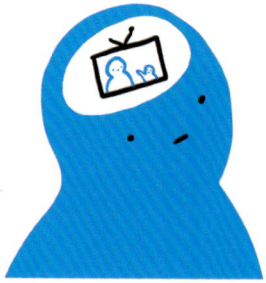

MOCKED BY A CHILD ON NATIONAL TELEVISION?

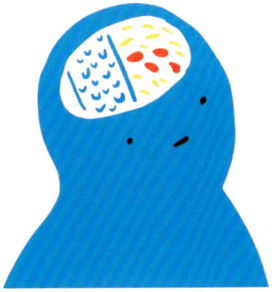

FREAK CHEESE-GRATER ACCIDENT?

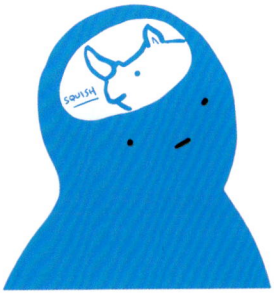

TRAMPLED BY A RHINO?

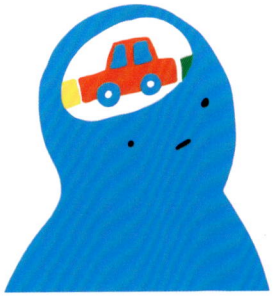

TRAFFIC JAM WHEN YOU REALLY NEED TO PEE?

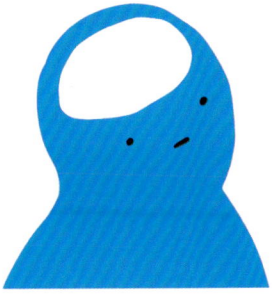

BLANKING ON YOUR PIN NUMBER?

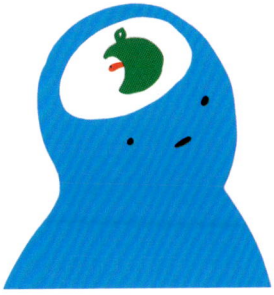

FINDING HALF A WORM IN YOUR APPLE?

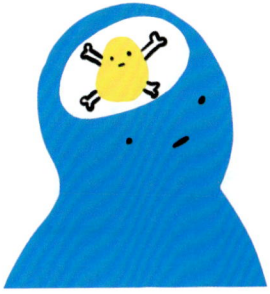

BEING ALLERGIC TO POTATOES?

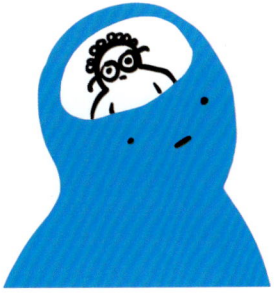

TOLD OFF BY A GRANDMA WHO ISN'T YOUR GRANDMA?

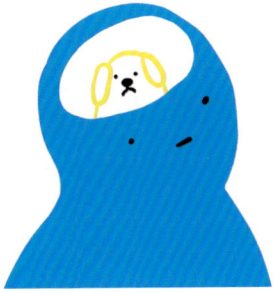

DISAPPOINTING A LABRADOR?

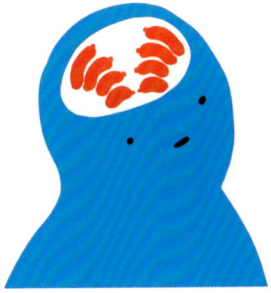

SAUSAGES INSTEAD OF FINGERS?

I MEANT, WHAT'S THE WORST THAT CAN HAPPEN WITH THE BOOK?

WELL, THEN YOU SHOULD HAVE BEEN WAAAAAAAY MORE SPECIFIC.

YOU CAN'T EVEN DRAW HANDS!

I LITERALLY HAVE NO IDEA WHAT YOU'RE TALKING ABOUT!

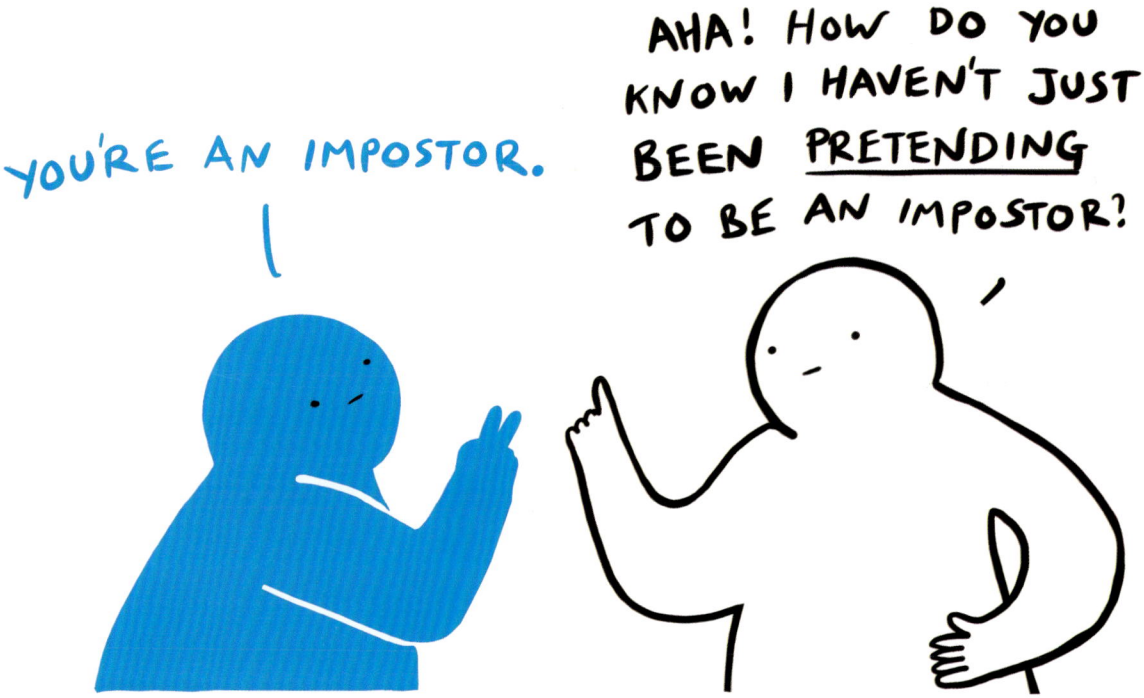
YOU'RE AN IMPOSTOR.
AHA! HOW DO YOU KNOW I HAVEN'T JUST BEEN PRETENDING TO BE AN IMPOSTOR?

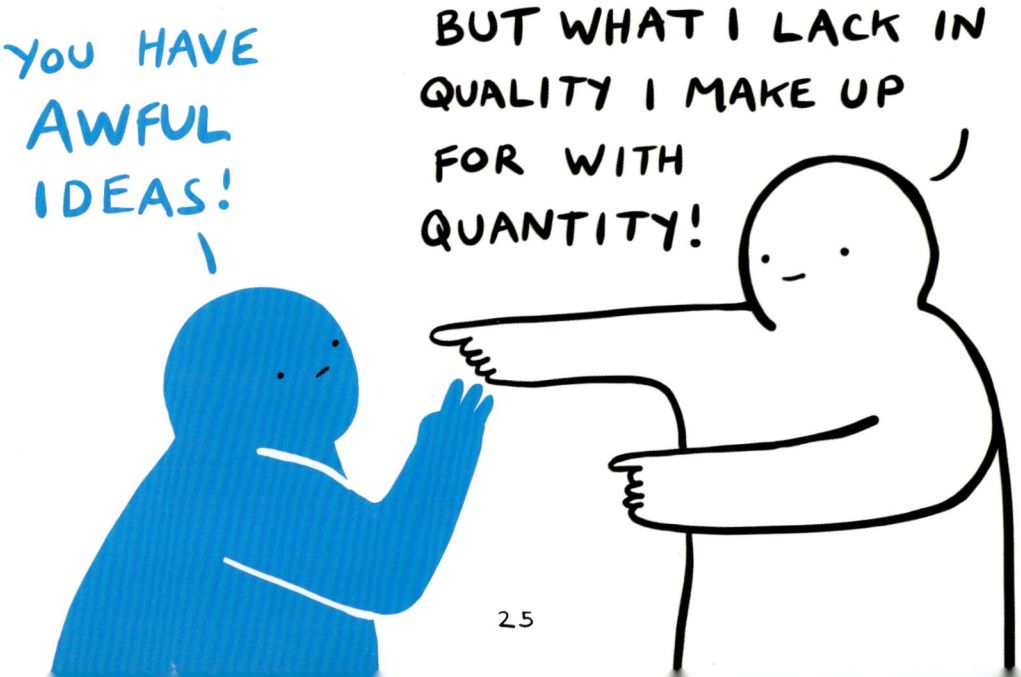
YOU HAVE AWFUL IDEAS!
BUT WHAT I LACK IN QUALITY I MAKE UP FOR WITH QUANTITY!

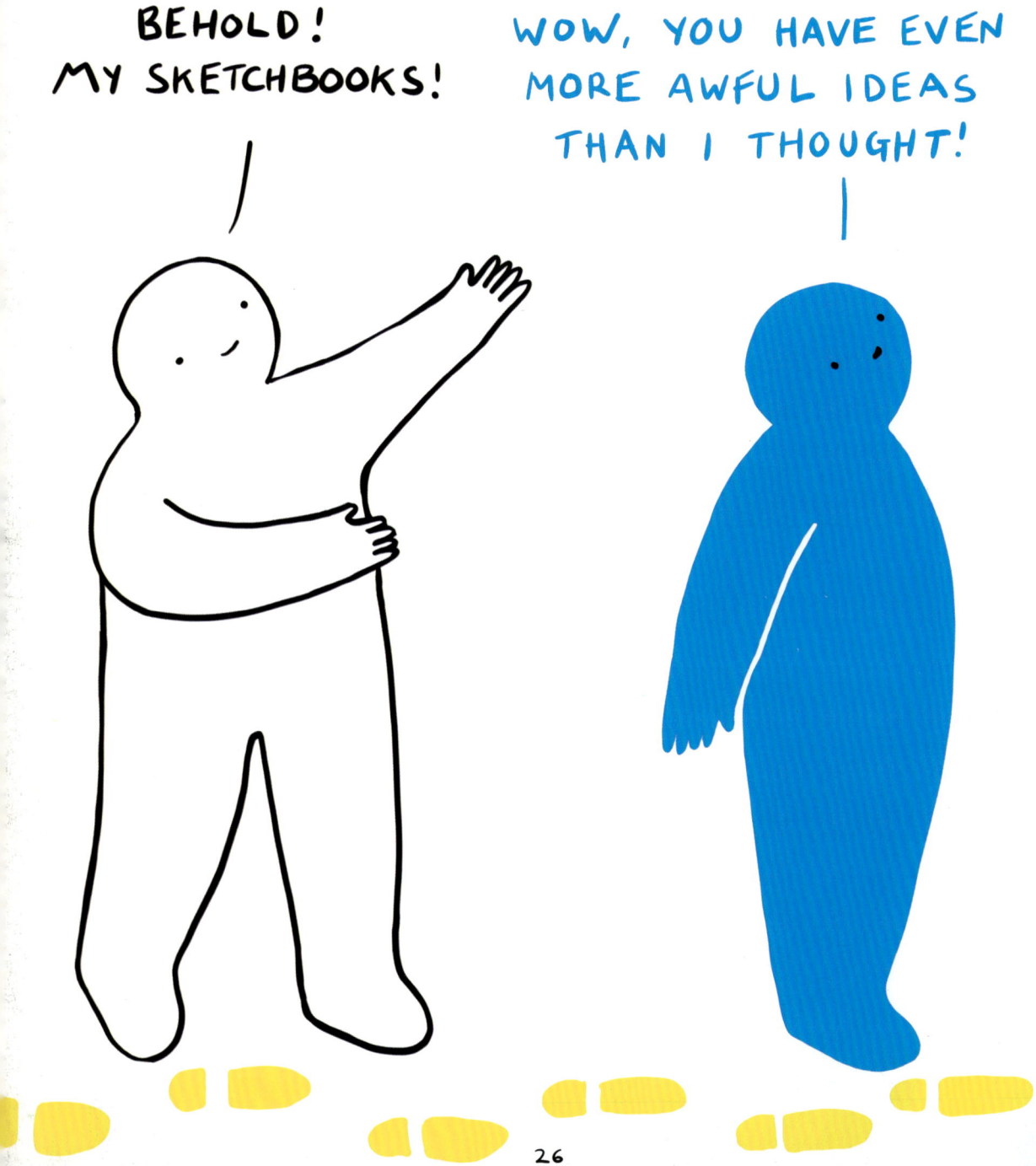
BEHOLD!
MY SKETCHBOOKS!
WOW, YOU HAVE EVEN MORE AWFUL IDEAS THAN I THOUGHT!

IF
YOU
CAN
READ
THIS
YOU
ARE
HOLD

TOOTHACHE
DEDICATIONS
TOXIC POSITIVITY
LEARNING
PUPPIES
OVERTHINKING
FAILURES

FLEXIBILITY
POTATO
SELFISHNESS
SUNBURN
MEMORIES
SOUL-SEARCHING
BURNOUT
CAKE

SAUSAGES
DARKNESS
SWEET RELIEF
TRAMPOLINING
FALLING OVER
INSPIRATION
ANXIETY
FUNNY-SHAPED CLOUDS

ING
THE
BOOK
THE
WRONG
WAY
ROUND

DISAPPOINTMENT
THE PATRIARCHY
DINOSAURS
SELF-HATRED
BAD DANCING
APATHY
JOY

HUGS
THE JOYS OF COMPOSTING
FEAR
THE BEES
TIME
BIG OLD TREES
THERAPY

PUMPKINS
THE INTERNET
OUTER SPACE
DEEP SADNESS
GROWTH
SANDWICHES
MUSIC

WHY'S THIS ONE SO BIG?
OH, THE DEDICATION FOR THE BOOK HAS BEEN DRIVING ME CRAZY.
IF
YOU
CAN
READ
ICHE
DEDICATIONS
TOXIC POSITIVITY
FLEXIBILITY
POTATO
SELFISHNESS
SUNBURN
SAUSAGES
DARKNESS
SWEET RELIEF
TRAMPOLINING

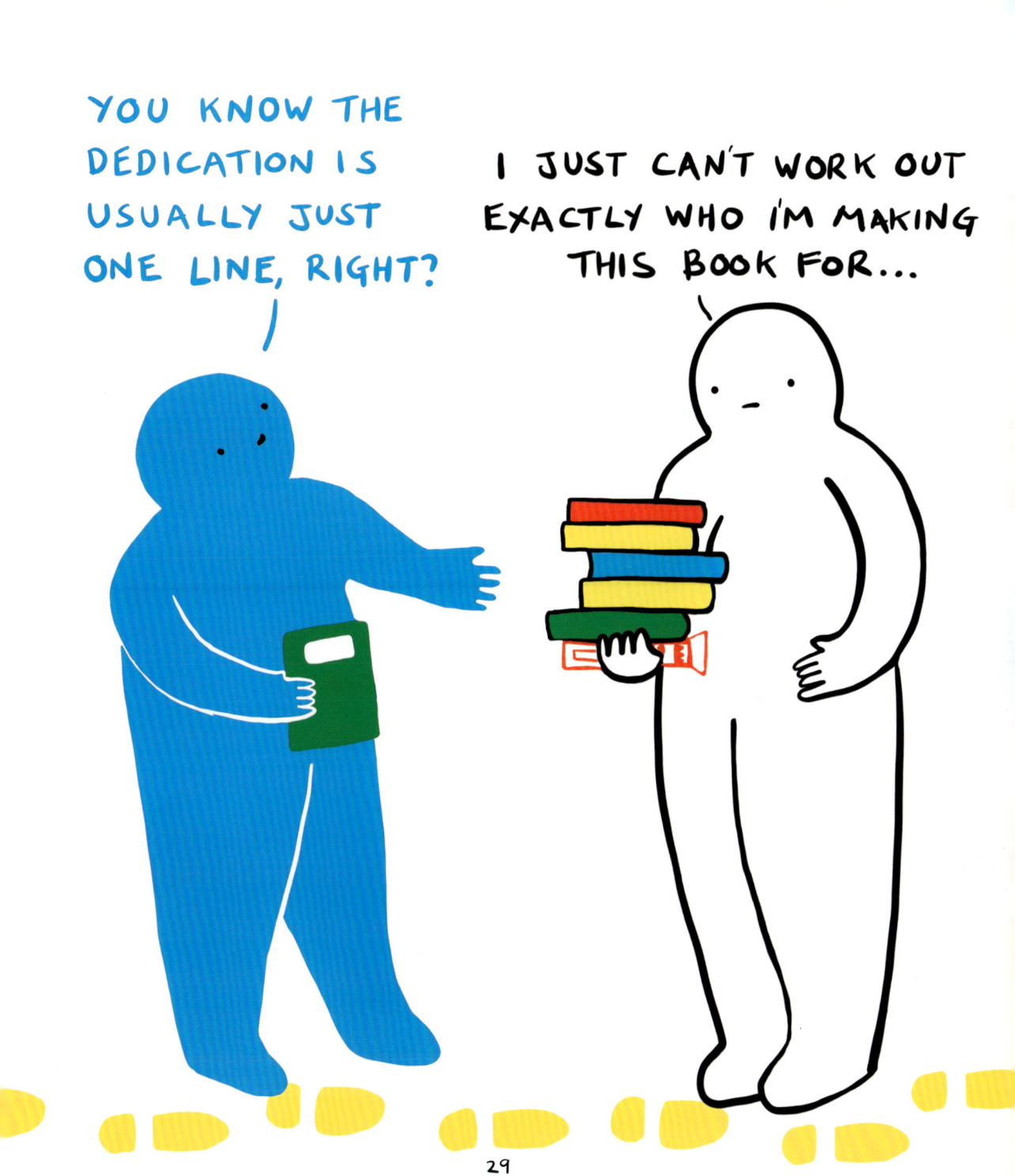
YOU KNOW THE DEDICATION IS USUALLY JUST ONE LINE, RIGHT?
I JUST CAN'T WORK OUT EXACTLY WHO I'M MAKING THIS BOOK FOR...

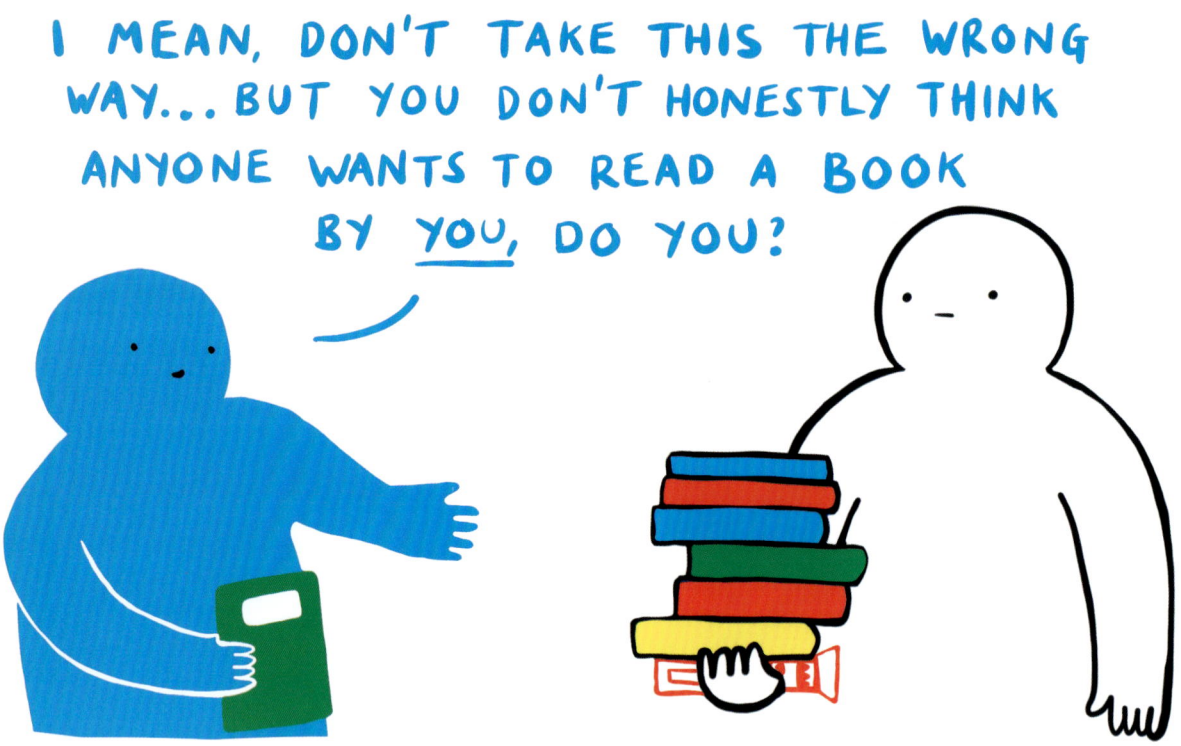

WELL, HOPE SAID-

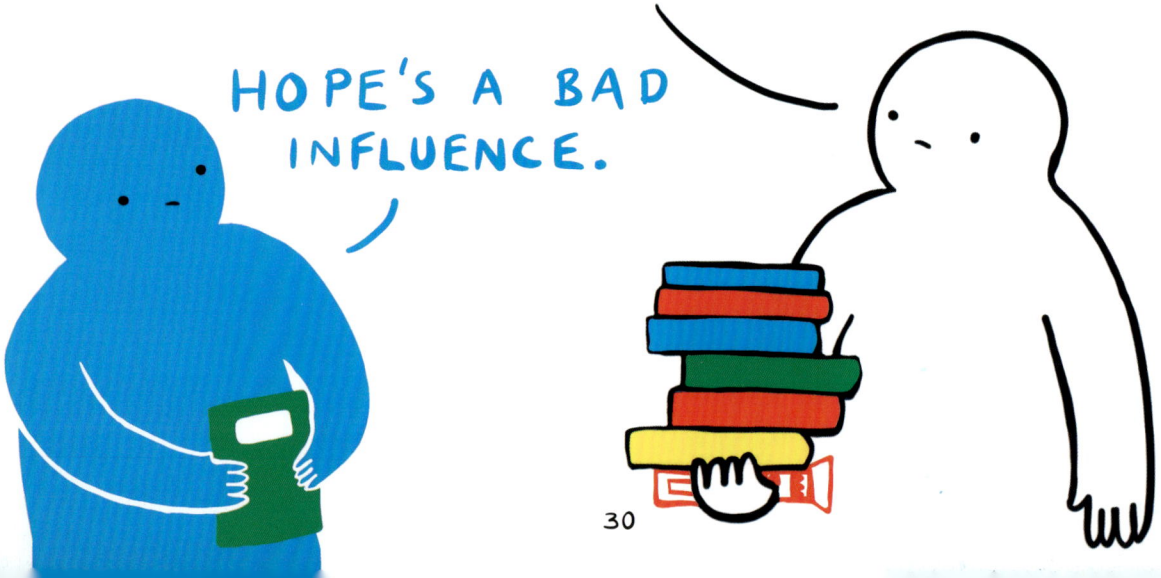

NOW, LET'S TAKE A LOOK AT THESE.

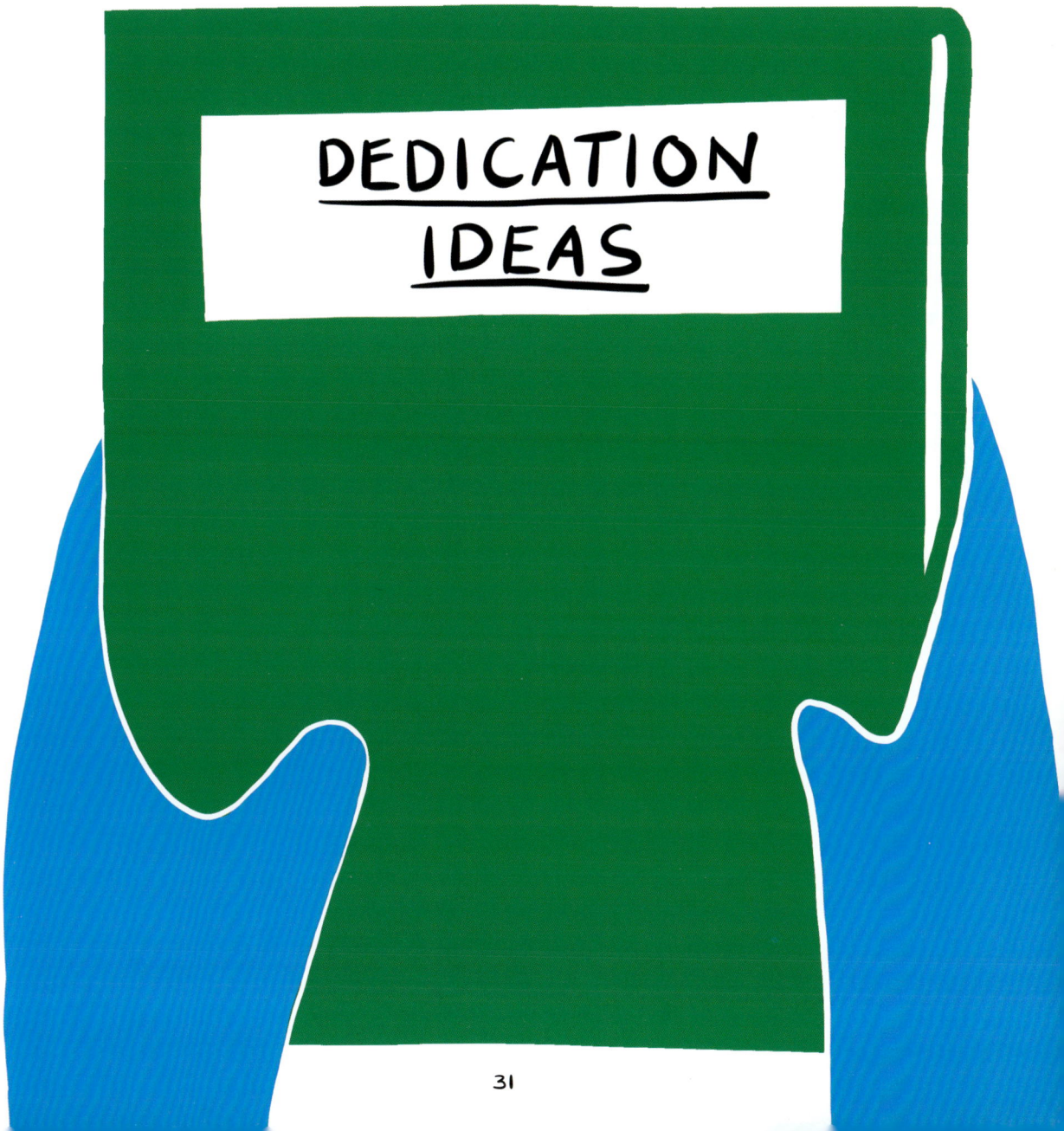

BRAVE WORRIERS

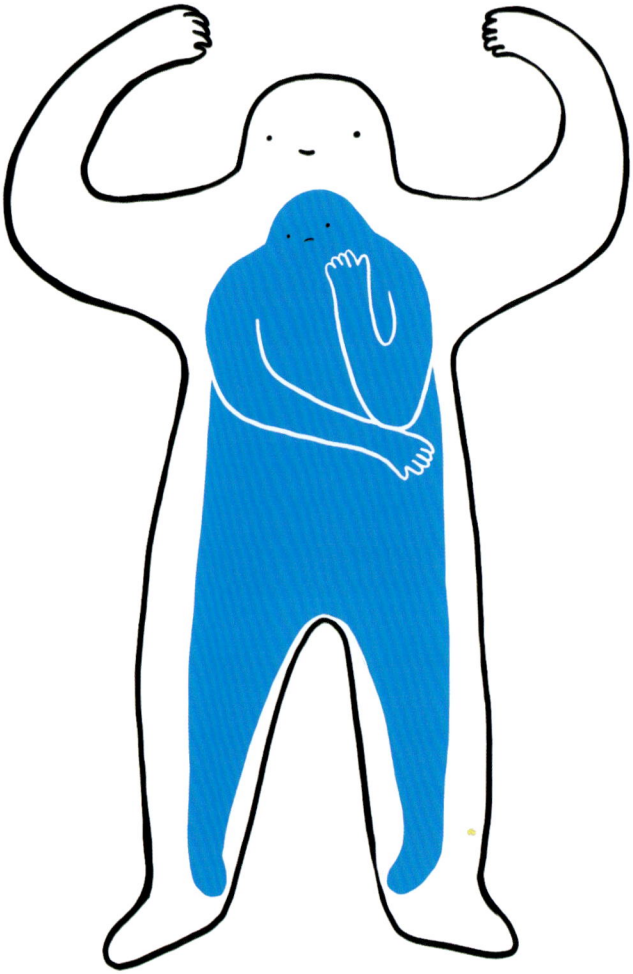

THIS BOOK IS FOR YOU

FEELERS OF

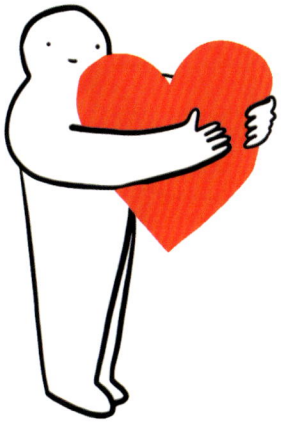

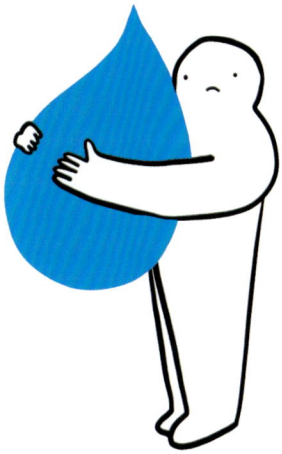

MANY FEELINGS

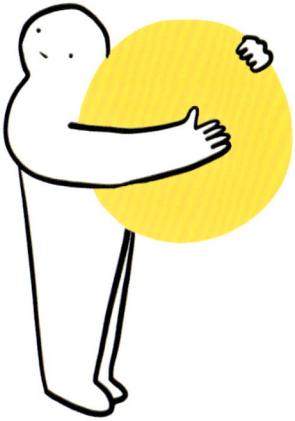

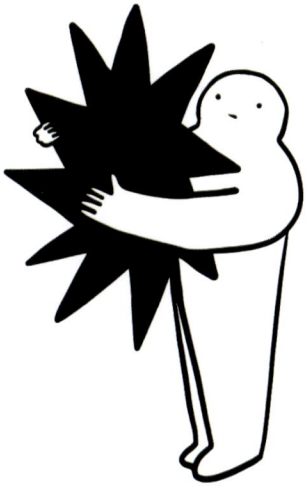

THIS BOOK IS FOR YOU

THOSE WHO READ

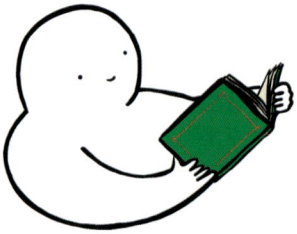

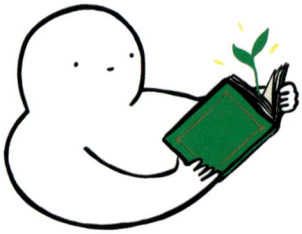

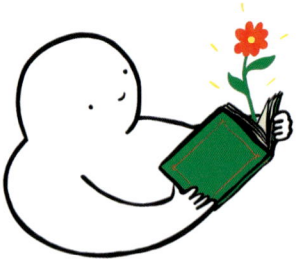

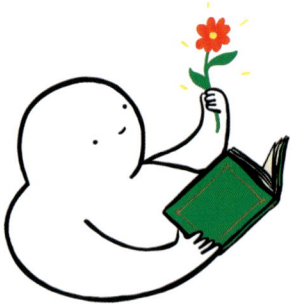

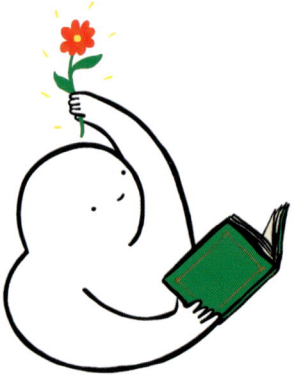

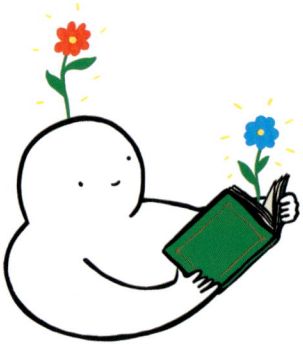

THIS BOOK IS FOR YOU

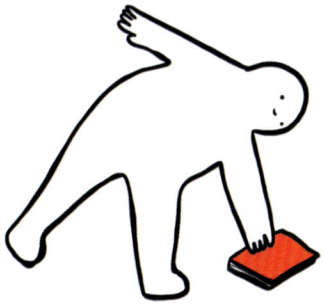

THOSE

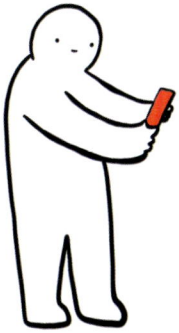

WHO

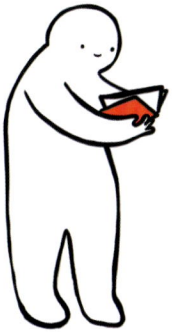

READ

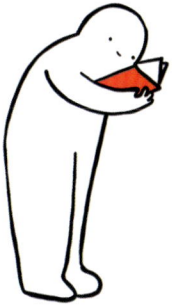

TOO

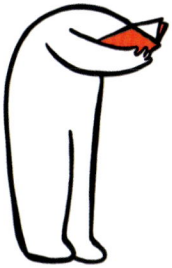

MUCH

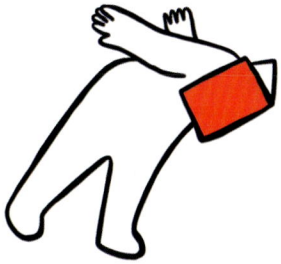

INTO

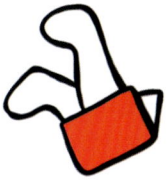

THINGS

THIS BOOK IS FOR YOU

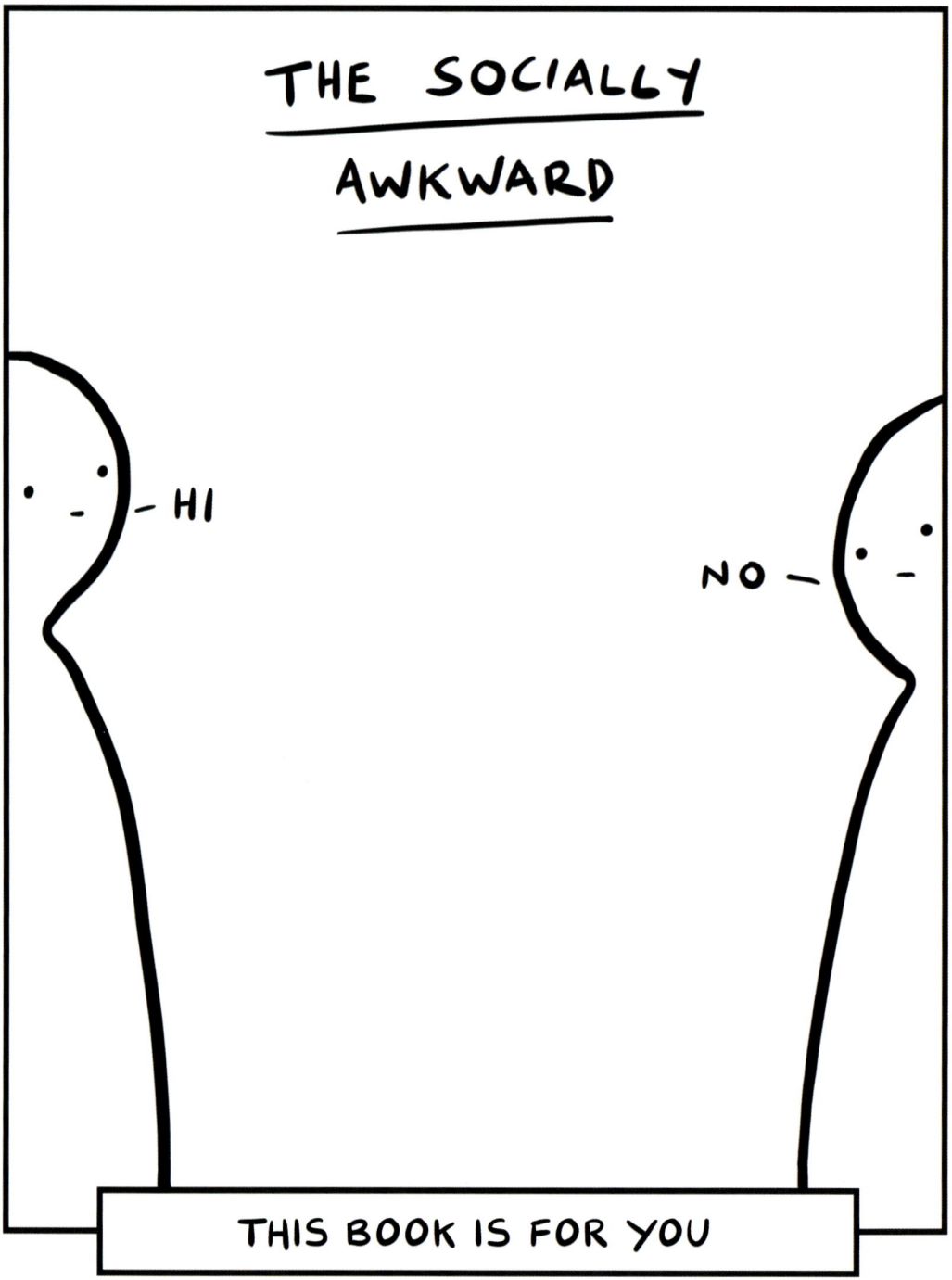
THE SOCIALLY AWKWARD
HI
NO
THIS BOOK IS FOR YOU

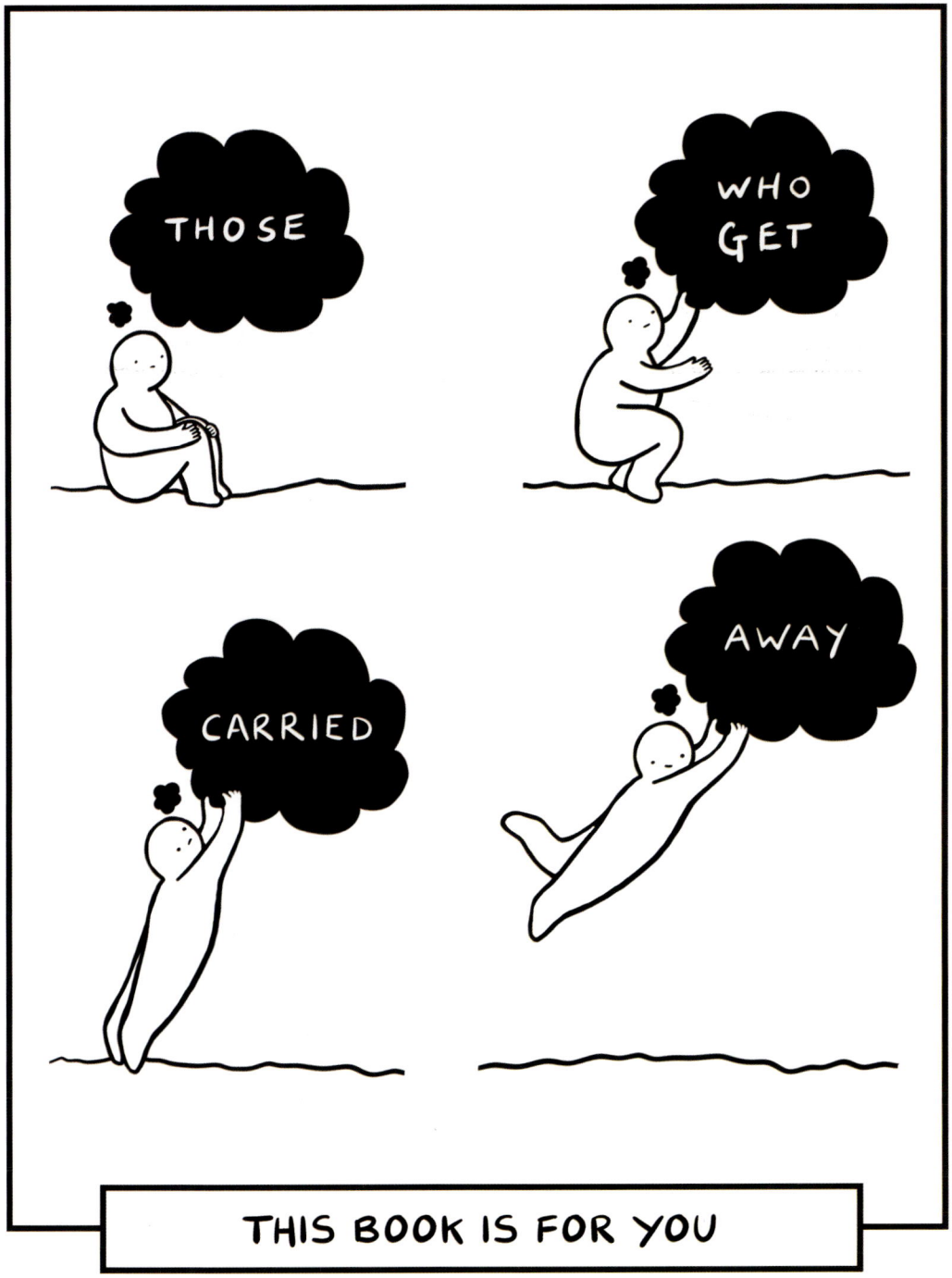
THOSE
WHO GET
CARRIED
AWAY
THIS BOOK IS FOR YOU

THE HEAVYHEARTED

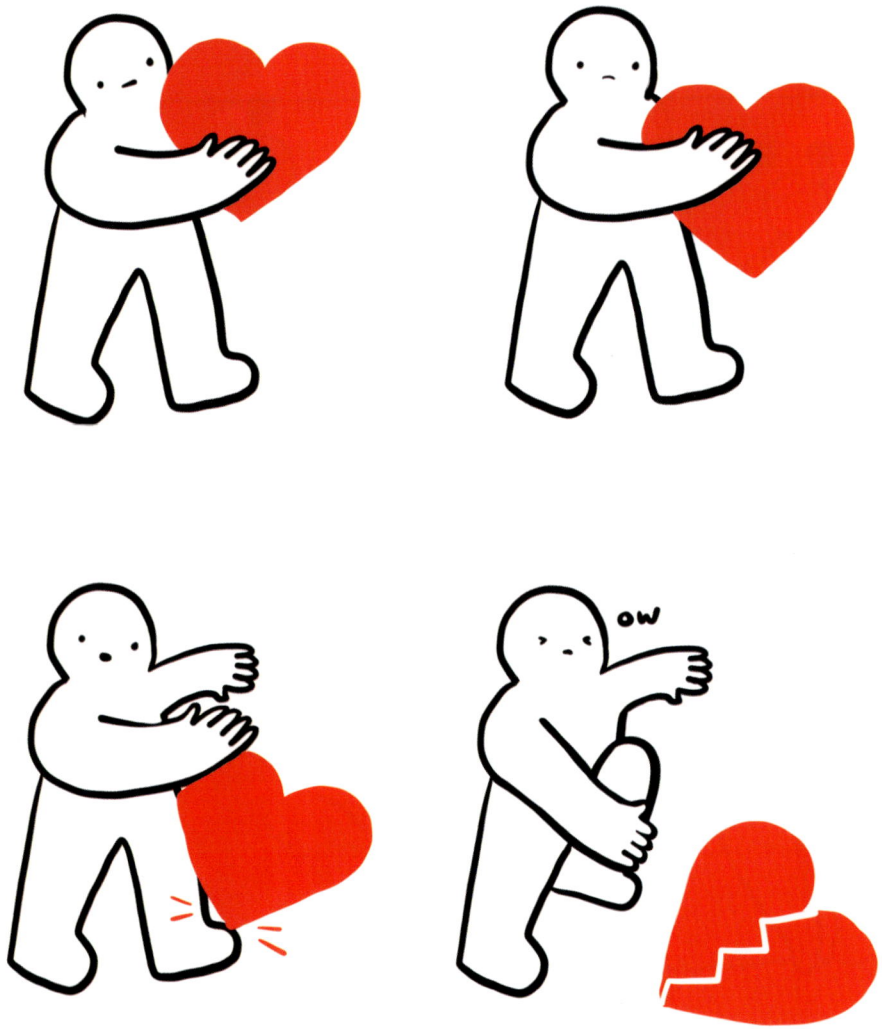

THIS BOOK IS FOR YOU

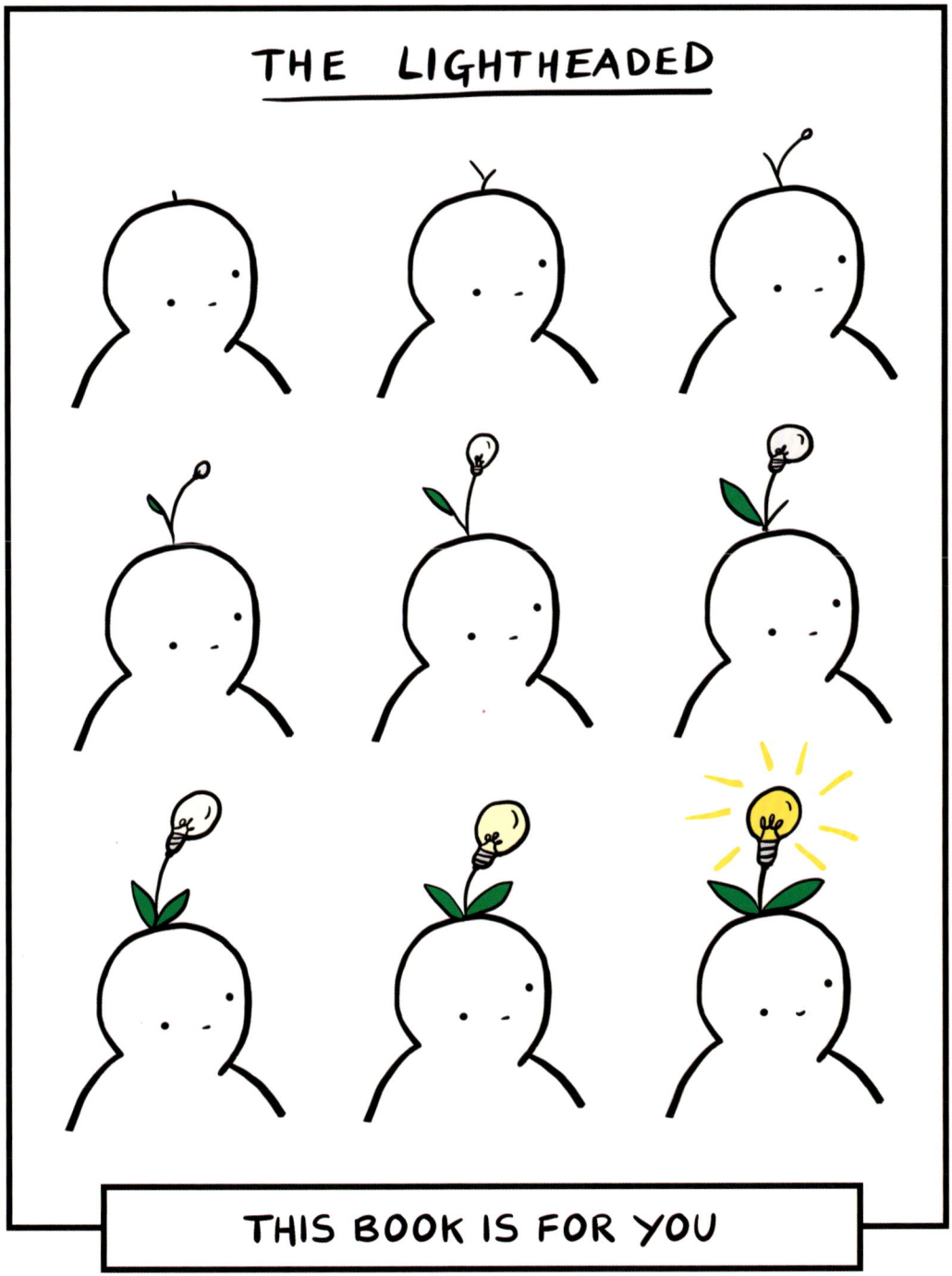
THE LIGHTHEADED
THIS BOOK IS FOR YOU

PEOPLE WHO BUY BOOKS BUT NEVER READ THEM

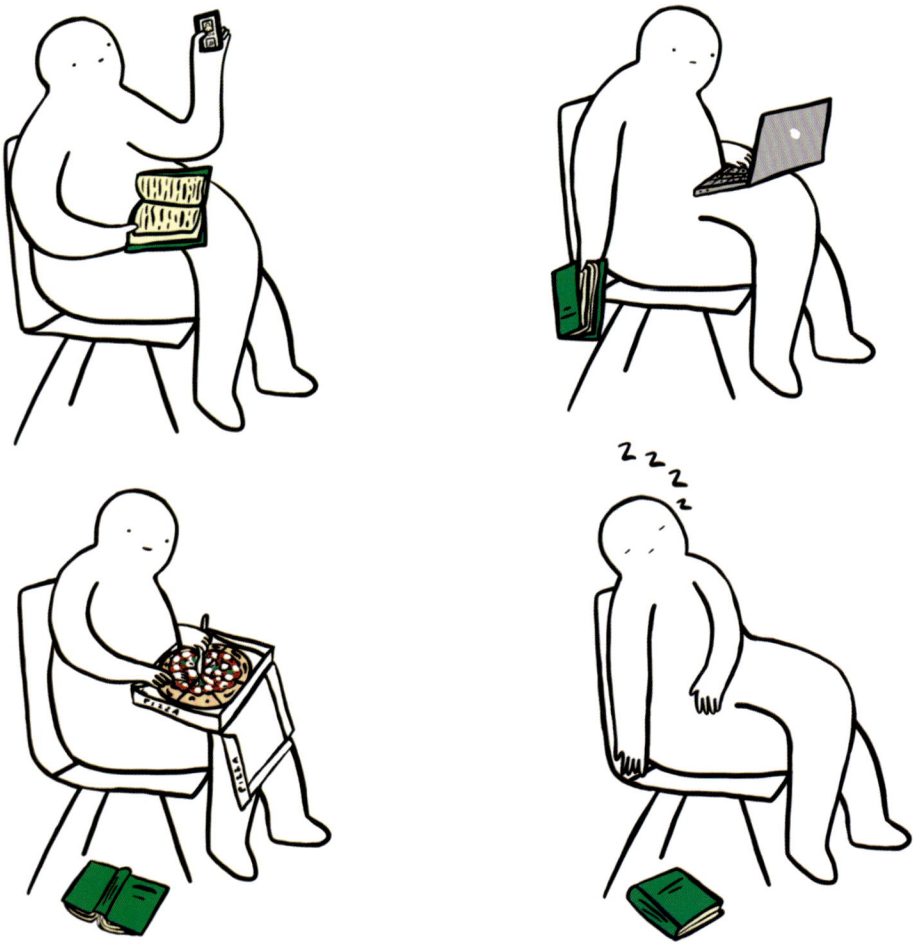

THIS BOOK IS FOR YOU

PEOPLE WHO READ BOOKS BUT NEVER BUY THEM

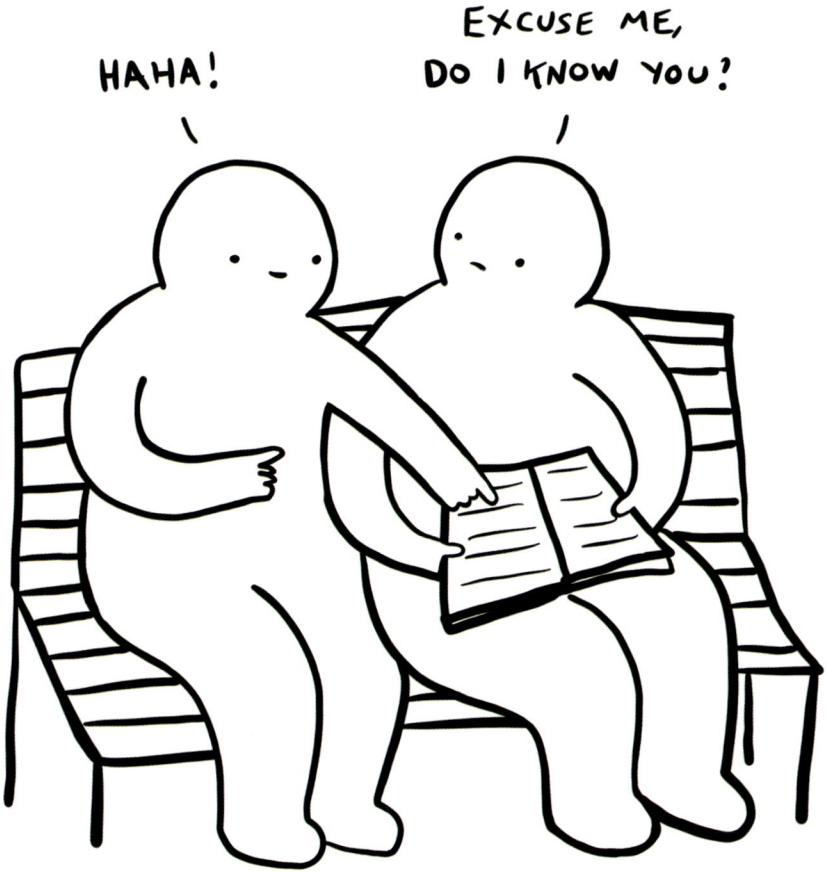

THIS BOOK IS FOR YOU

GOT ANY CONSTRUCTIVE CRITICISM?

NO, BUT COULD I INTEREST YOU IN SOME DESTRUCTIVE CRITICISM? IT'S MY SPECIALTY!

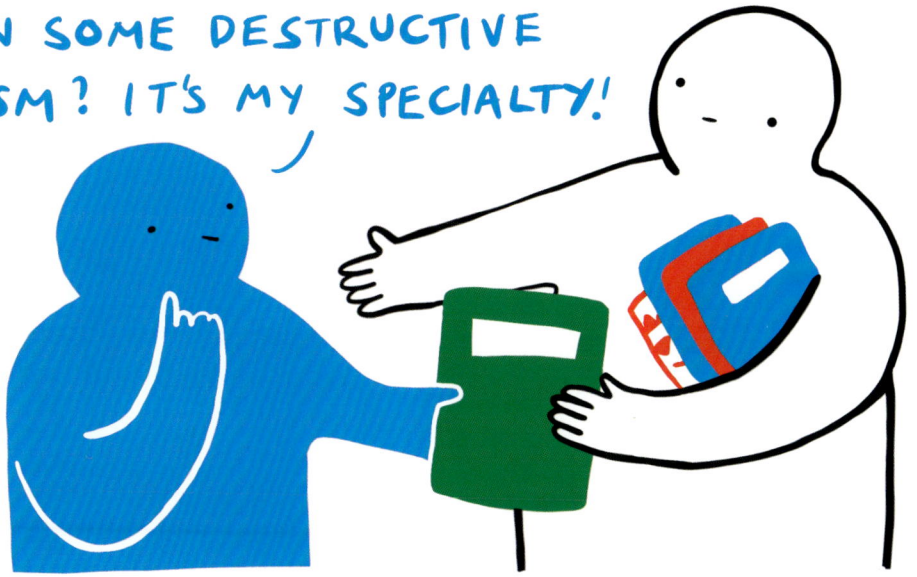

I MISS HOPE!

BUT YOU'VE GOT ME! HOPE AND I, WE'RE NOT THAT DIFFERENT, YOU KNOW?

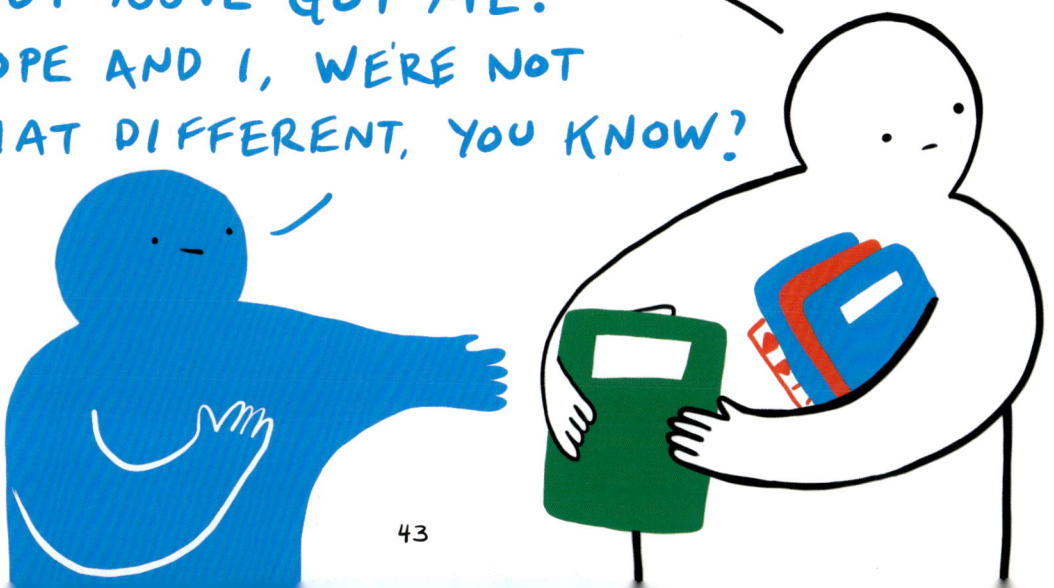

YOU'RE JOKING, RIGHT? YOU'RE, LIKE, COMPLETE OPPOSITES!

HOPE AND I BOTH JUST WANT THE BEST FOR YOU.

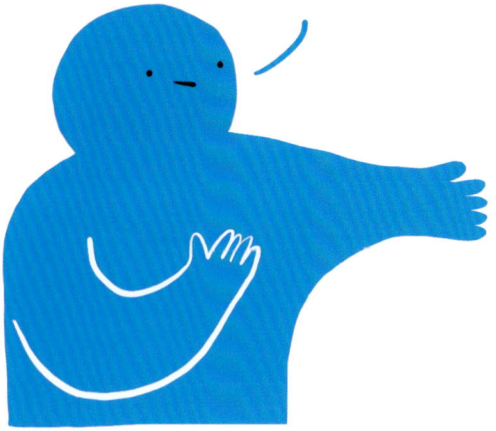

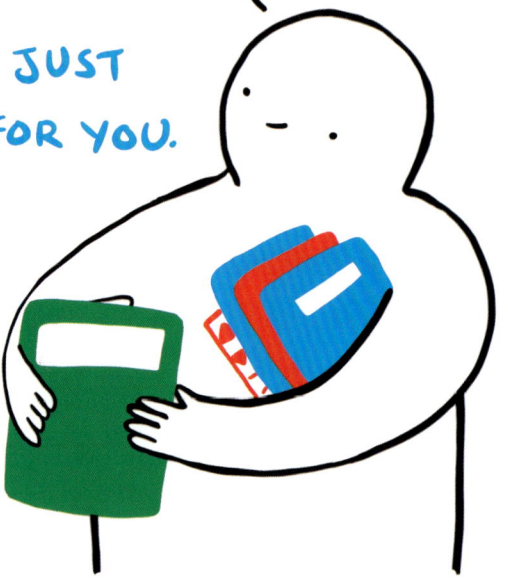

BUT I DON'T WANT YOU TO GET HURT. HOPE HAS LET YOU DOWN SO MANY TIMES IN THE PAST.

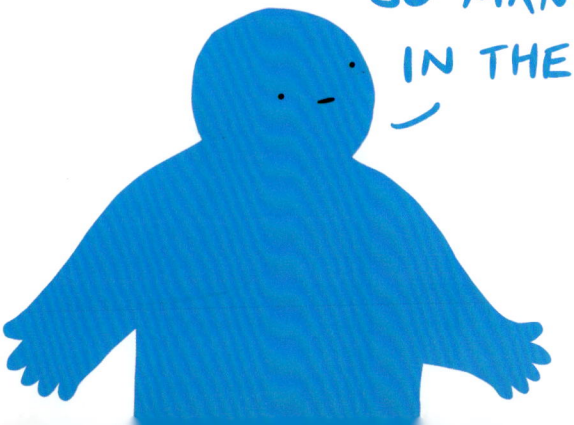

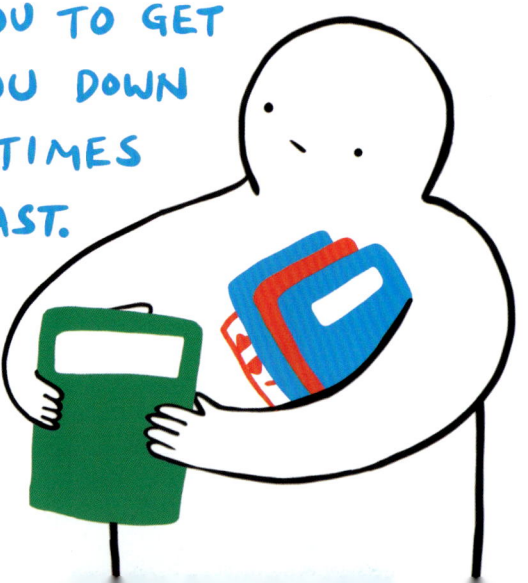

AND MAKING BOOKS IS HARD, EVEN FOR REALLY SMART PEOPLE, SO IMAGINE HOW HARD IT WILL BE FOR YOU!

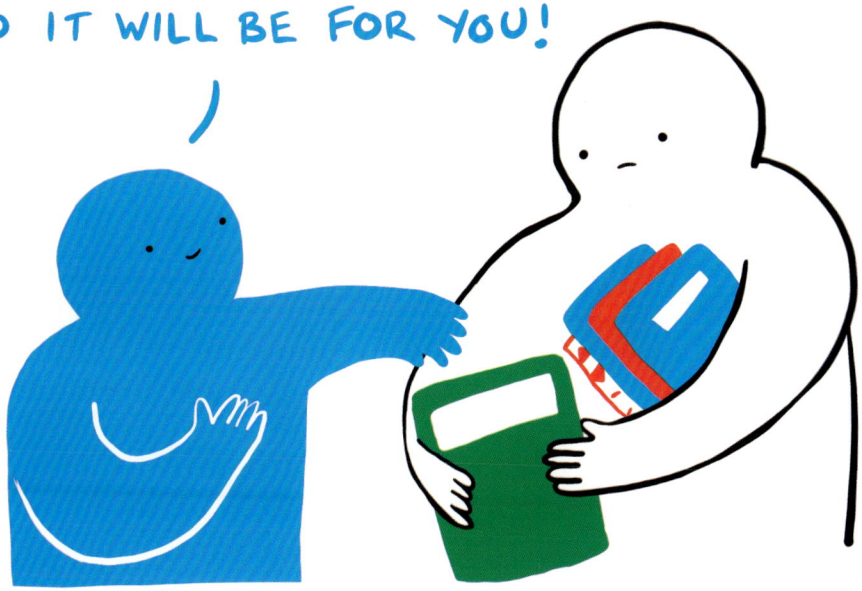

YOU WANT MY ADVICE?

"IF YOU DON'T TRY, YOU CAN'T FAIL."

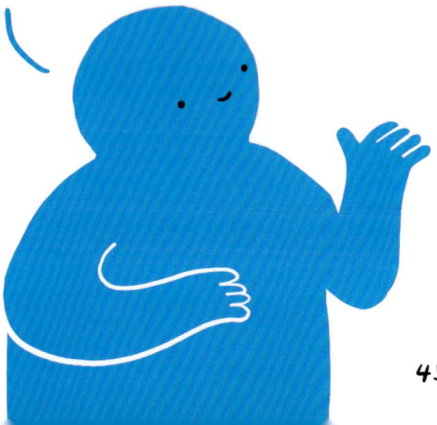

NOT REALLY.

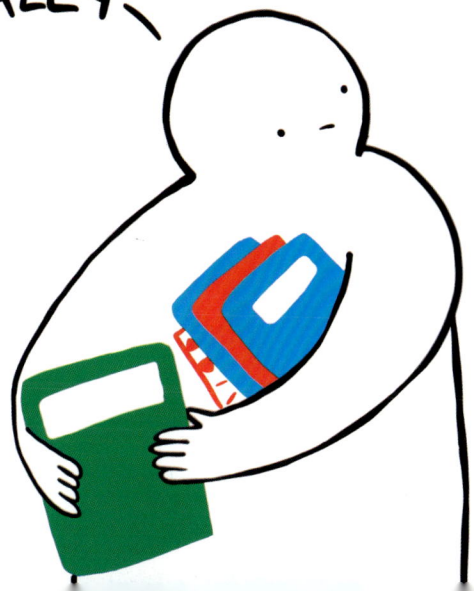

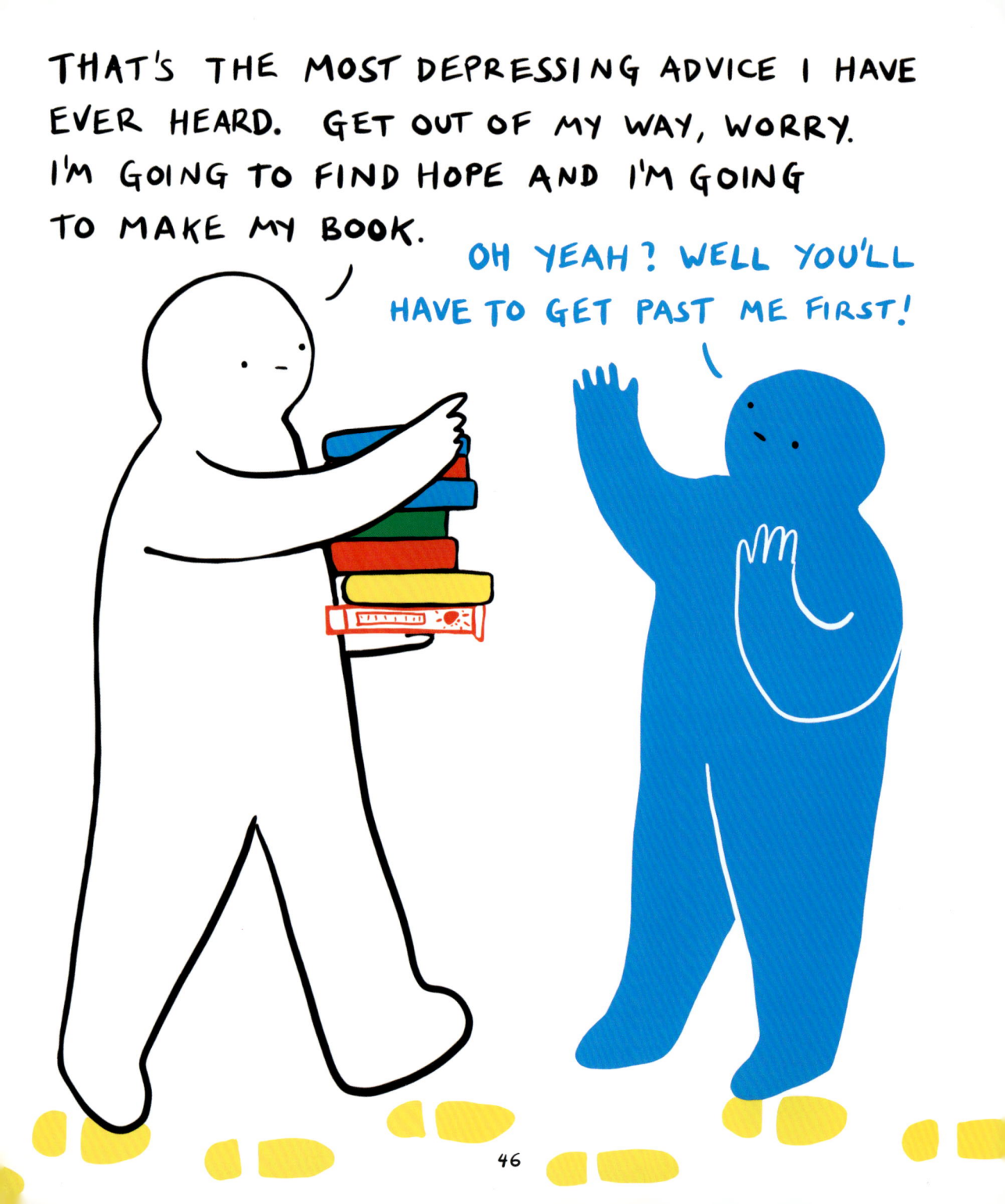
THAT'S THE MOST DEPRESSING ADVICE I HAVE EVER HEARD. GET OUT OF MY WAY, WORRY. I'M GOING TO FIND HOPE AND I'M GOING TO MAKE MY BOOK.
OH YEAH? WELL YOU'LL HAVE TO GET PAST ME FIRST!

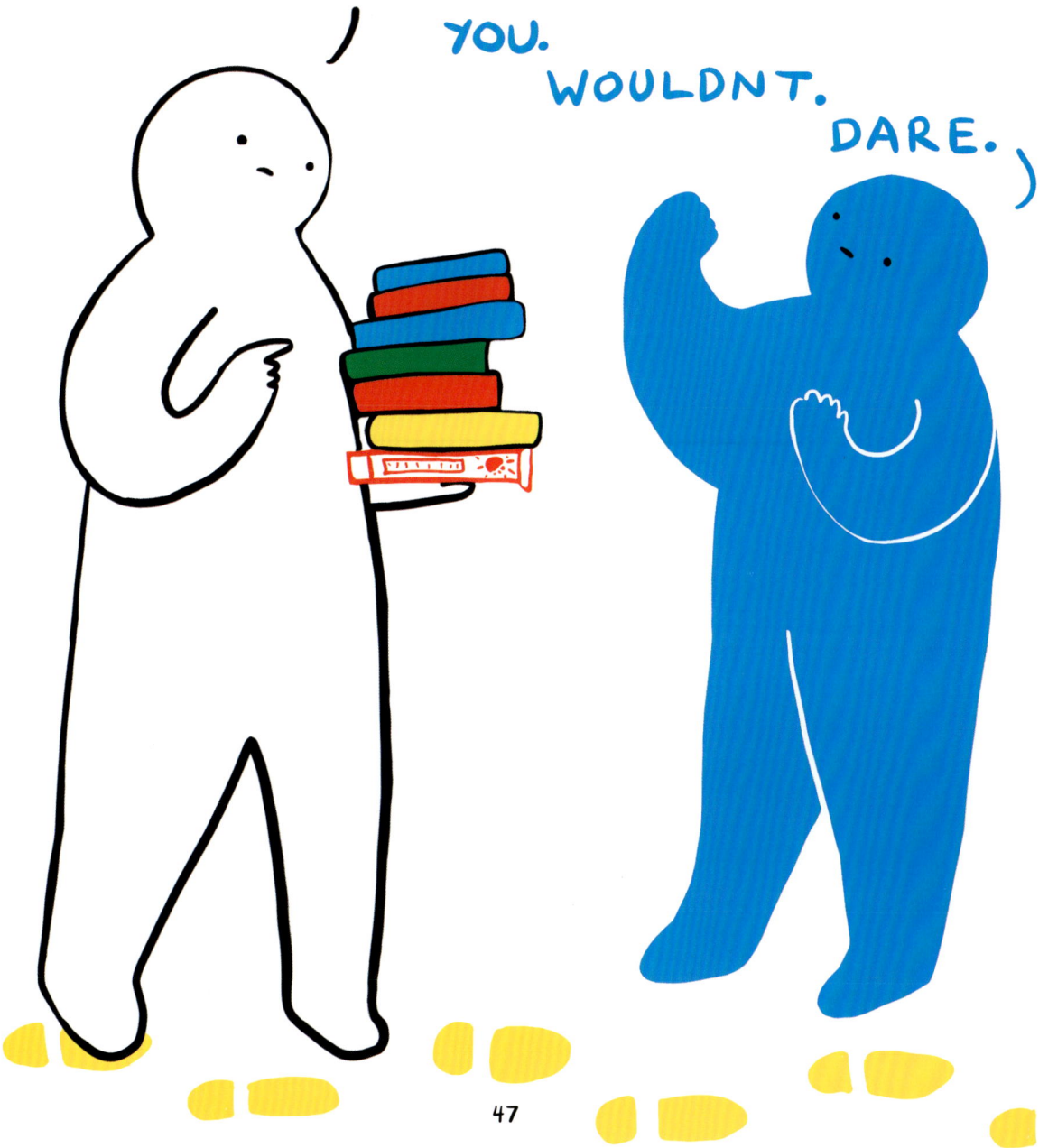
WORRY, I'M WARNING YOU. STEP ASIDE OR I'LL DO SOME DEEP BREATHING EXERCISES AND MAKE MYSELF A NICE CUP OF TEA.
YOU. WOULDNT. DARE.

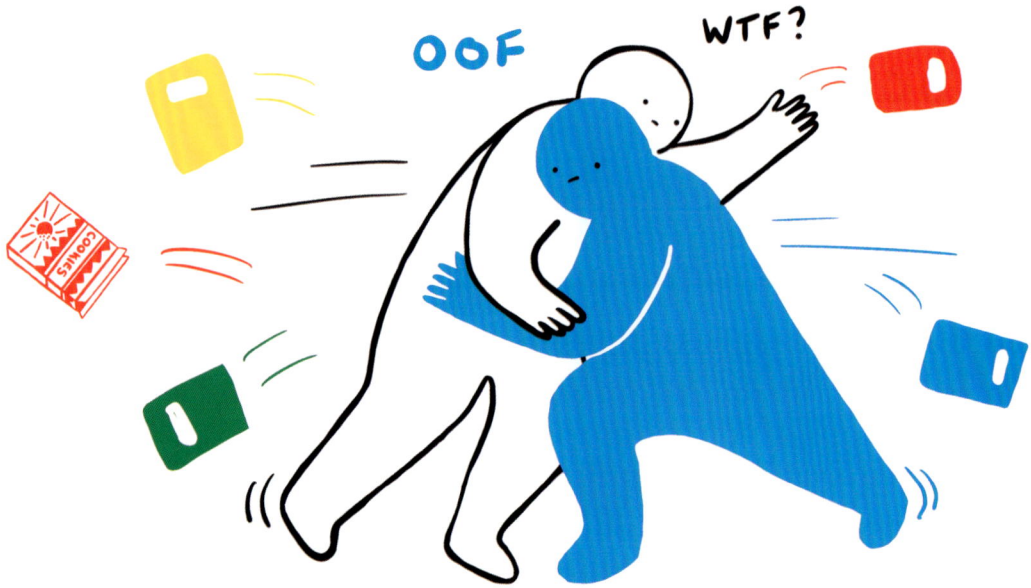
OOF
WTF?
COOKIES

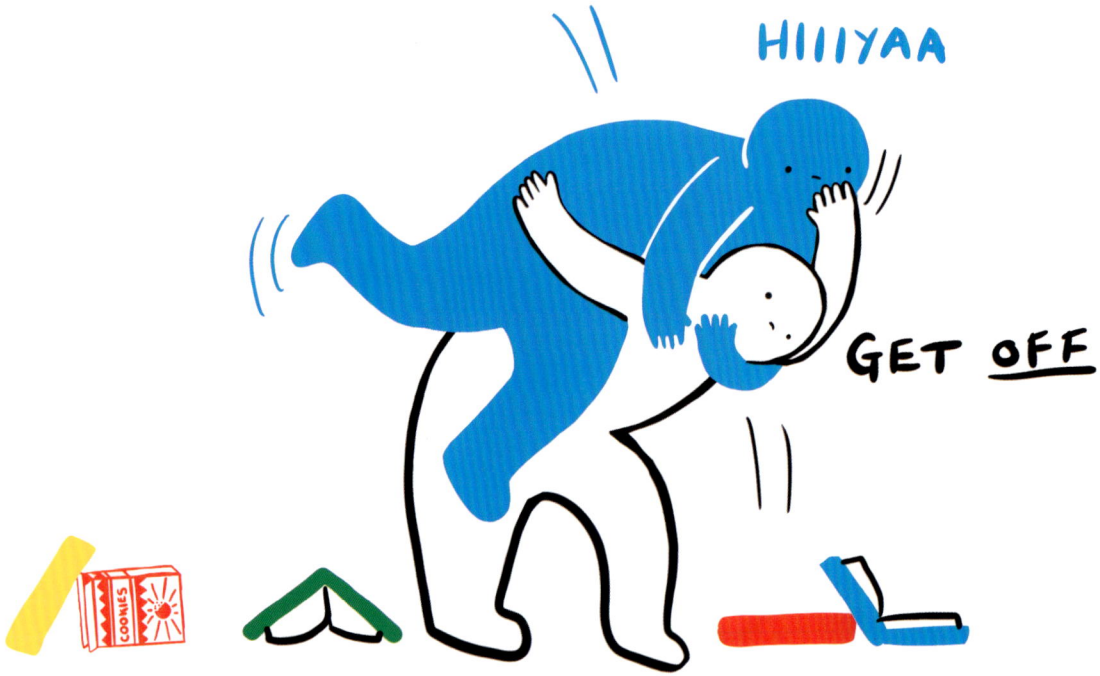
HIIIYAA
GET OFF
COOKIES

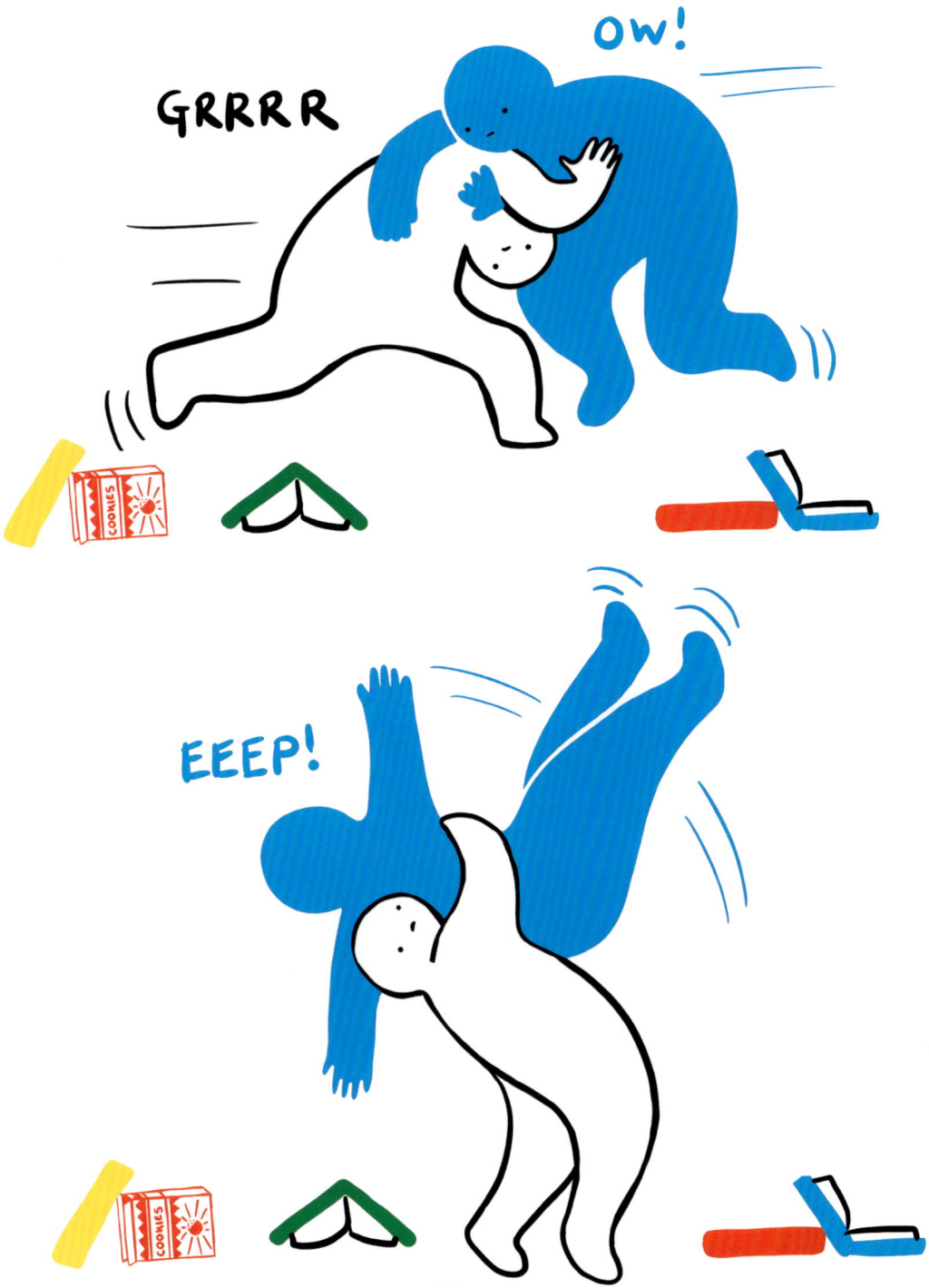
GRRRR
OW!
COOKIES
EEEP!
COOKIES

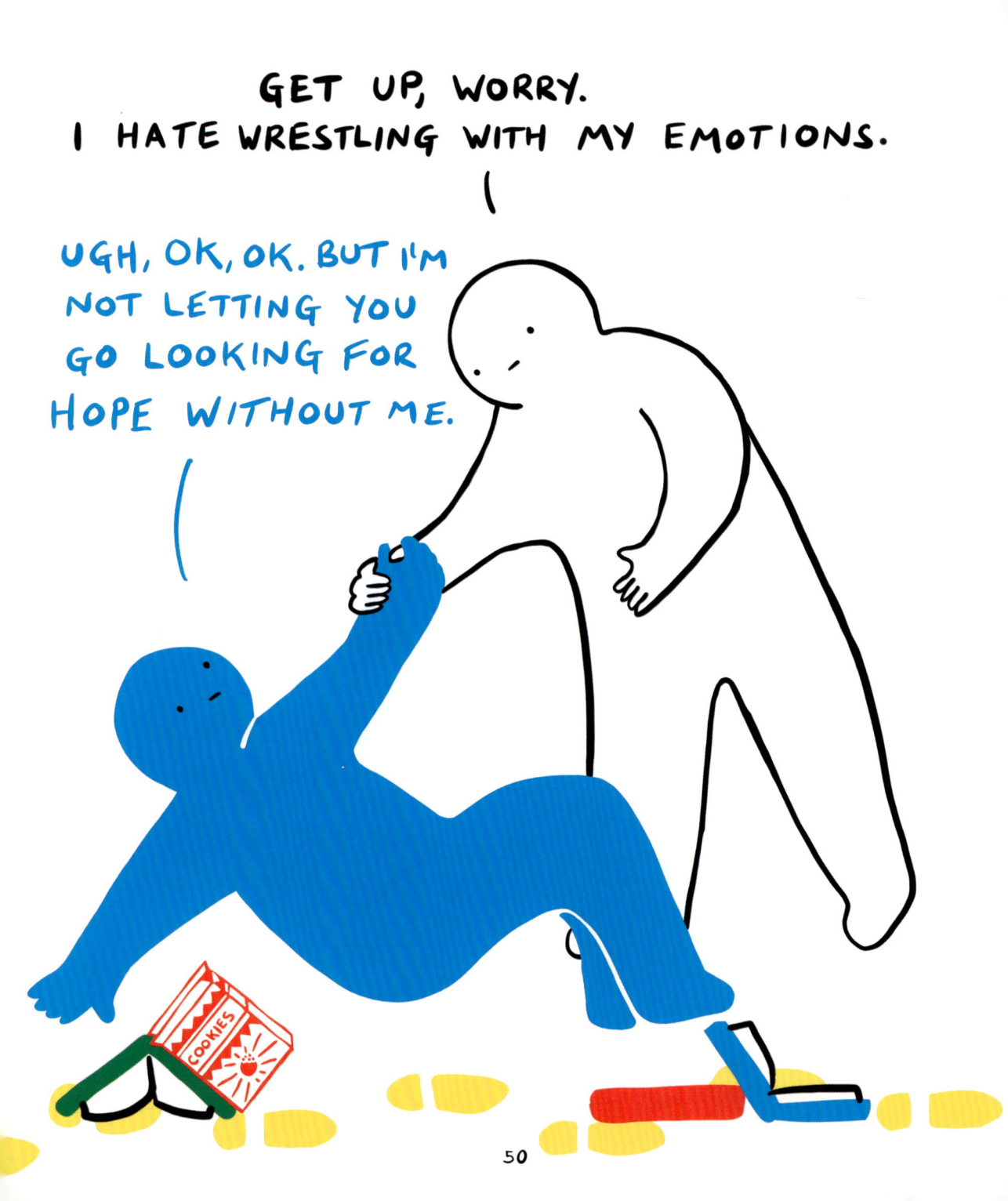
GET UP, WORRY.
I HATE WRESTLING WITH MY EMOTIONS.
UGH, OK, OK. BUT I'M NOT LETTING YOU GO LOOKING FOR HOPE WITHOUT ME.
COOKIES

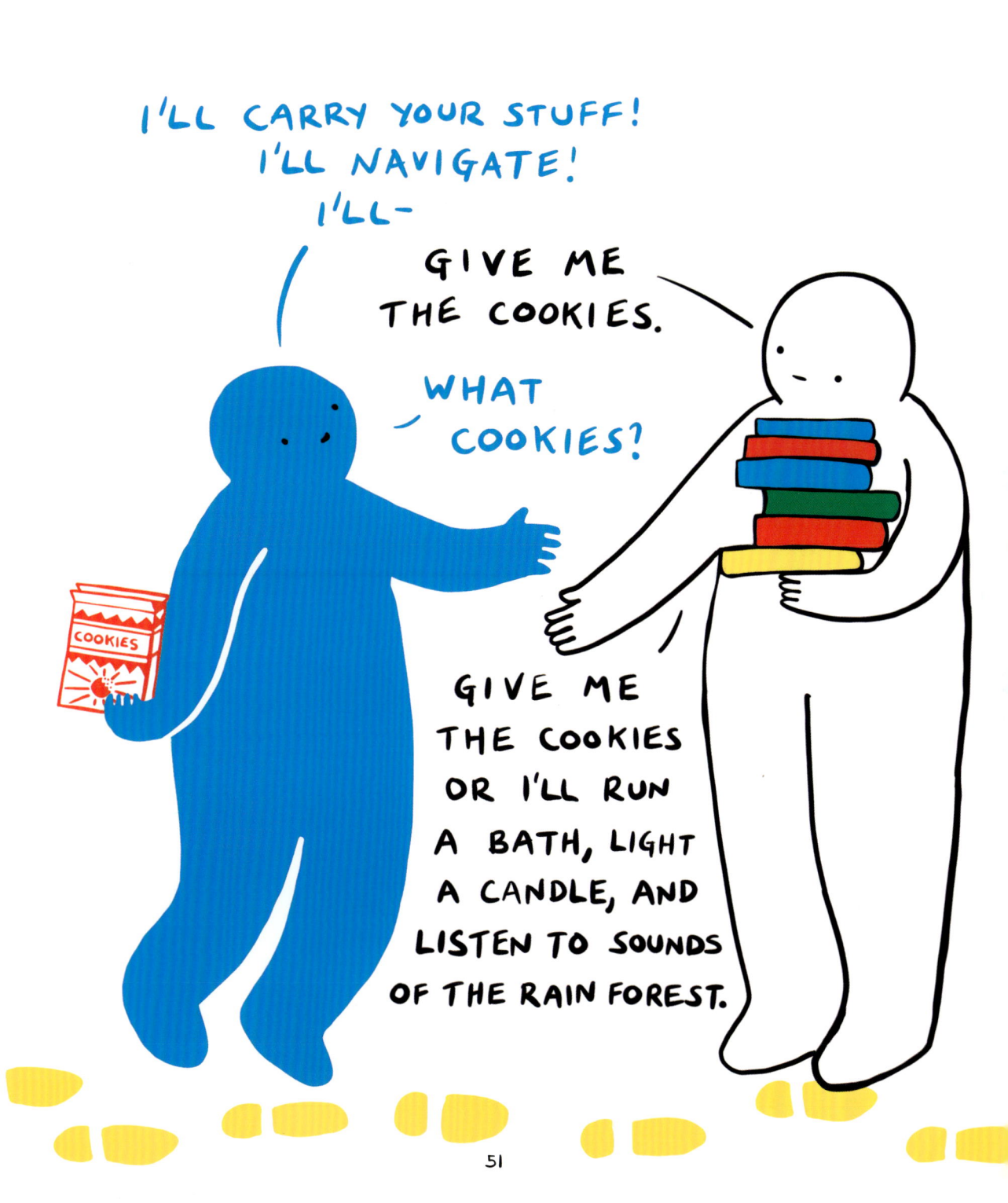
I'LL CARRY YOUR STUFF!
I'LL NAVIGATE!
I'LL-
GIVE ME THE COOKIES.
WHAT COOKIES?
COOKIES
GIVE ME THE COOKIES OR I'LL RUN A BATH, LIGHT A CANDLE, AND LISTEN TO SOUNDS OF THE RAIN FOREST.

SIGH FINE. I'LL GIVE YOU THE COOKIES ON TWO CONDITIONS: 1. I AM COMING WITH YOU TO FIND HOPE.

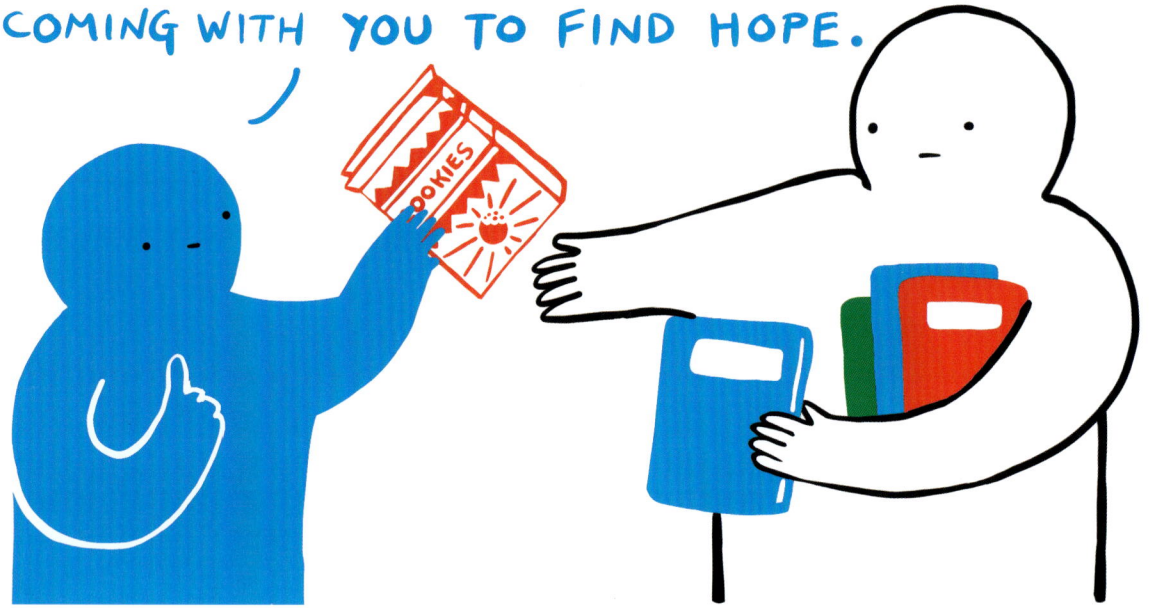

2. I GET TO EDIT YOUR BOOK ON THE WAY. JUDGING BY WHAT I'VE SEEN SO FAR, YOU NEED ALL THE HELP YOU CAN GET.

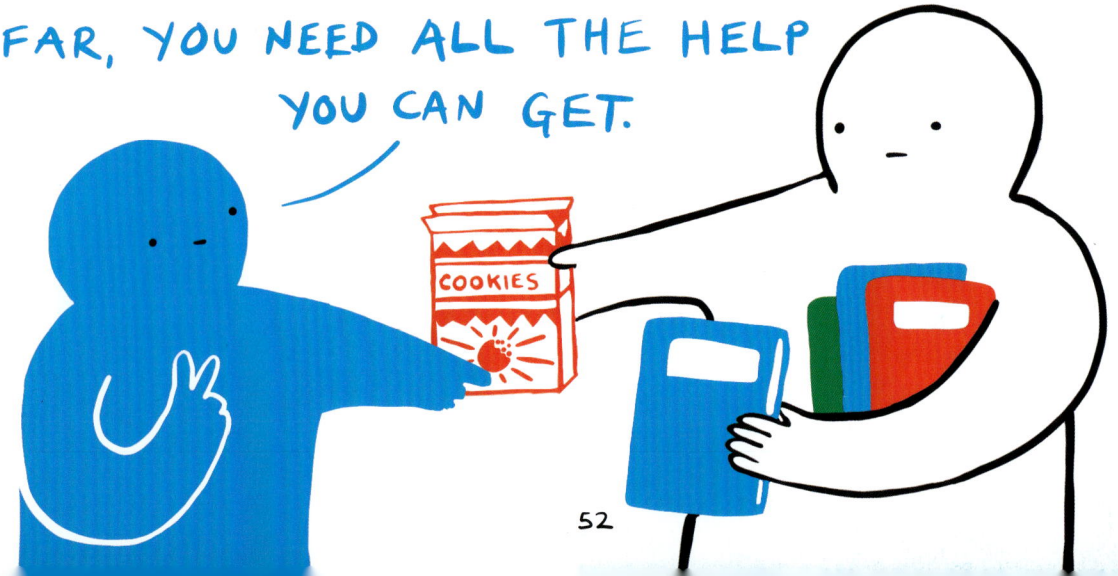

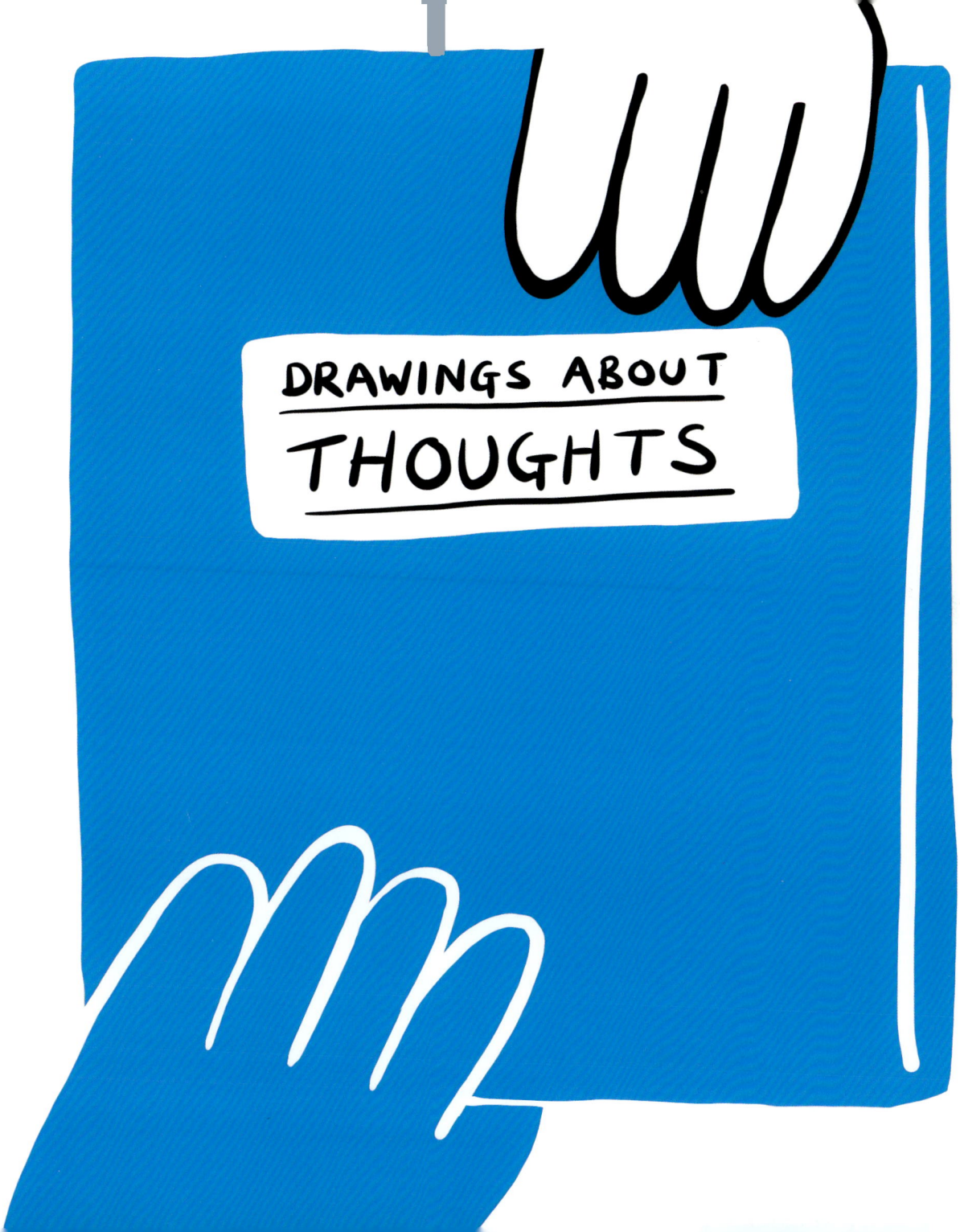
DRAWINGS ABOUT
THOUGHTS

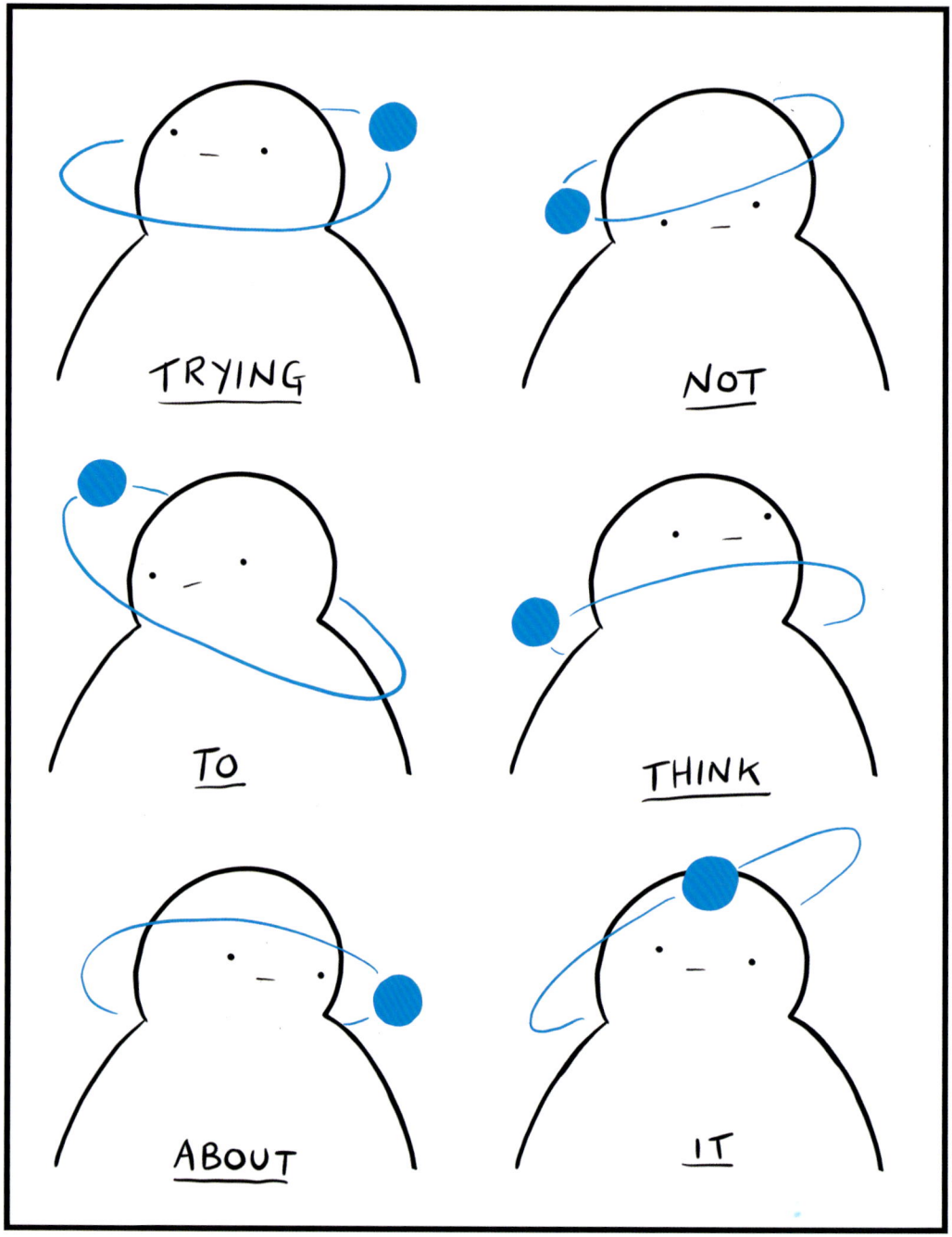

MOSTLY FAILING.

ME TRYING TO GET OUT OF MY OWN HEAD

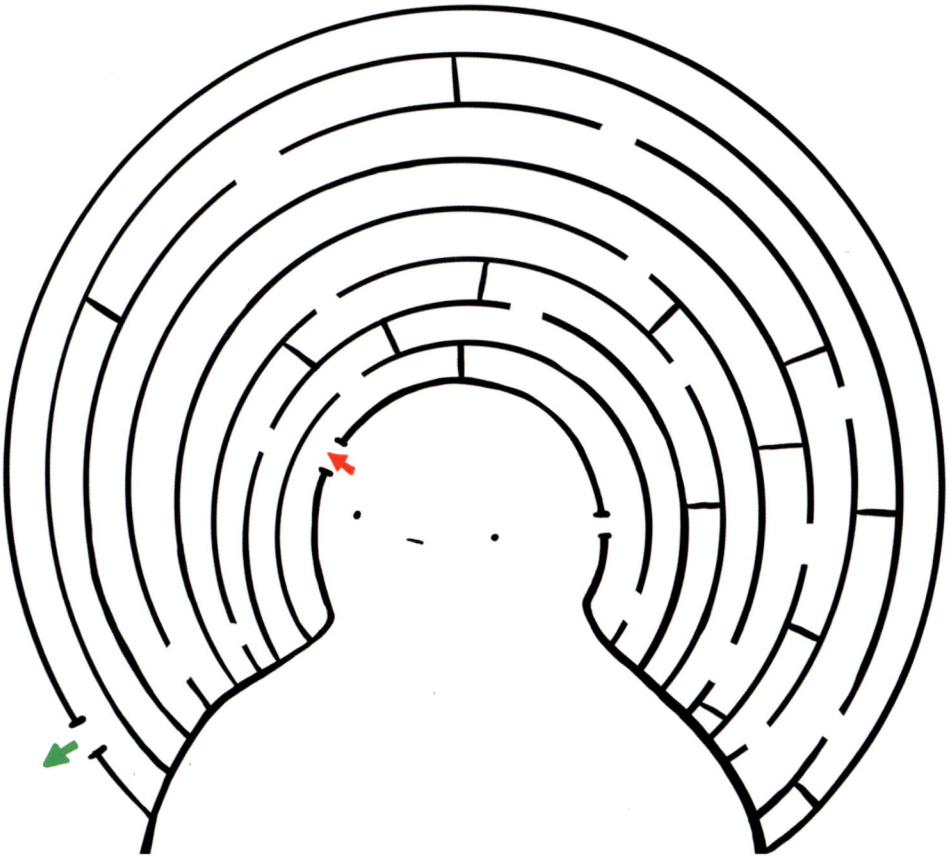

PLAY ALONG AT HOME.

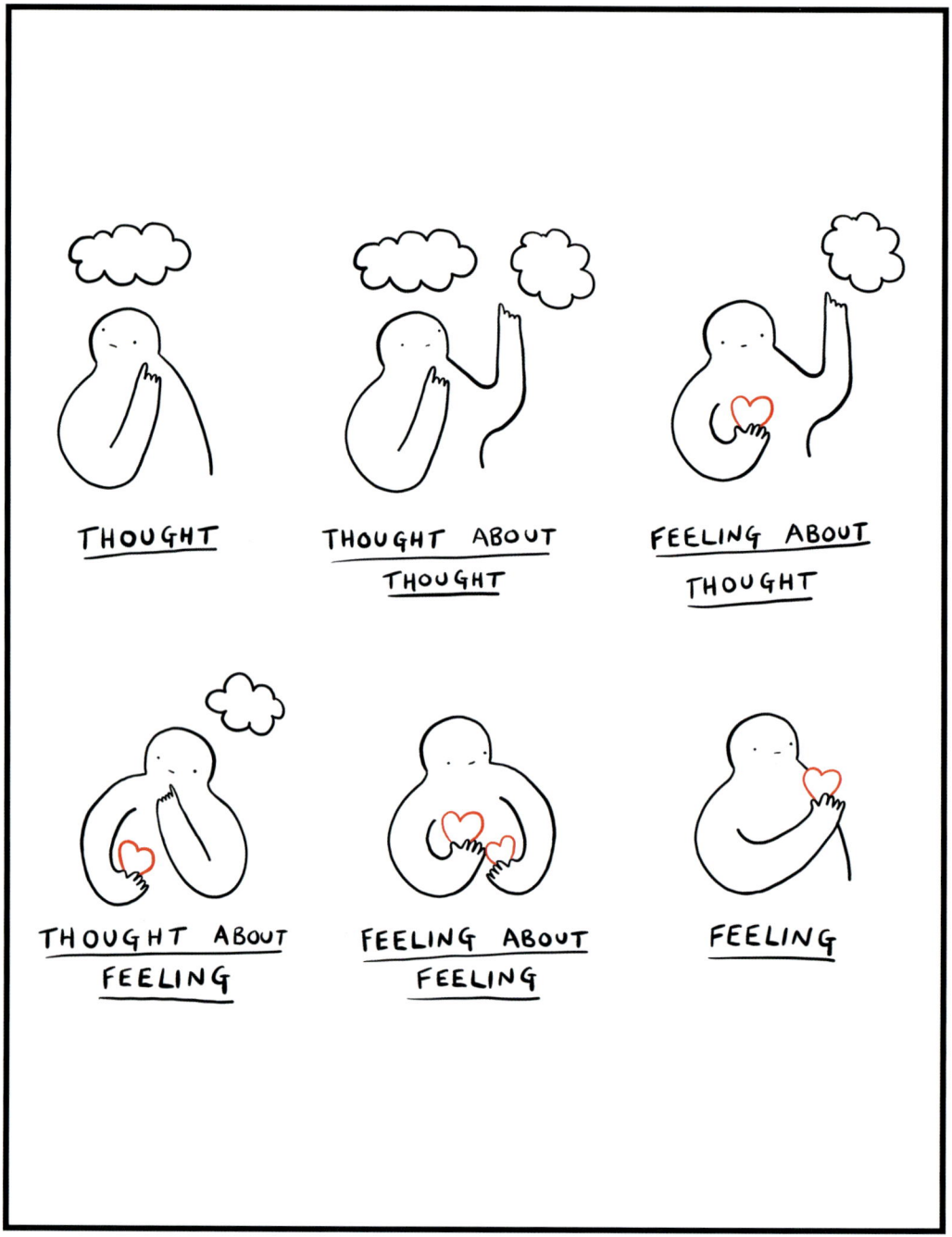
THOUGHT
THOUGHT ABOUT THOUGHT
FEELING ABOUT THOUGHT
THOUGHT ABOUT FEELING
FEELING ABOUT FEELING
FEELING

PROCESSING.

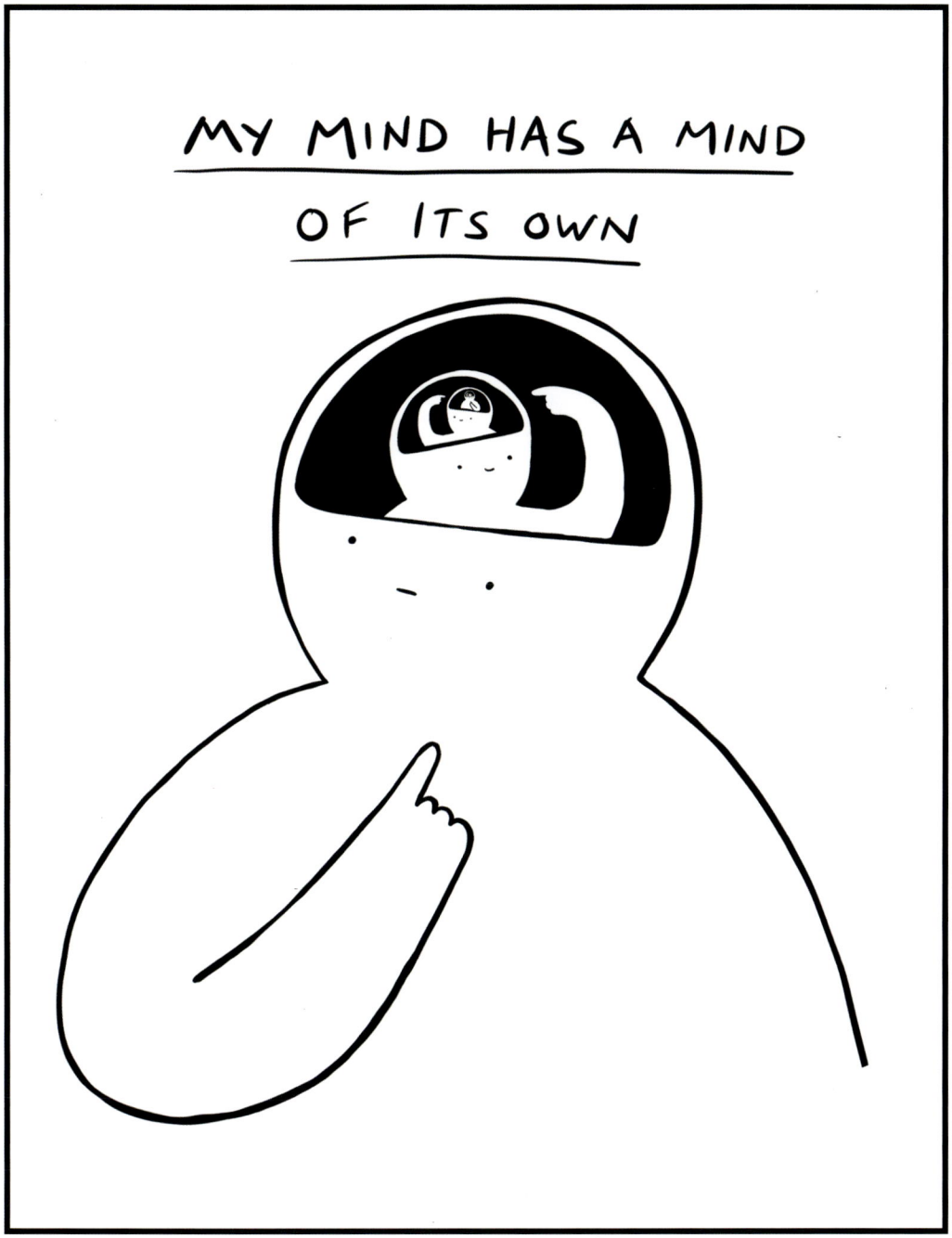

AND SO ON.

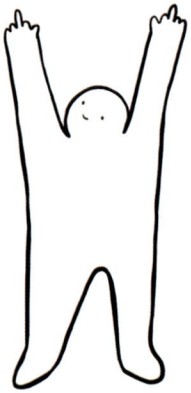

NOT TODAY,
DARK THOUGHTS

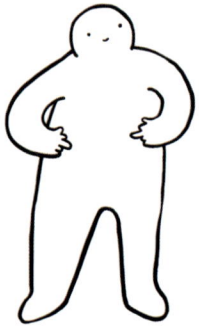

NOT TODAY,
SELF-DOUBT

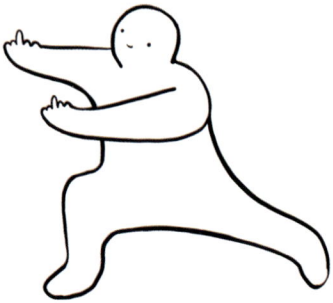

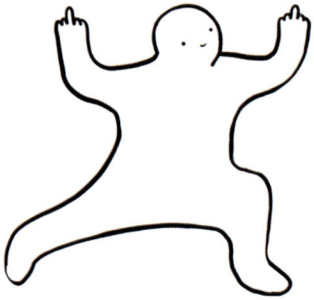

NOT TODAY, AVOIDING MY ACTUAL RESPONSIBILITIES
AND INSTEAD DOING SMALL, MEANINGLESS TASKS
AROUND THE HOUSE IN ORDER TO DISTRACT MYSELF
FROM THE FACT THAT MY LIFE IS A MESS

NOT TODAY.

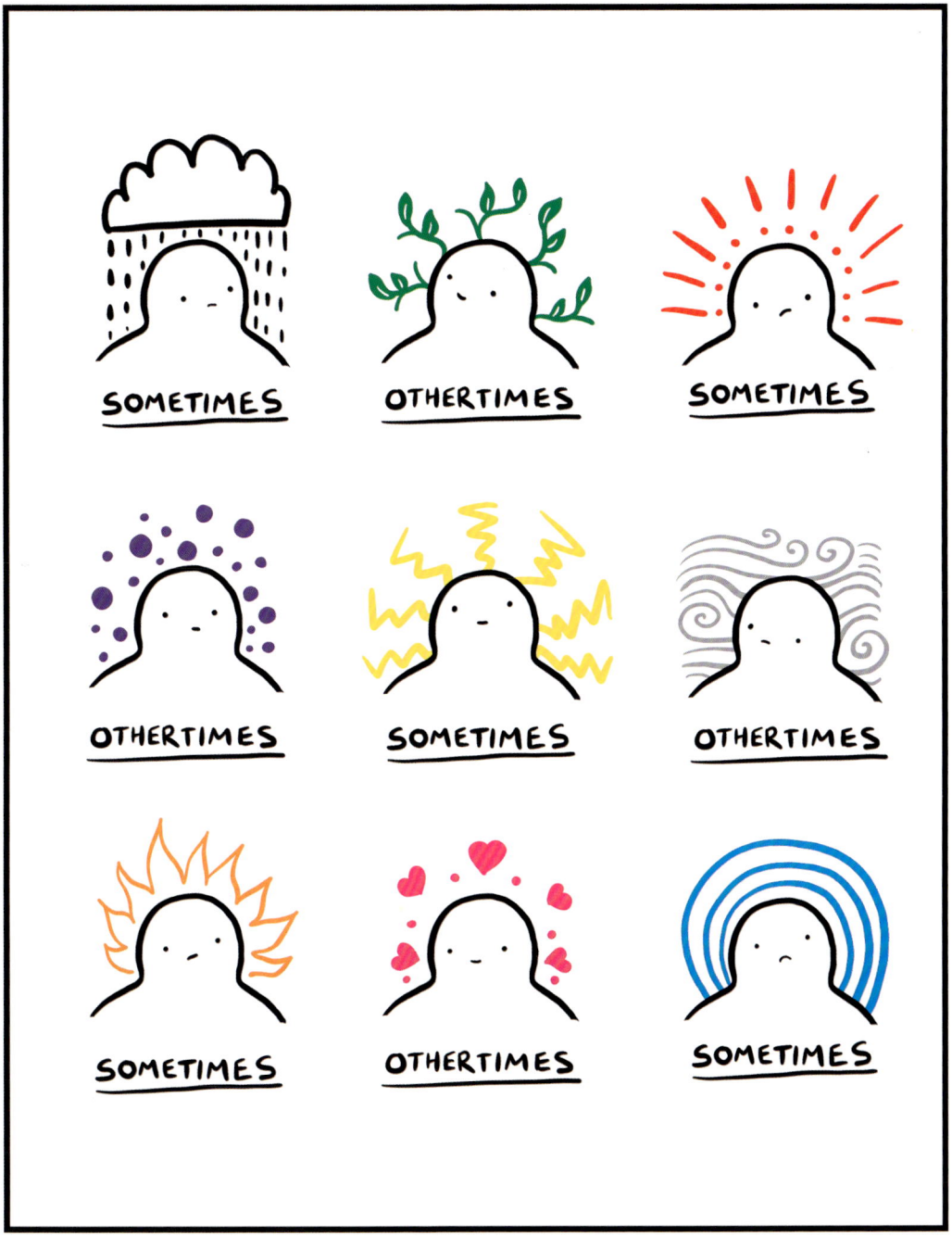

MENTAL HEALTH.

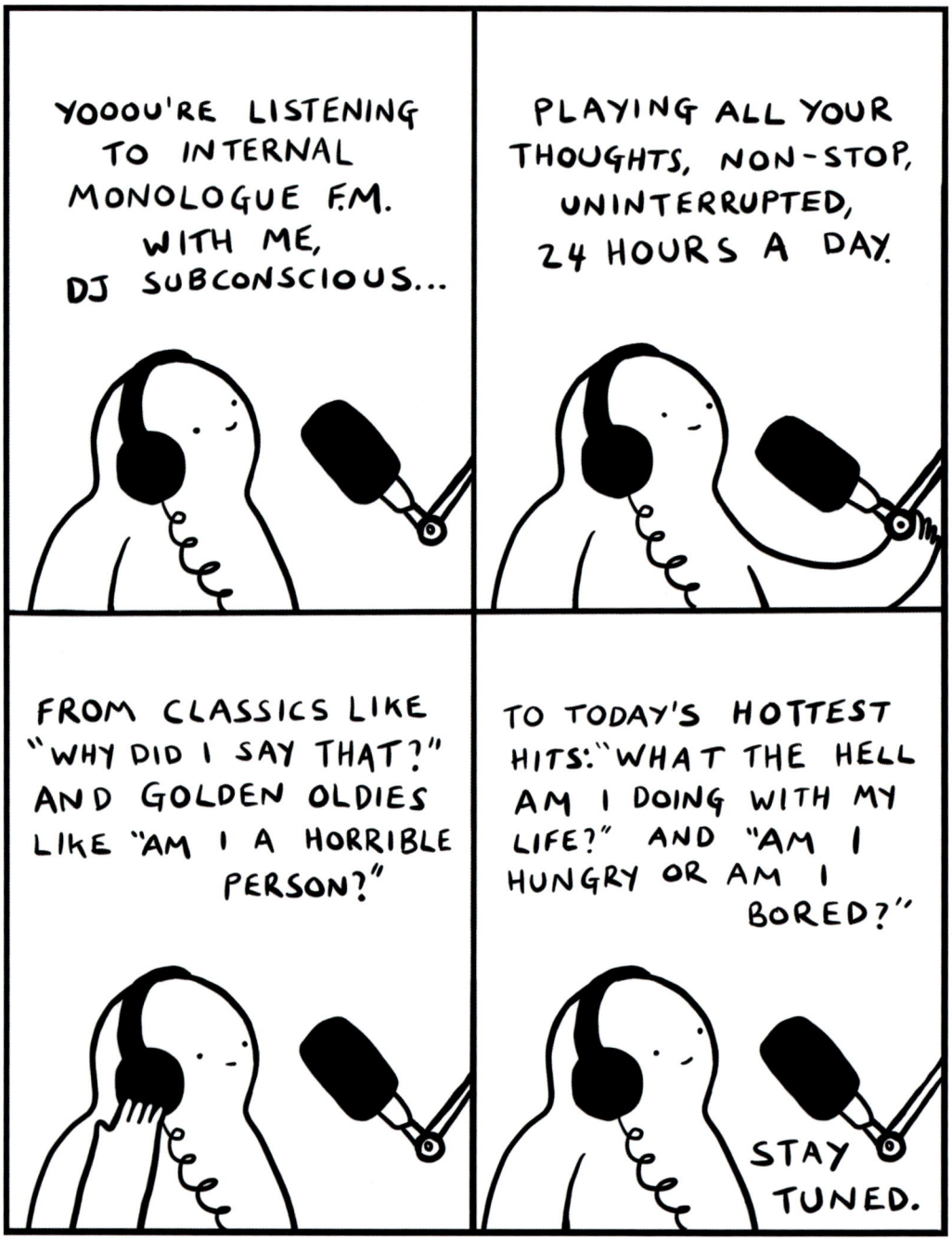

NONSTOP BANGERS.

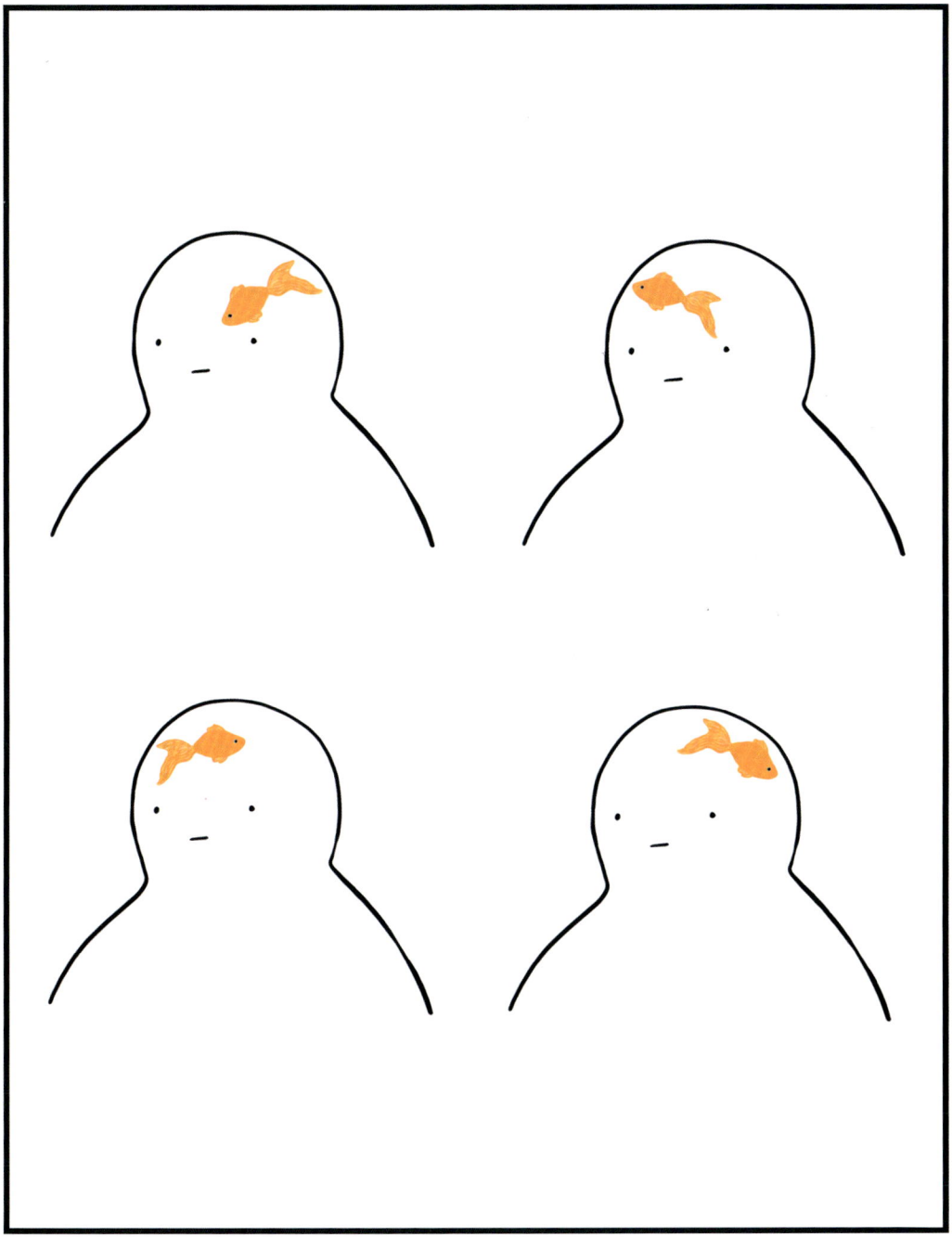

HERE WE GO AGAIN.

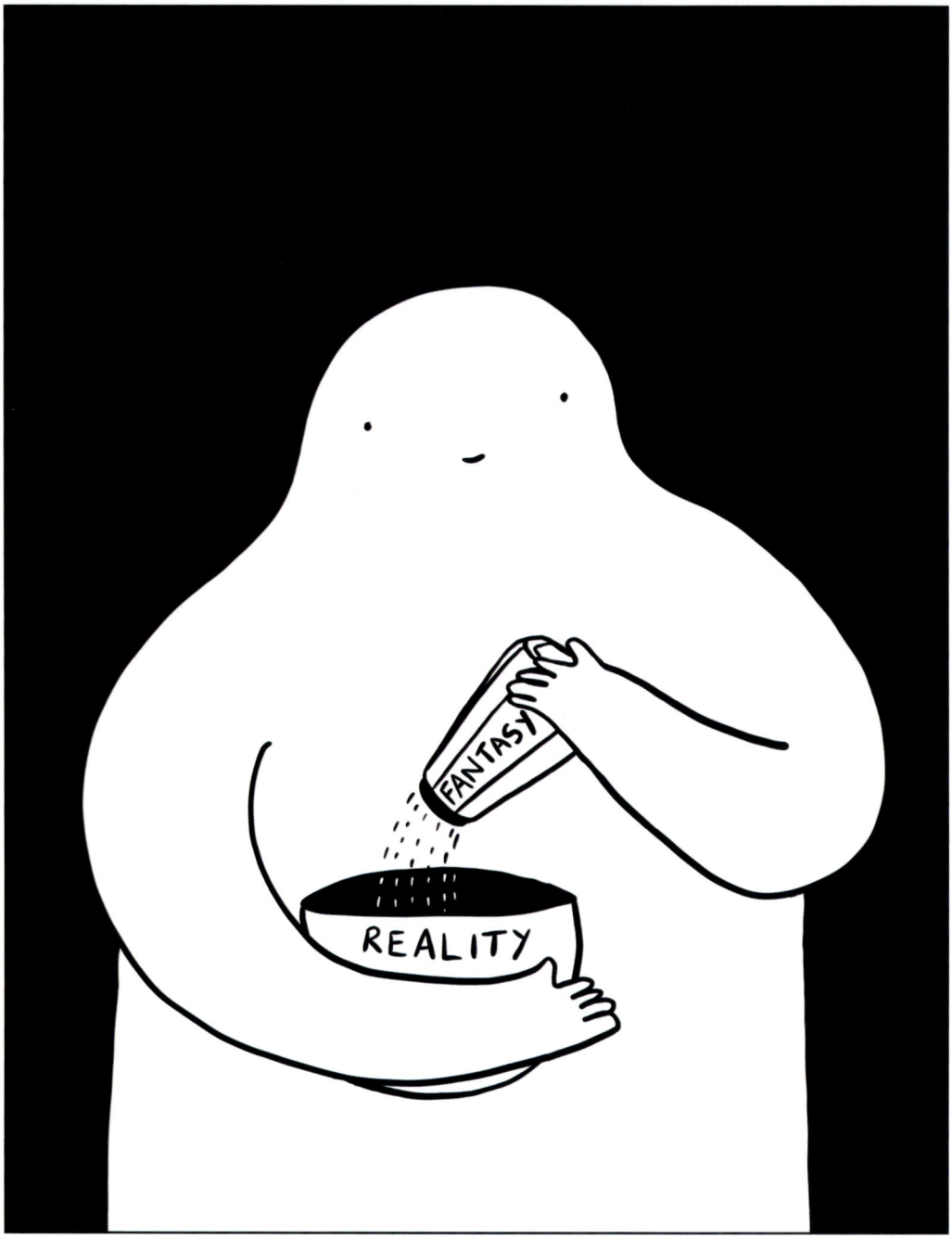

SECRET INGREDIENT.

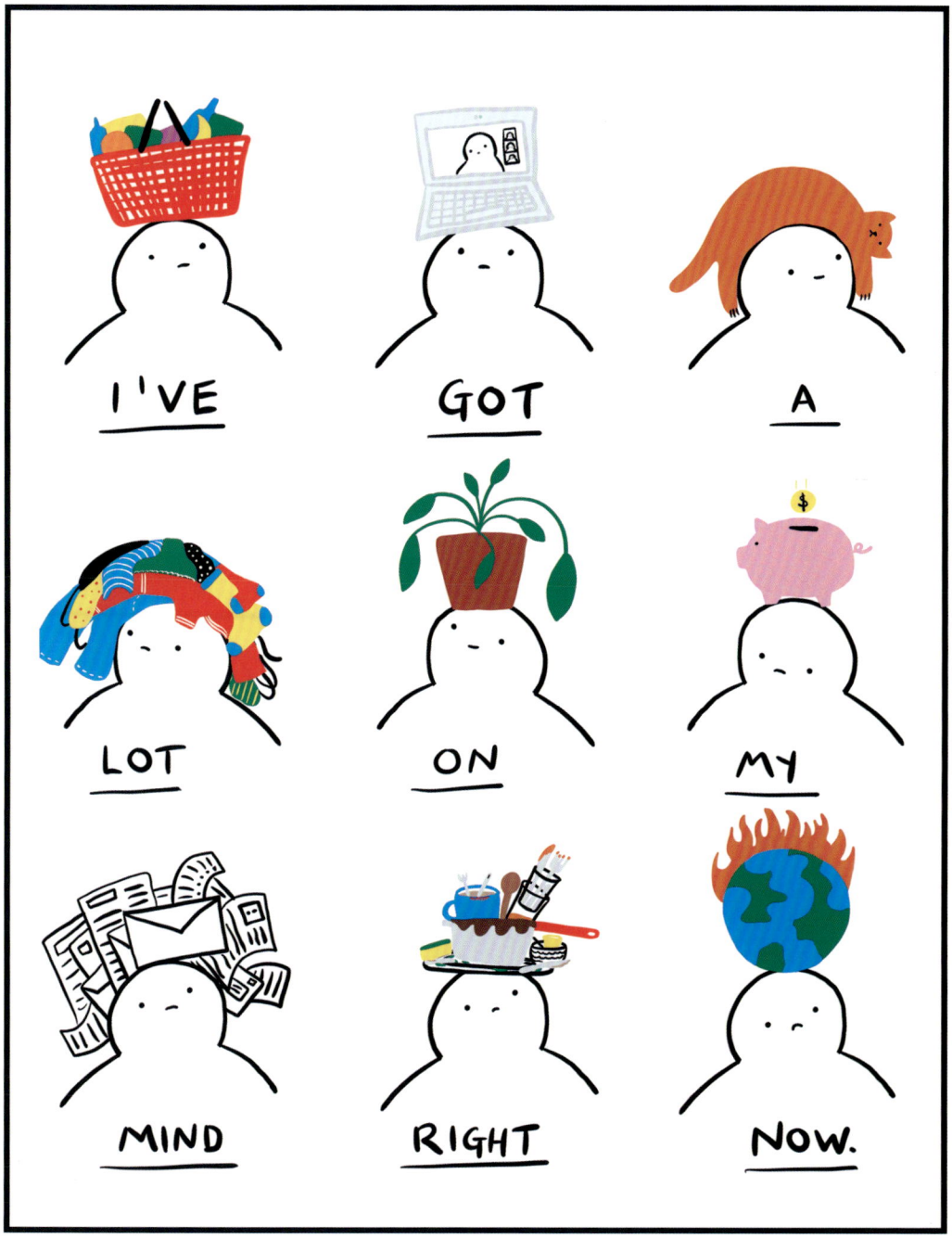

MENTAL LOAD.

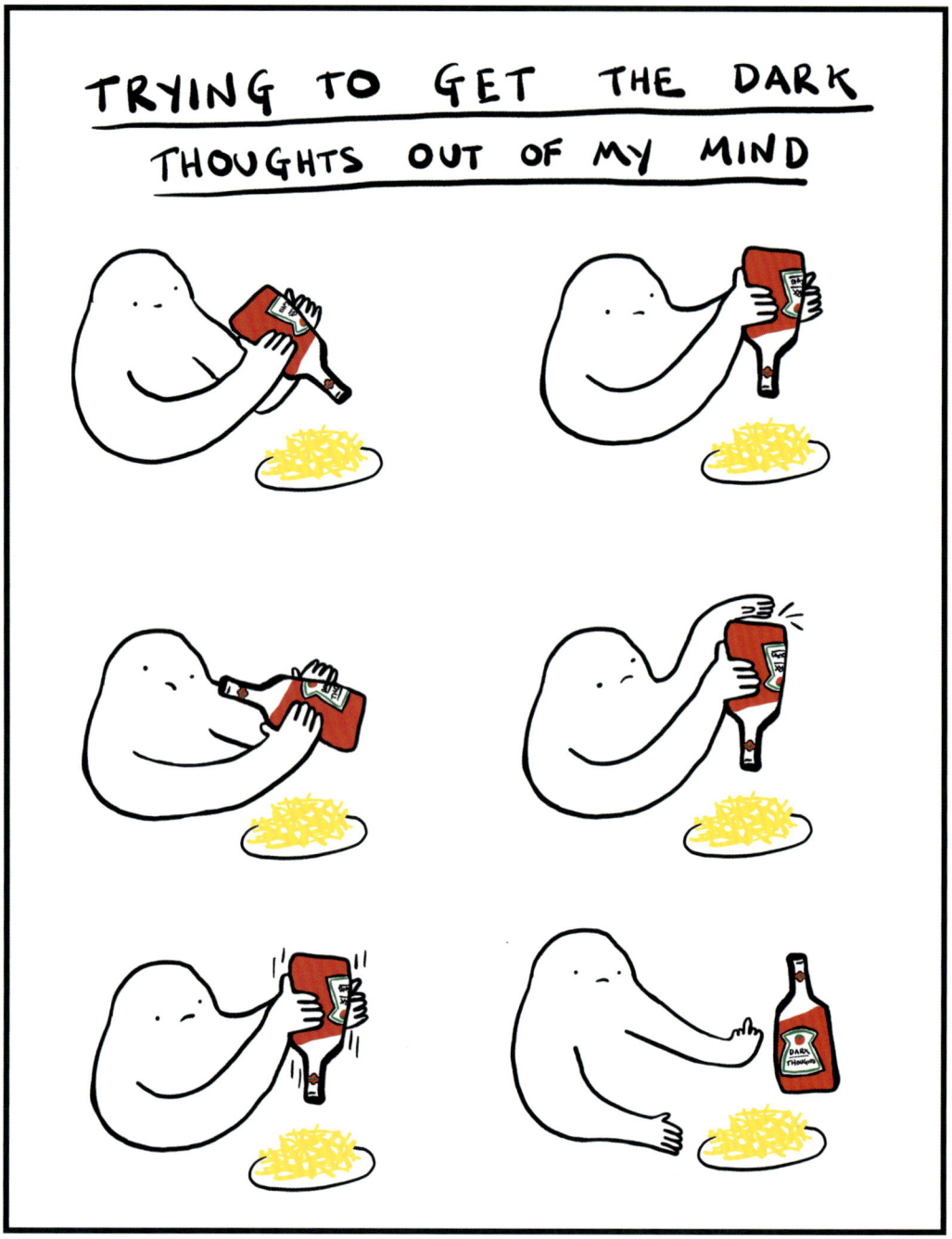

SAUCE OF FRUSTRATION.

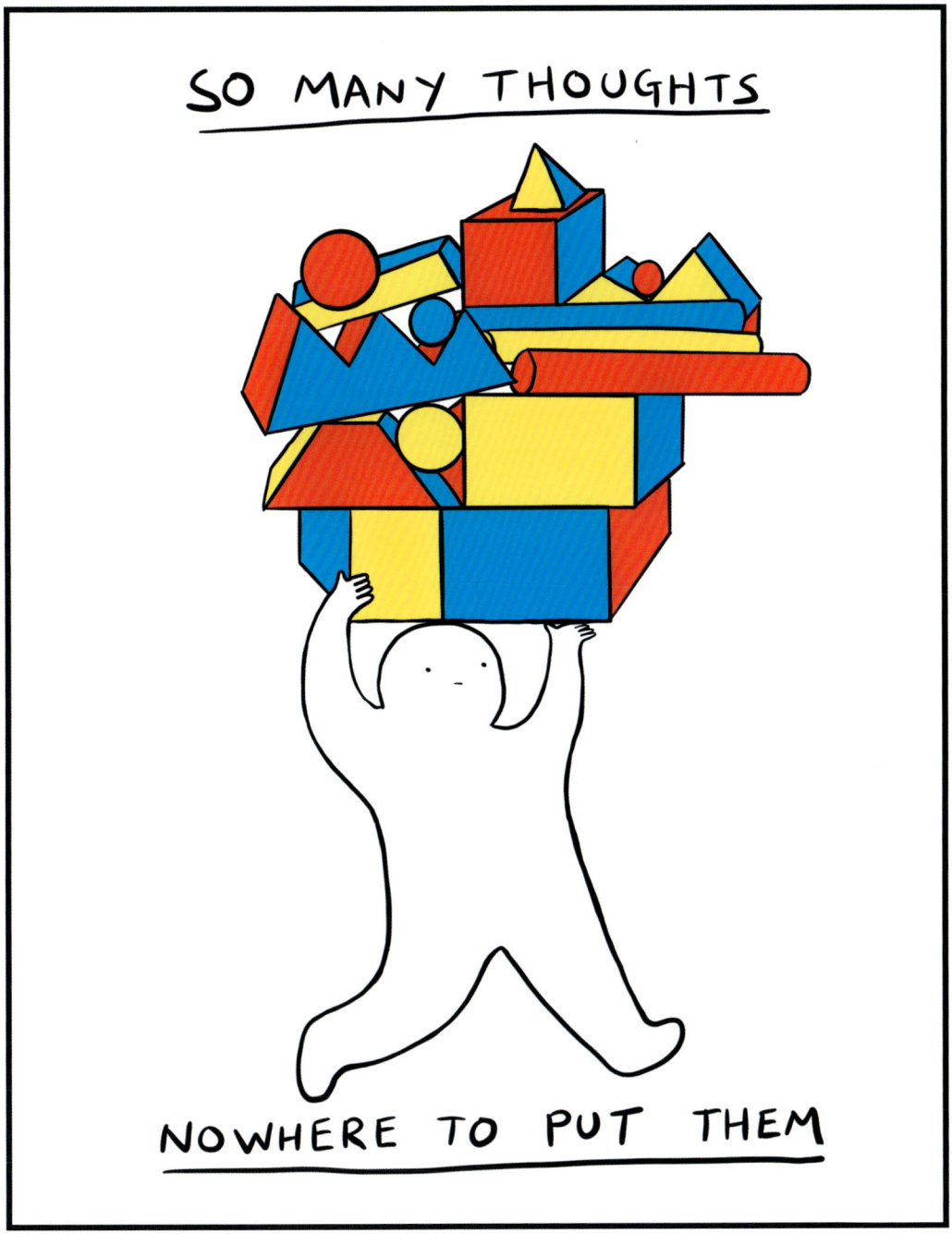

NEED MORE HEADSPACE.

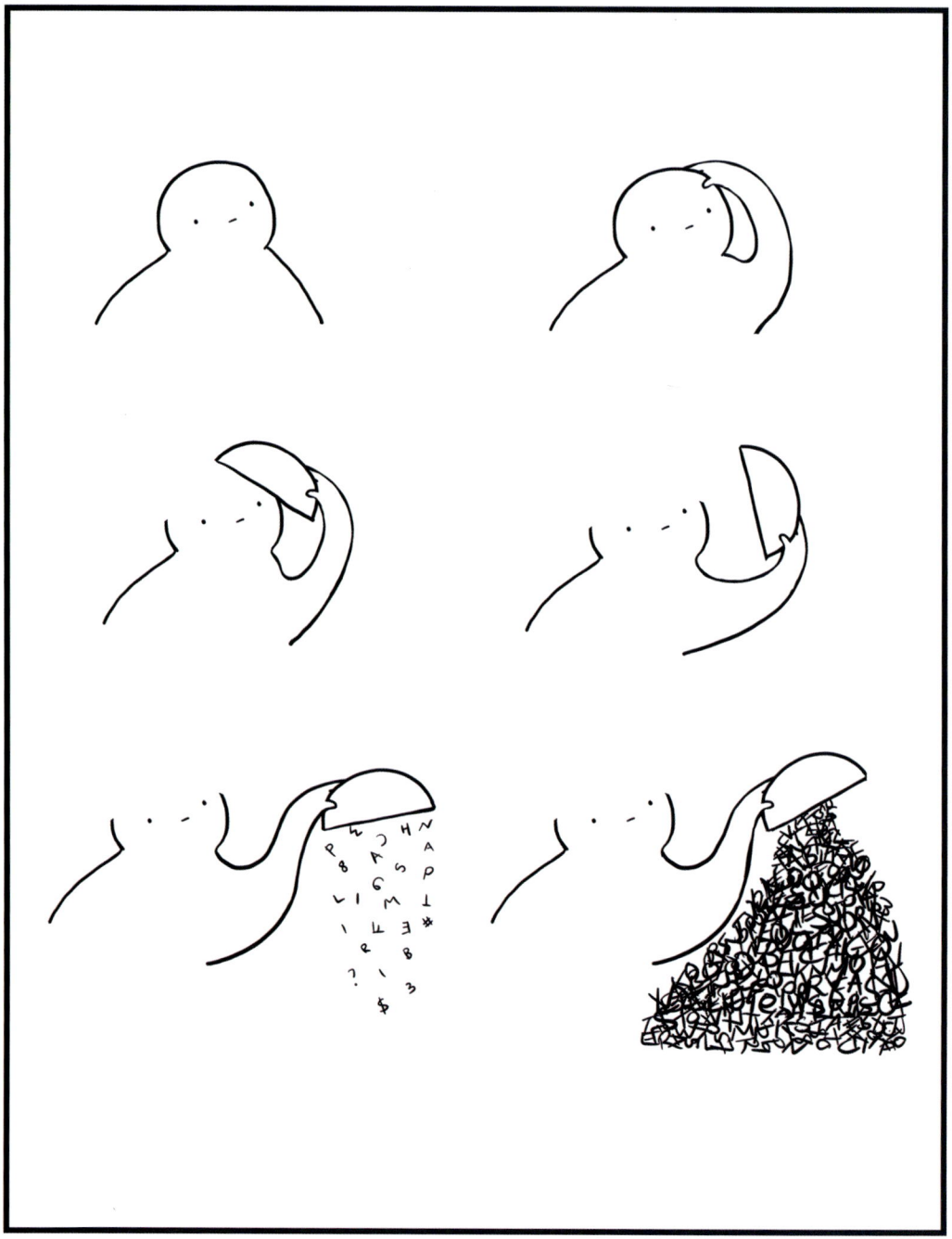

MINDFULL.

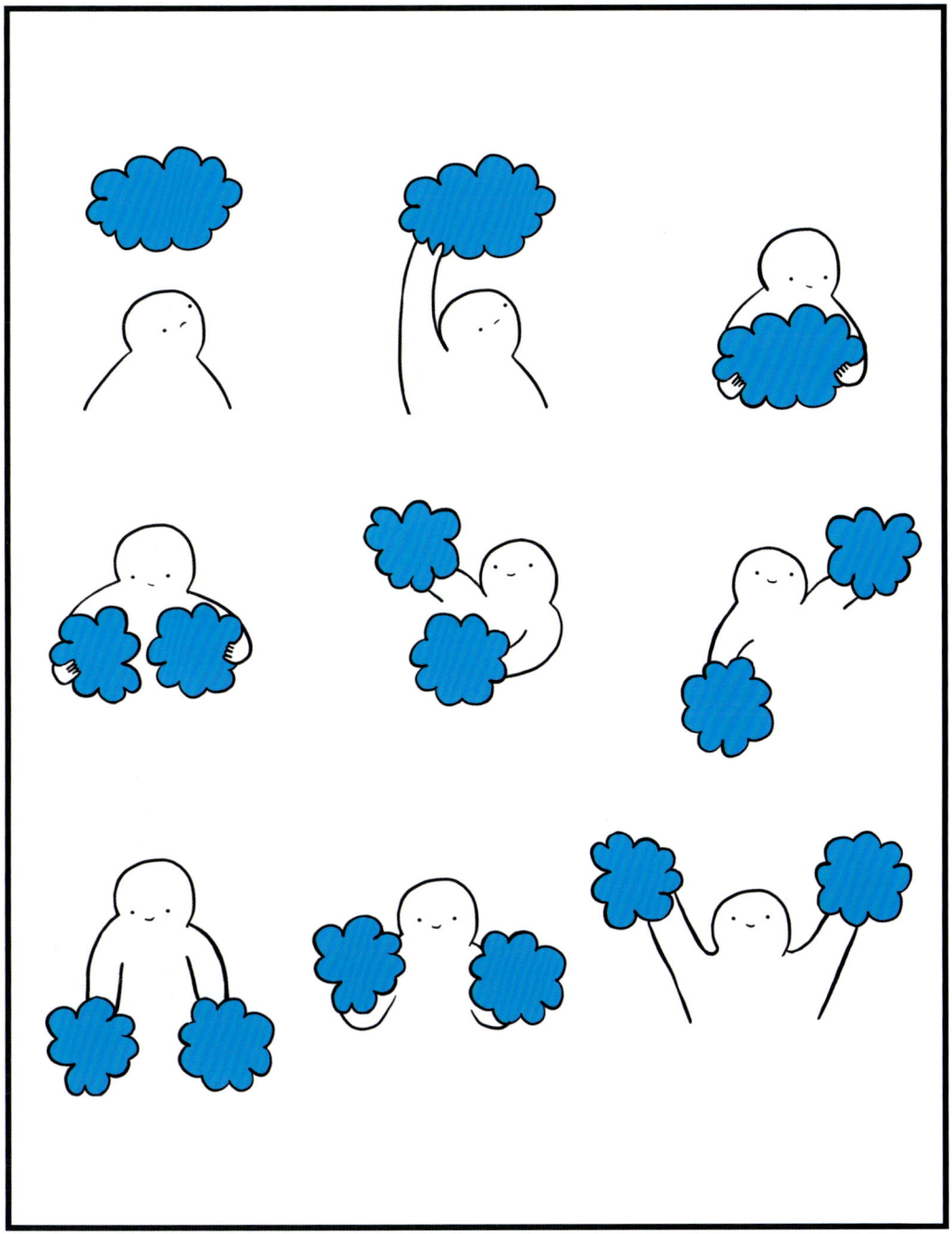

SELF-ENCOURAGEMENT.

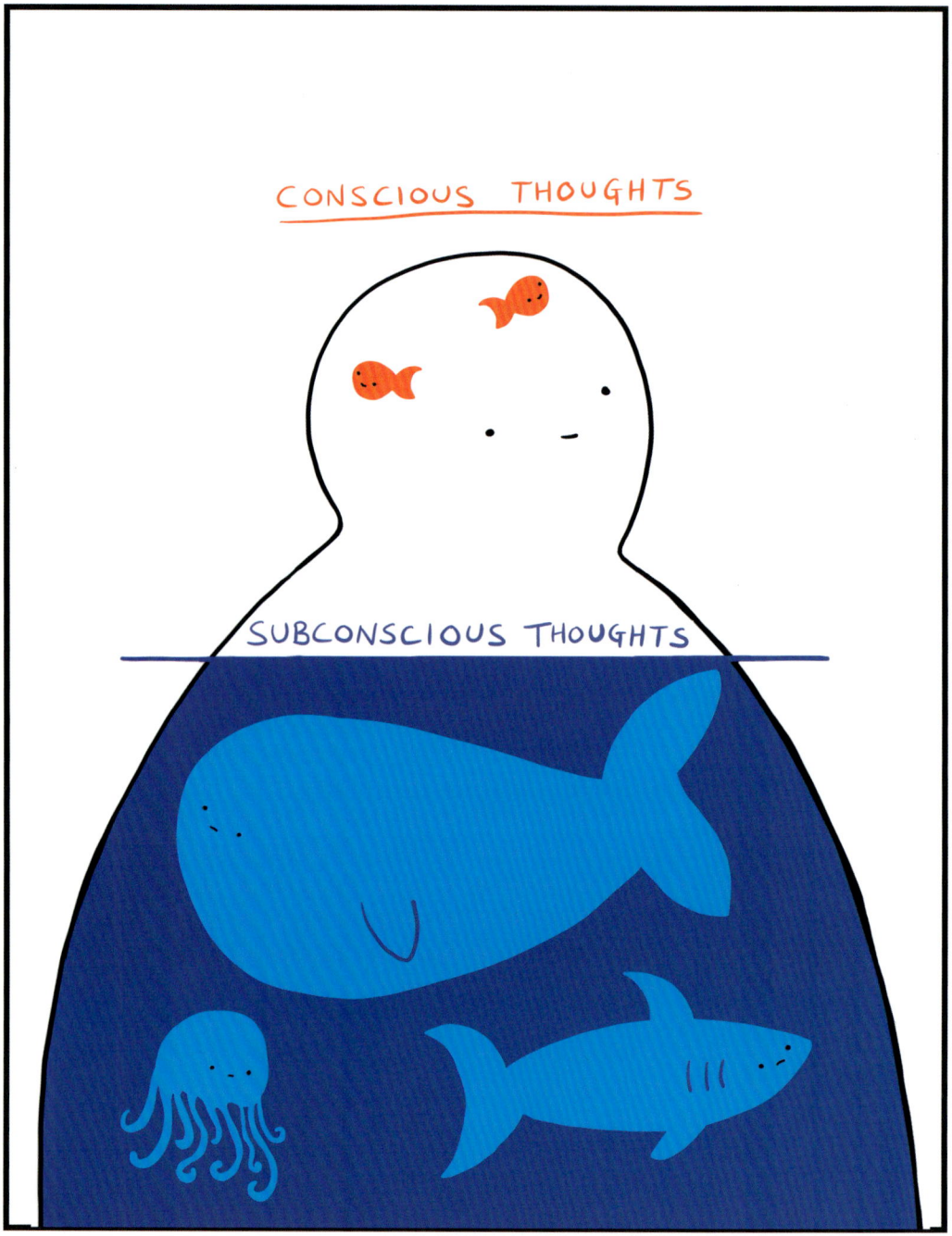

SCHOOL OF THOUGHT.

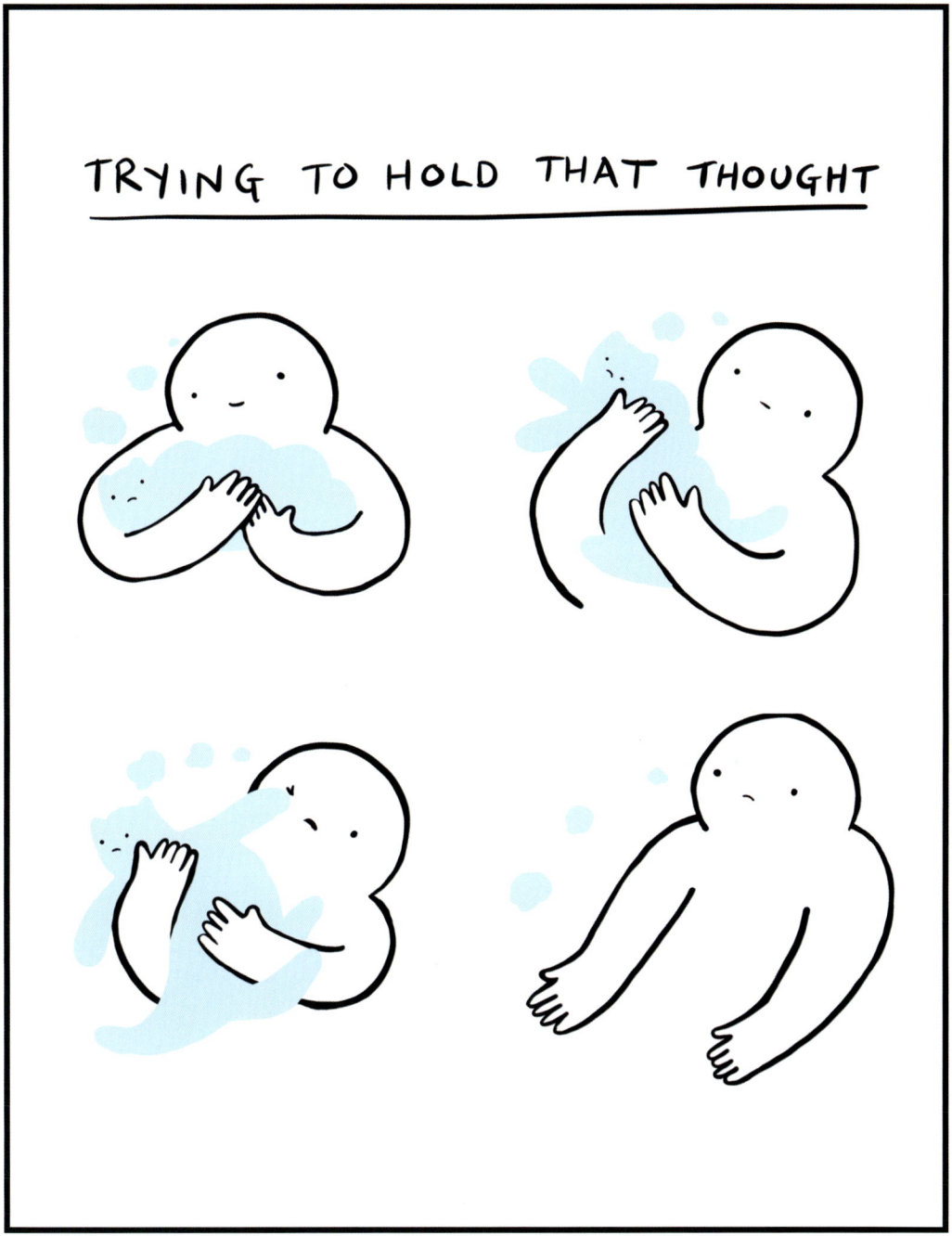

THOUGHTS DON'T LIKE BEING HELD.

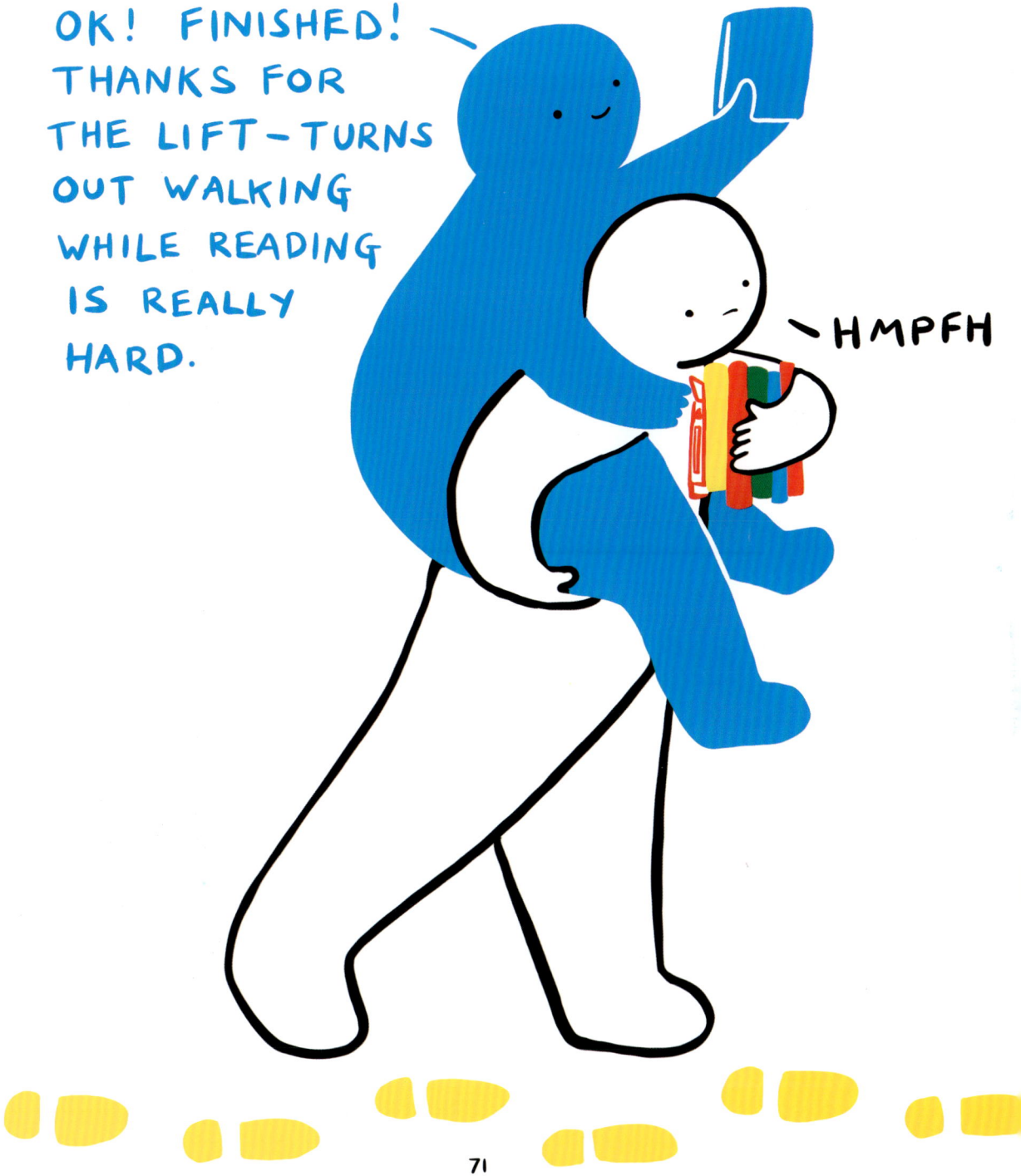
OK! FINISHED! THANKS FOR THE LIFT - TURNS OUT WALKING WHILE READING IS REALLY HARD.
HMPFH

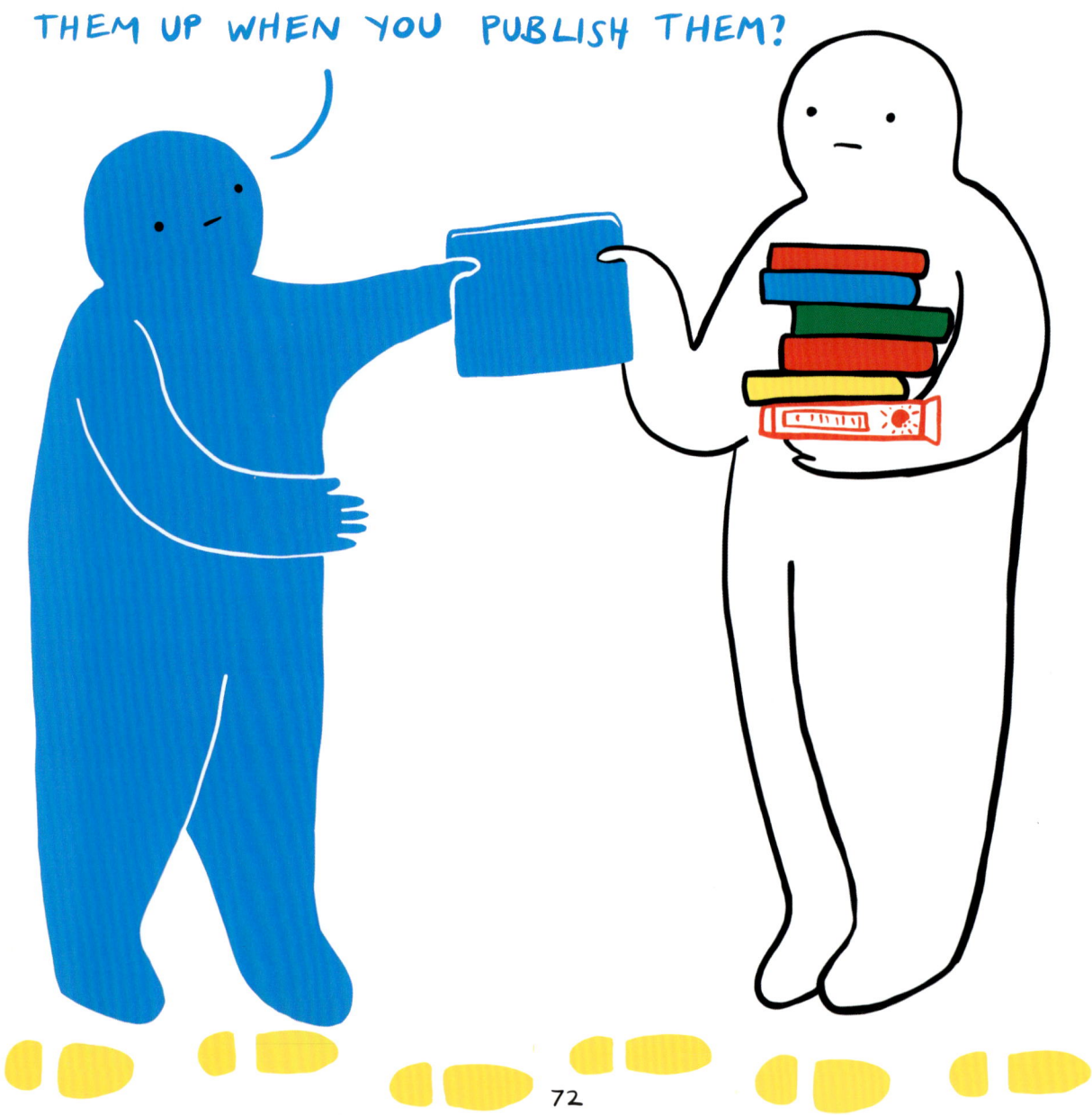
SOME OF THESE SKETCHES ARE OK FOR A ROUGH DRAFT - I'M GUESSING YOU'LL WORK WITH A TRAINED ILLUSTRATOR TO DRAW THEM UP WHEN YOU PUBLISH THEM?

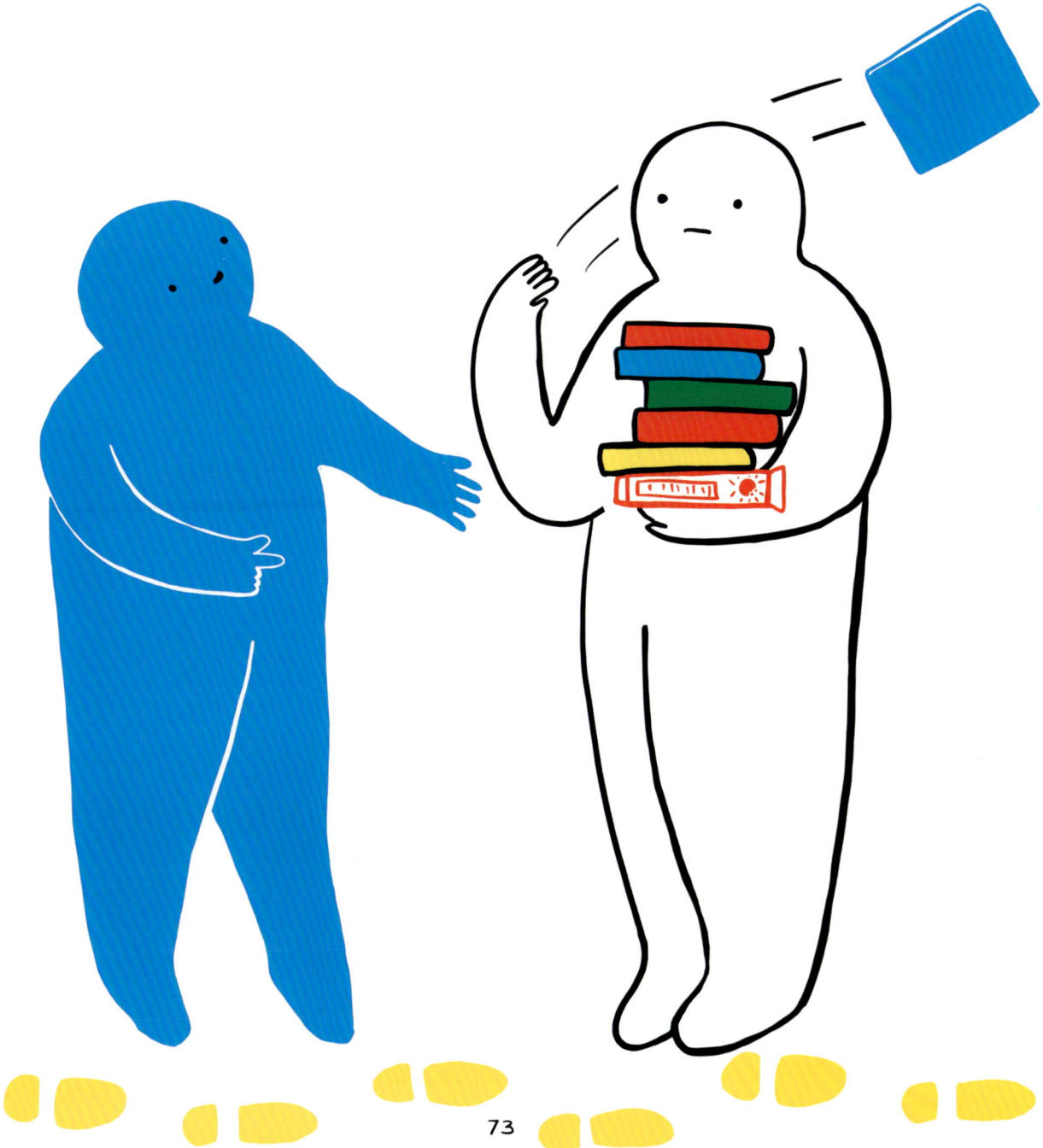

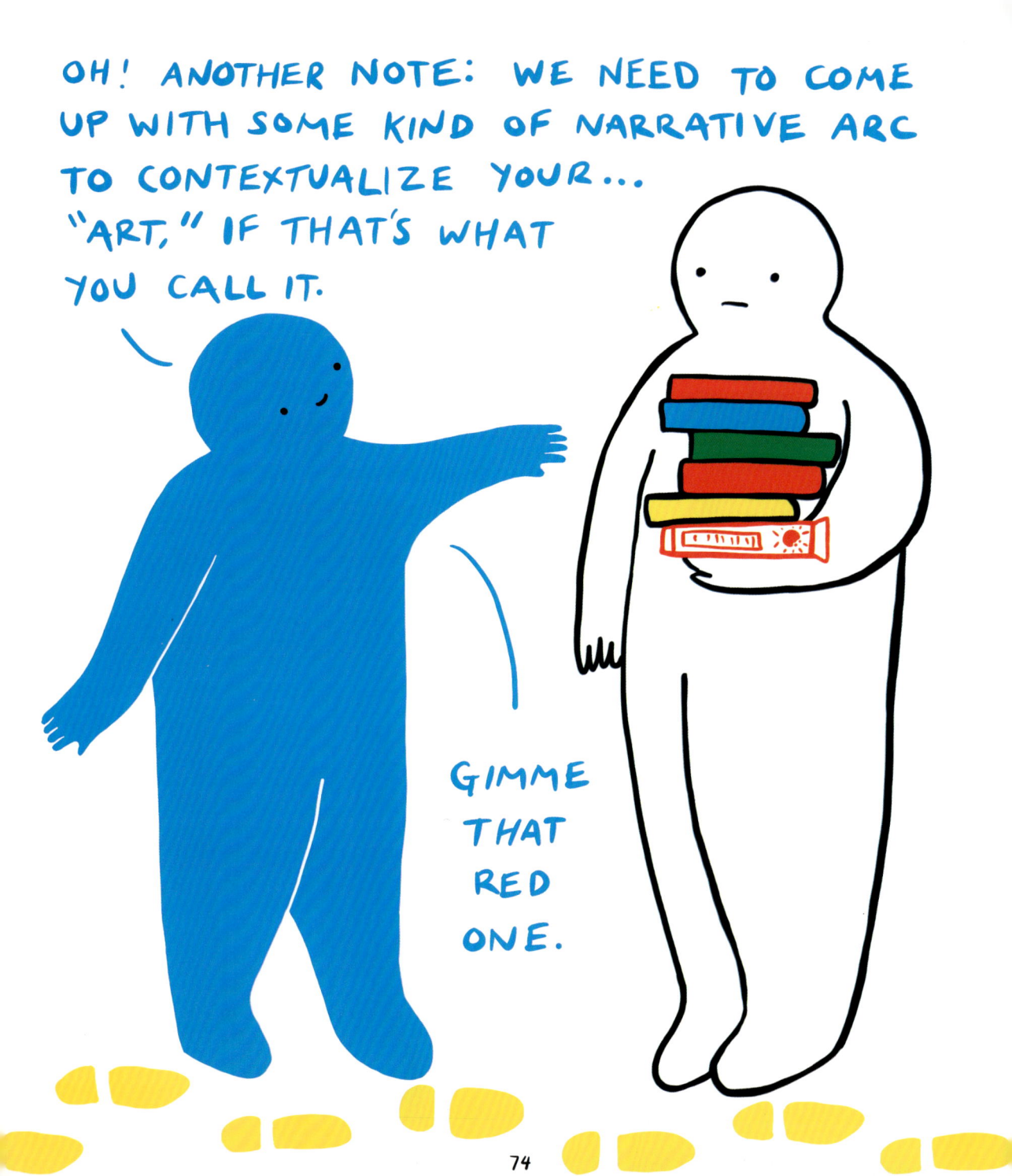
OH! ANOTHER NOTE: WE NEED TO COME UP WITH SOME KIND OF NARRATIVE ARC TO CONTEXTUALIZE YOUR... "ART," IF THAT'S WHAT YOU CALL IT.
GIMME THAT RED ONE.

DRAWINGS ABOUT FEELINGS

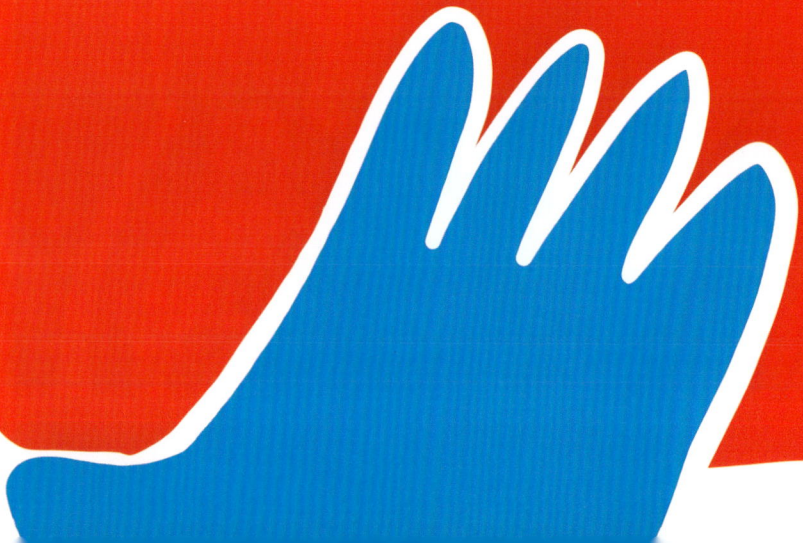

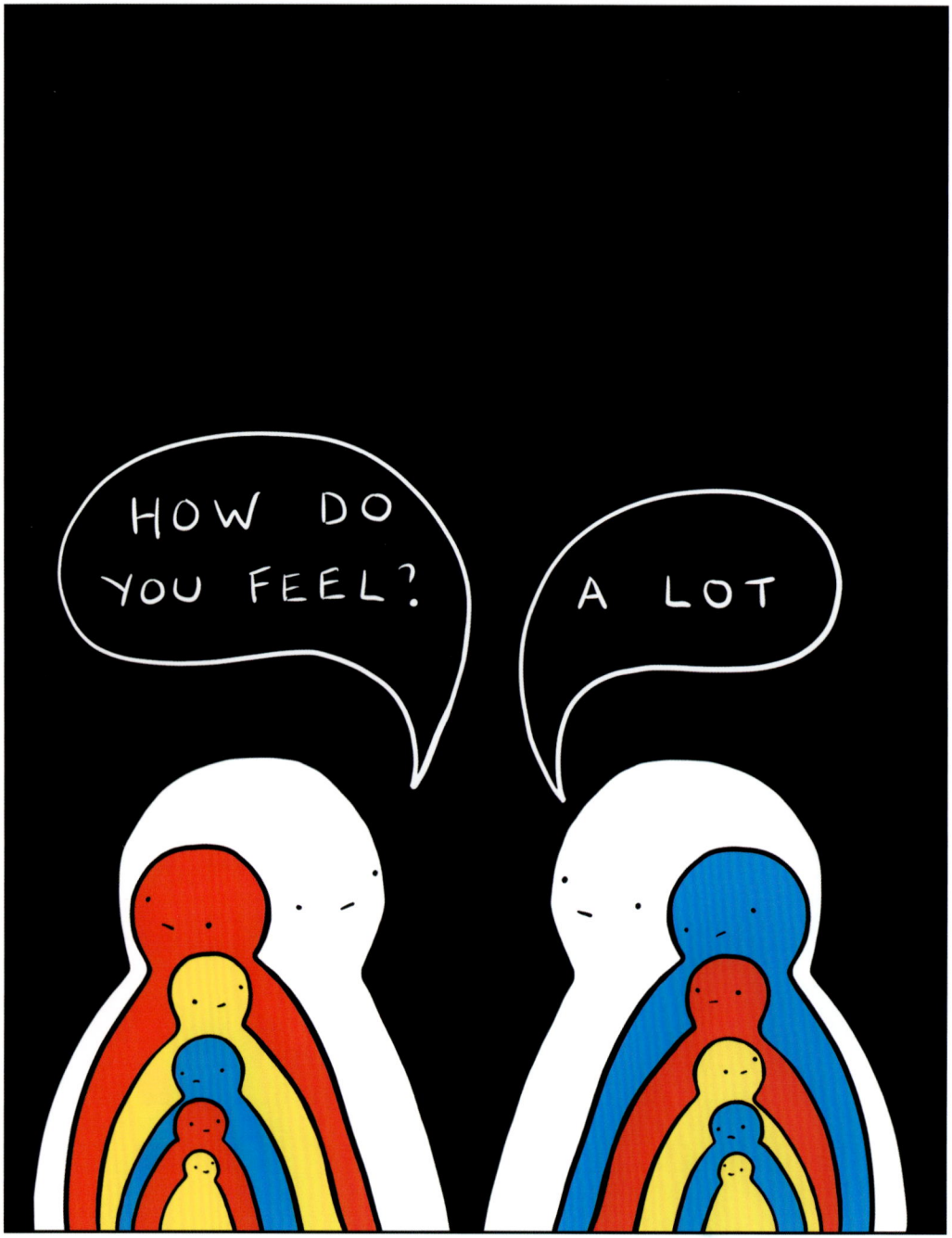

AND OFTEN.

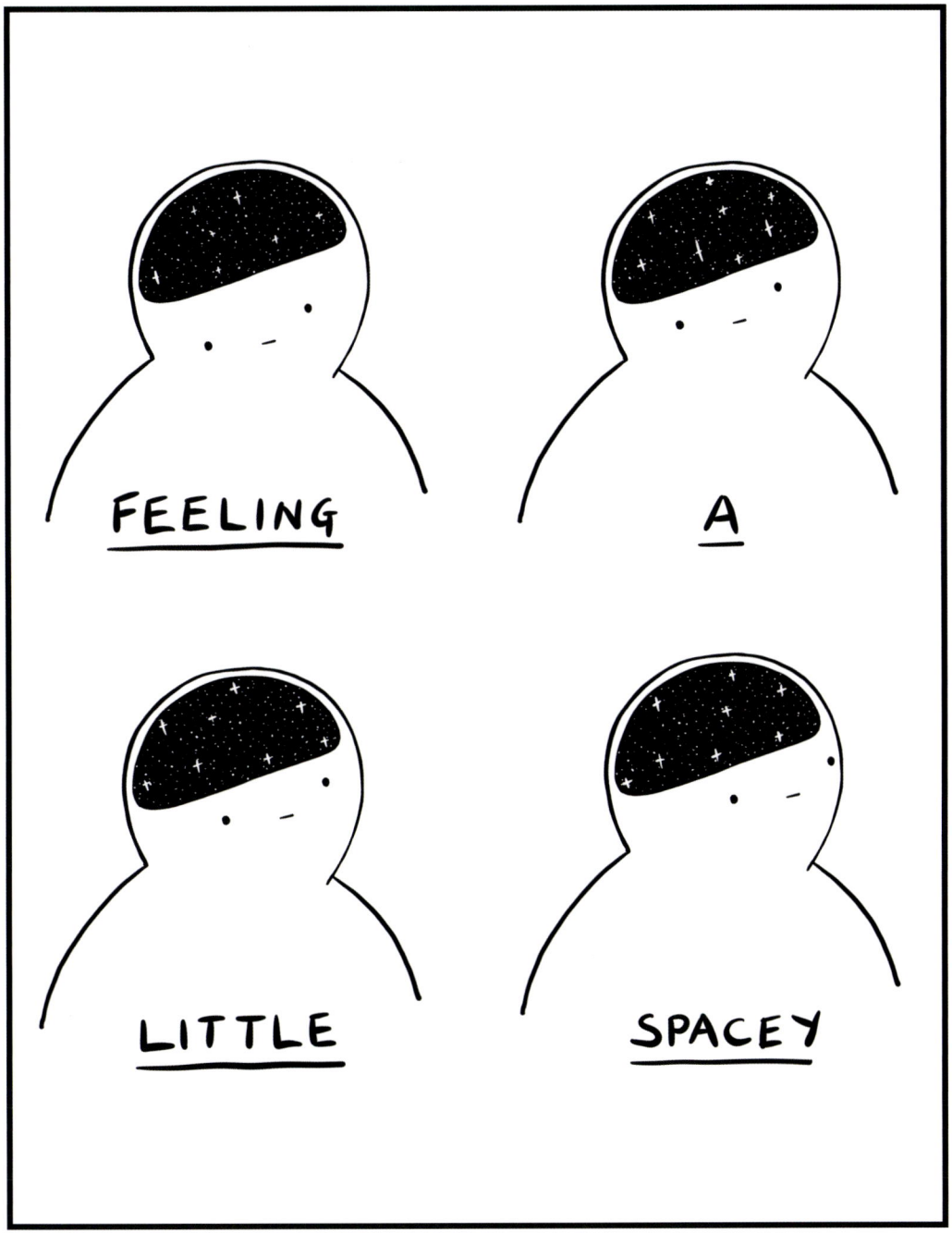

HOUSTON, WE HAVE A PROBLEM.

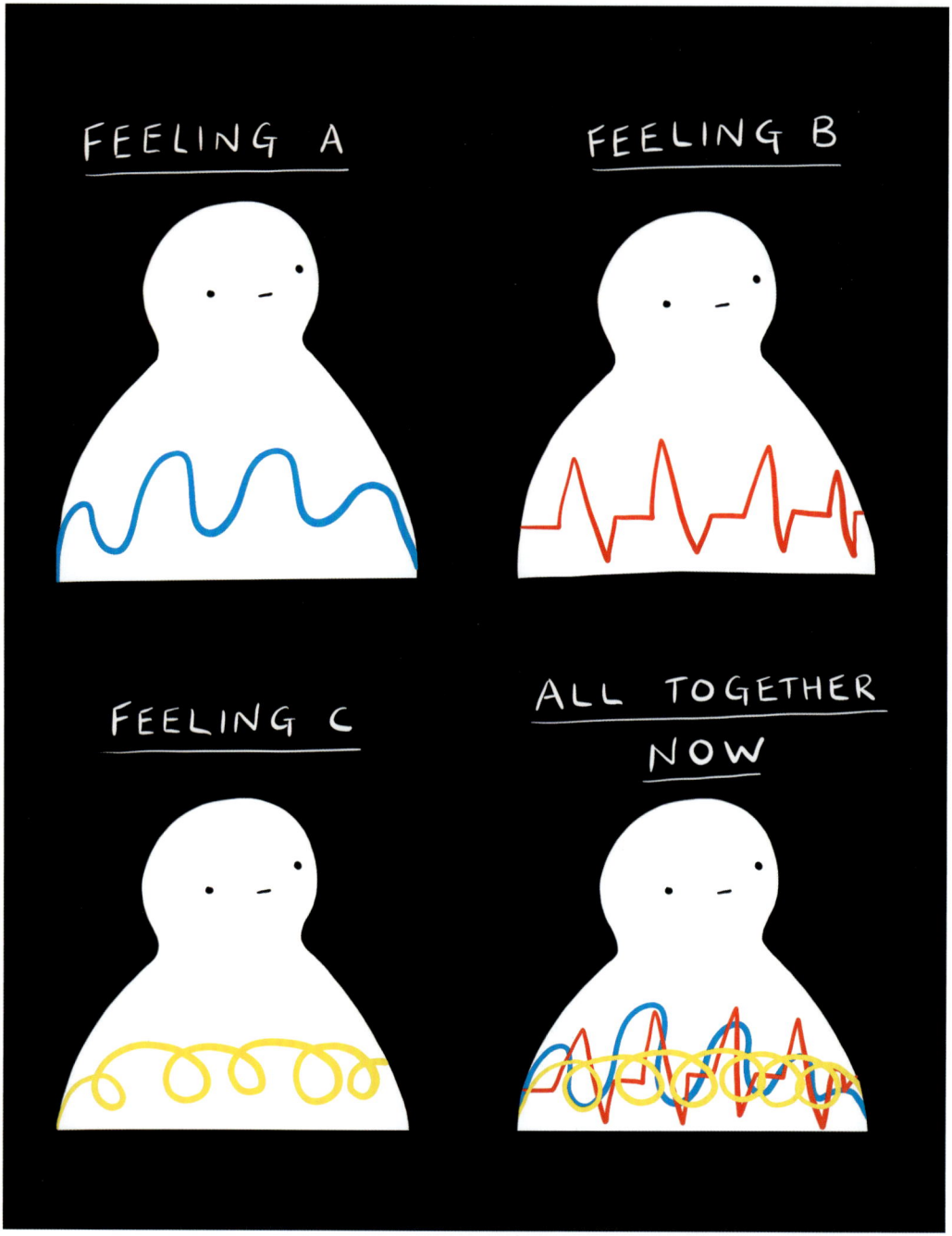

COMPOSITION.

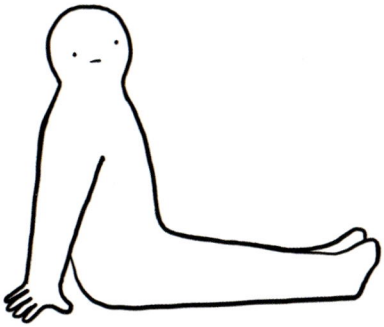

GET UP

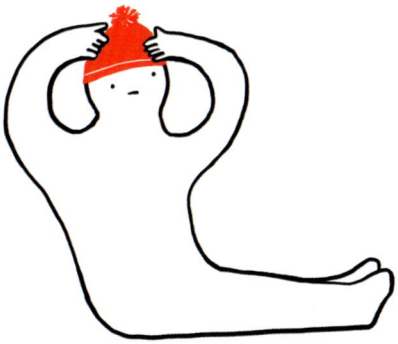

GET DRESSED

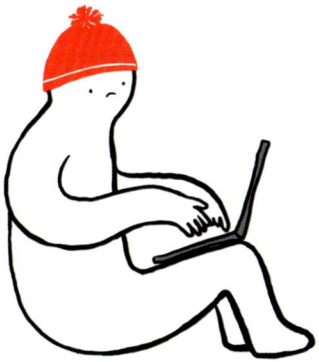

GET STRESSED

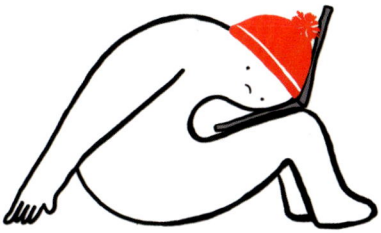

GET DEPRESSED

#BLESSED

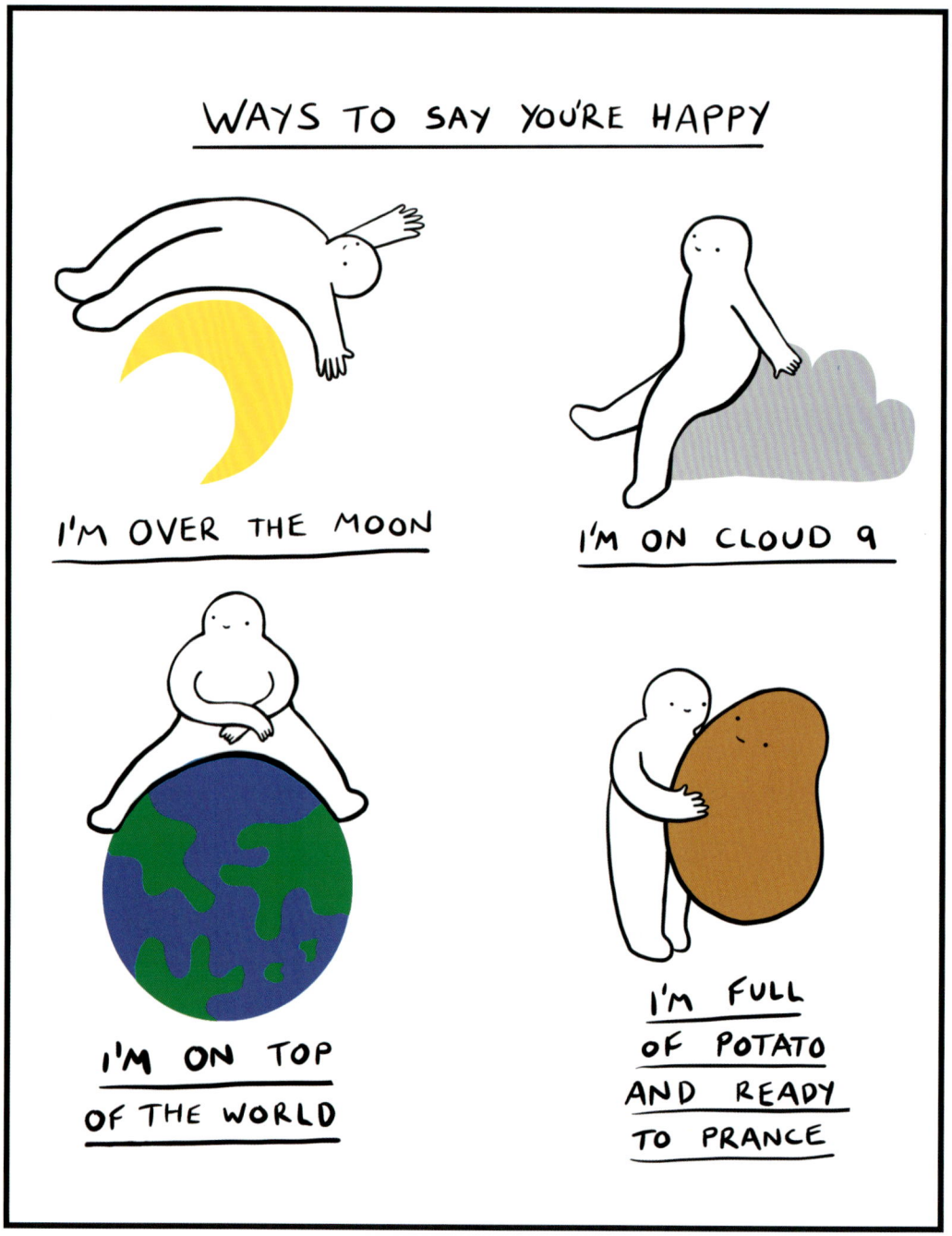

I MADE ONE OF THEM UP.

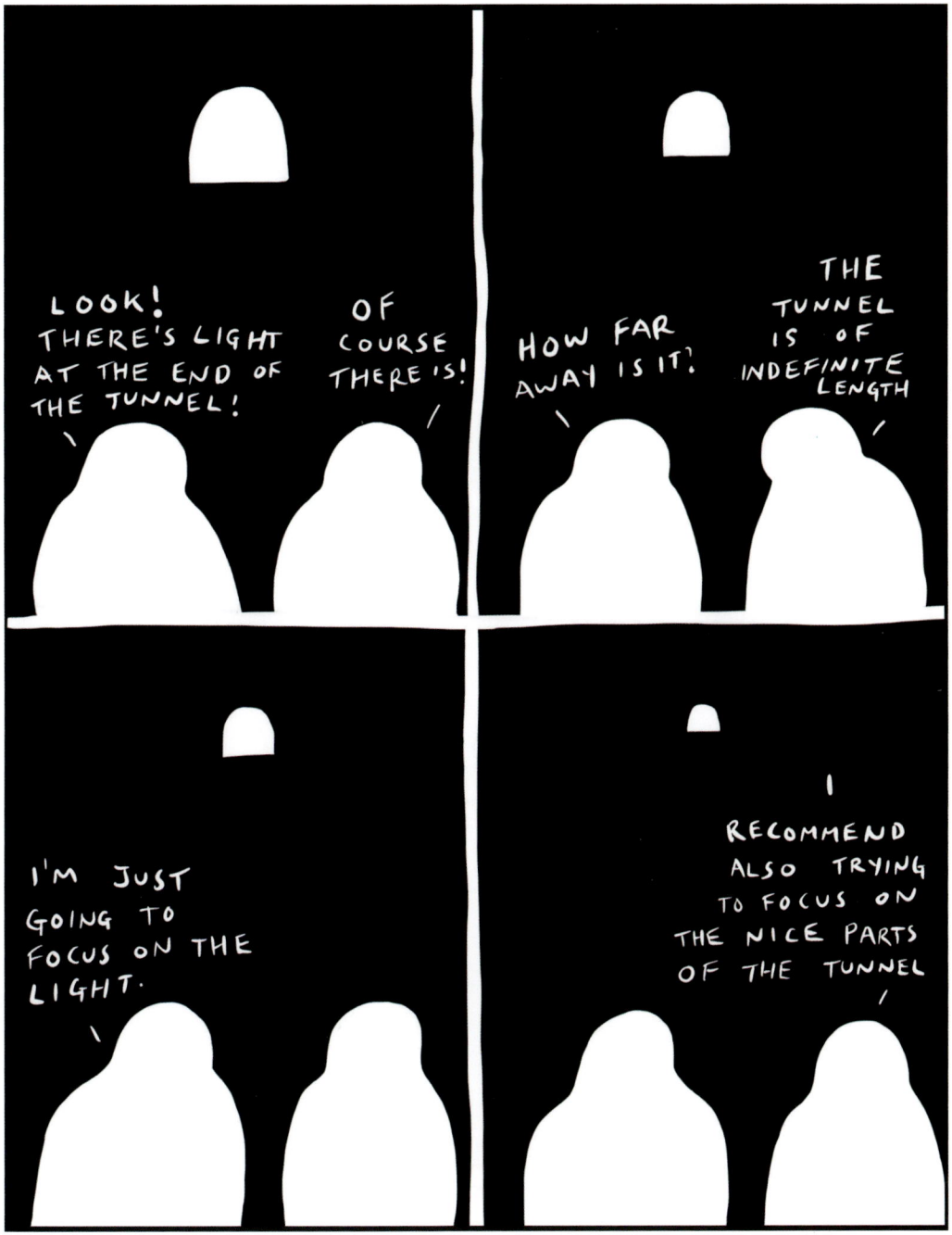

TUNNEL VISION.

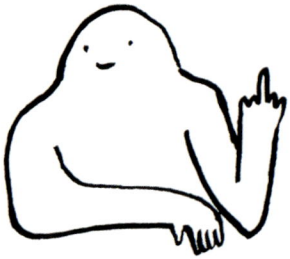

KINDEST REGARDS

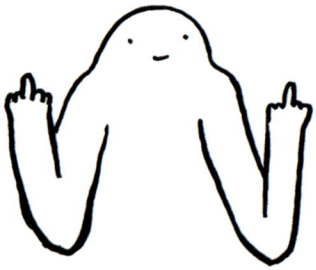

KIND REGARDS

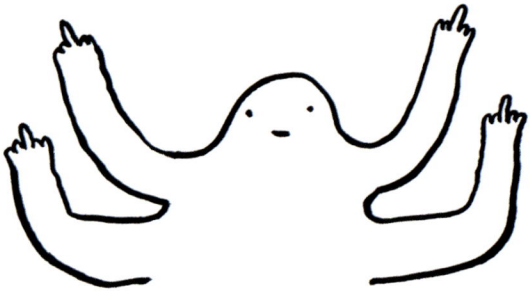

REGARDS

I LOOK FORWARD TO YOUR REPLY.

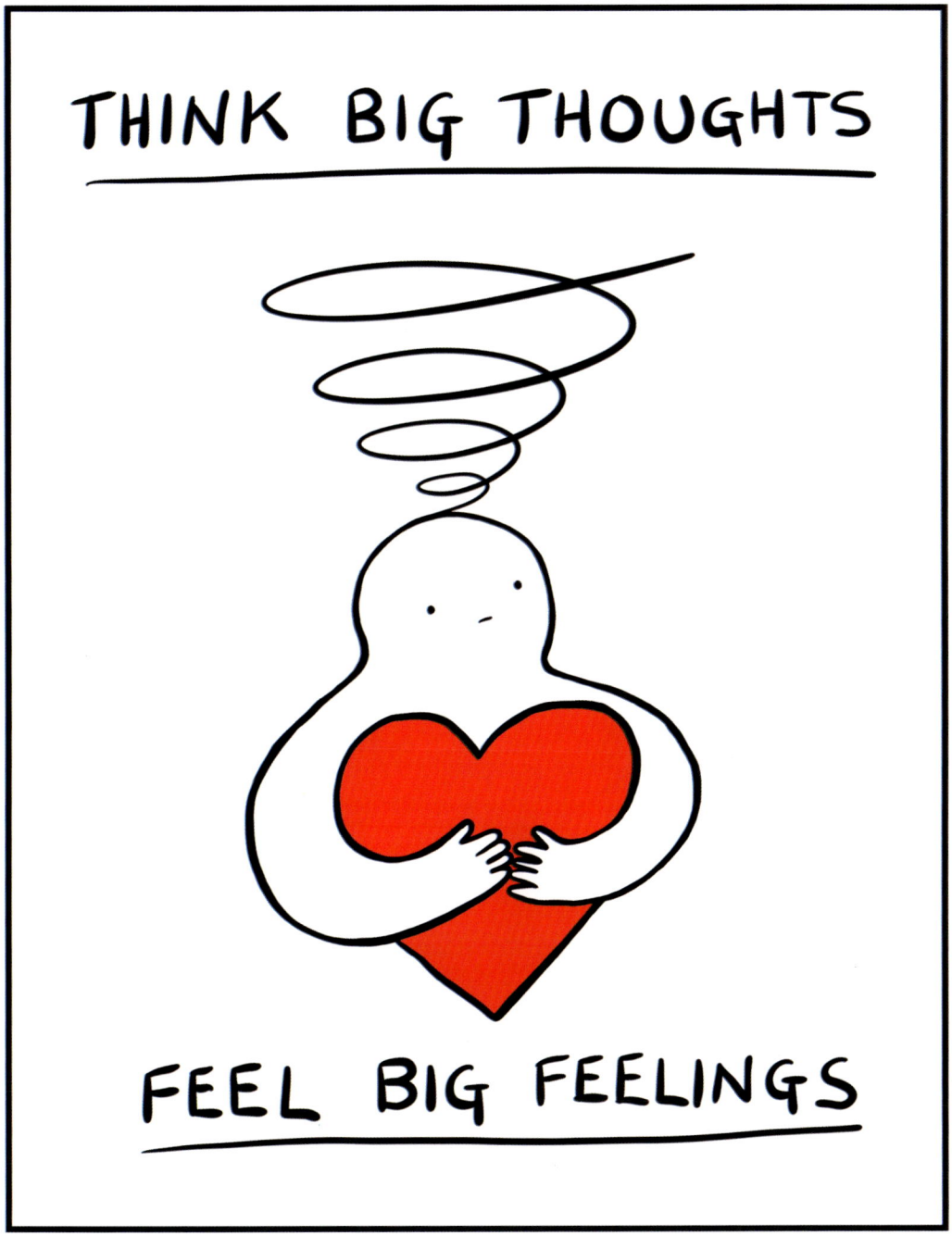

GO BIG OR GO HOME.

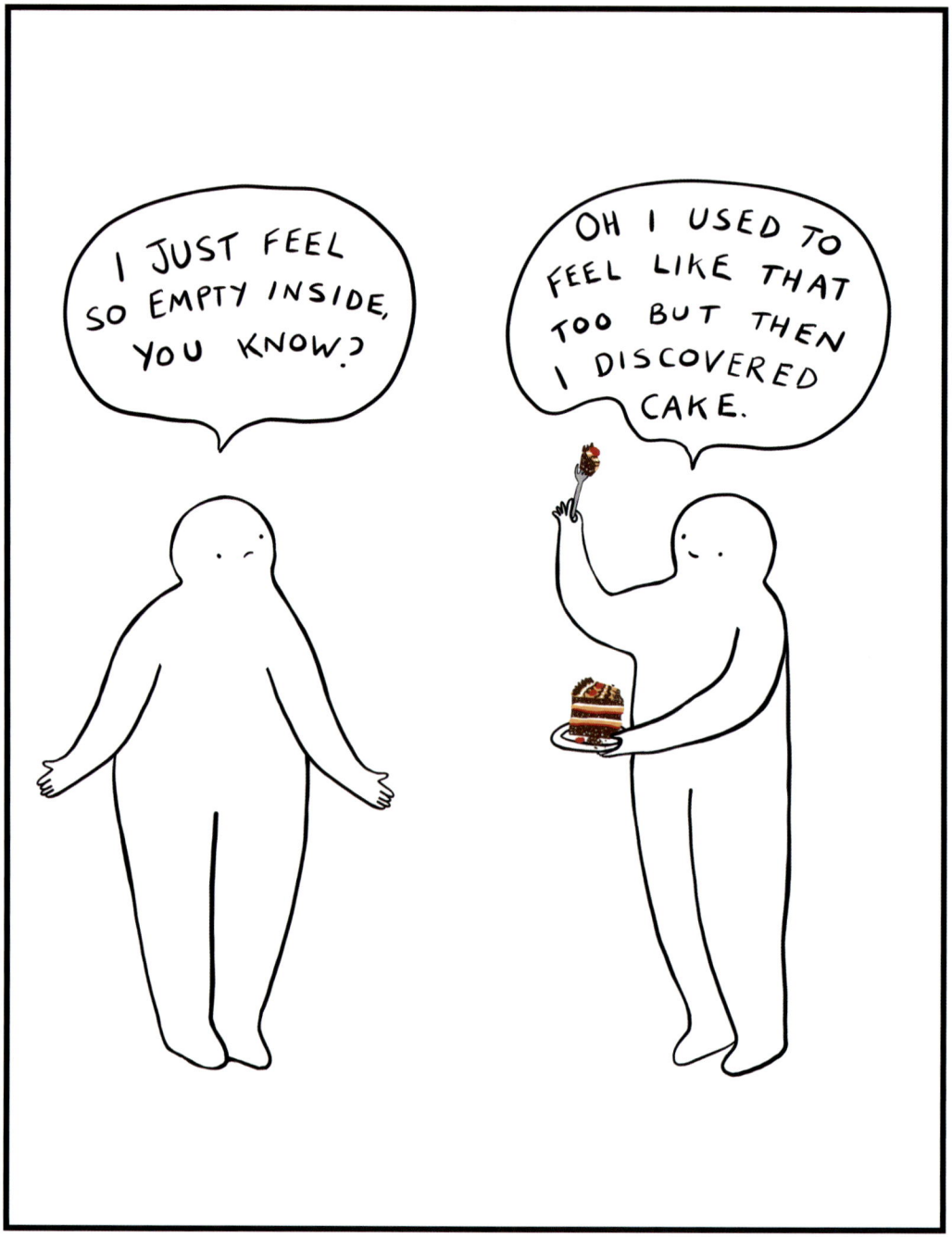

SLICE OF LIFE.

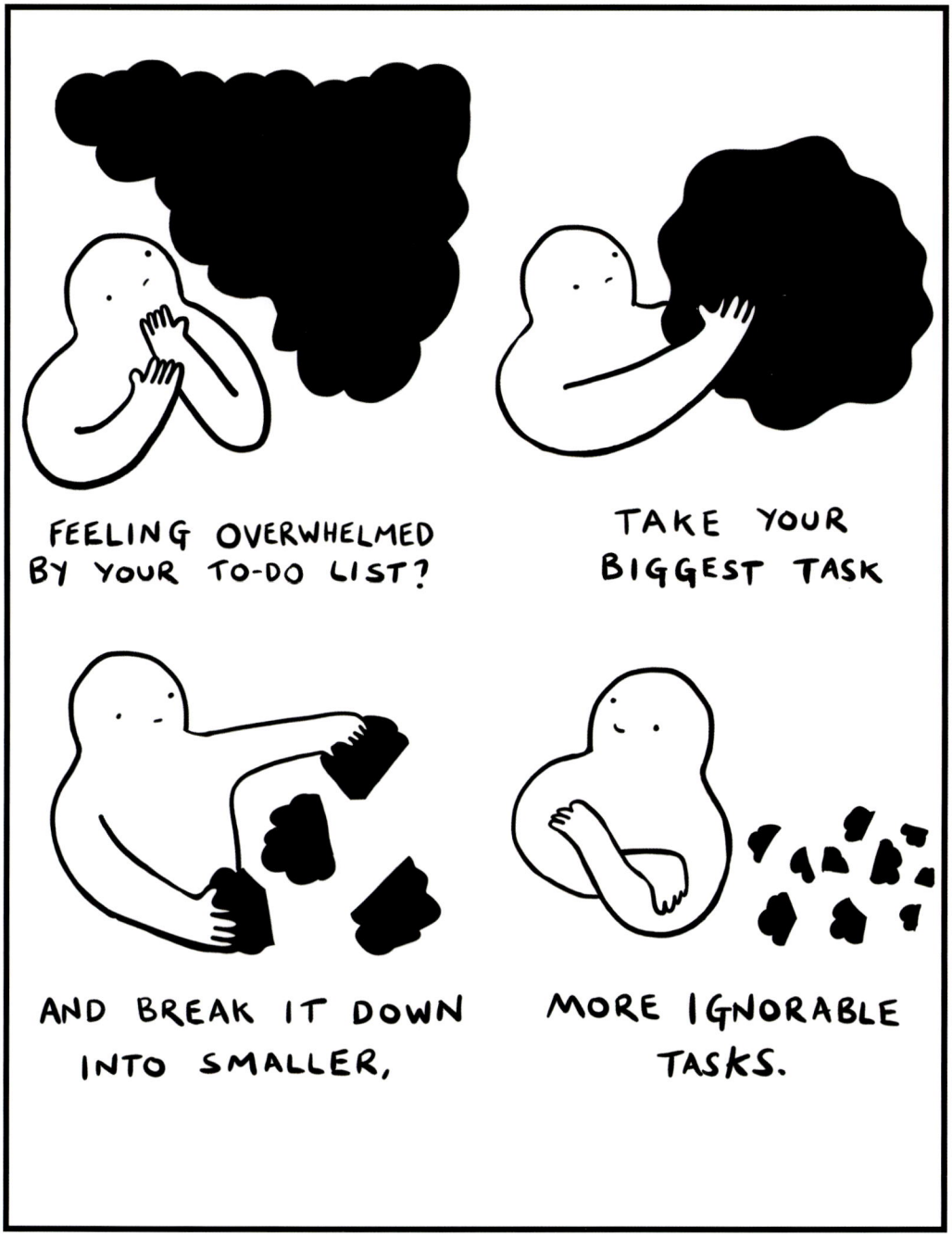
FEELING OVERWHELMED BY YOUR TO-DO LIST?
TAKE YOUR BIGGEST TASK
AND BREAK IT DOWN INTO SMALLER,
MORE IGNORABLE TASKS.

HOT TIP.

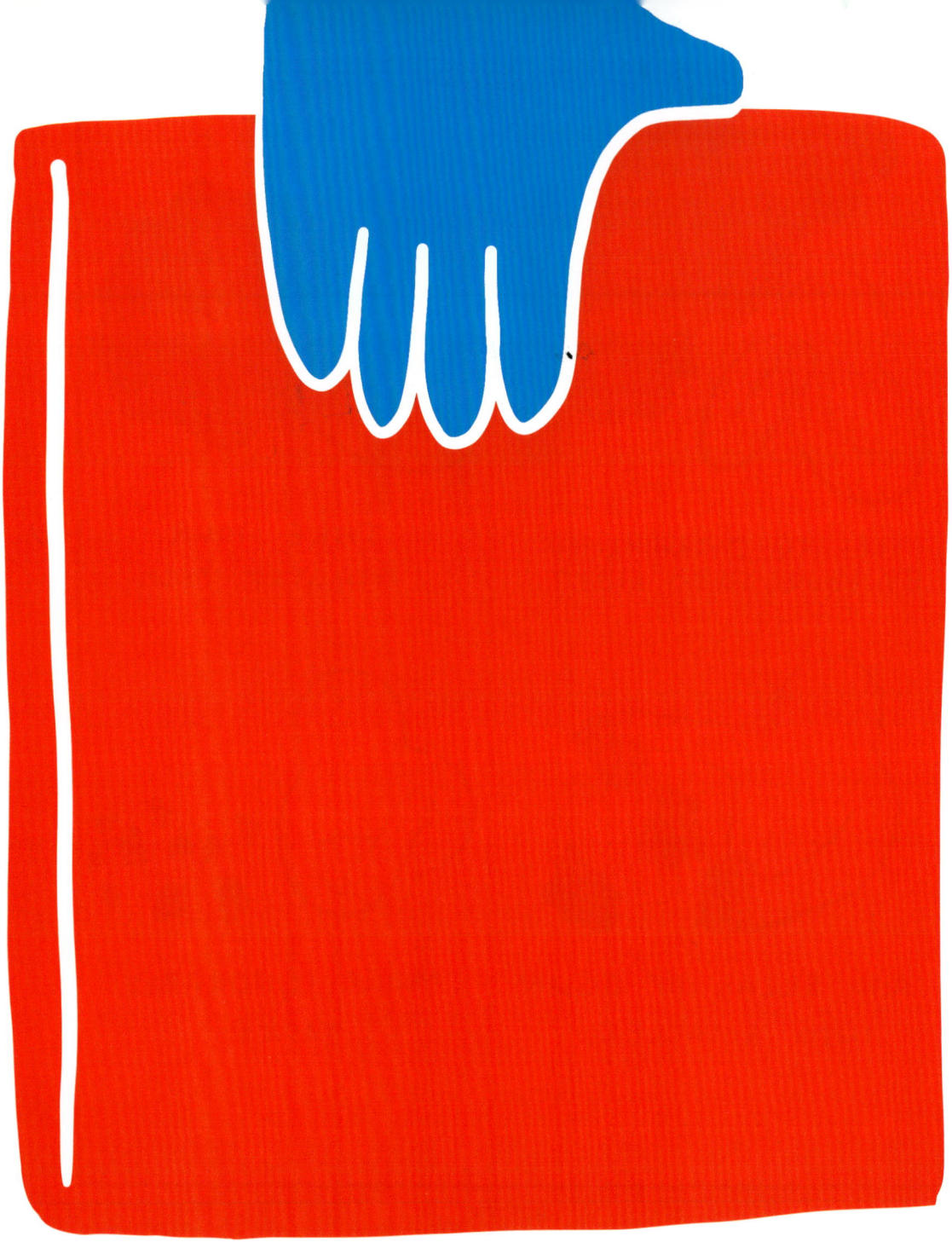

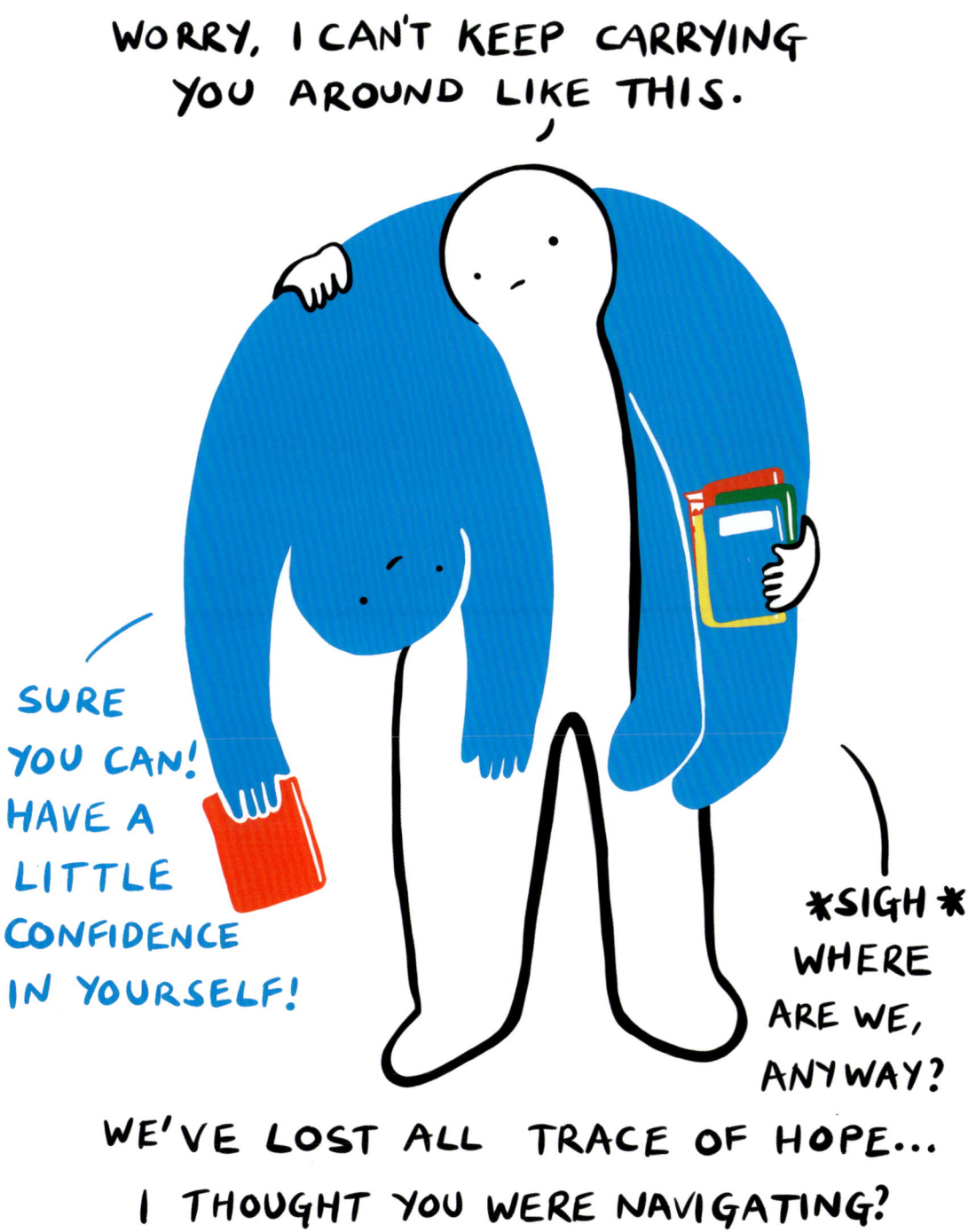
WORRY, I CAN'T KEEP CARRYING YOU AROUND LIKE THIS.
SURE YOU CAN! HAVE A LITTLE CONFIDENCE IN YOURSELF!
SIGH WHERE ARE WE, ANYWAY?
WE'VE LOST ALL TRACE OF HOPE...
I THOUGHT YOU WERE NAVIGATING?

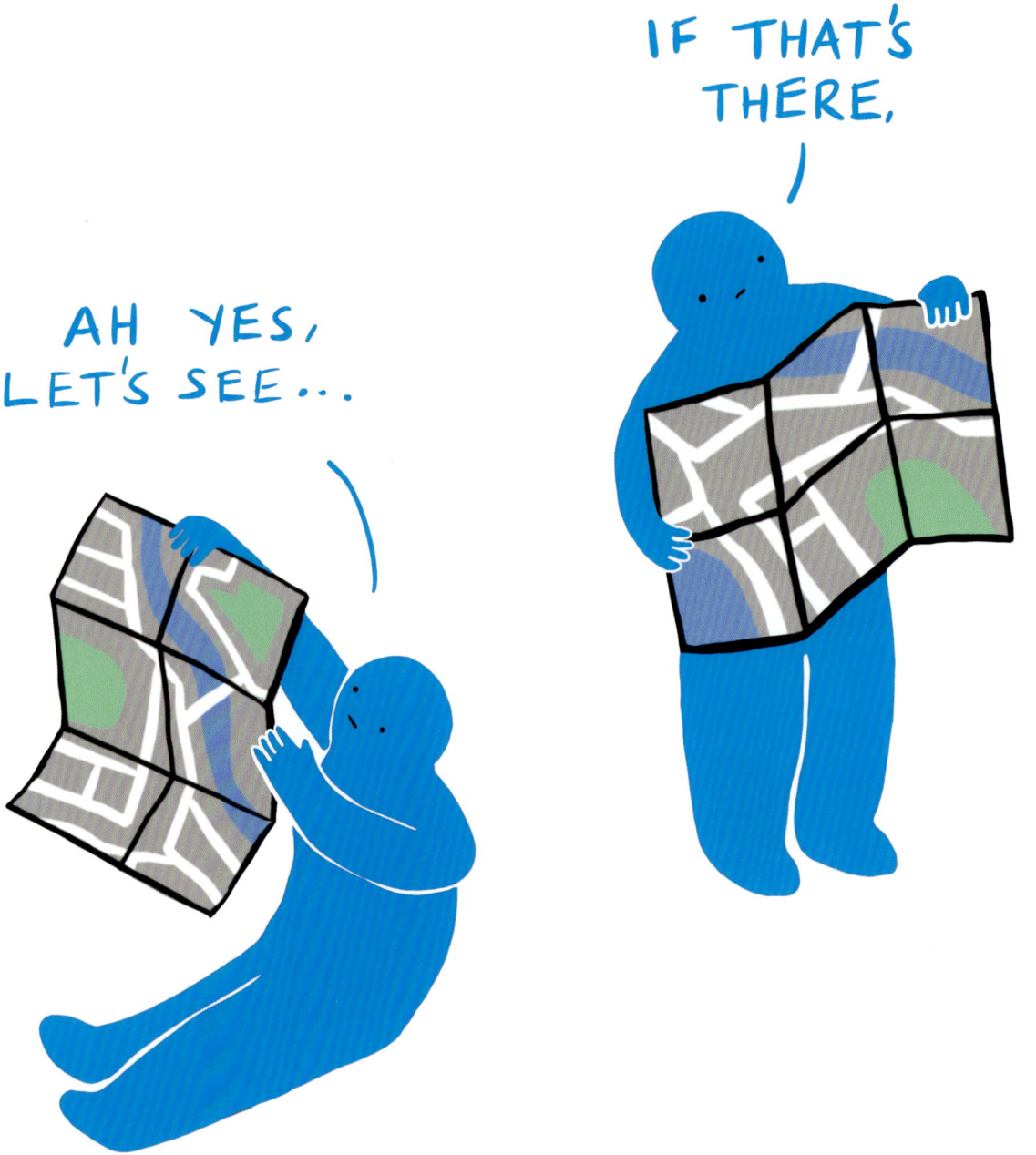
AH YES, LET'S SEE...
IF THAT'S THERE,

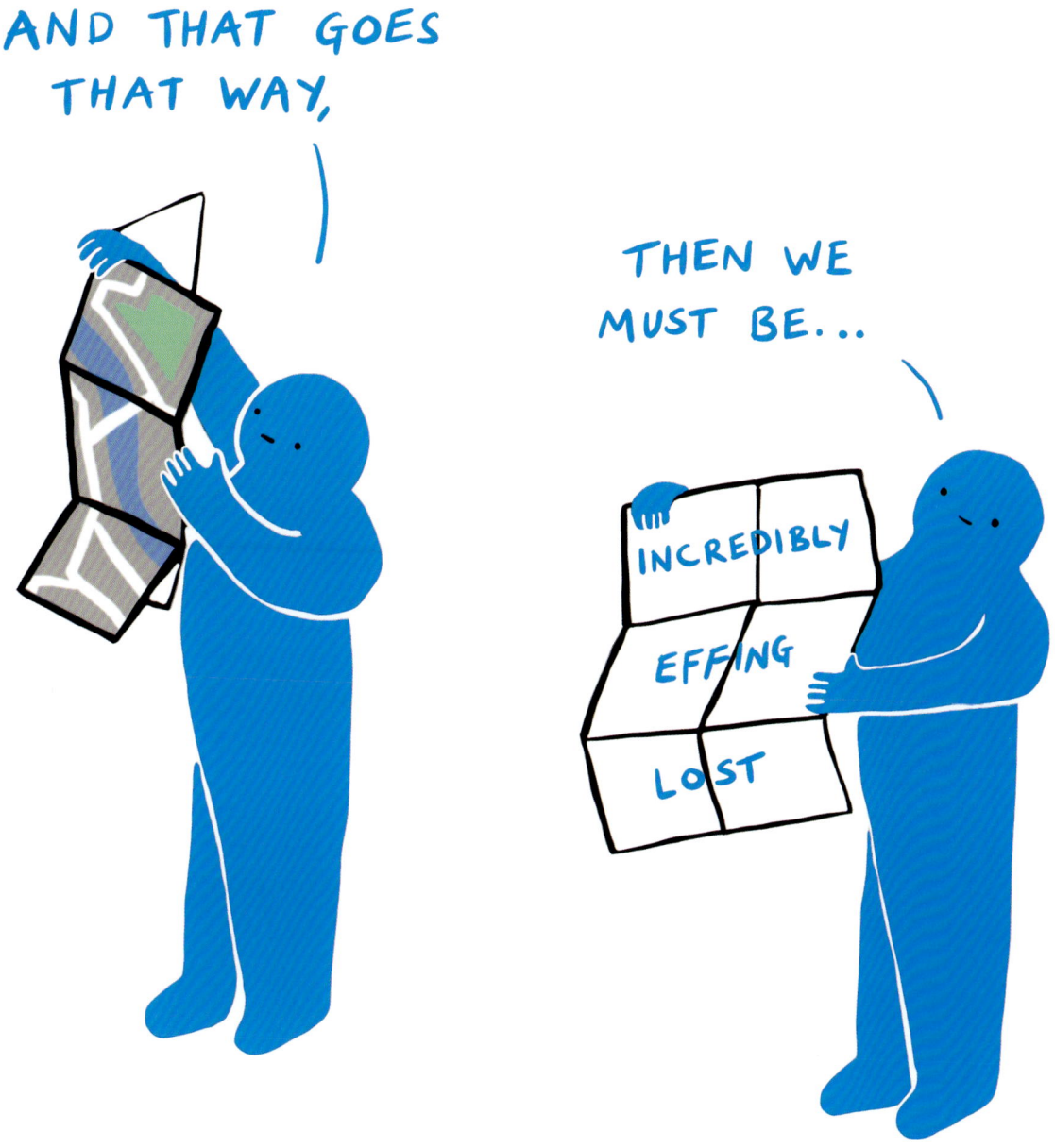
AND THAT GOES THAT WAY,
THEN WE MUST BE...
INCREDIBLY
EFFING
LOST

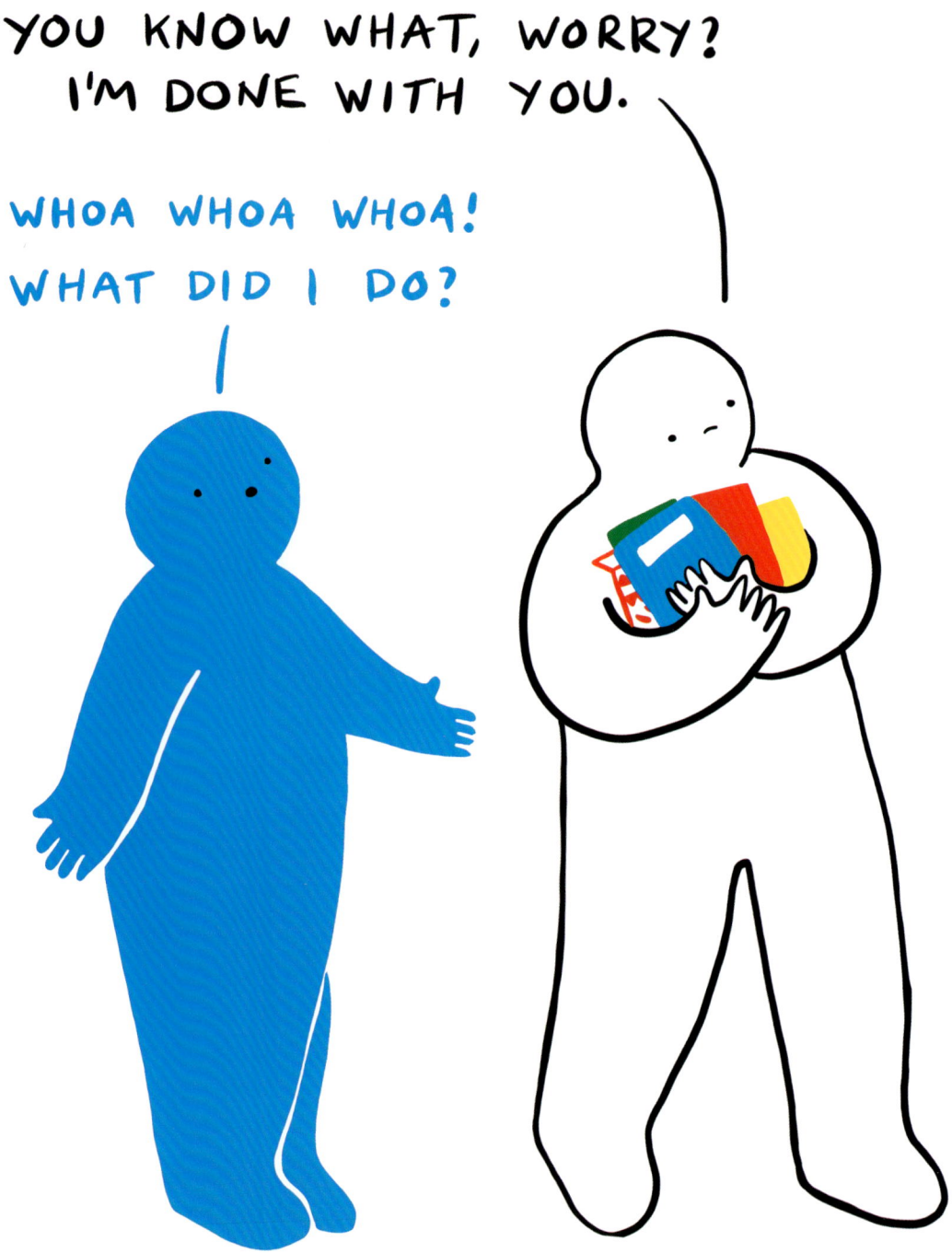
YOU KNOW WHAT, WORRY? I'M DONE WITH YOU.
WHOA WHOA WHOA! WHAT DID I DO?

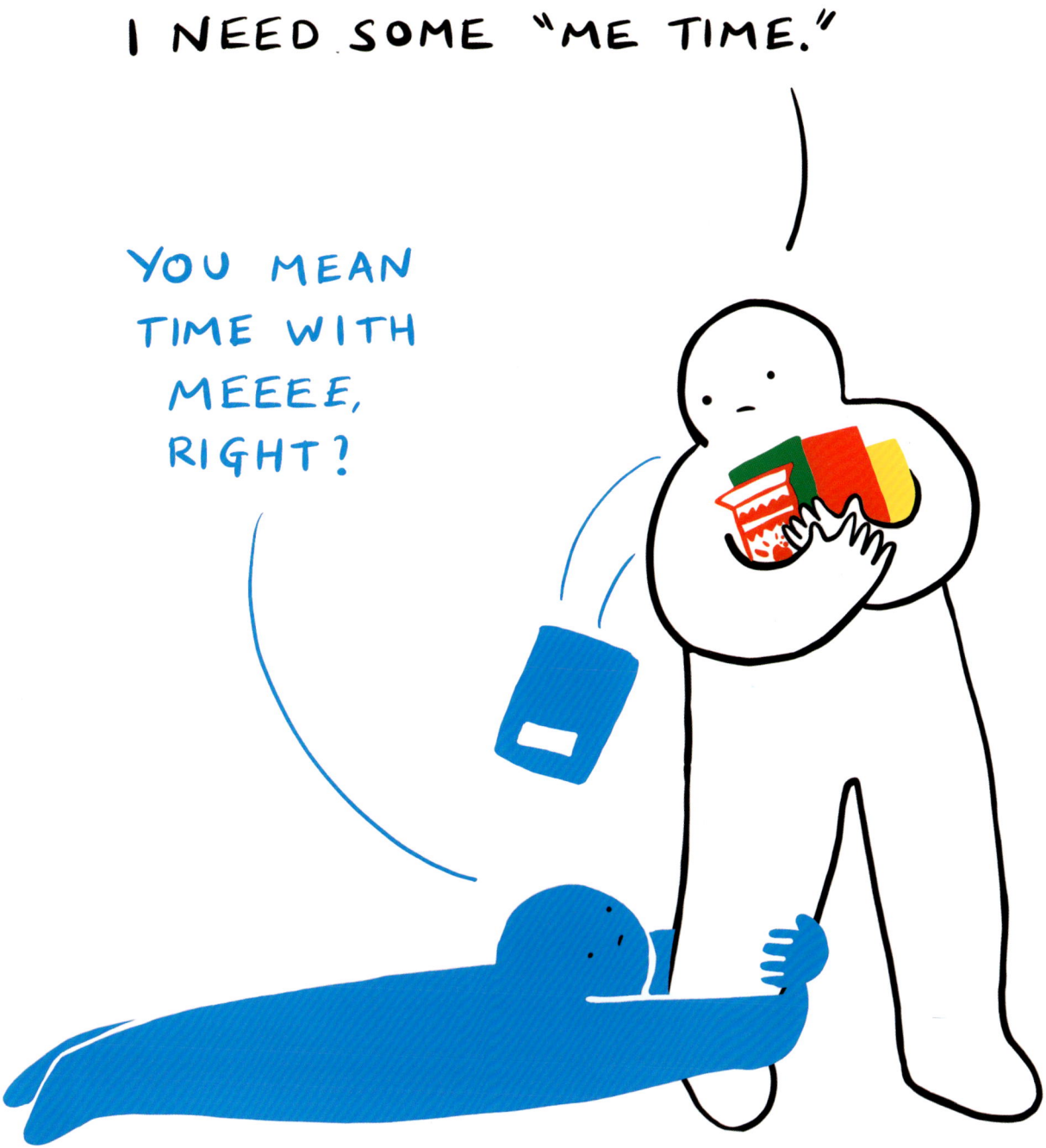
I NEED SOME "ME TIME."
YOU MEAN TIME WITH MEEEE, RIGHT?

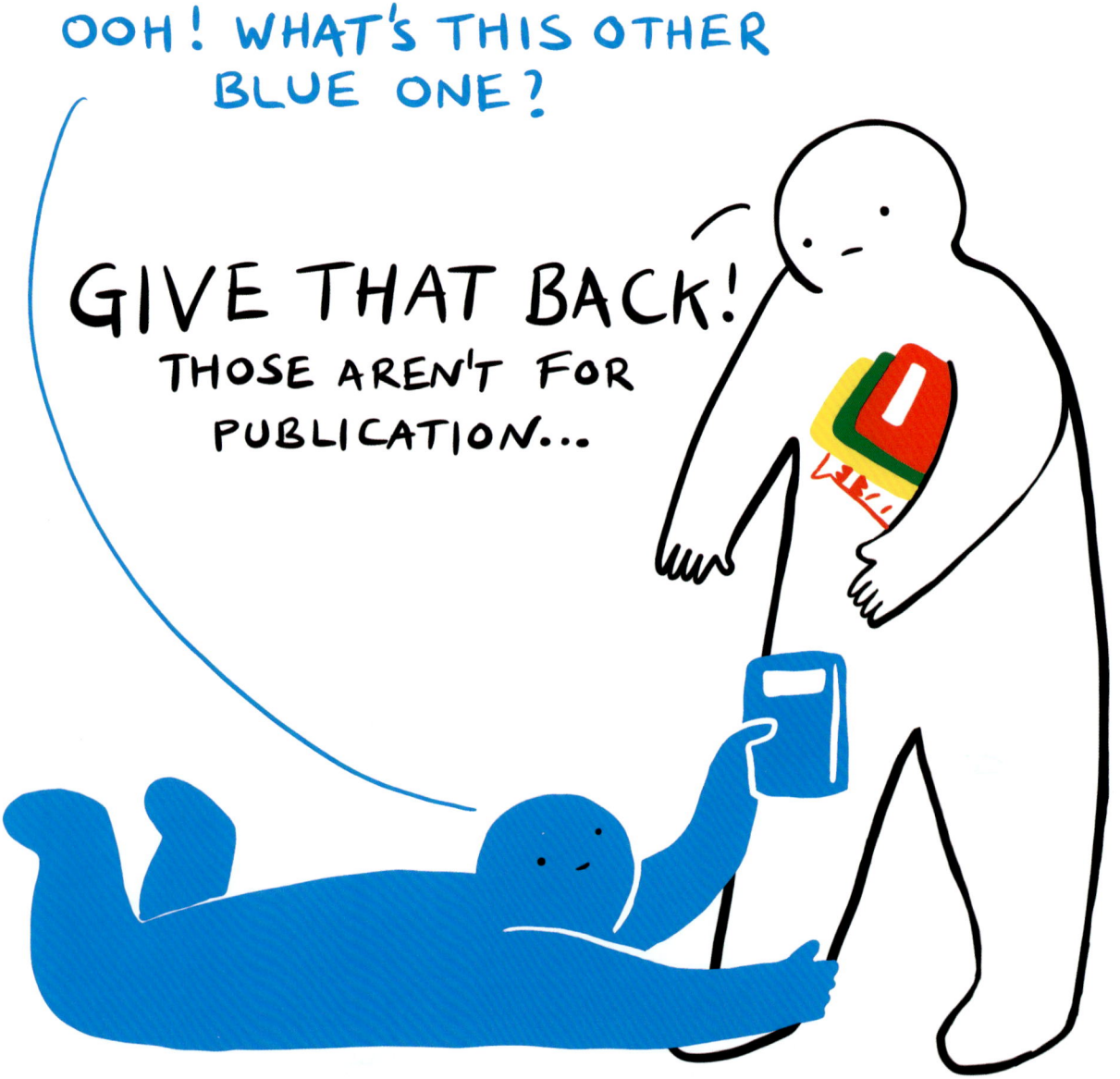
OOH! WHAT'S THIS OTHER BLUE ONE?
GIVE THAT BACK!
THOSE AREN'T FOR PUBLICATION...

THESE ARE ABOUT... ME?

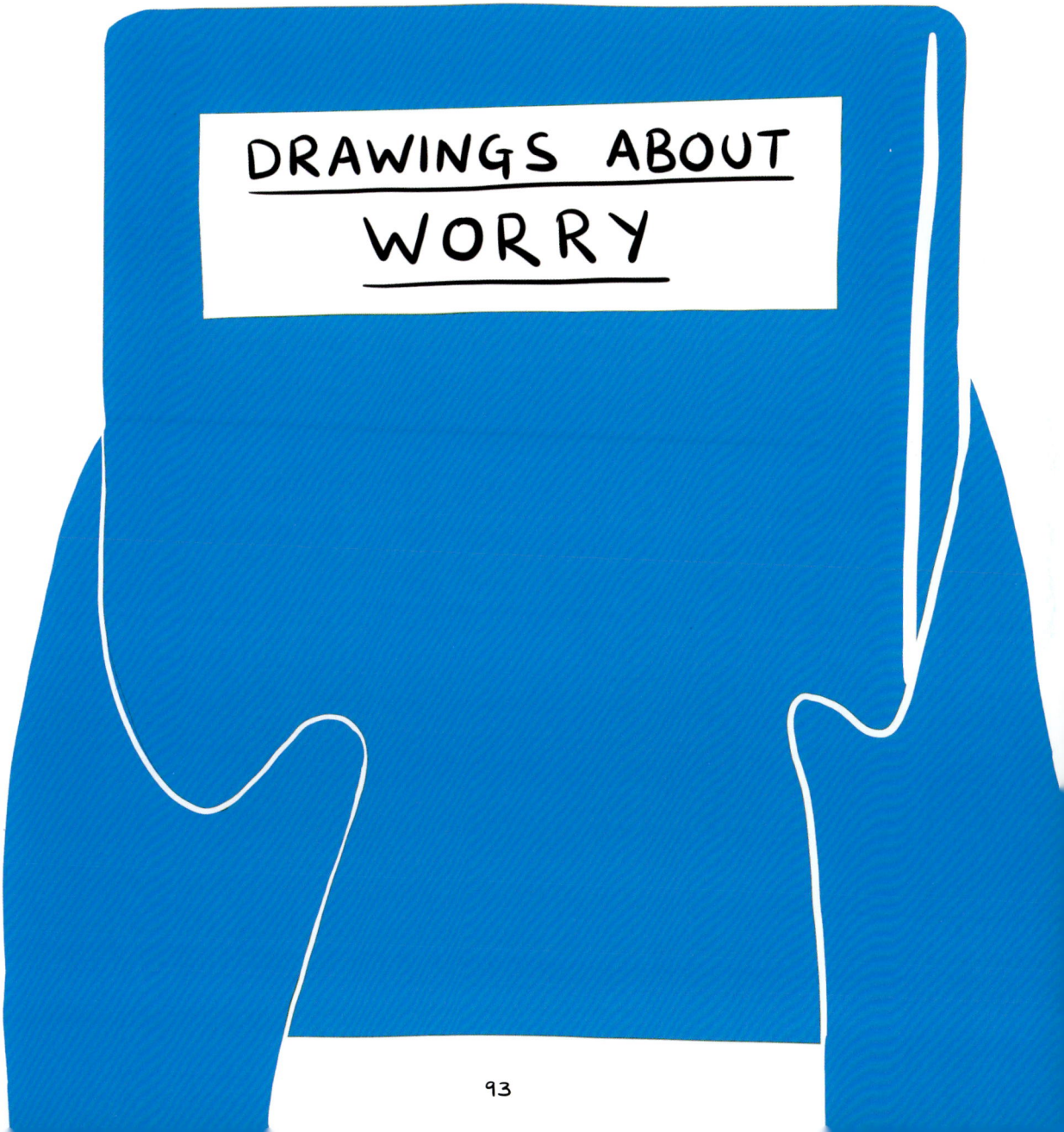

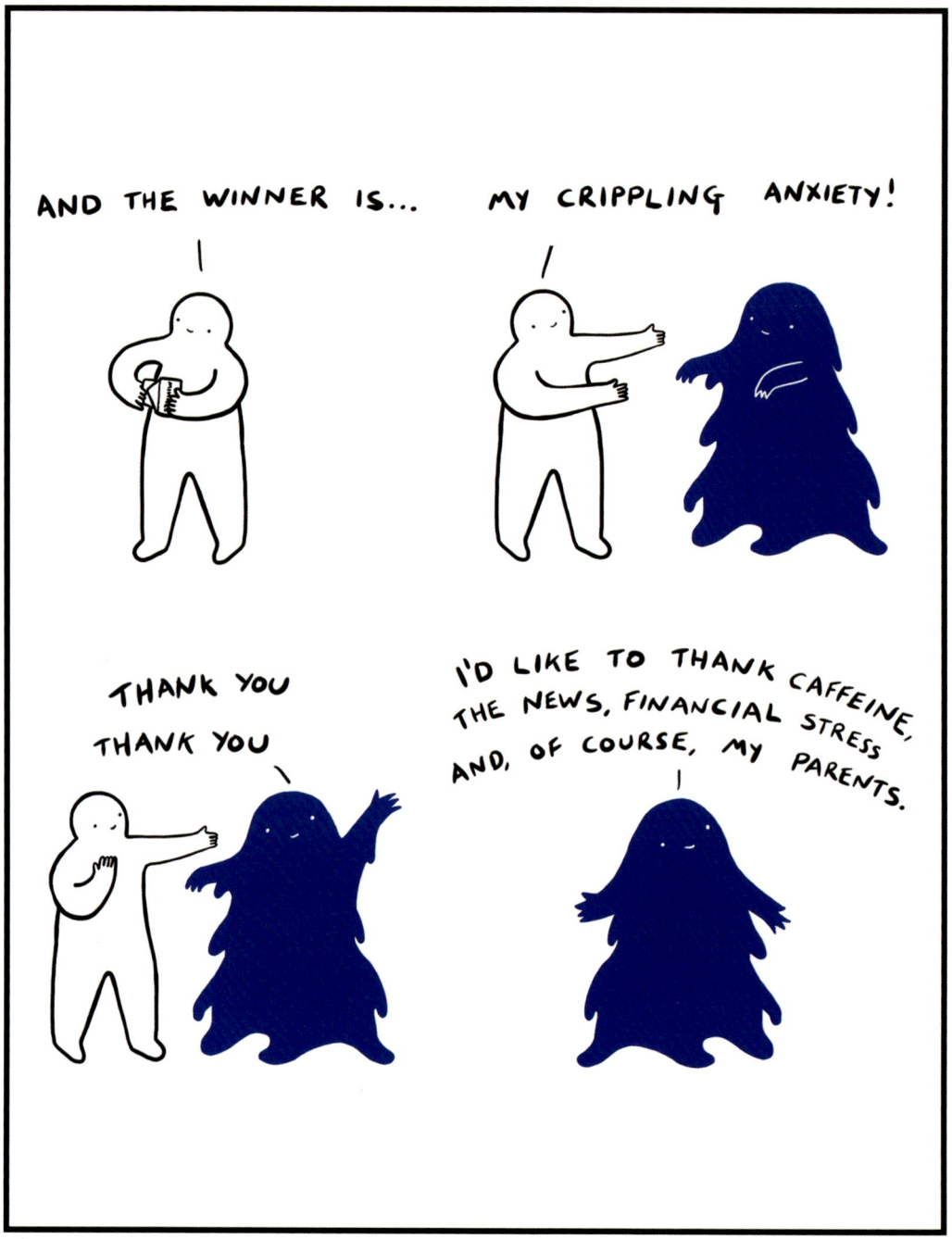

ACCEPTANCE SPEECH.

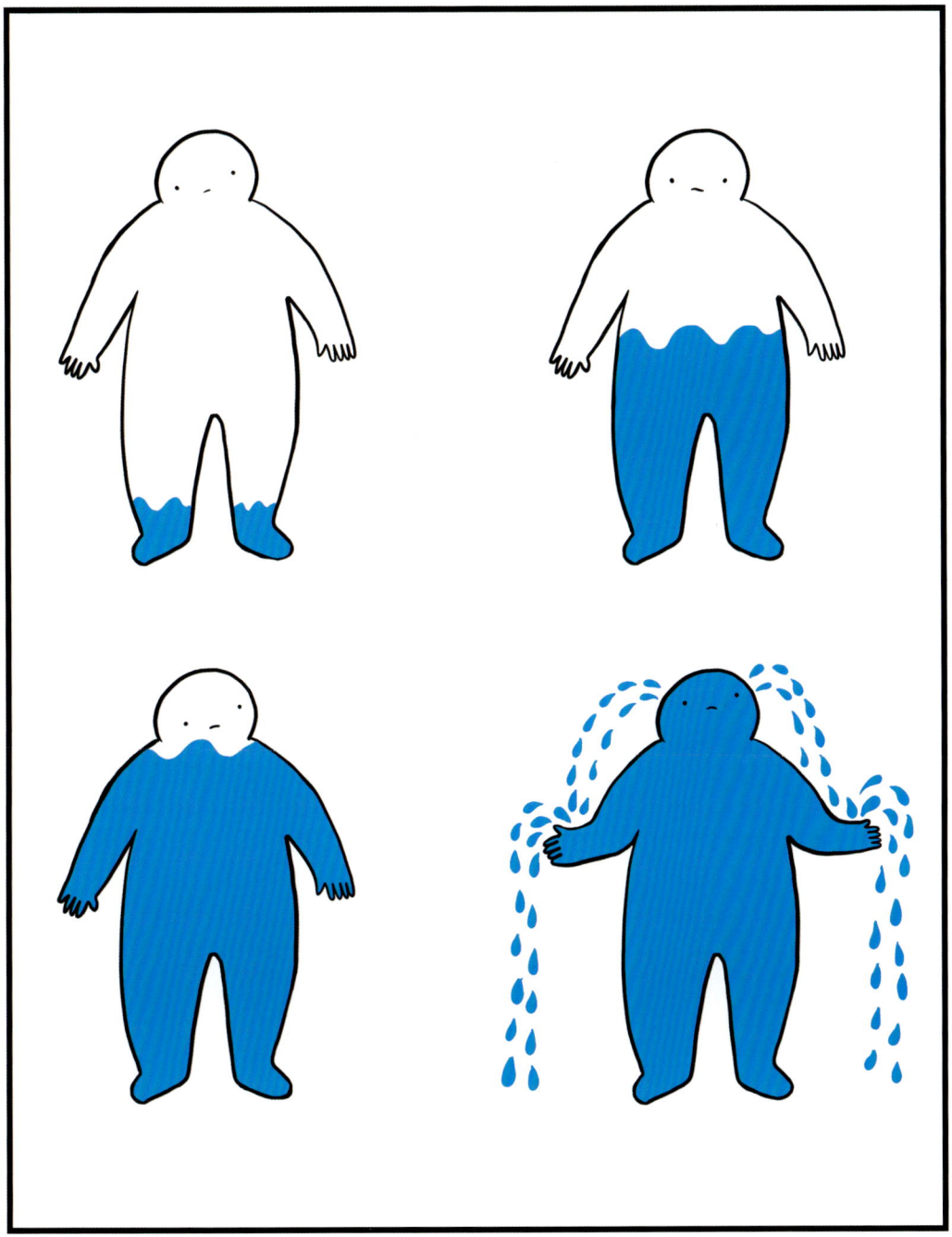

WATER FEATURE.

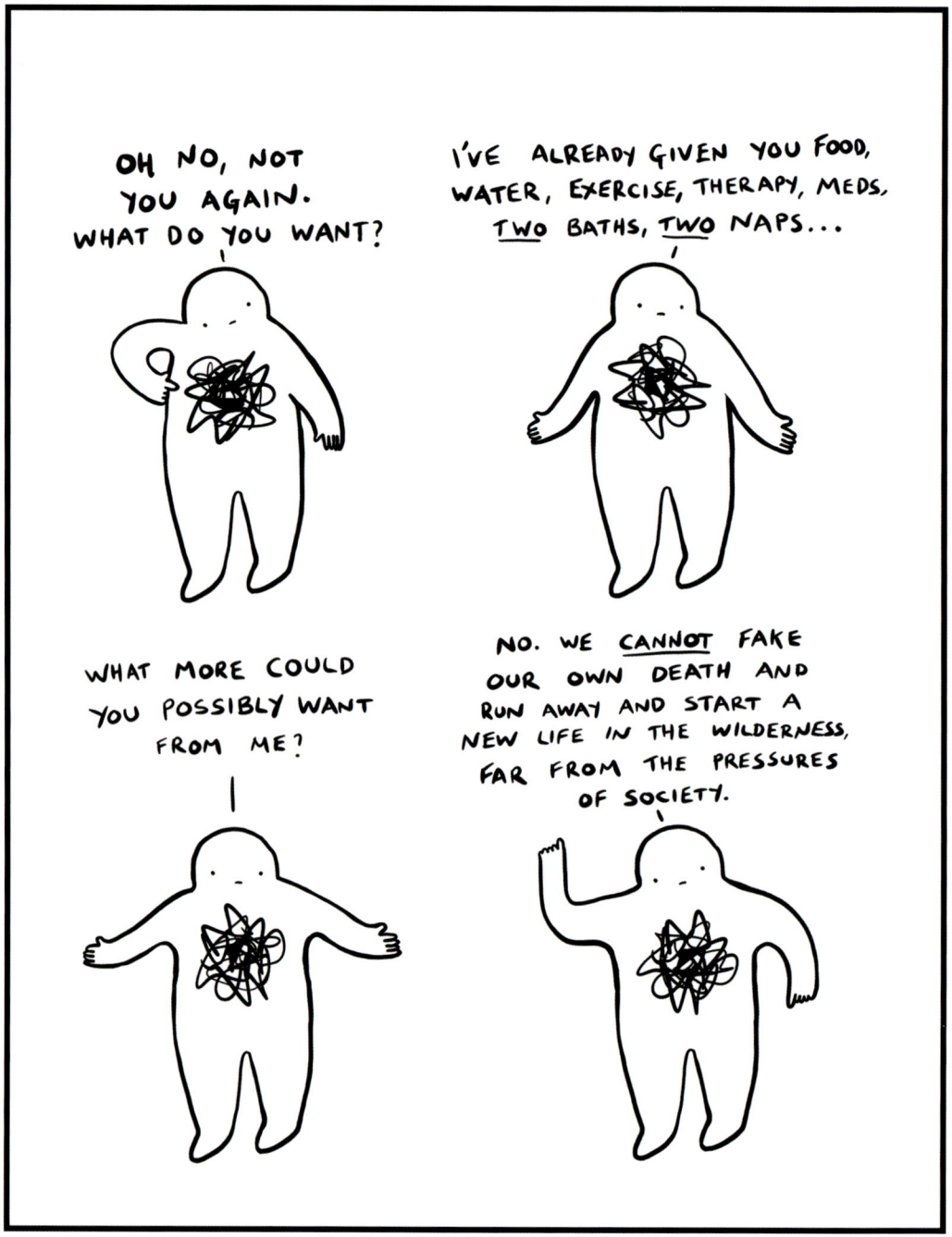

AS MUCH AS WE MIGHT WANT TO.

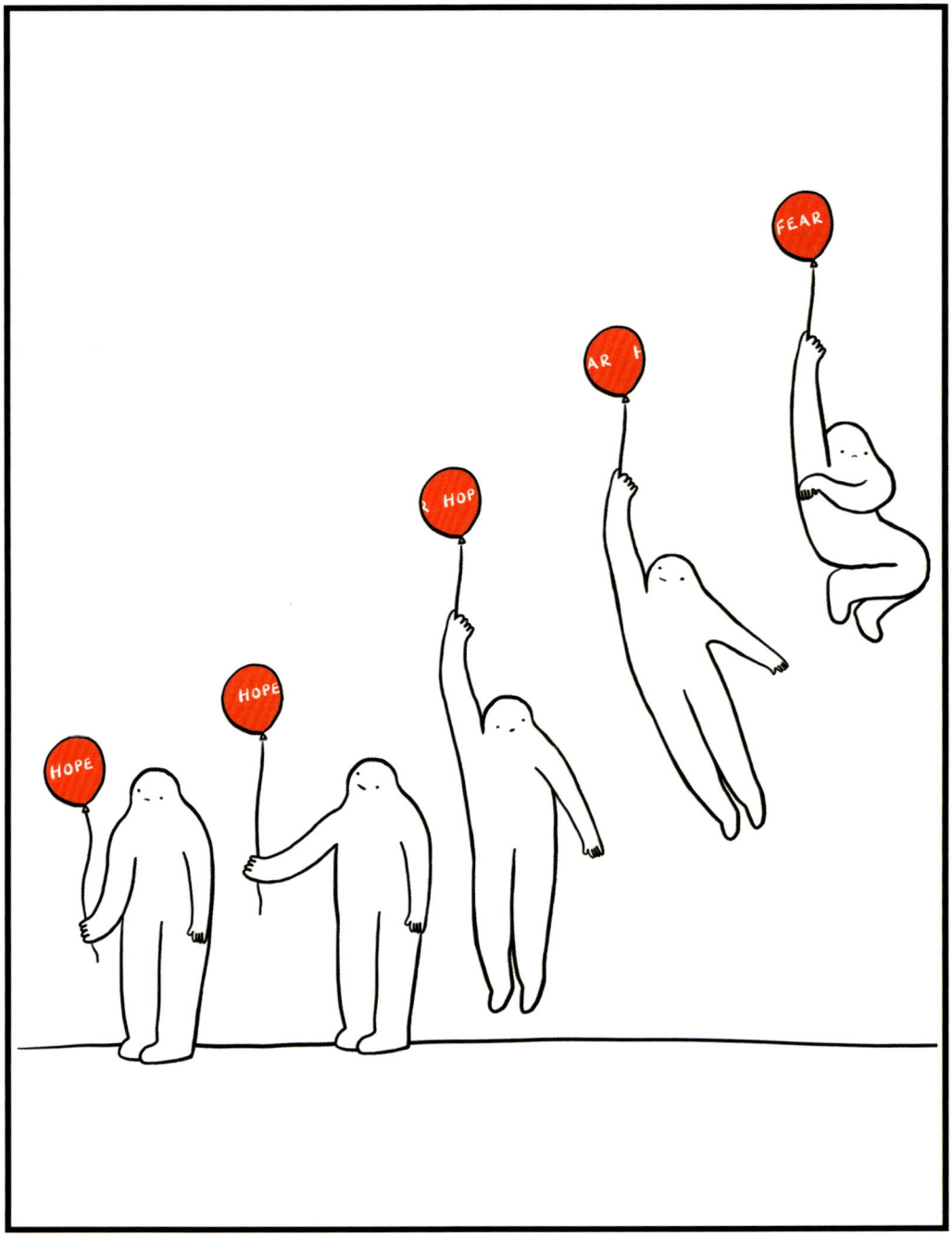

ON THE RISE.

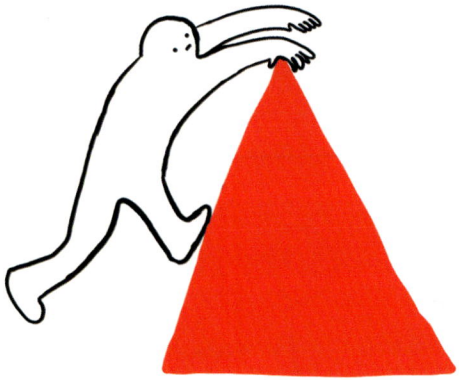

OVER THE SPIKE OF ANXIETY

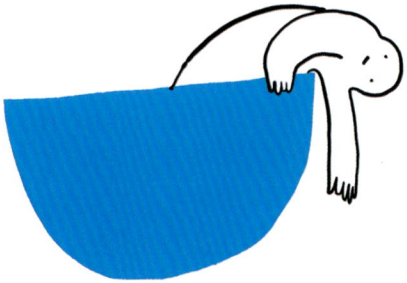

OUT OF THE PIT OF DESPAIR

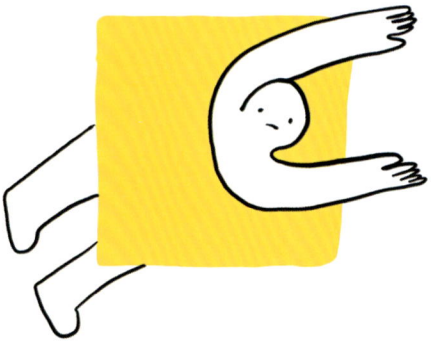

THROUGH THE FOG OF DOUBT

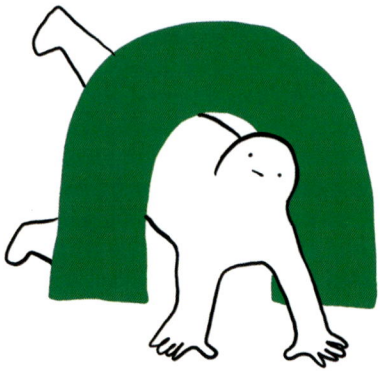

TIME FOR BREAKFAST!

MORNING!

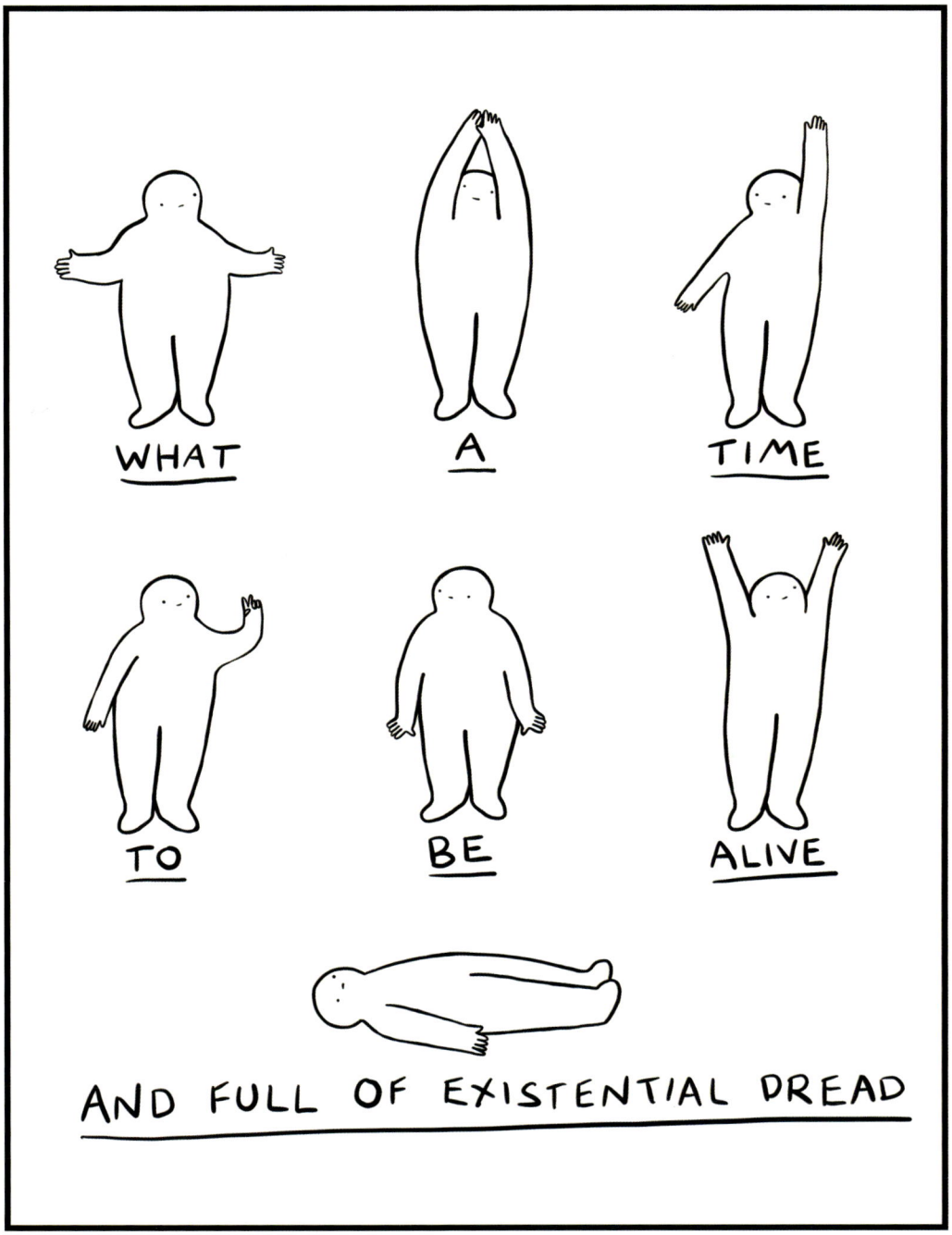

LIVING IN THE NOW.

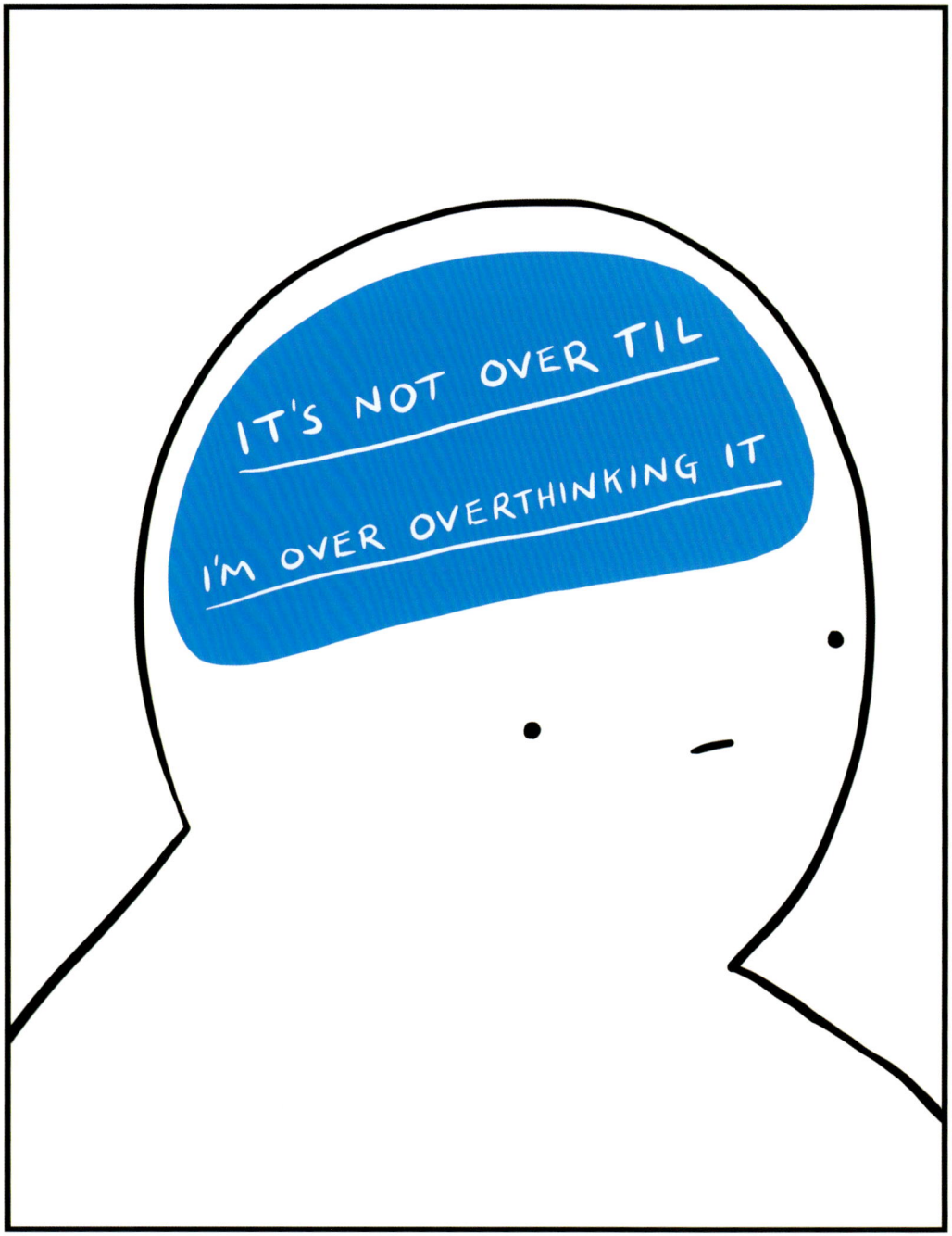

OVERTHOUGHT.

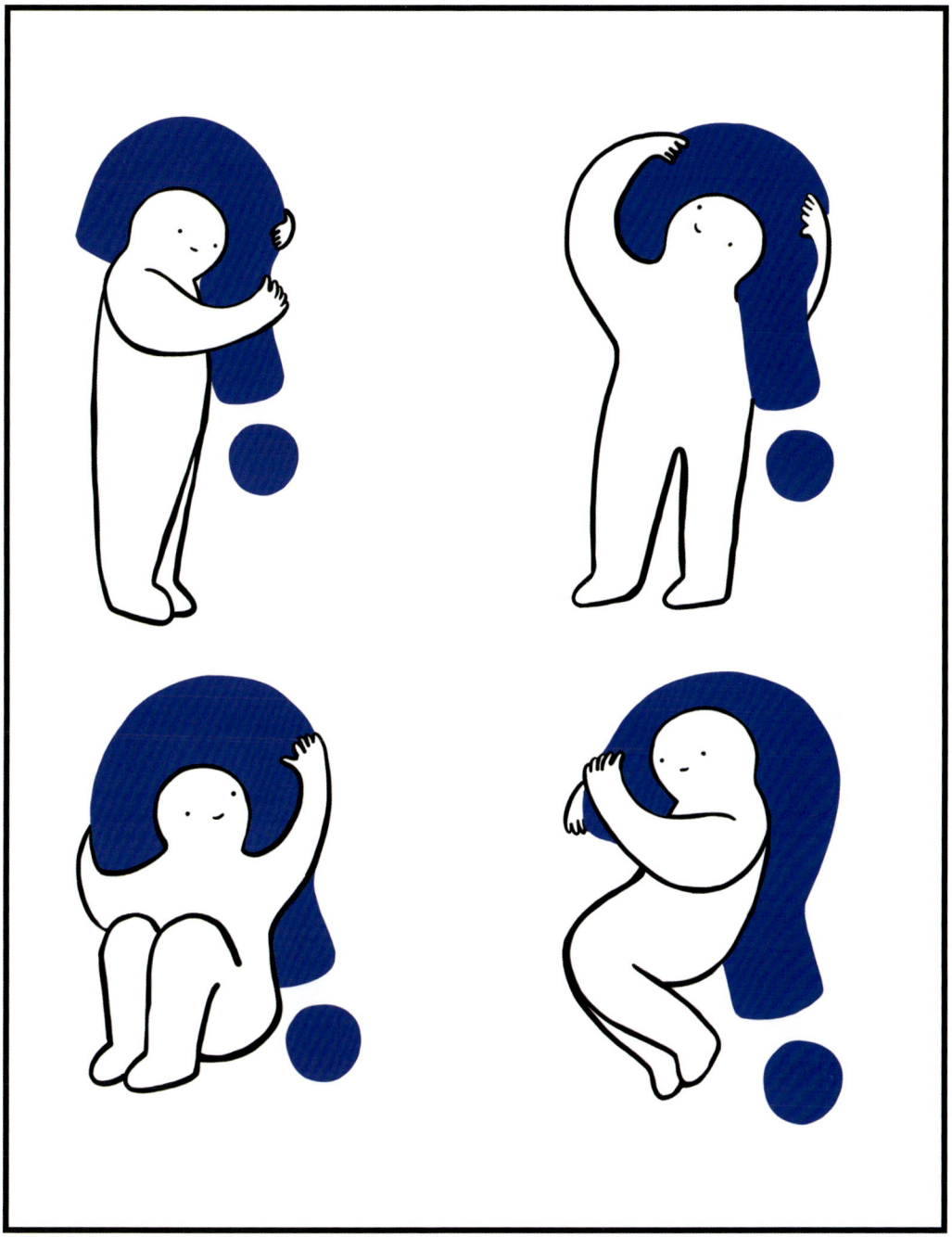

EMBRACING UNCERTAINTY.

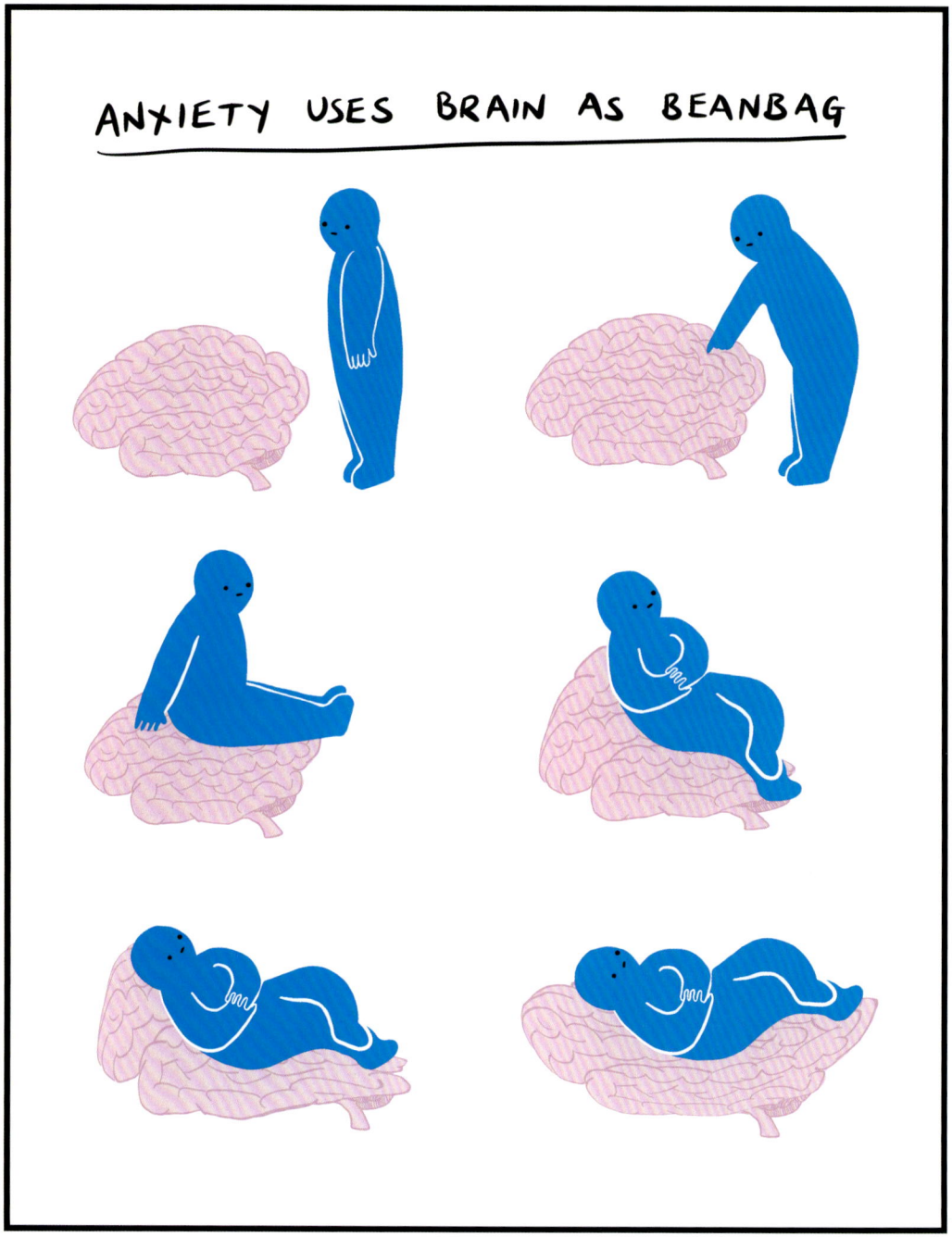

STRUGGLES TO GET BACK UP AGAIN.

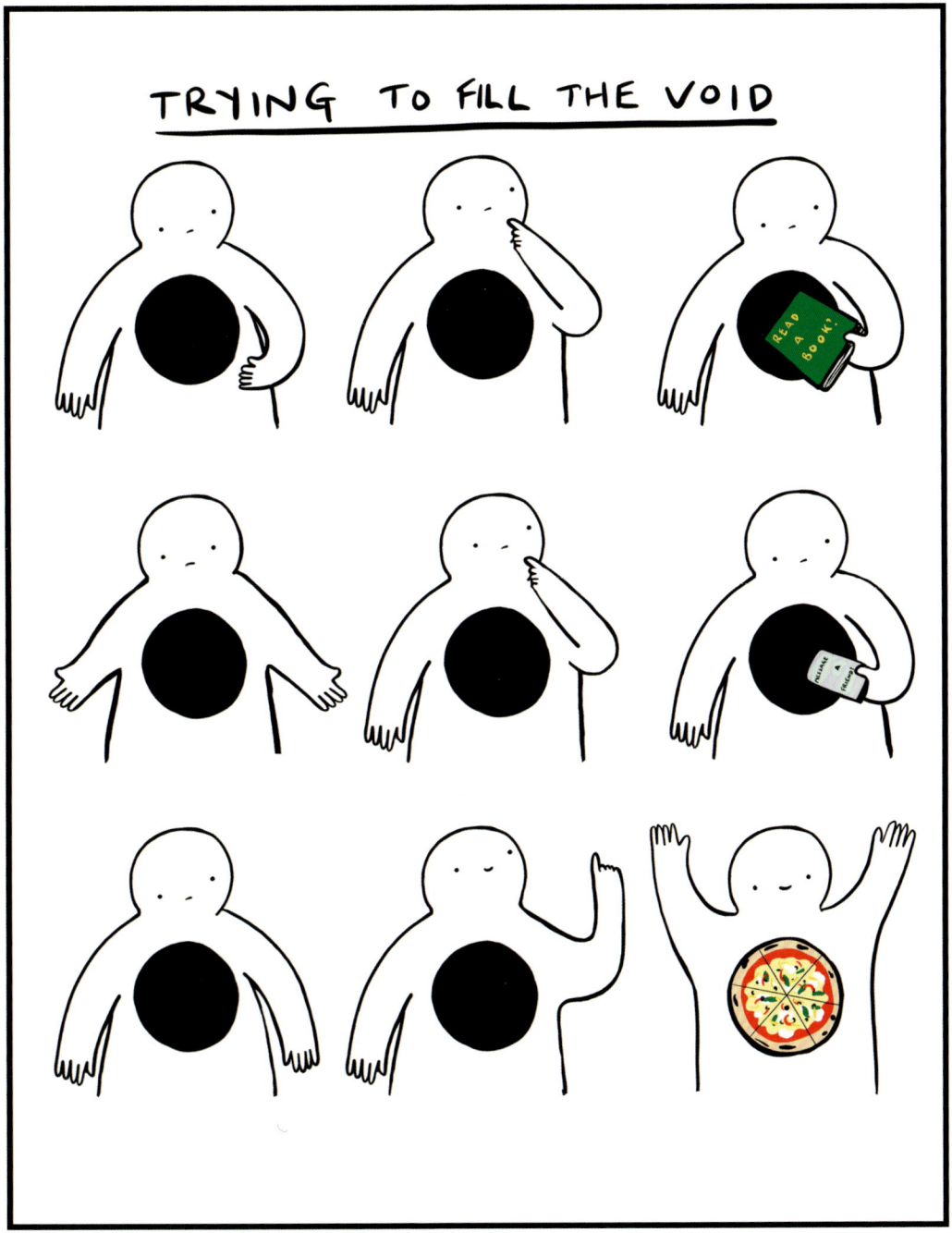

PERFECT FIT.

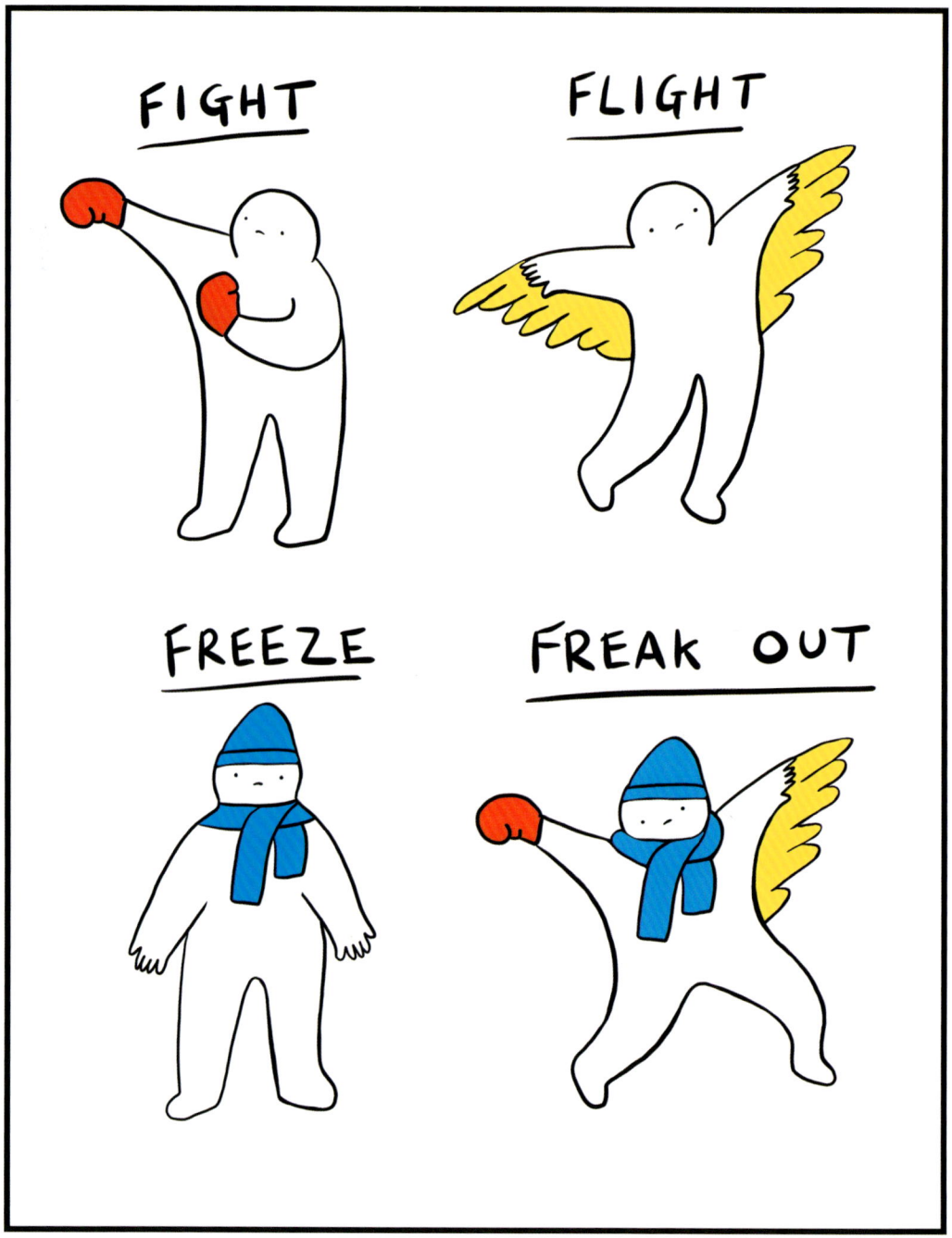

FOUR OPTIONS.

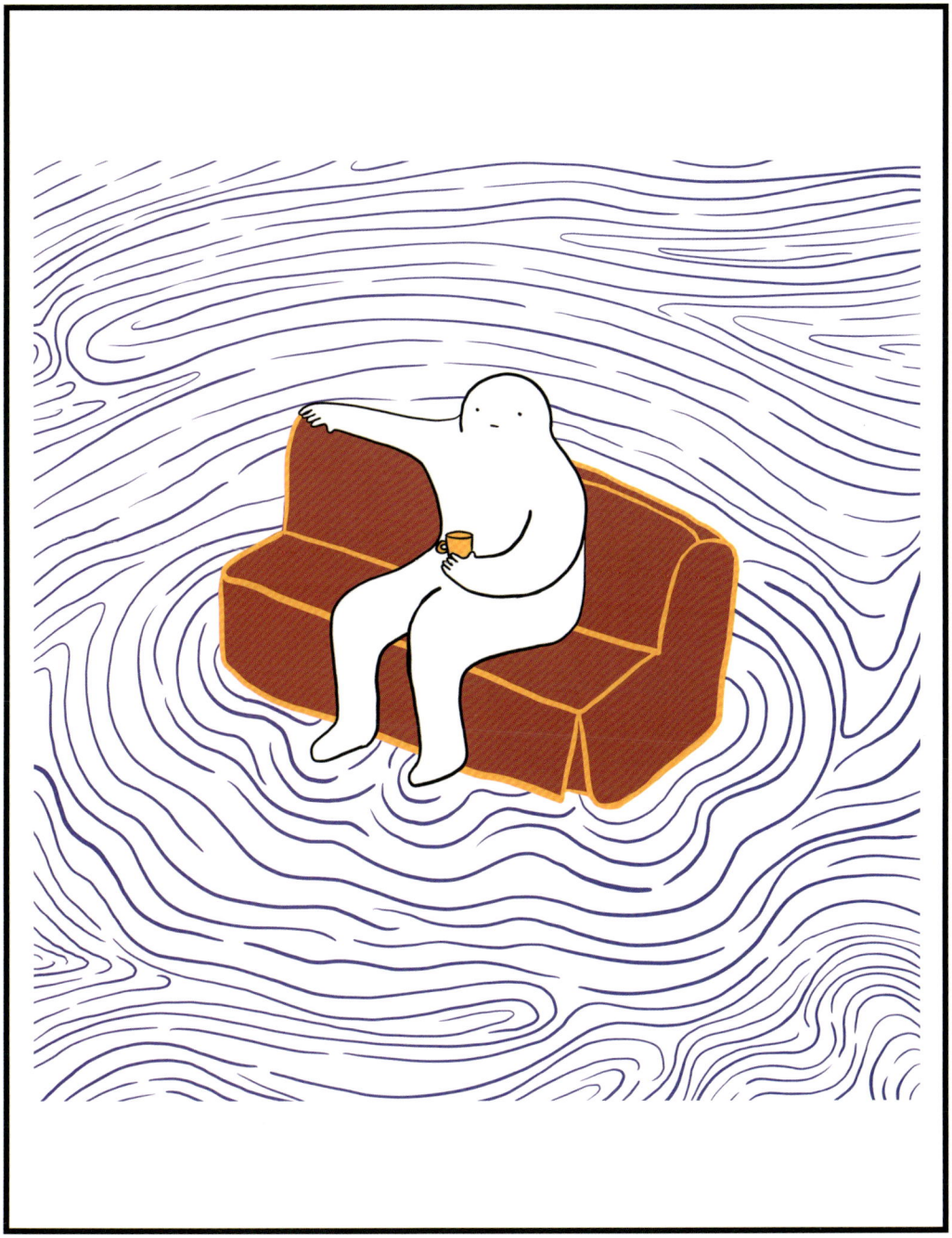

AT SEA.

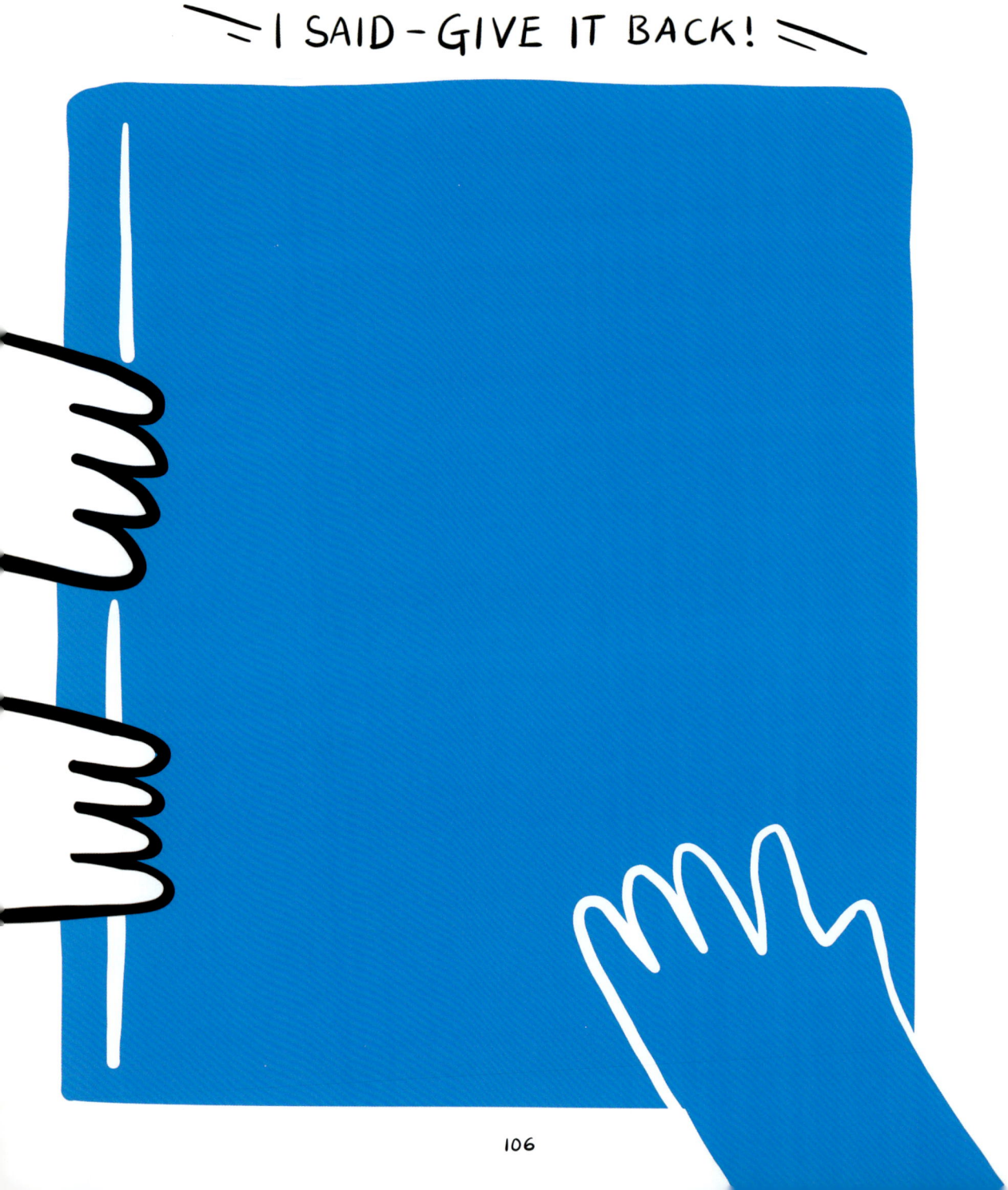
I SAID - GIVE IT BACK!

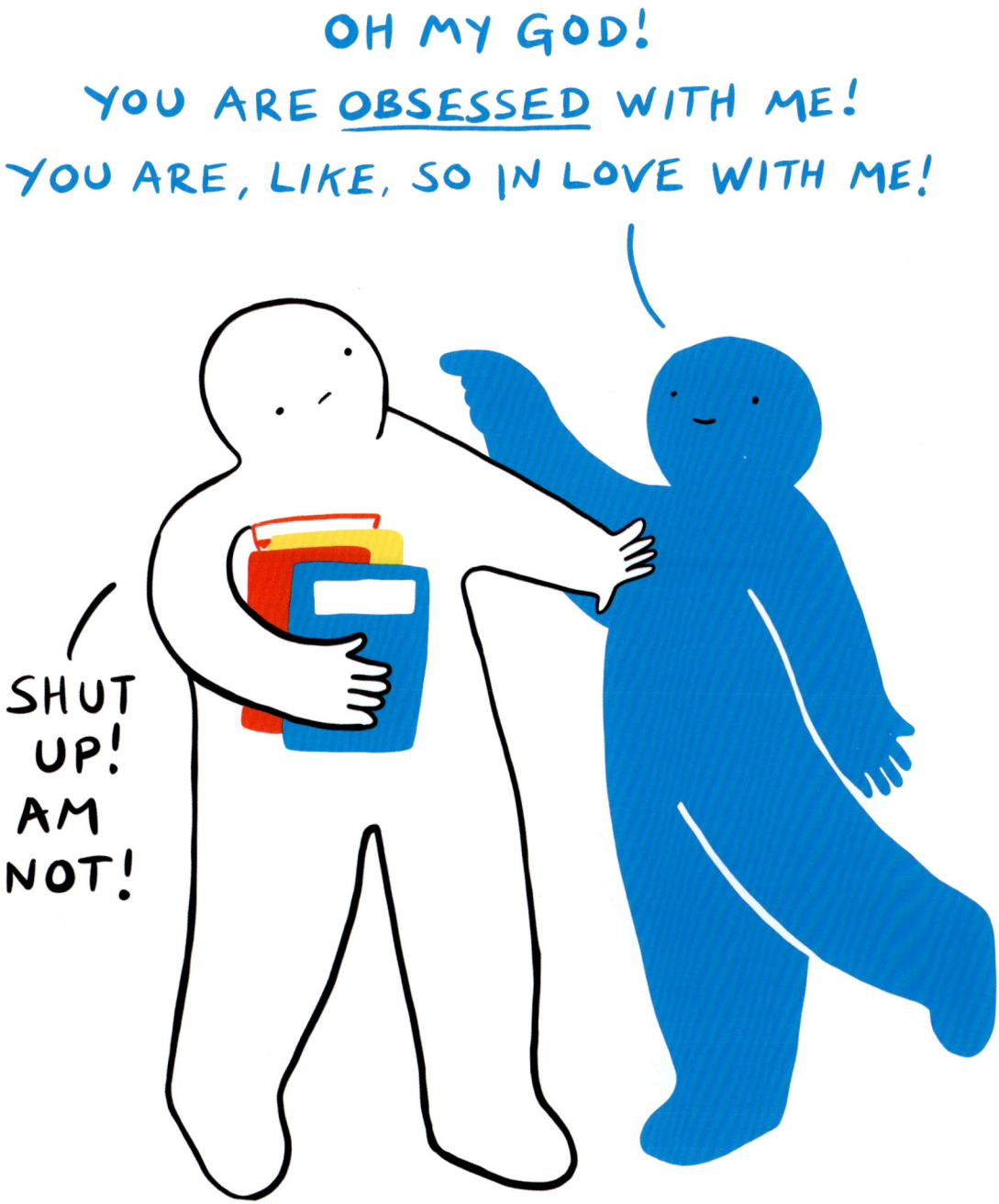
OH MY GOD!
YOU ARE OBSESSED WITH ME!
YOU ARE, LIKE, SO IN LOVE WITH ME!
SHUT UP! AM NOT!

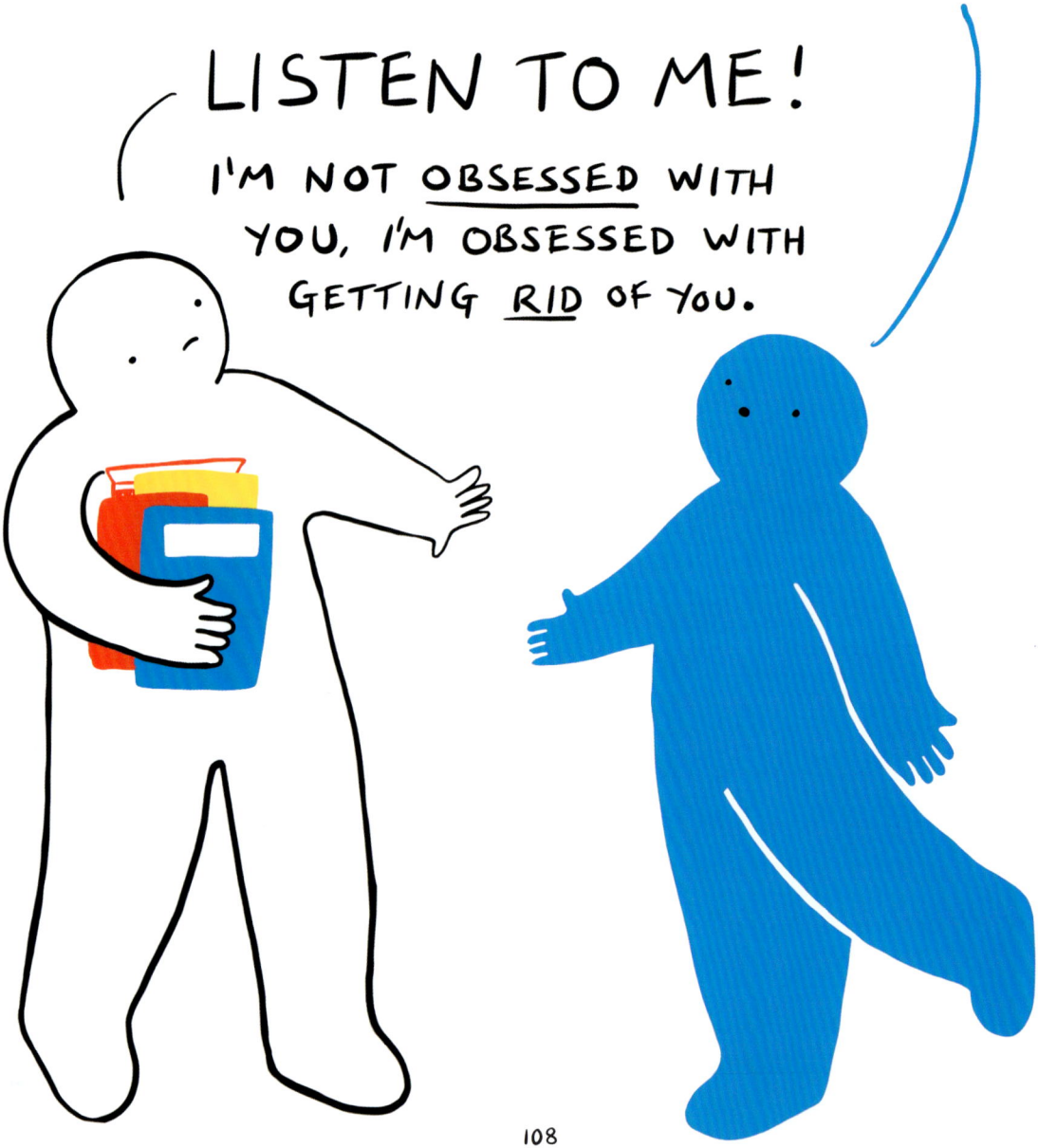
LOOK, I'M FLATTERED, BUT TO BE HONEST, YOU'RE NOT REALLY MY TYPE. YOU'RE TOO - WHAT'S THE WORD? ANXIOUS?
LISTEN TO ME!
I'M NOT OBSESSED WITH YOU, I'M OBSESSED WITH GETTING RID OF YOU.

(THIS PAGE HAS BEEN INTENTIONALLY LEFT BLANK IN ORDER TO REPRESENT A STUNNED AND AWKWARD SILENCE.)

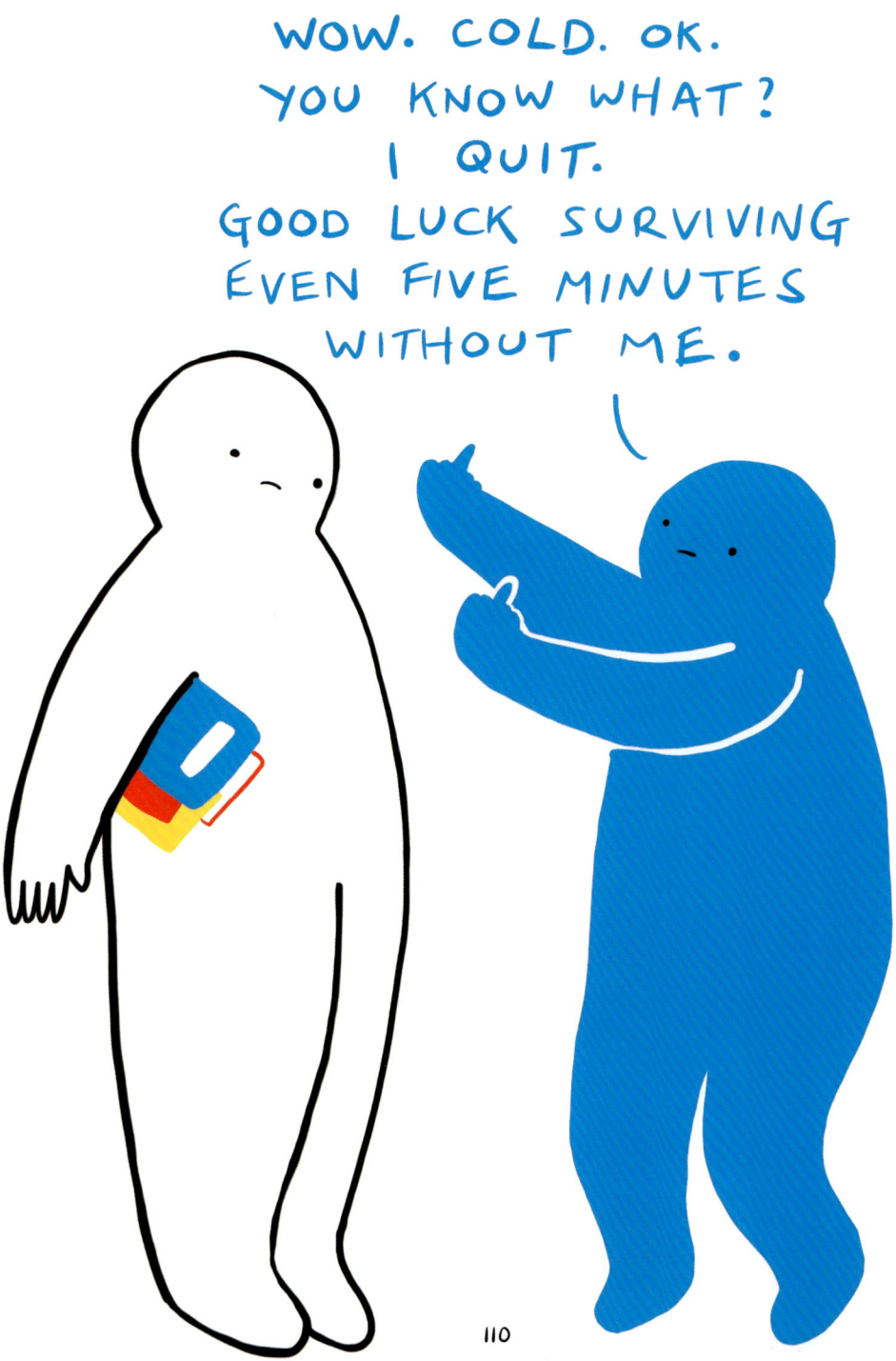
WOW. COLD. OK.
YOU KNOW WHAT?
I QUIT.
GOOD LUCK SURVIVING
EVEN FIVE MINUTES
WITHOUT ME.

AND DON'T EVEN THINK ABOUT TRYING TO FOLLOW ME – I'M A MASTER OF STEALTH AND – OH SHIT!

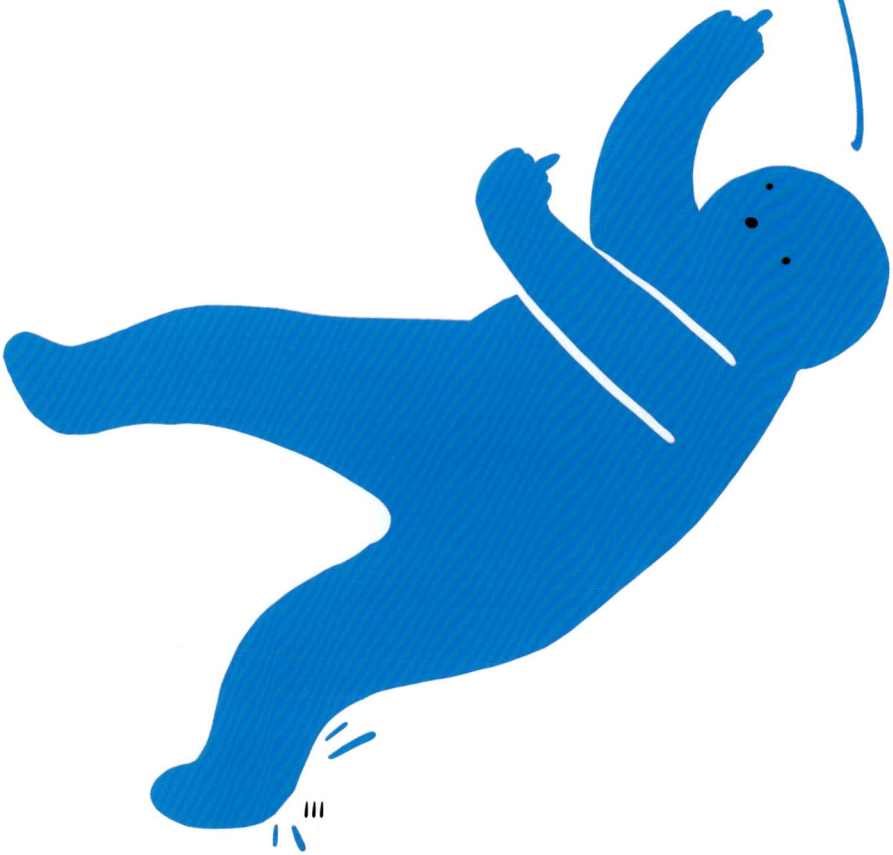

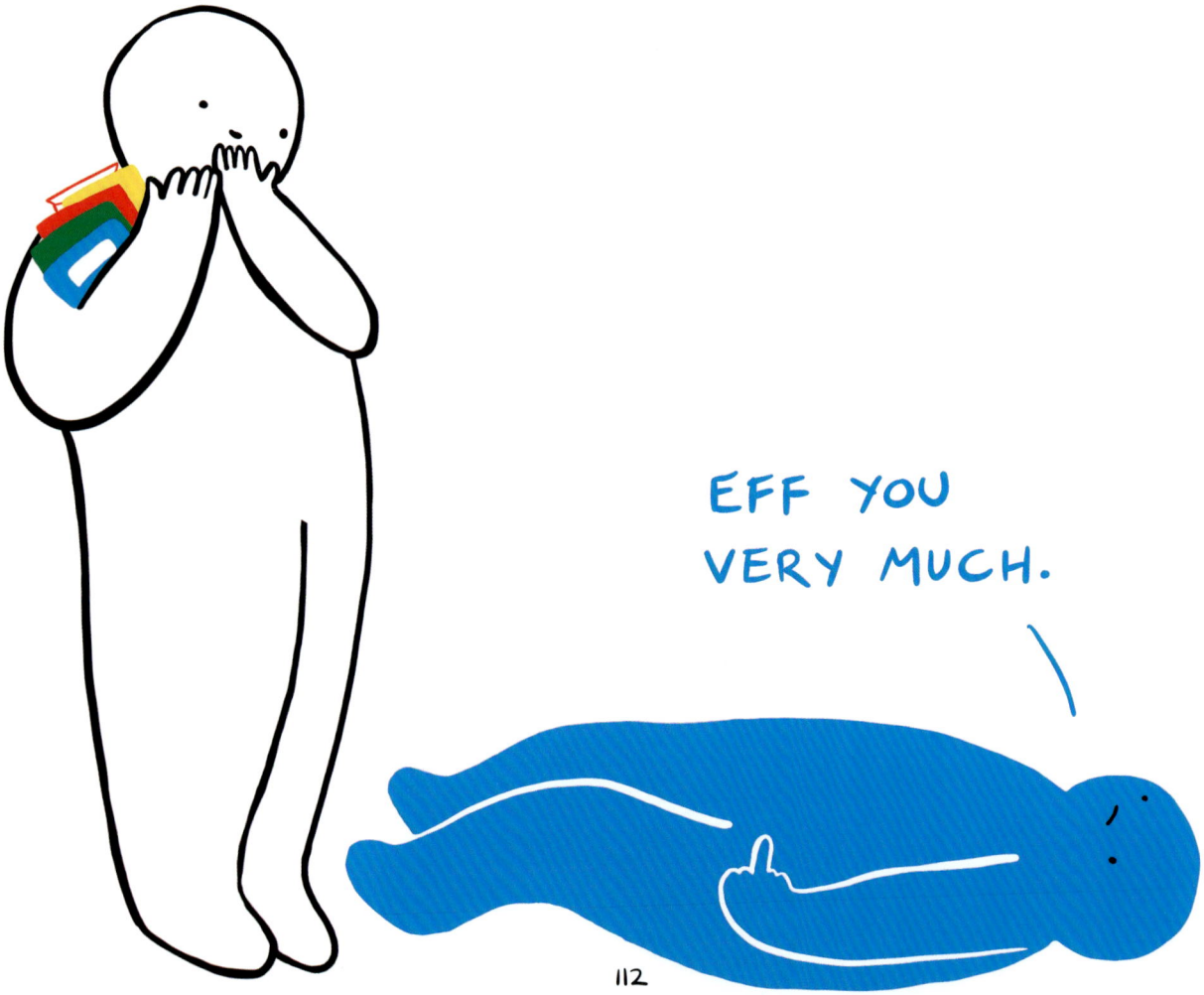
EFF YOU
VERY MUCH.

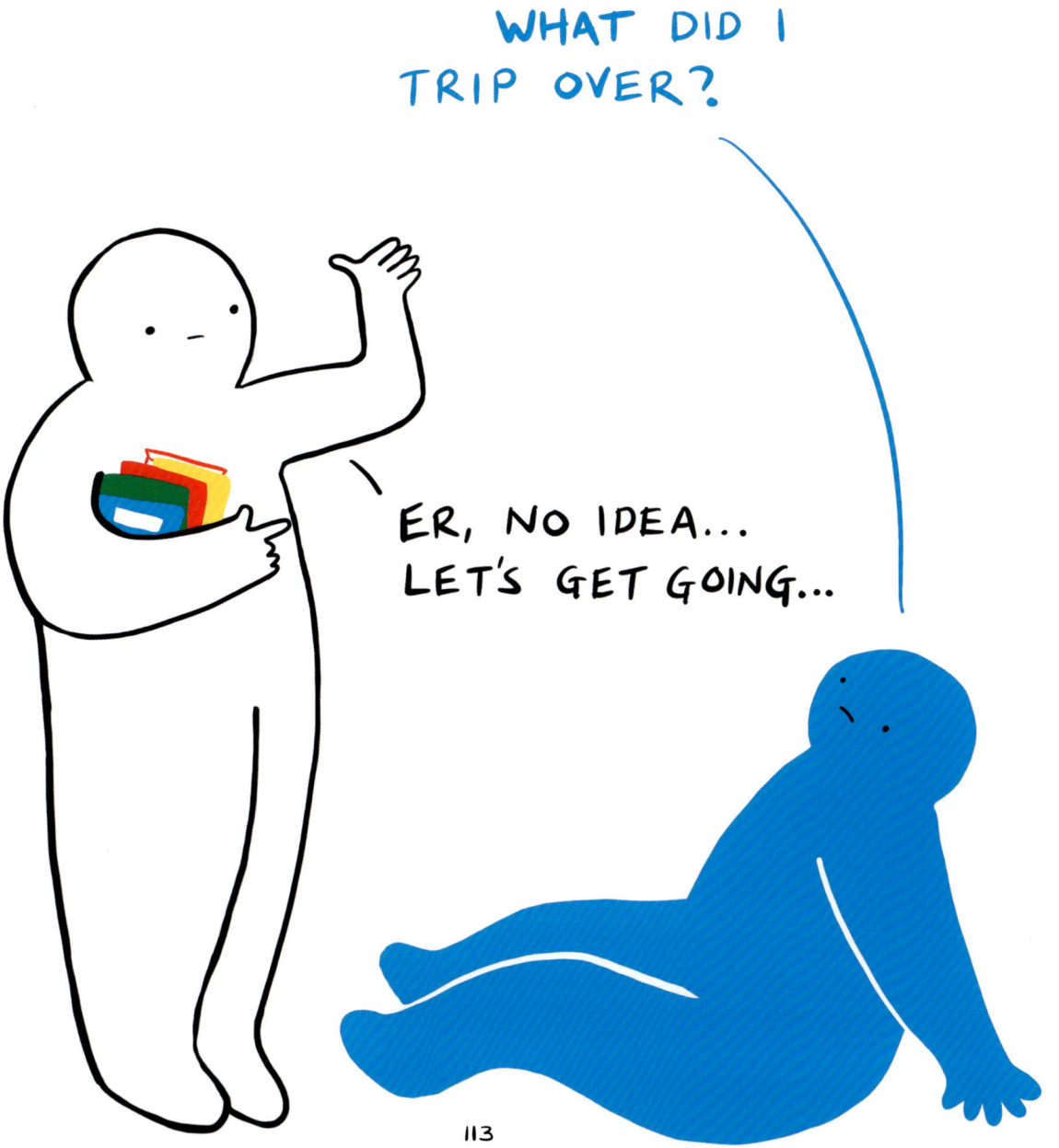
WHAT DID I TRIP OVER?
ER, NO IDEA... LET'S GET GOING...

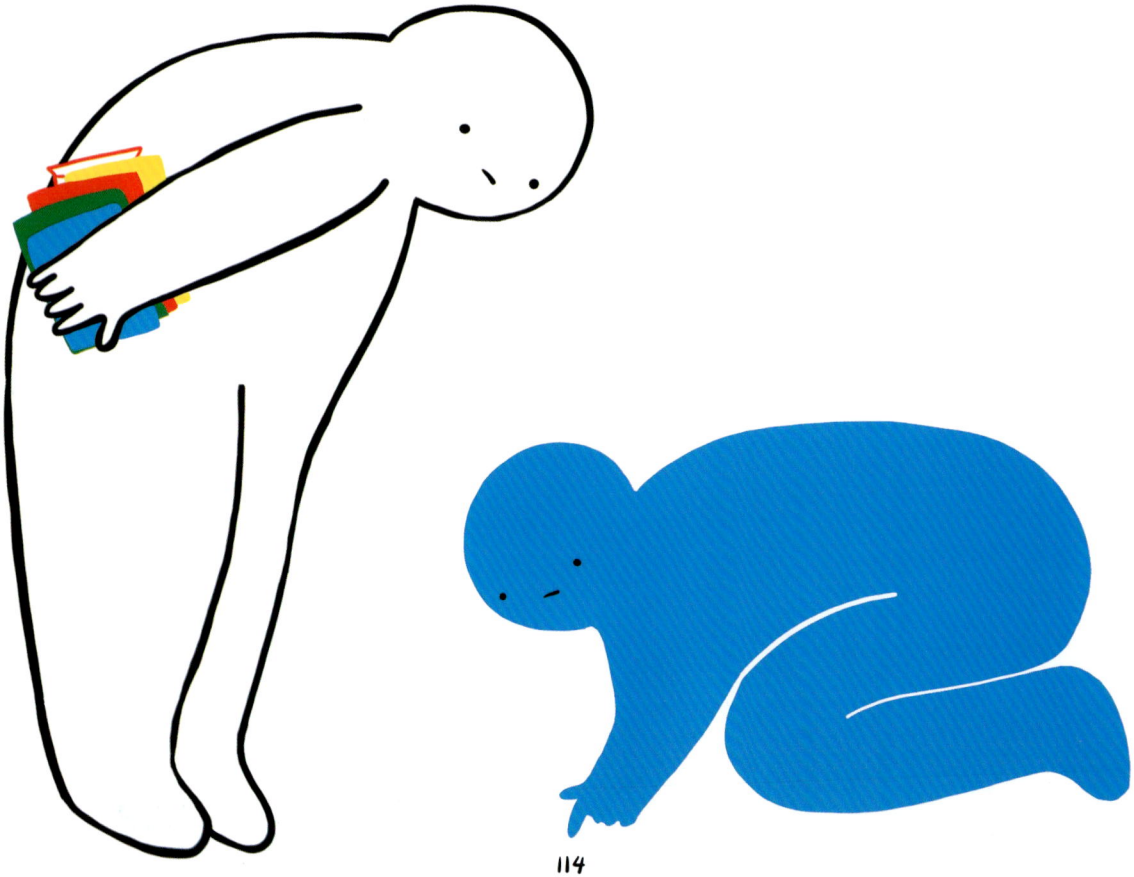

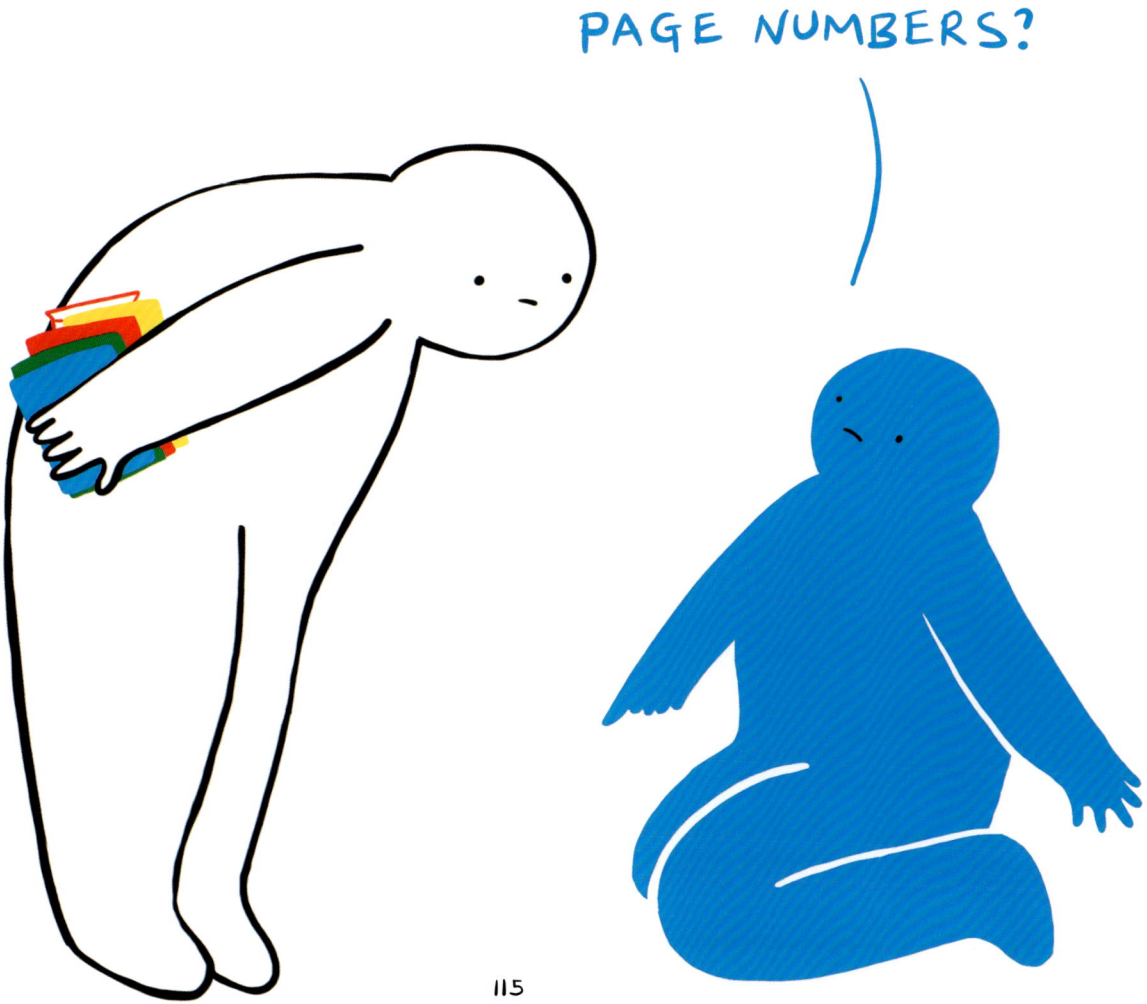
PAGE NUMBERS?

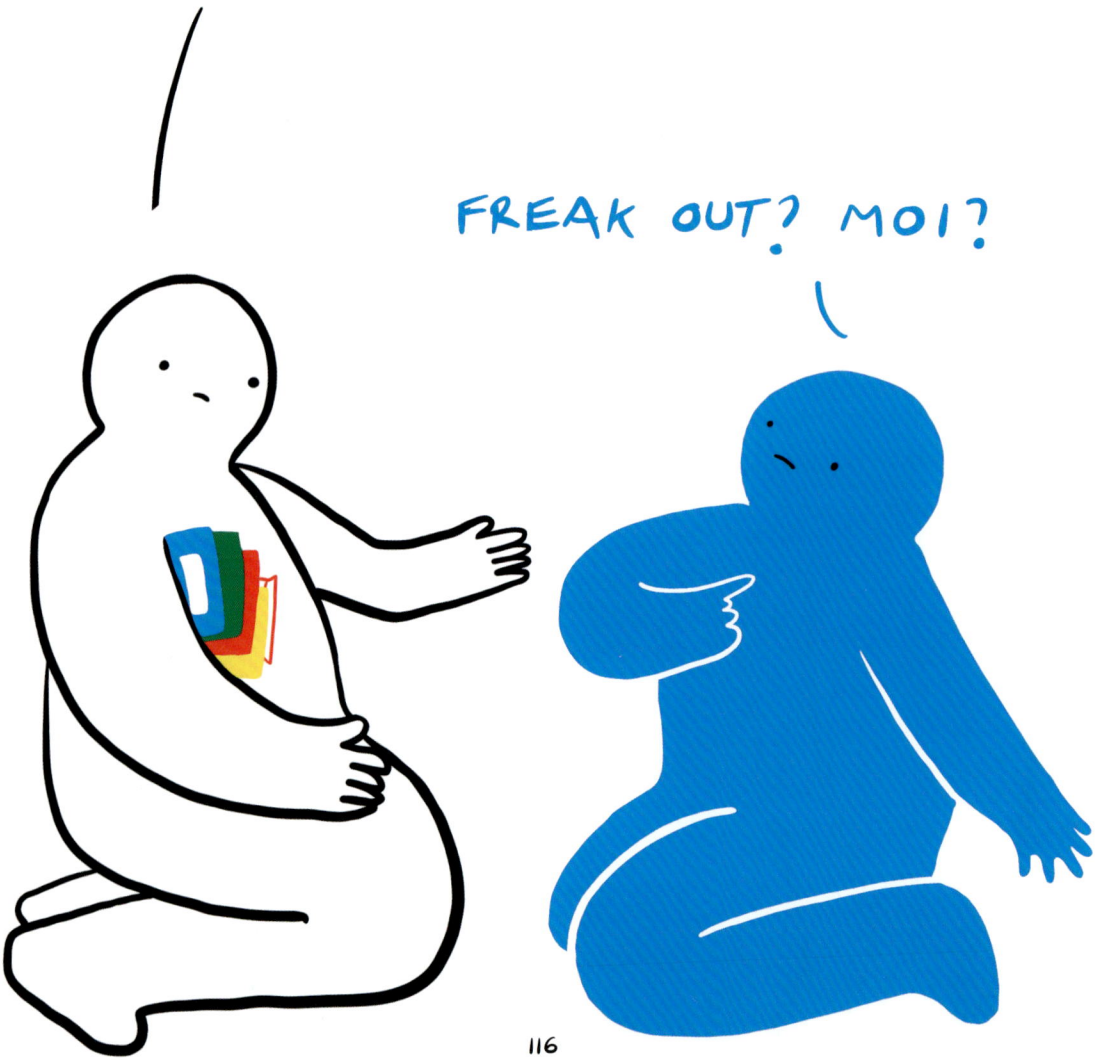
WORRY, I'M GOING TO TELL YOU SOMETHING, BUT YOU HAVE TO PROMISE ME YOU WON'T FREAK OUT.
FREAK OUT? MOI?

I JUST DON'T WANT YOU TO WORRY...

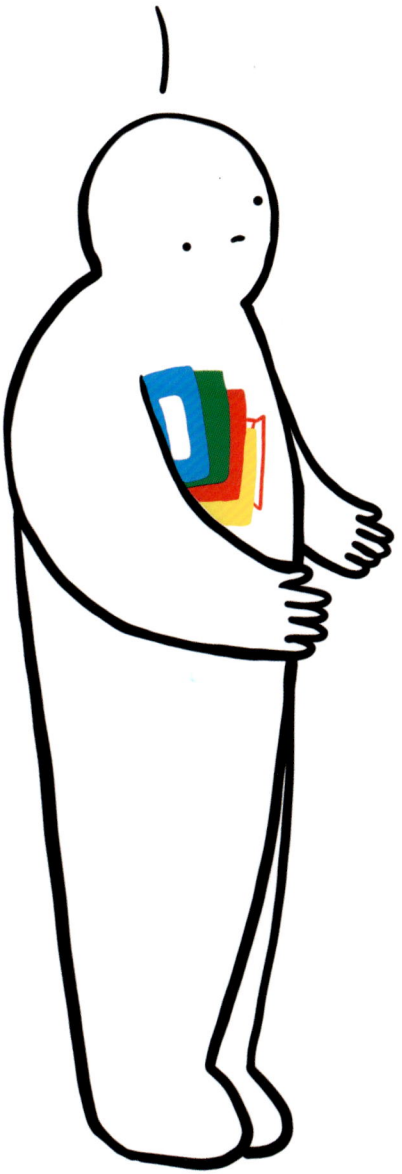

I SWEAR, IF ONE MORE PERSON TELLS ME TO STOP WORRYING, I'LL PROBABLY HAVE A PANIC ATTACK.

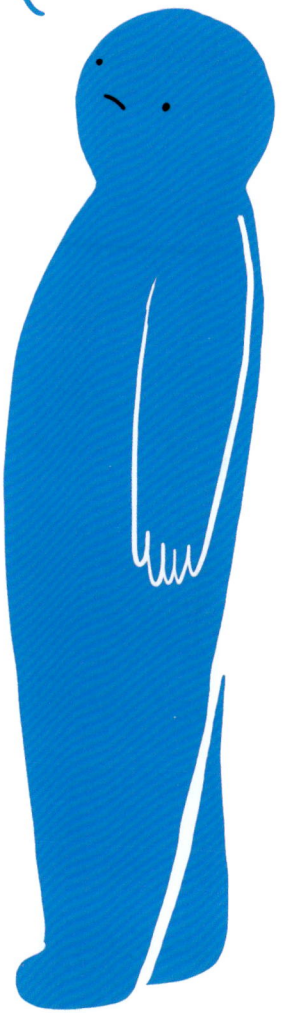

OK. HERE GOES: YOU AND I ARE IN THE BOOK - MY BOOK - IT'S CALLED "THIS BOOK IS FOR YOU" AND, ER, WE'RE IN IT... RIGHT NOW.

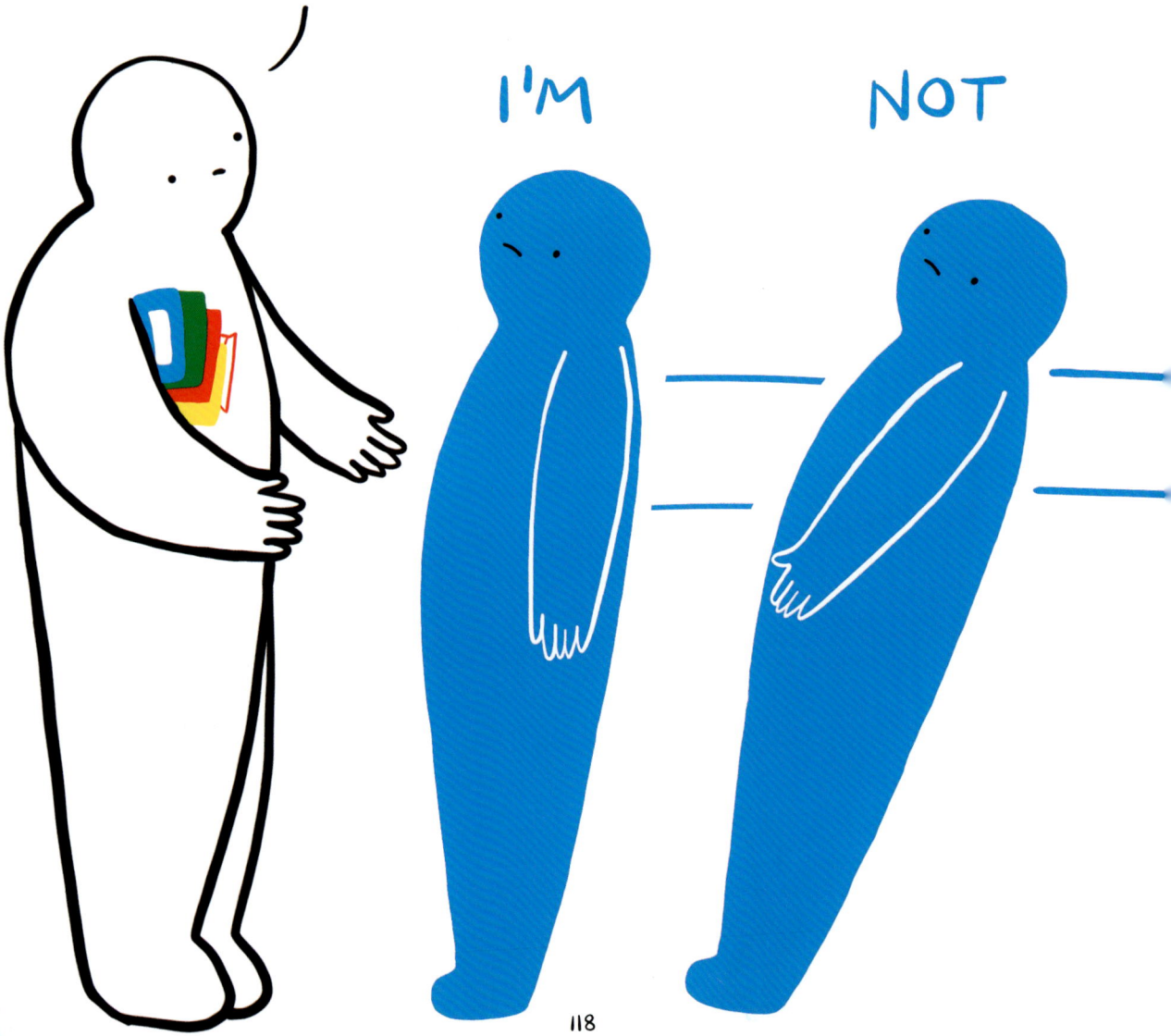

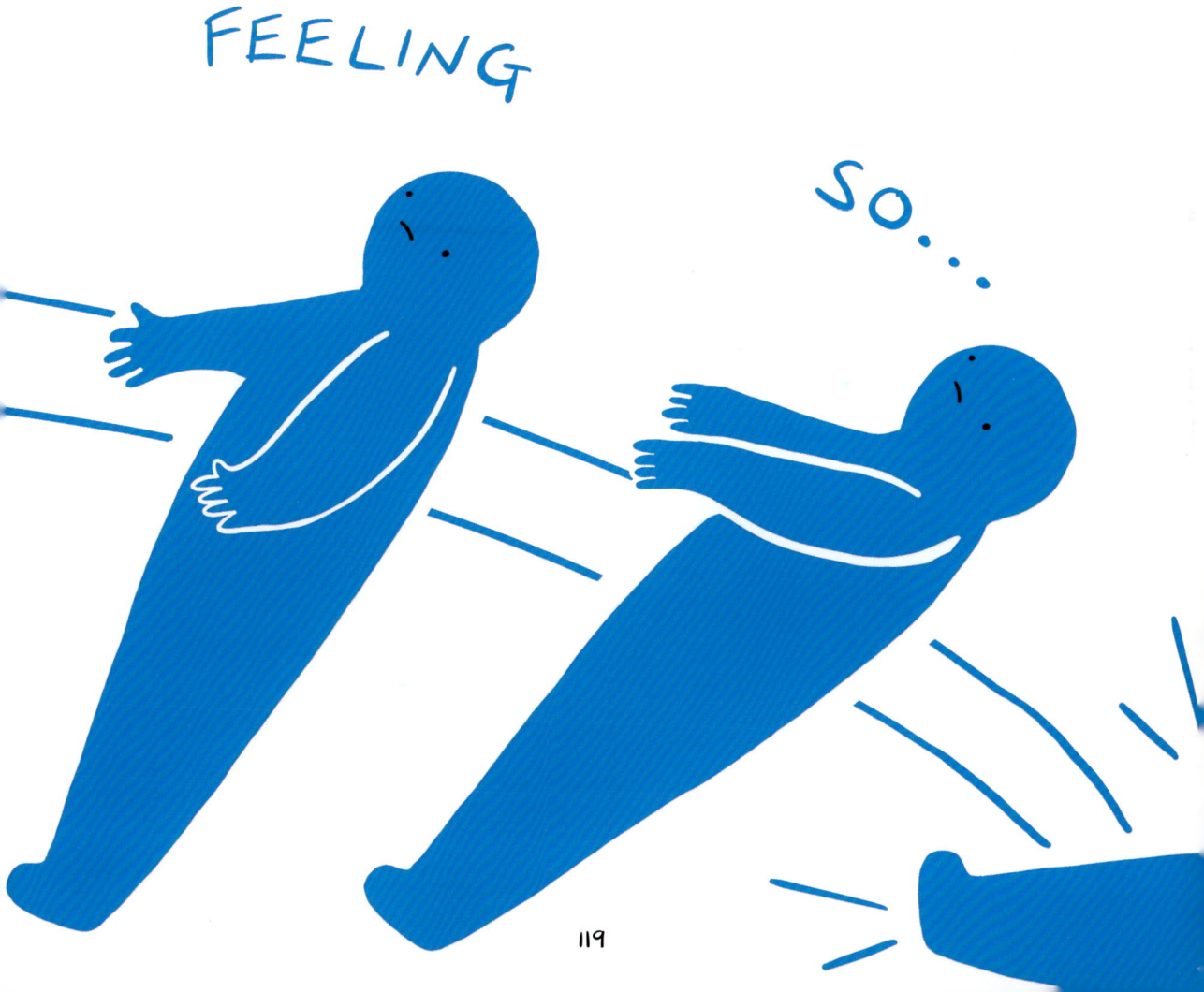
FEELING
SO...

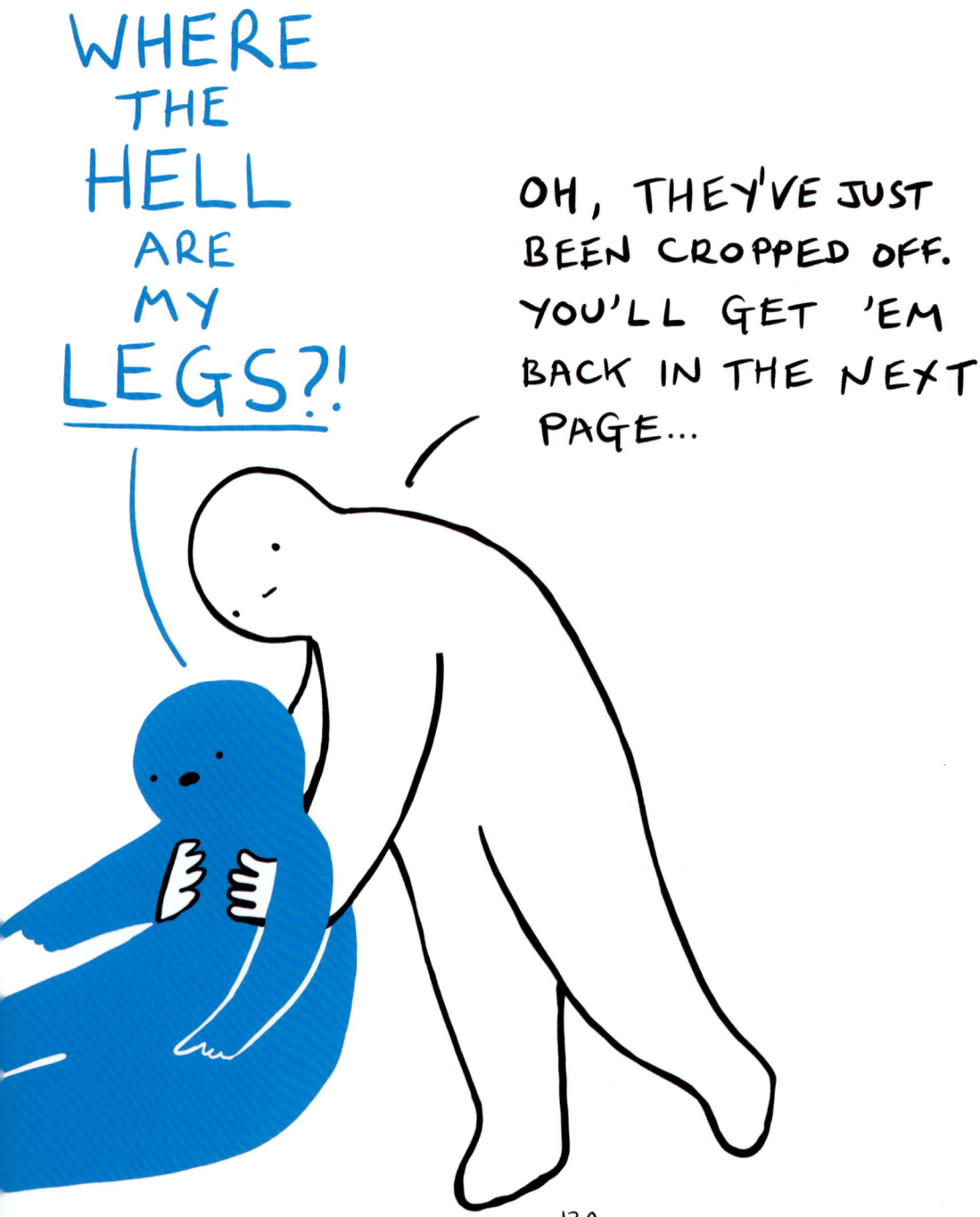
WHERE THE HELL ARE MY LEGS?!
OH, THEY'VE JUST BEEN CROPPED OFF. YOU'LL GET 'EM BACK IN THE NEXT PAGE...

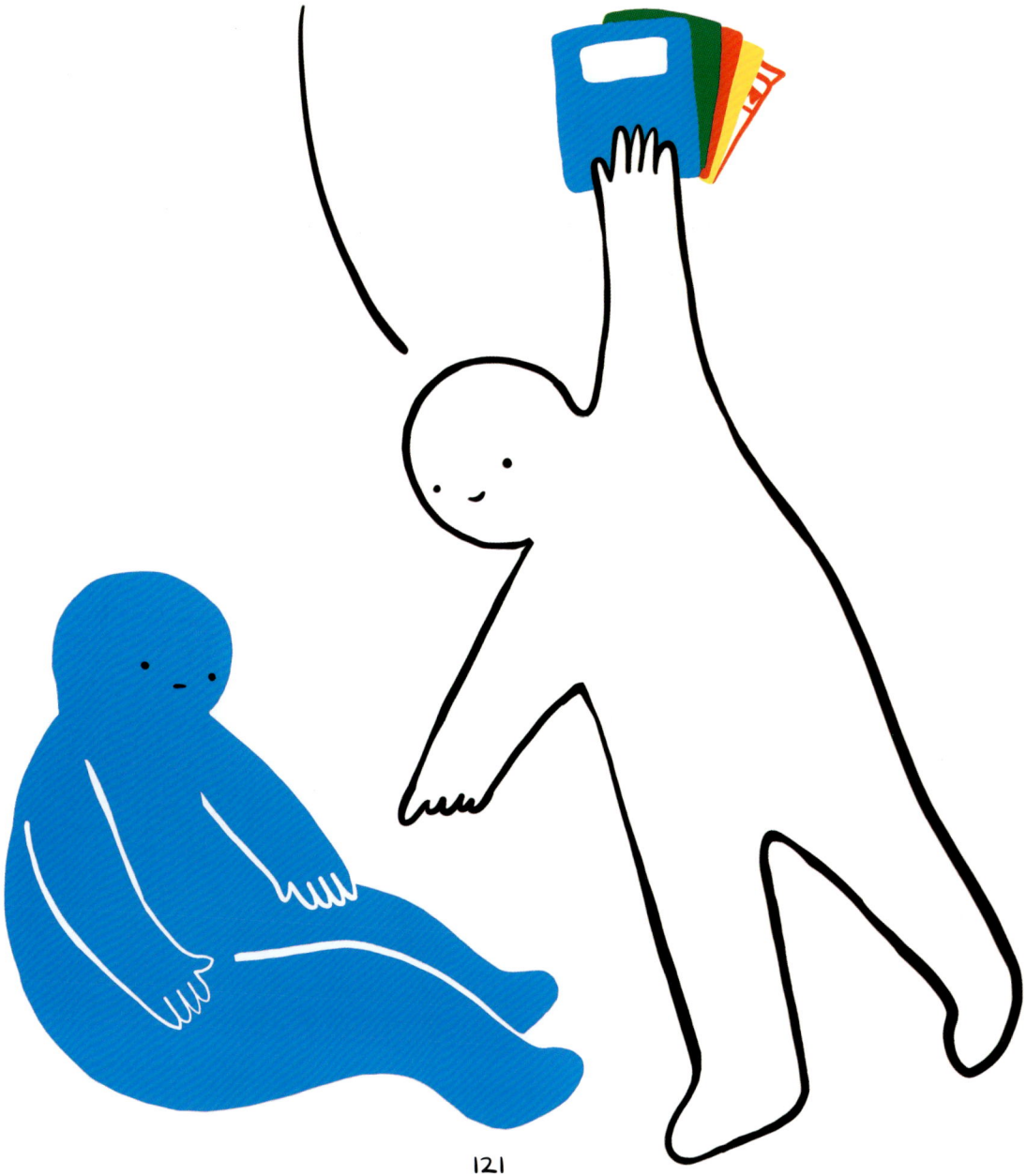
SEE? SO COOL! I LOVE BOOKS!
COME ON - I'LL SHOW YOU AROUND!

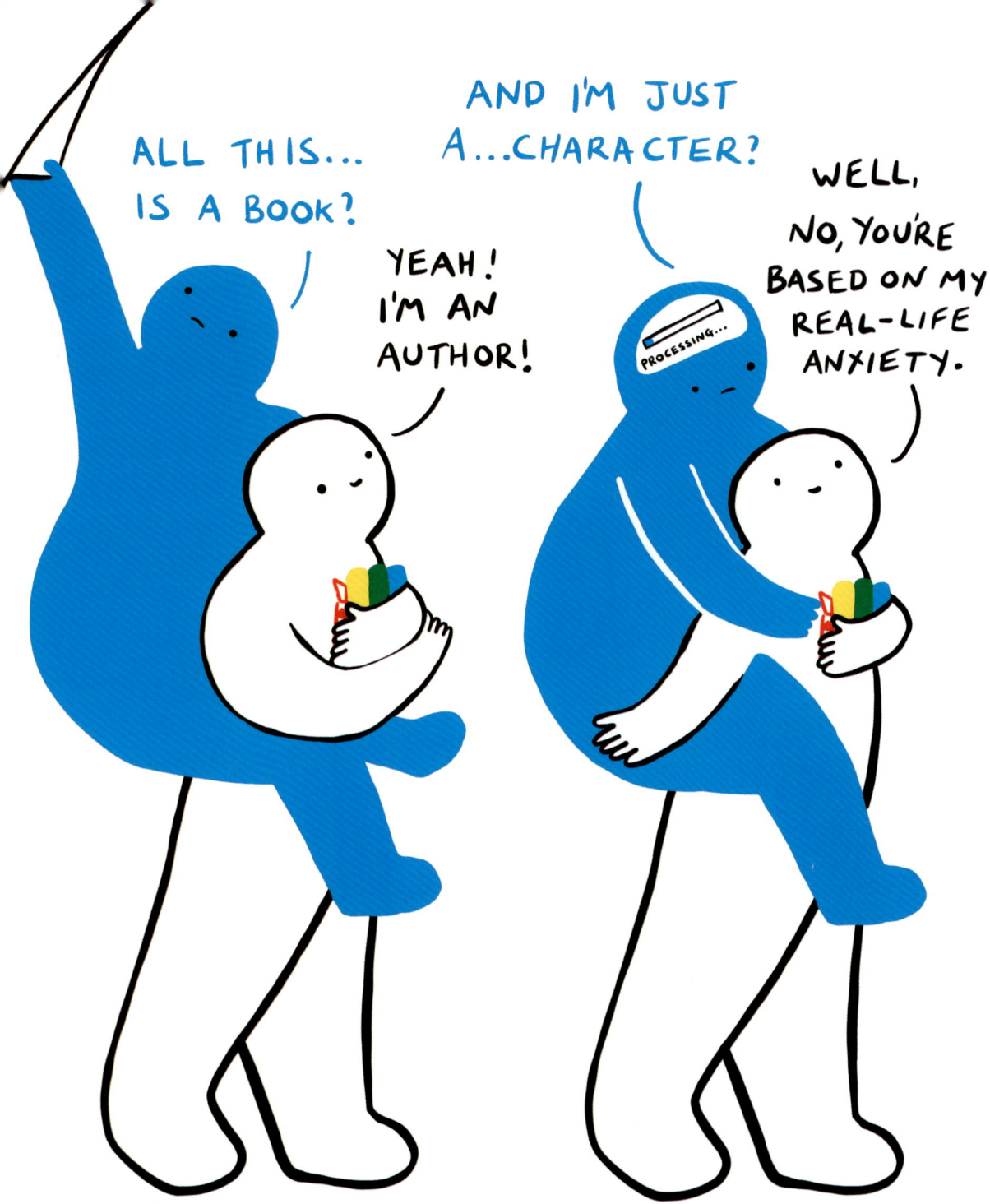
ALL THIS... IS A BOOK?
YEAH! I'M AN AUTHOR!
AND I'M JUST A...CHARACTER?
PROCESSING...
WELL, NO, YOU'RE BASED ON MY REAL-LIFE ANXIETY.

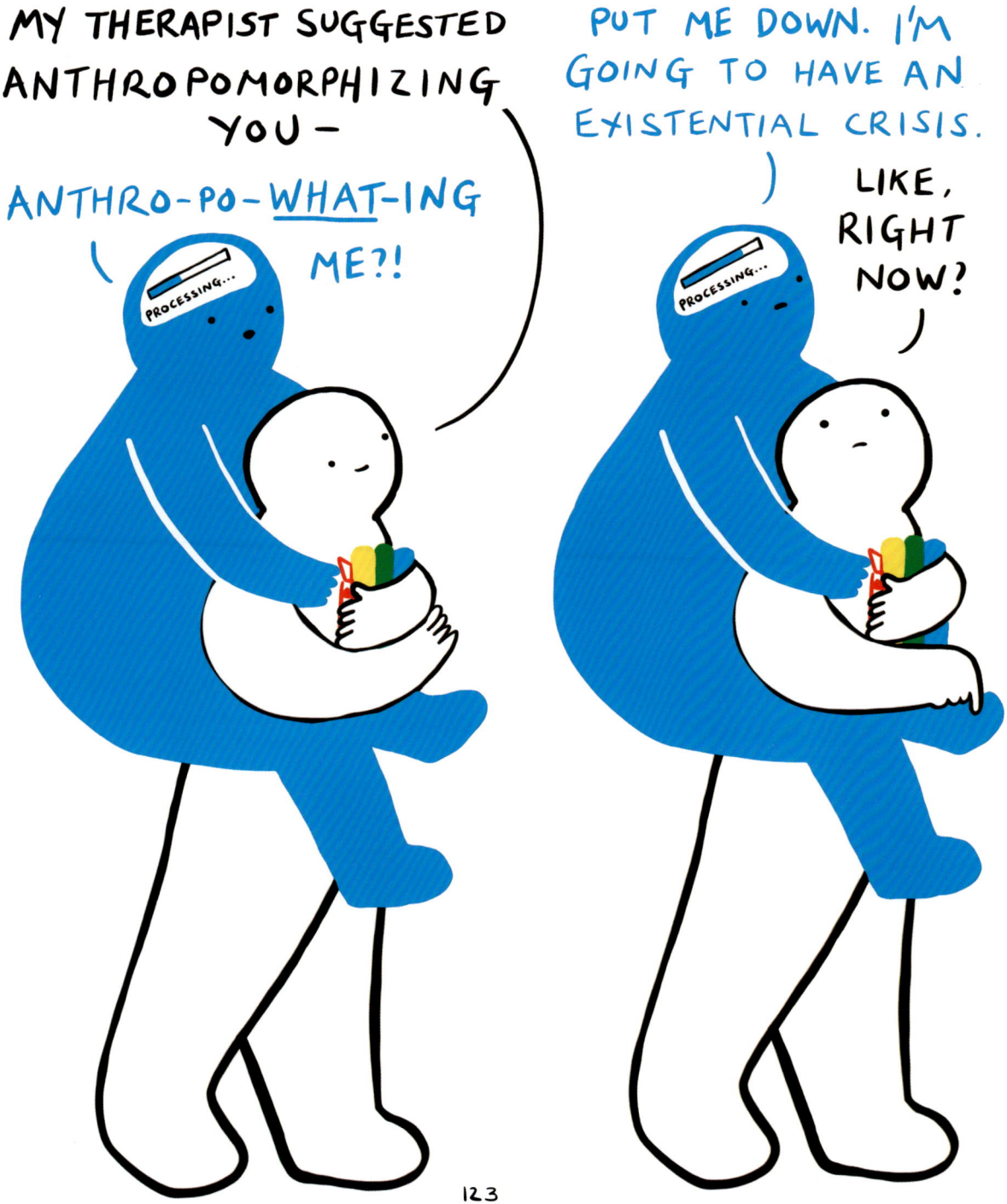
MY THERAPIST SUGGESTED ANTHROPOMORPHIZING YOU –
ANTHRO-PO-WHAT-ING ME?!
PROCESSING...
PUT ME DOWN. I'M GOING TO HAVE AN EXISTENTIAL CRISIS.
LIKE, RIGHT NOW?
PROCESSING...

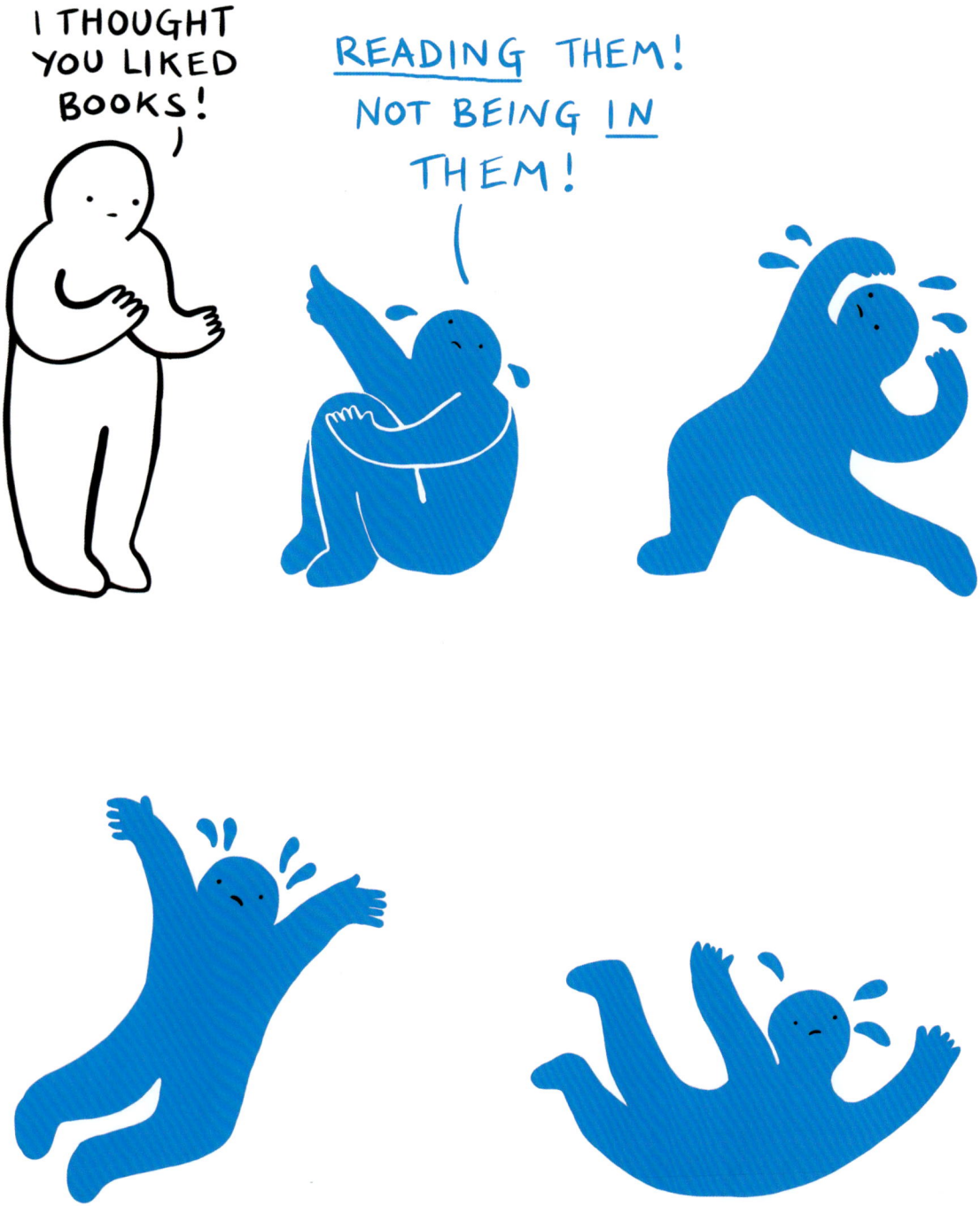
I THOUGHT YOU LIKED BOOKS!
READING THEM! NOT BEING IN THEM!

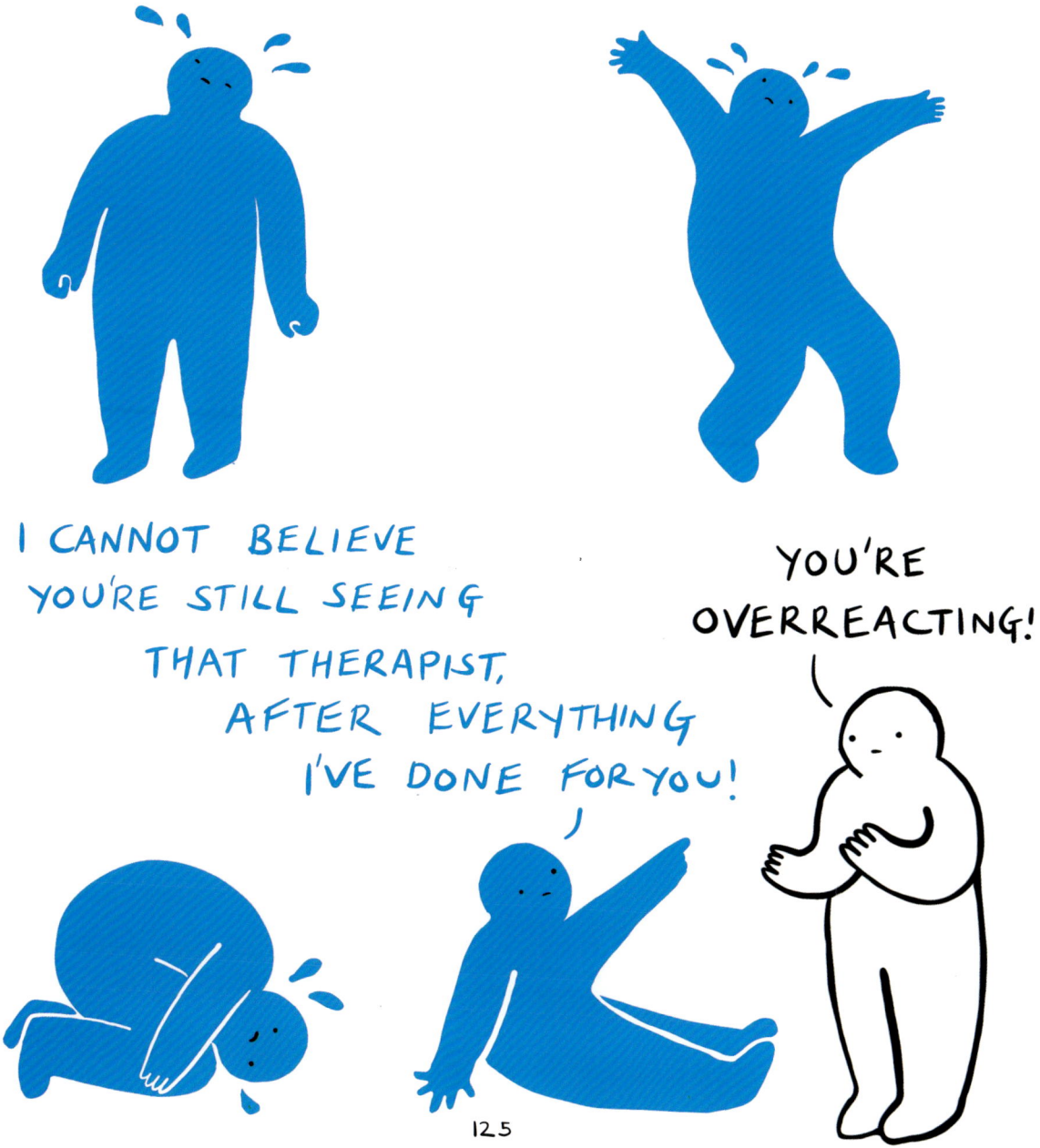
I CANNOT BELIEVE YOU'RE STILL SEEING THAT THERAPIST, AFTER EVERYTHING I'VE DONE FOR YOU!
YOU'RE OVERREACTING!

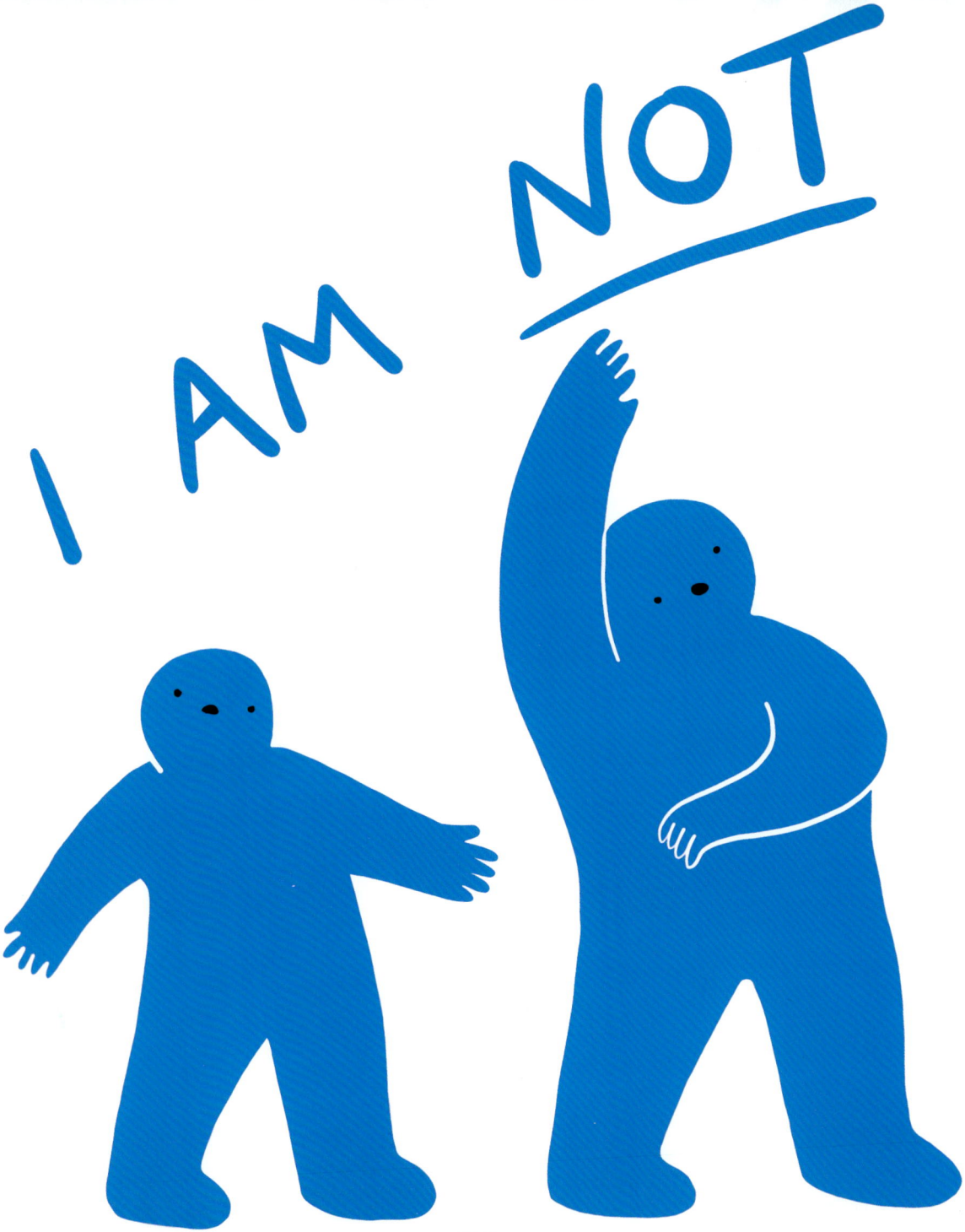
I AM NOT

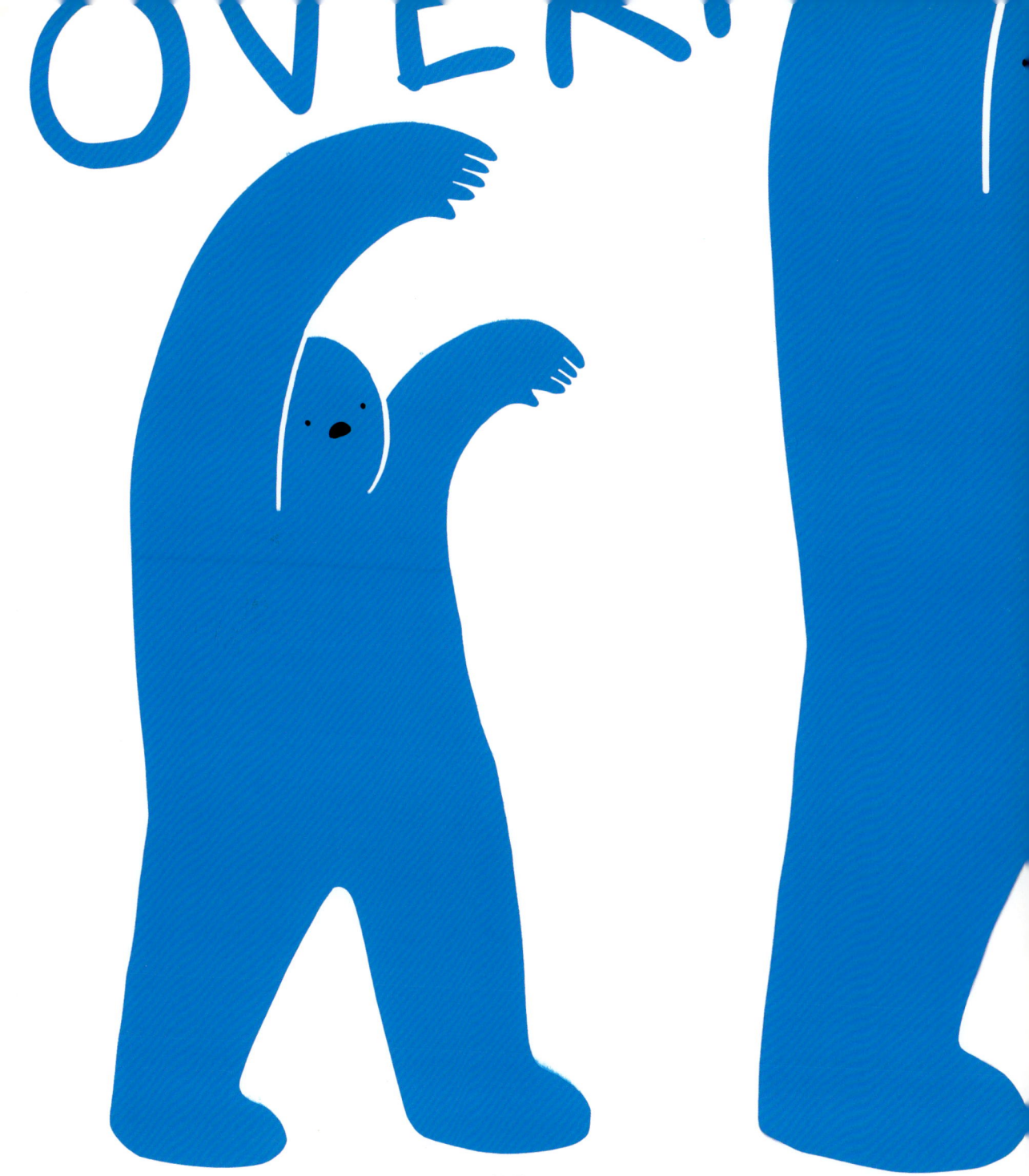
OVER

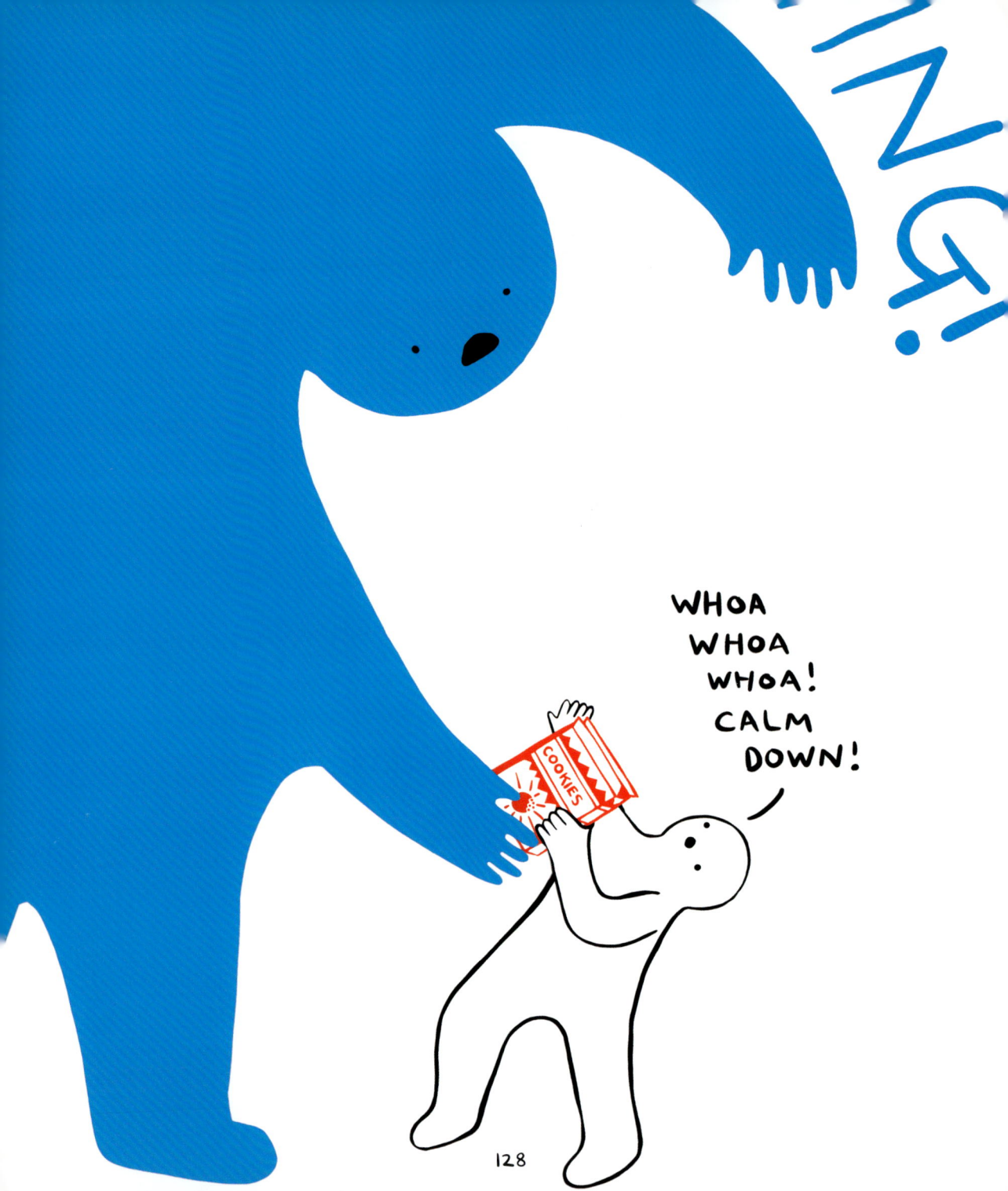
ING!
WHOA WHOA WHOA! CALM DOWN!
COOKIES

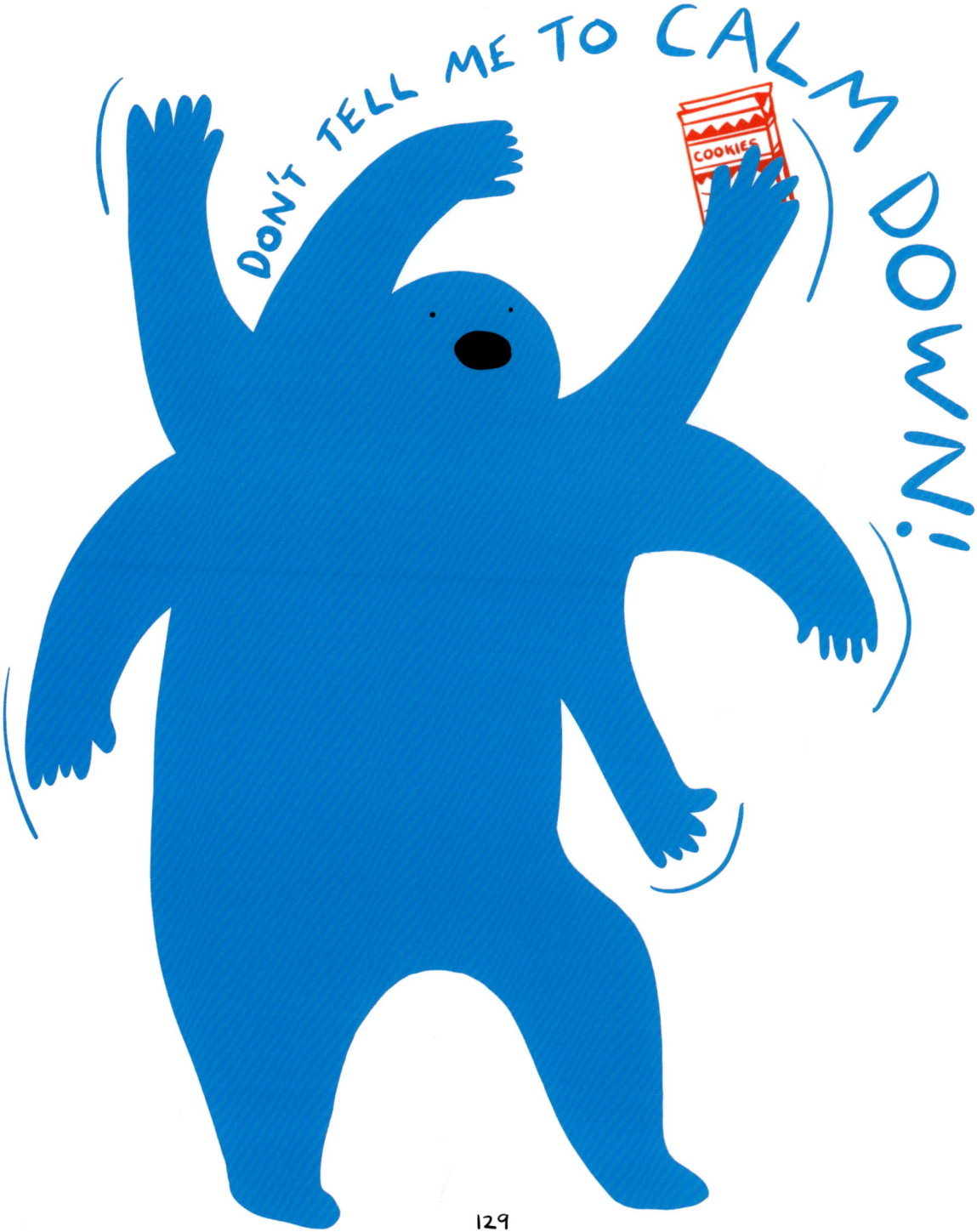
DON'T TELL ME TO CALM DOWN!
COOKIES

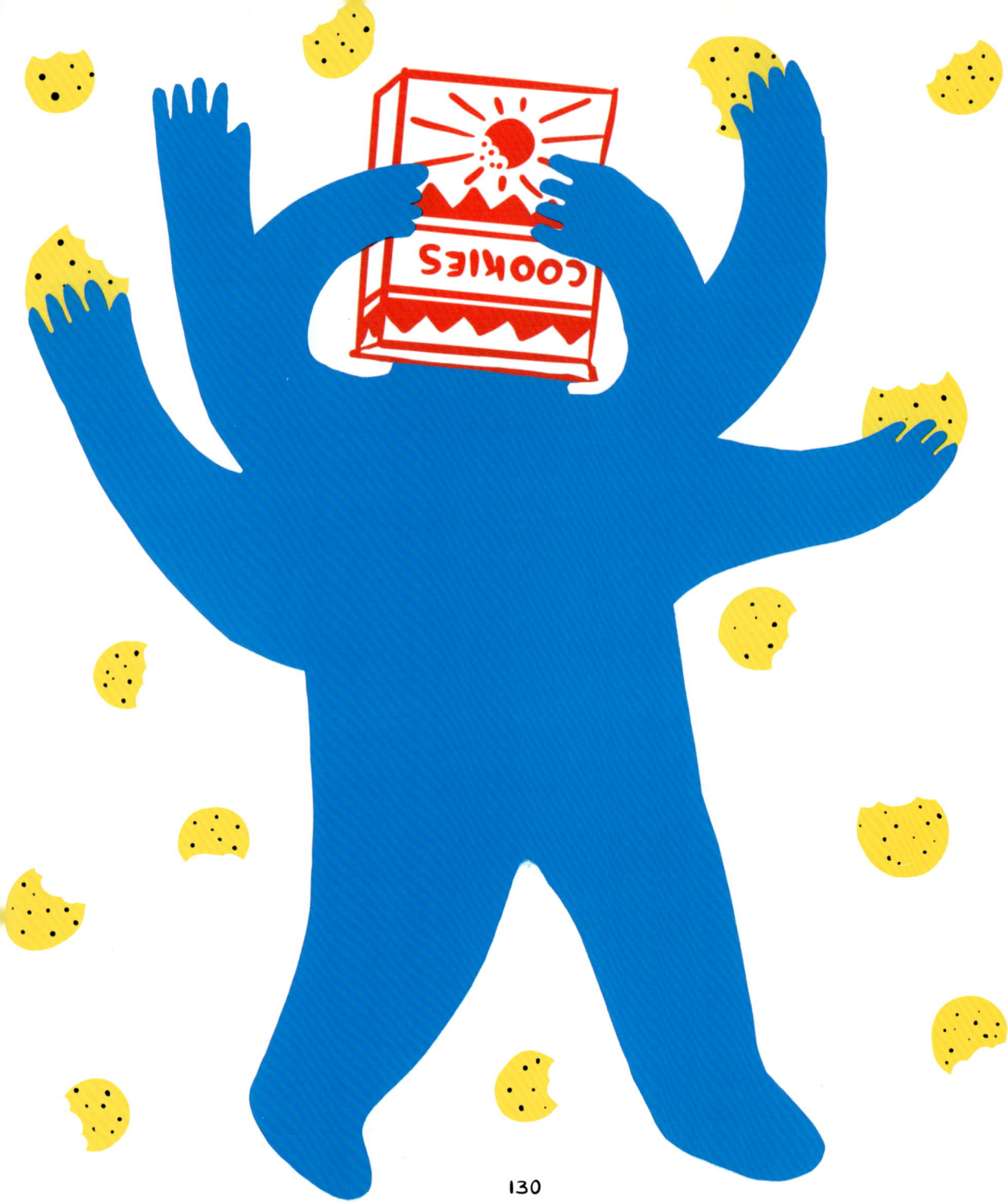
COOKIES

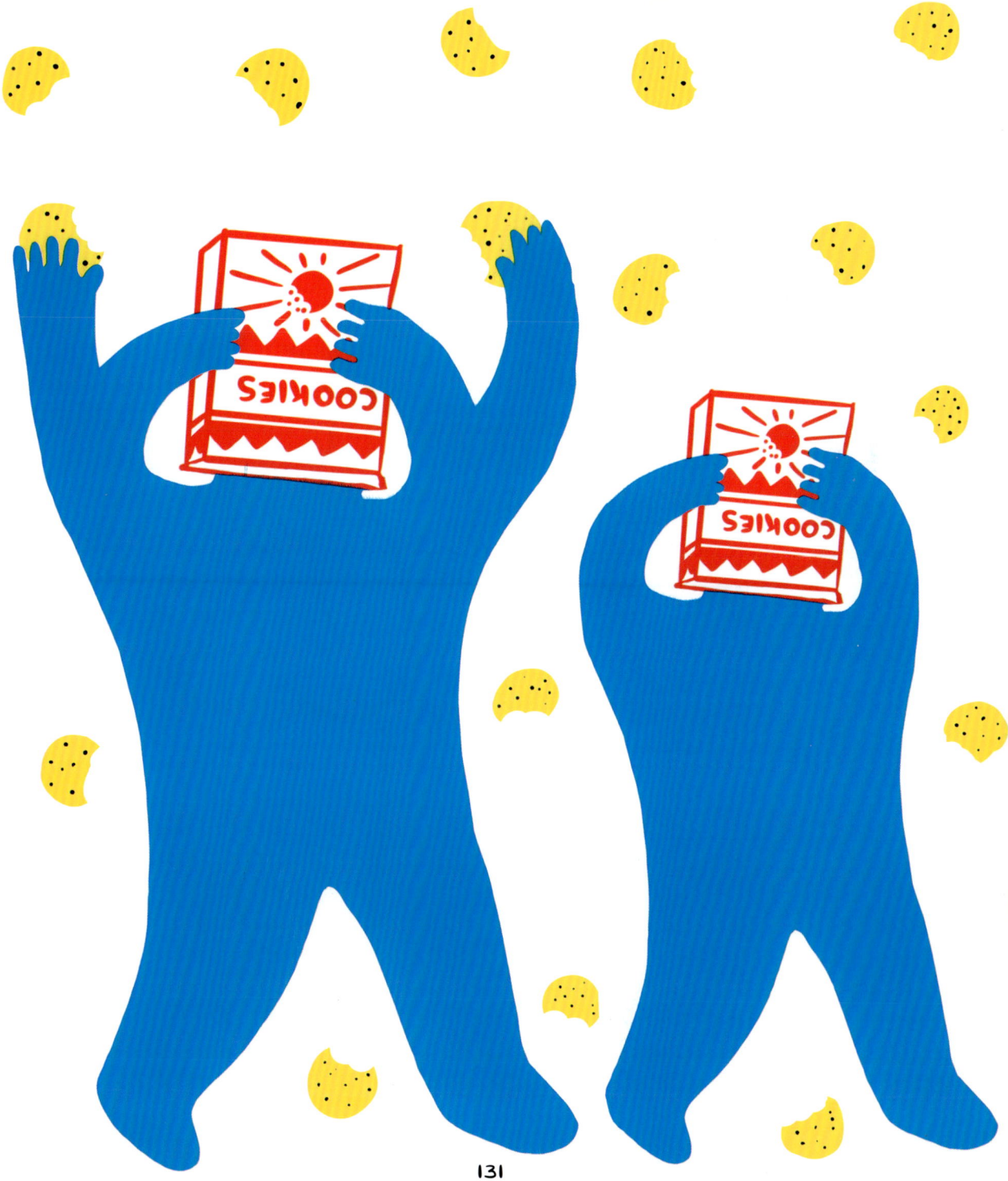
COOKIES
COOKIES

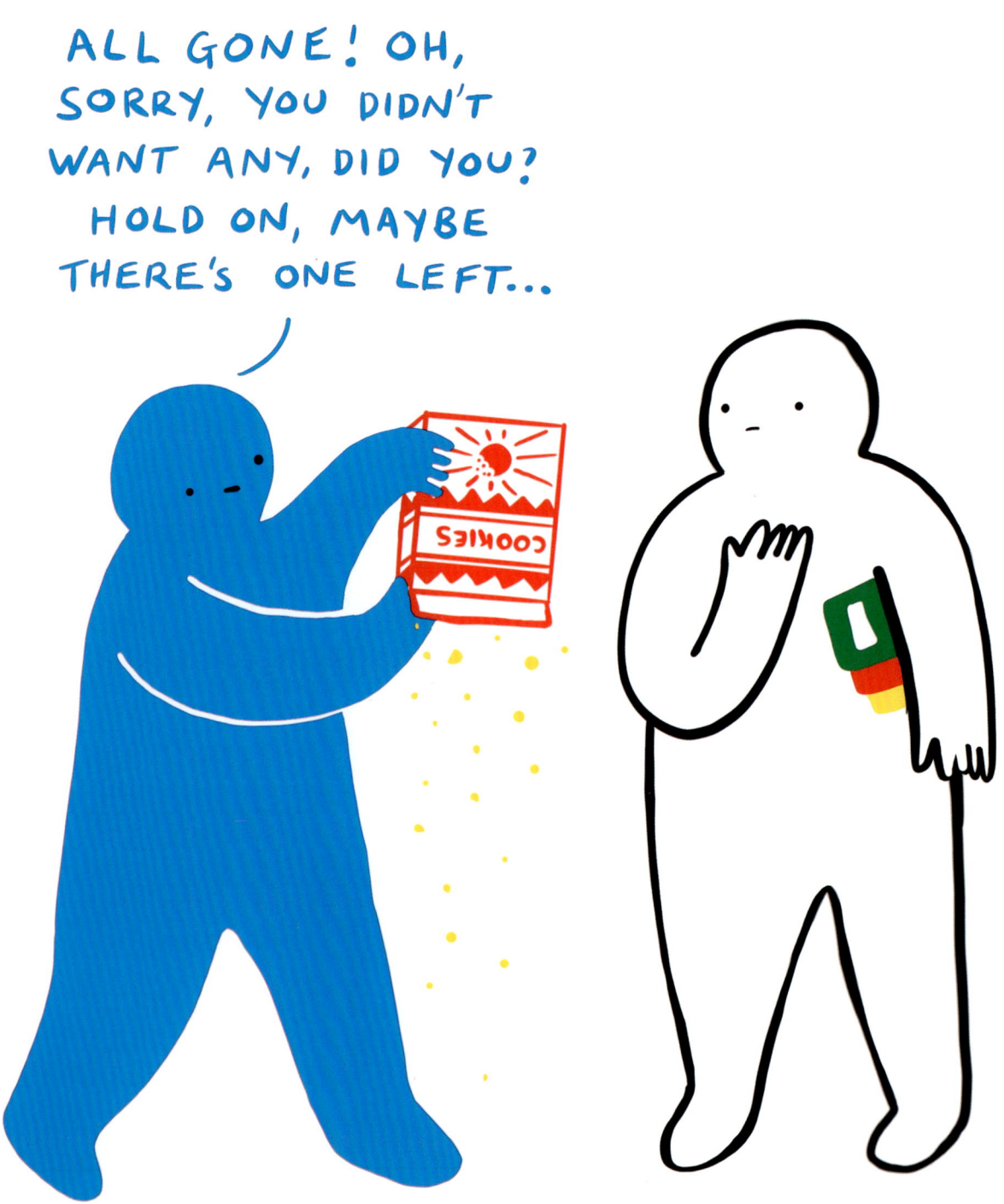
ALL GONE! OH, SORRY, YOU DIDN'T WANT ANY, DID YOU? HOLD ON, MAYBE THERE'S ONE LEFT...
COOKIES

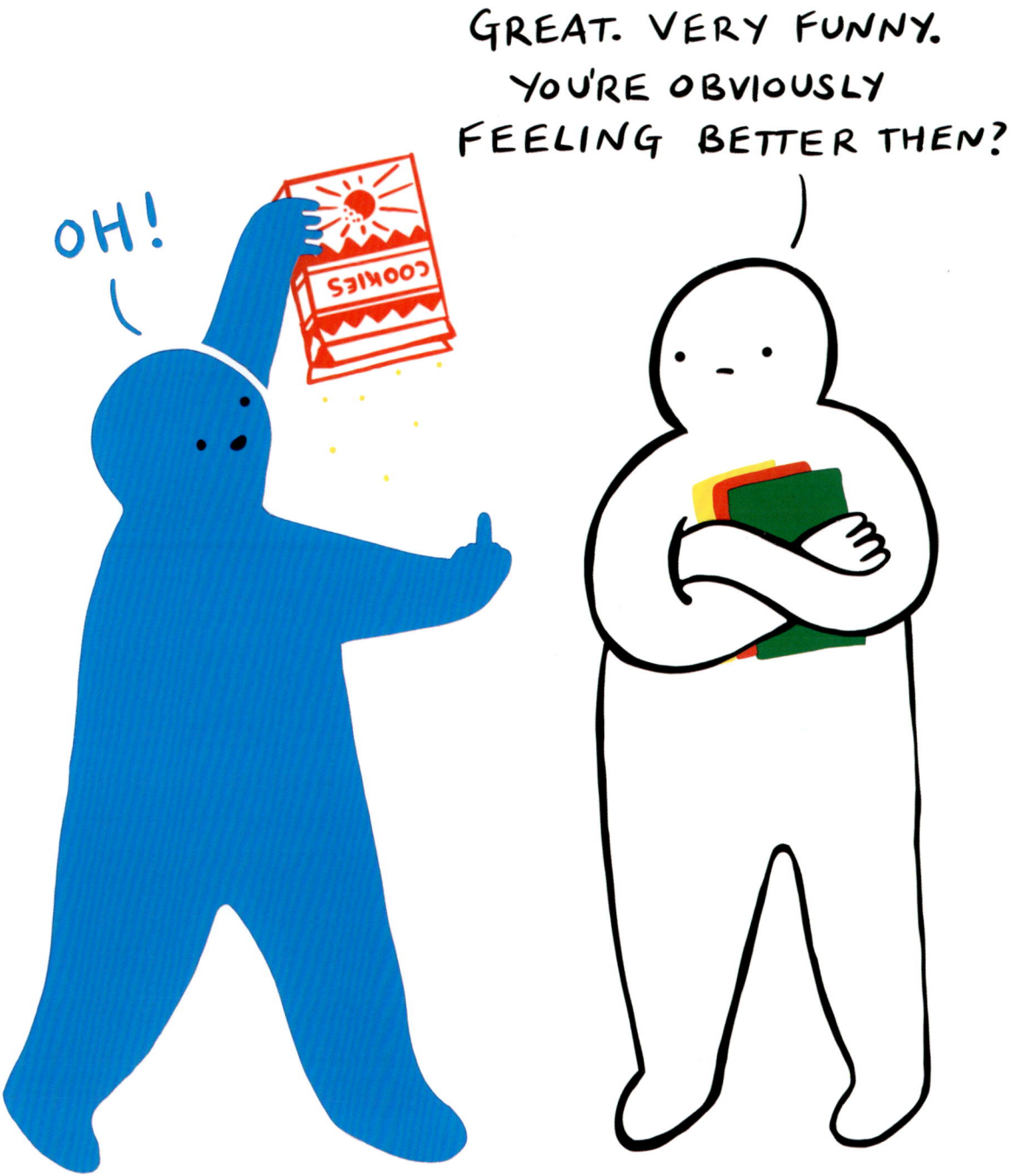
GREAT. VERY FUNNY. YOU'RE OBVIOUSLY FEELING BETTER THEN?
OH!
COOKIES

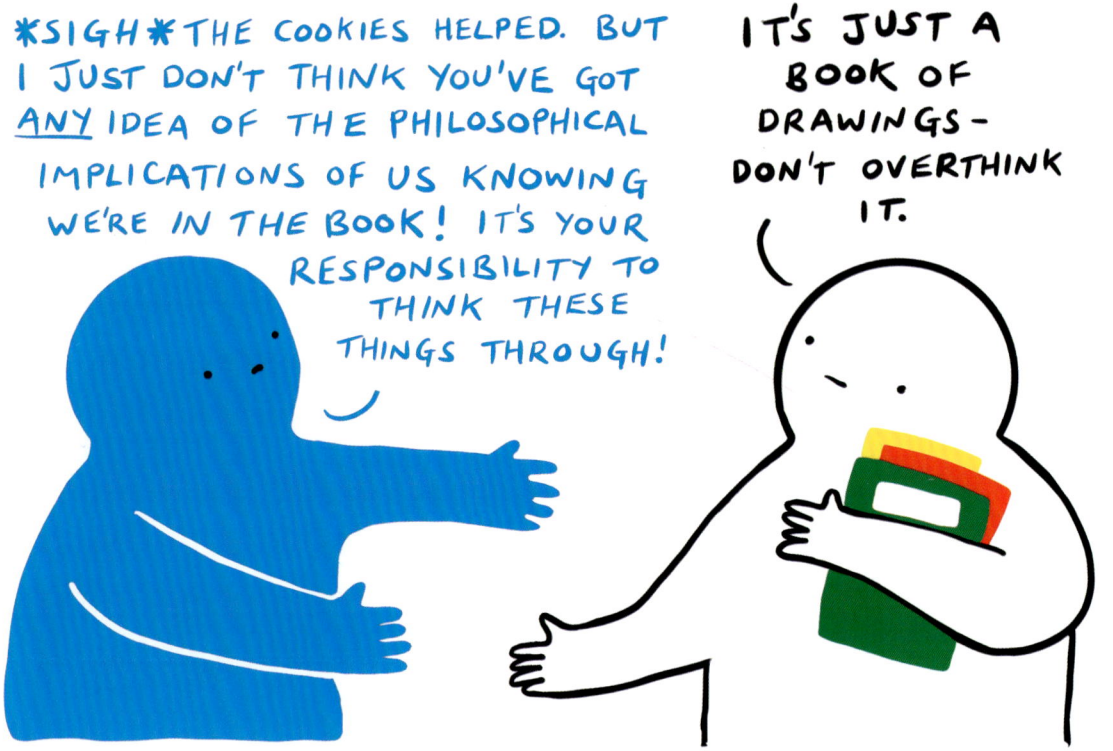
SIGH THE COOKIES HELPED. BUT I JUST DON'T THINK YOU'VE GOT ANY IDEA OF THE PHILOSOPHICAL IMPLICATIONS OF US KNOWING WE'RE IN THE BOOK! IT'S YOUR RESPONSIBILITY TO THINK THESE THINGS THROUGH!
IT'S JUST A BOOK OF DRAWINGS - DON'T OVERTHINK IT.

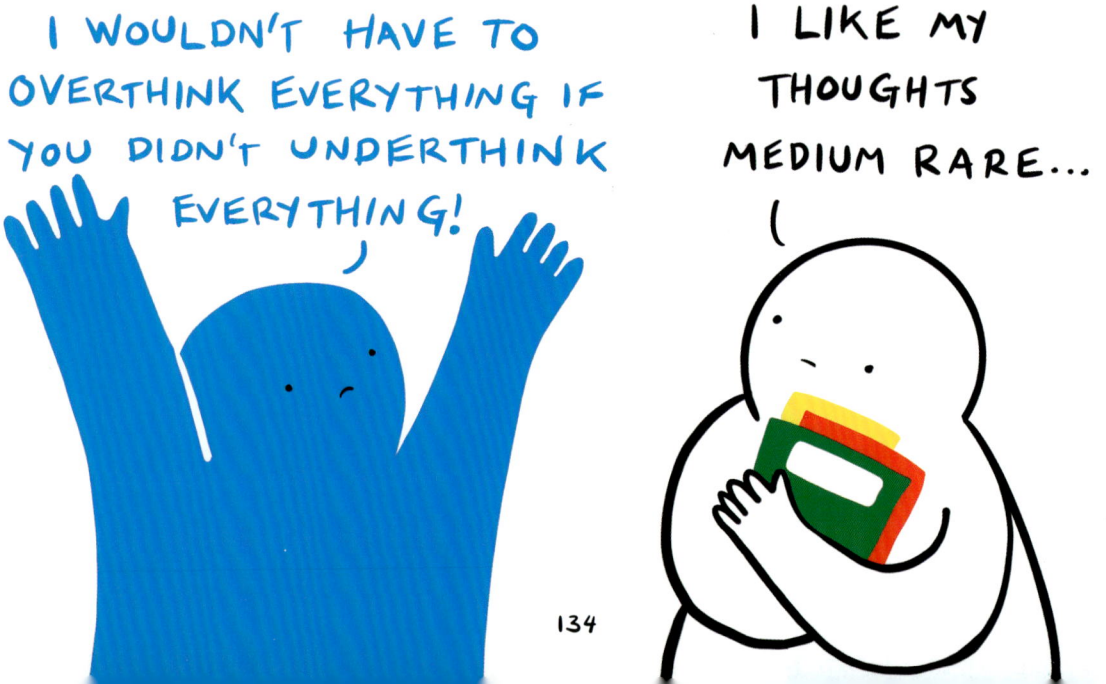
I WOULDN'T HAVE TO OVERTHINK EVERYTHING IF YOU DIDN'T UNDERTHINK EVERYTHING!
I LIKE MY THOUGHTS MEDIUM RARE...

BUT I AM SORRY I DIDN'T TELL YOU EARLIER. IF IT MAKES YOU FEEL ANY BETTER, YOU SHOULD KNOW THAT I COULDN'T HAVE MADE THIS BOOK WITHOUT YOU. I COULDN'T HAVE DONE ANY OF THIS WITHOUT YOU. YOU'RE A BIG PART OF MY STORY! IN FACT, YOU'RE ONE OF THE MAIN CHARACTERS!

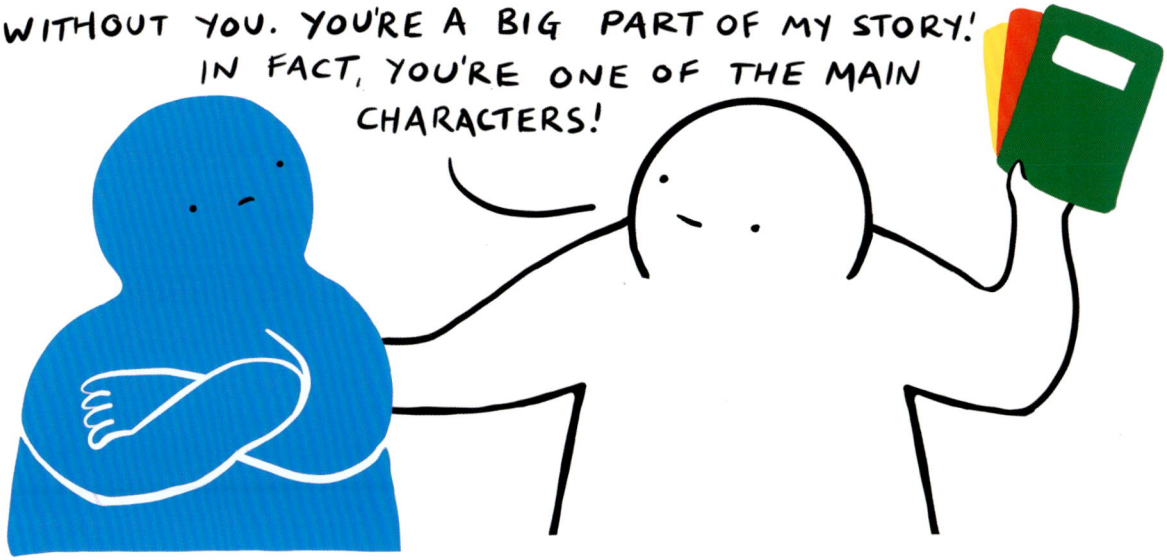

WAIT... I'M THE HERO?

I DIDN'T SAY HERO—

I'M THE HERO, AND YOU'RE MY SUPER ANNOYING BUT LOYAL SIDEKICK WHO FOLLOWS ME AROUND EVERYWHERE!

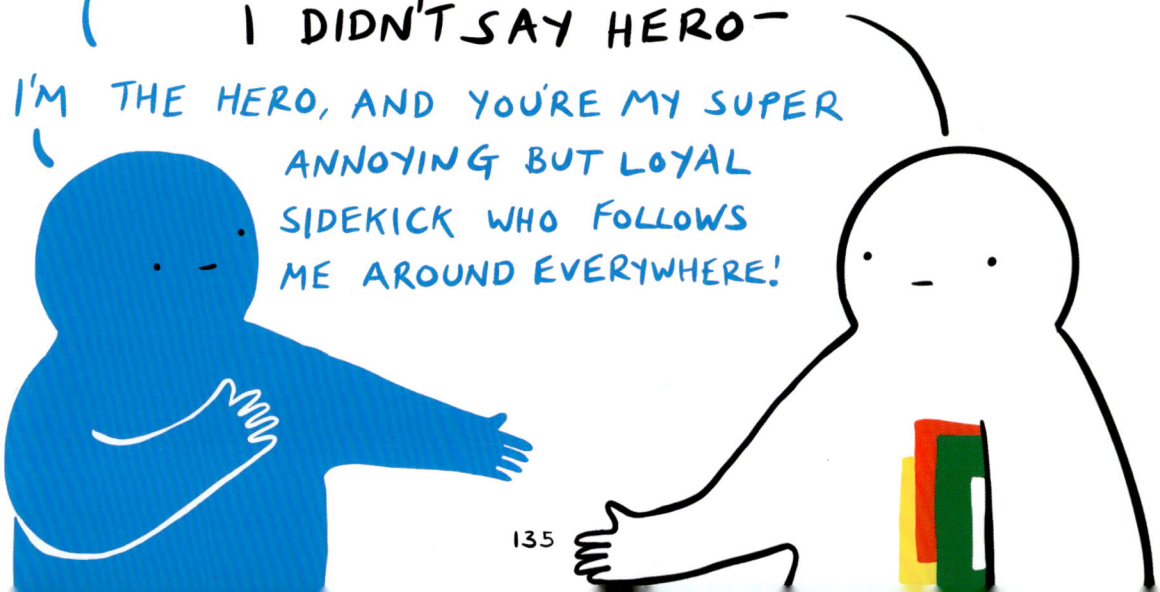

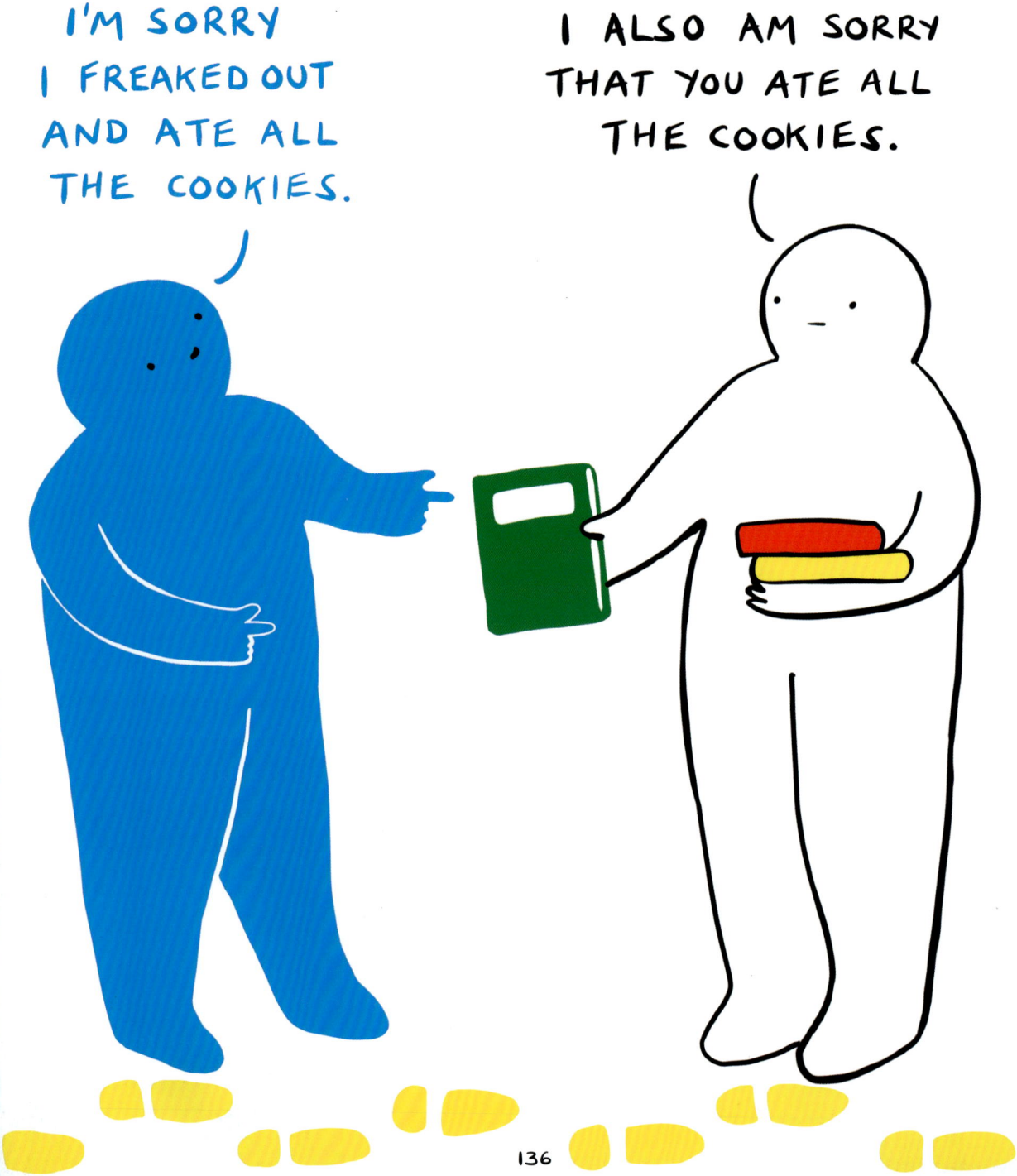
I'M SORRY I FREAKED OUT AND ATE ALL THE COOKIES.
I ALSO AM SORRY THAT YOU ATE ALL THE COOKIES.

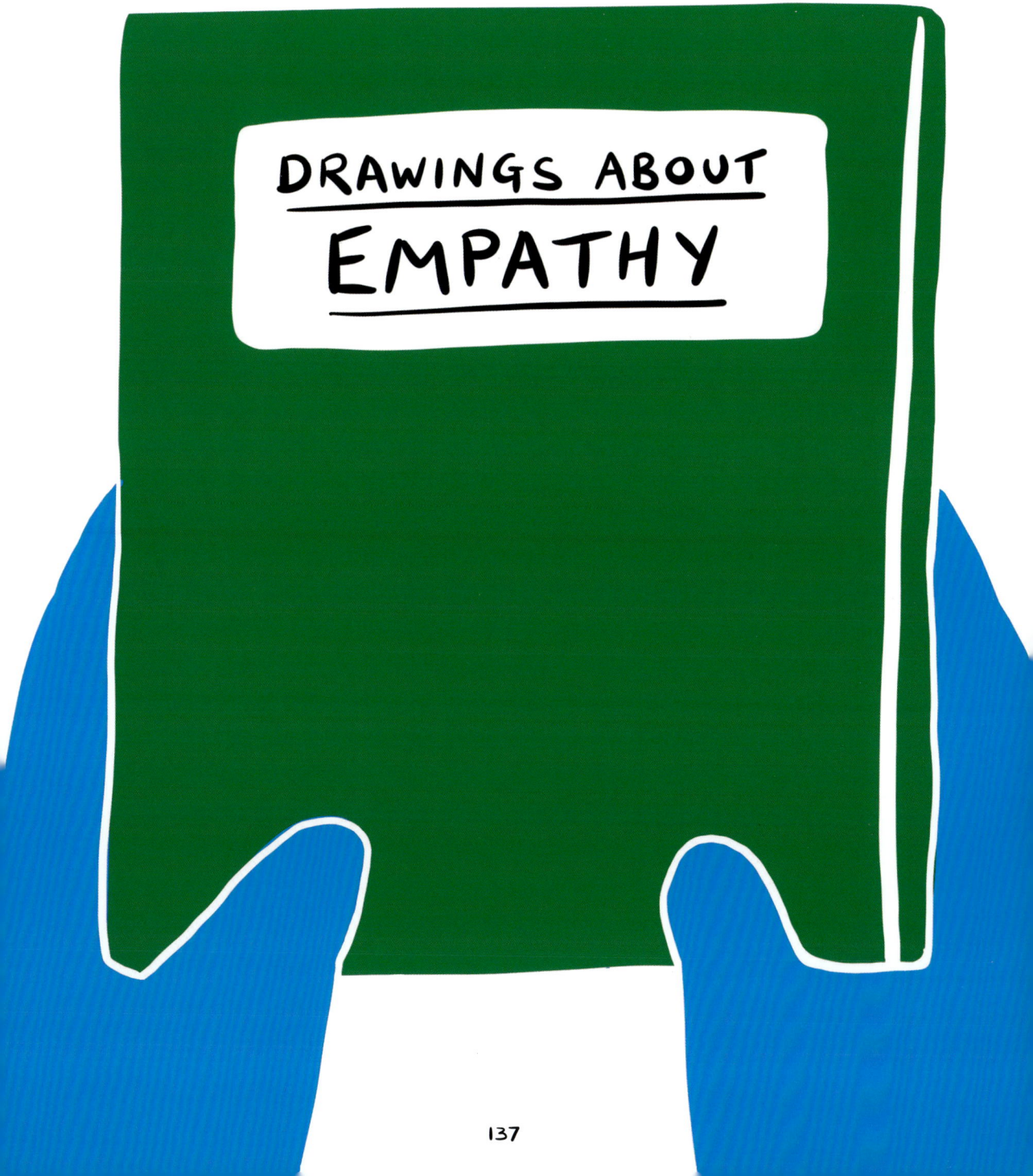
DRAWINGS ABOUT
EMPATHY

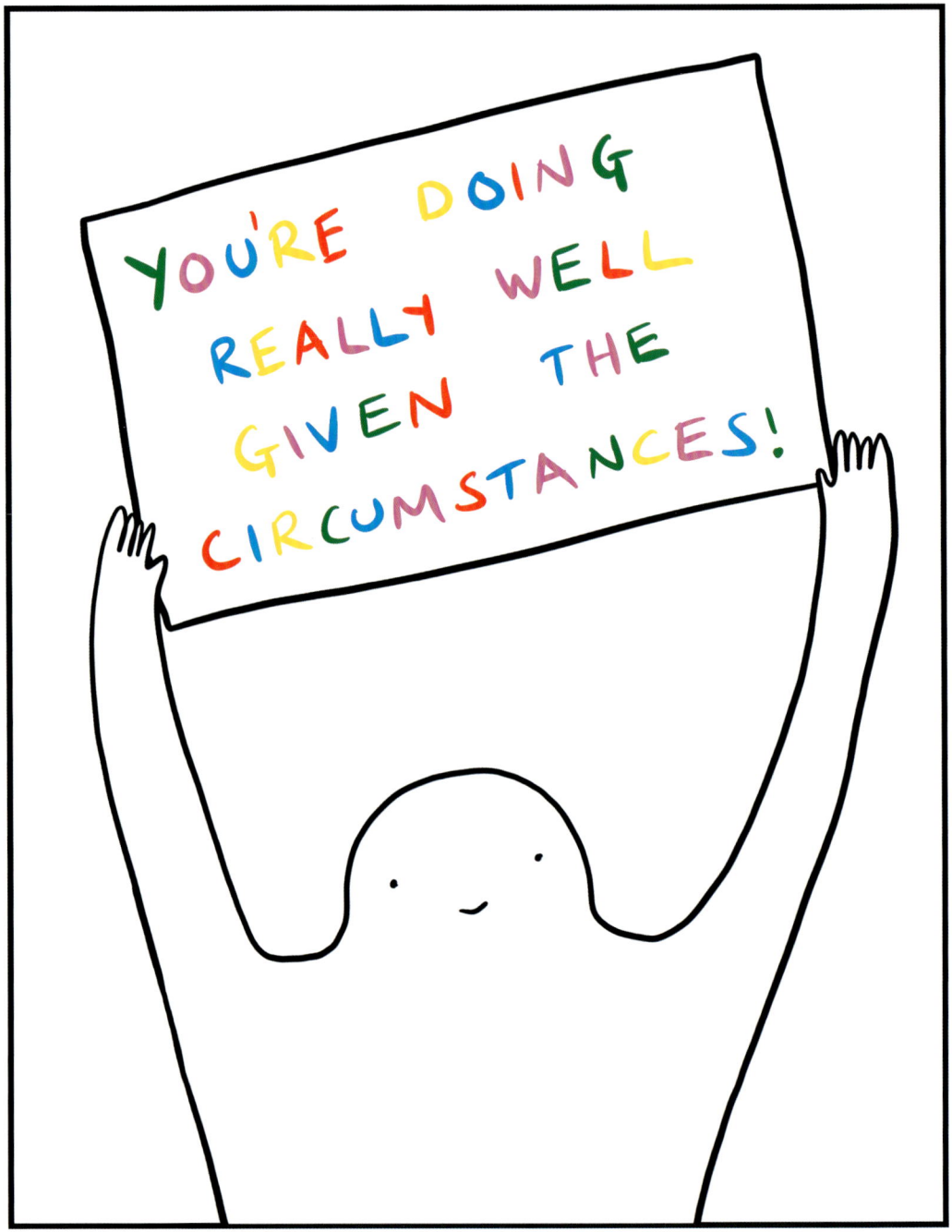

NOTE TO SELF.

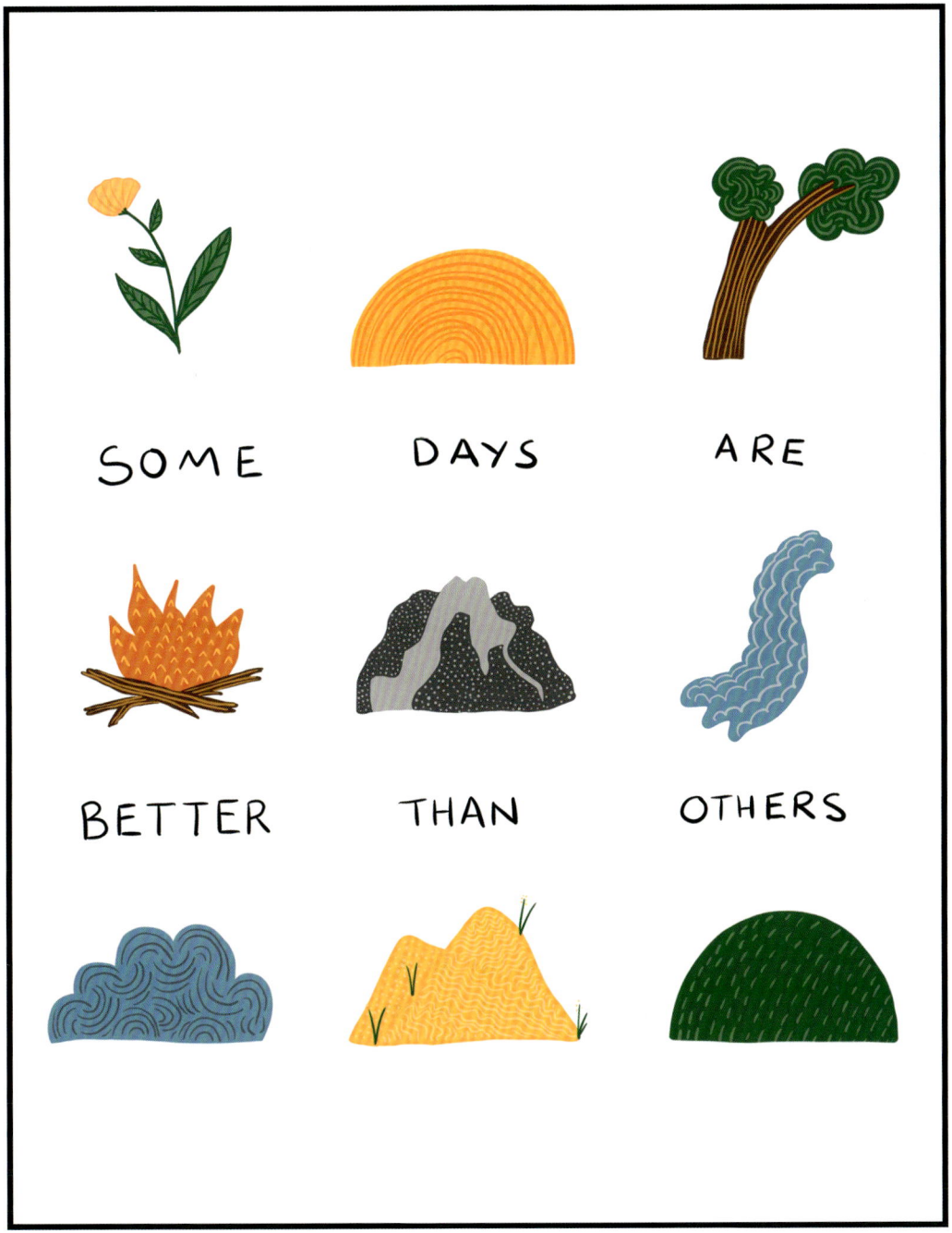

DAILY REMINDER.

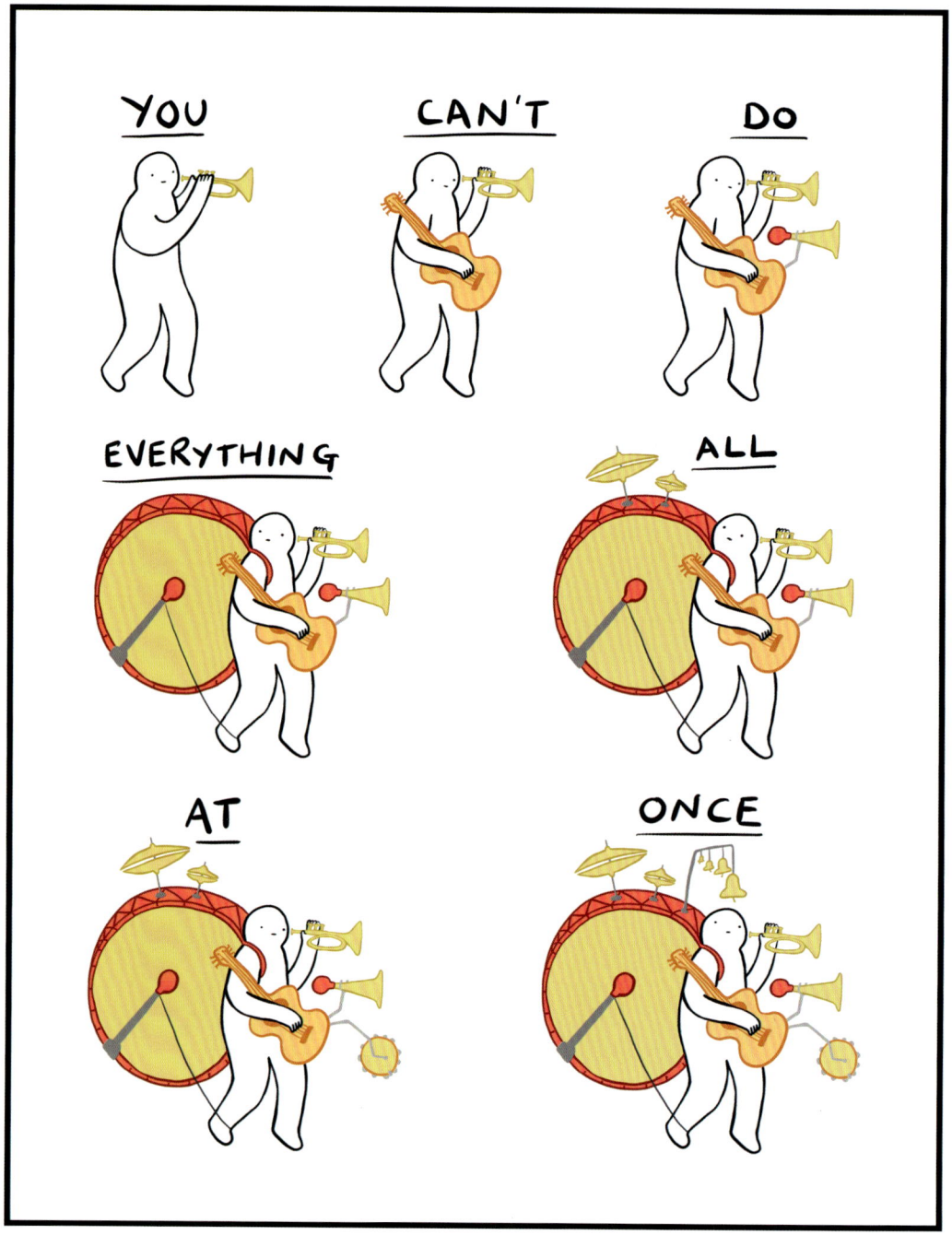

MULTI-INSTRUMENTAL HEALTH MATTERS.

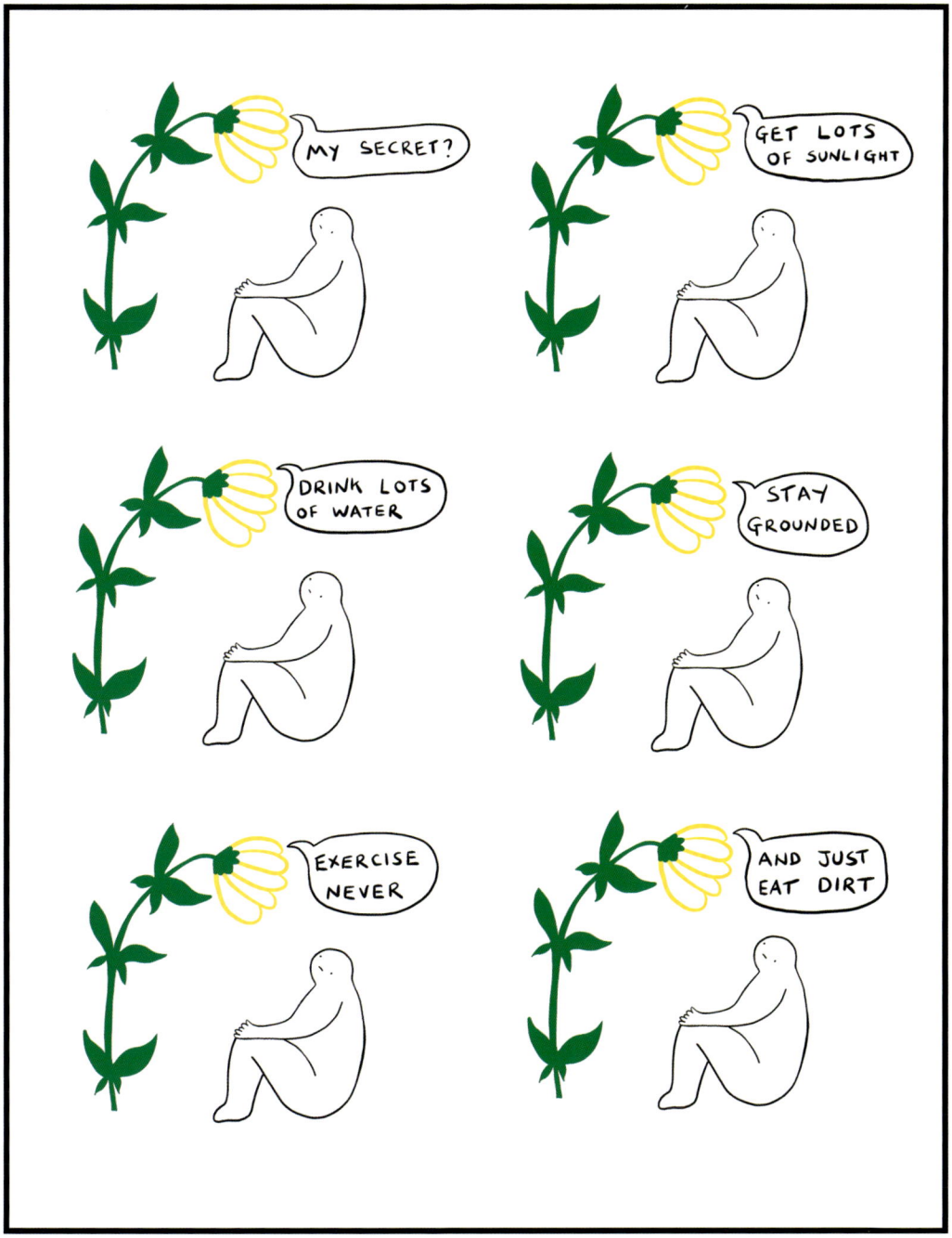

COMMUNING WITH NATURE.

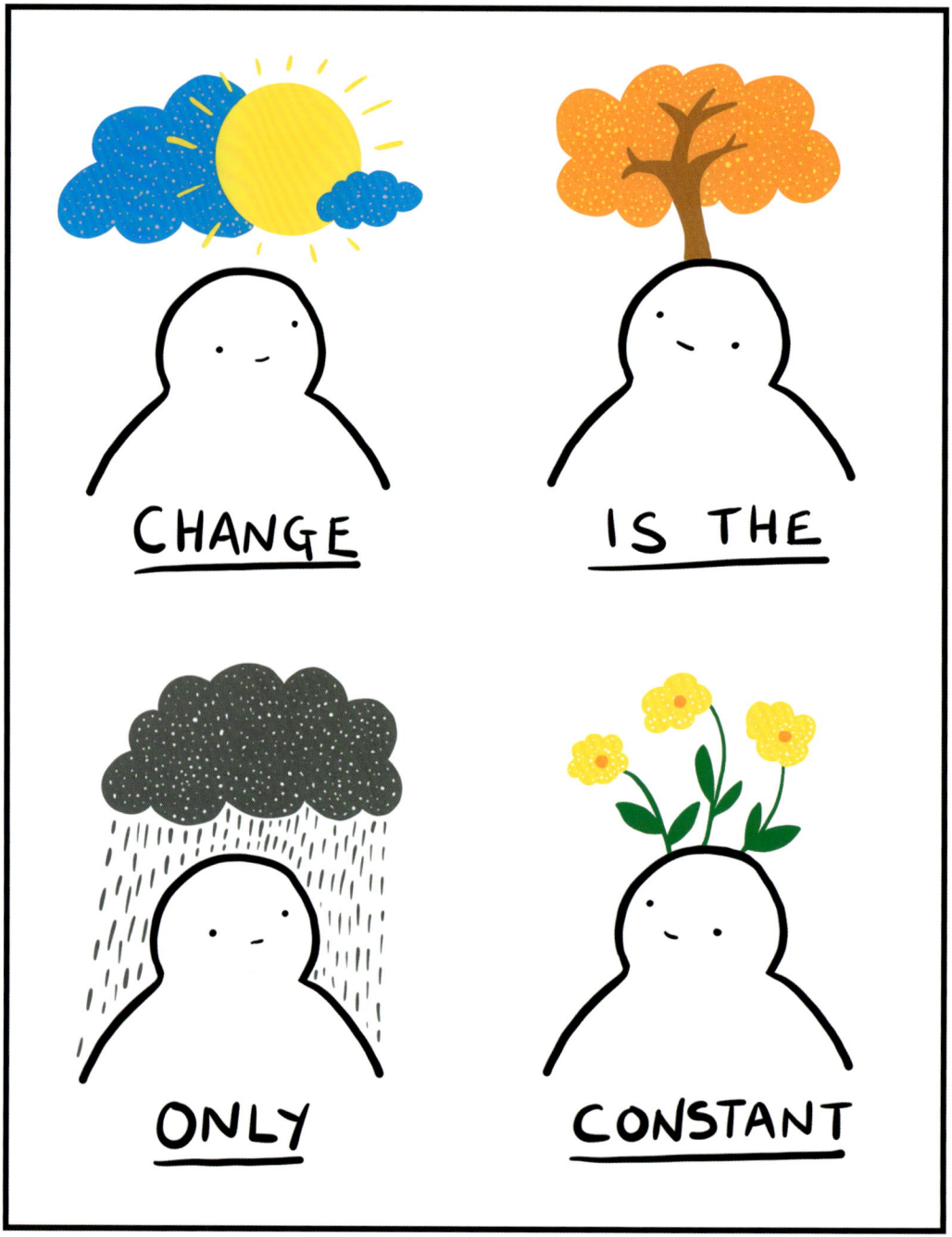

SEASON'S GREETINGS.

LIFE, LIKE A SAUSAGE DOG, IS VERY LONG AND VERY SHORT,

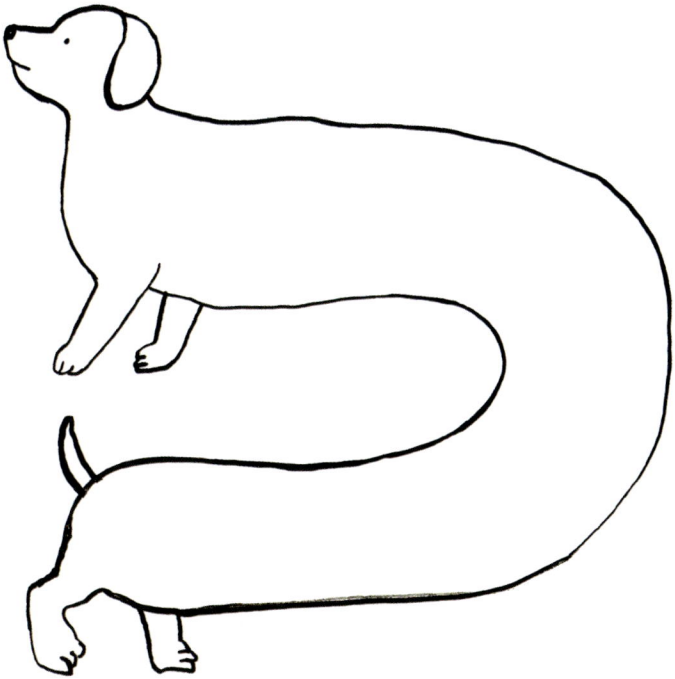

COMPLETELY WONDERFUL AND ABSOLUTELY RIDICULOUS.

AND FULL OF BACK PAIN.

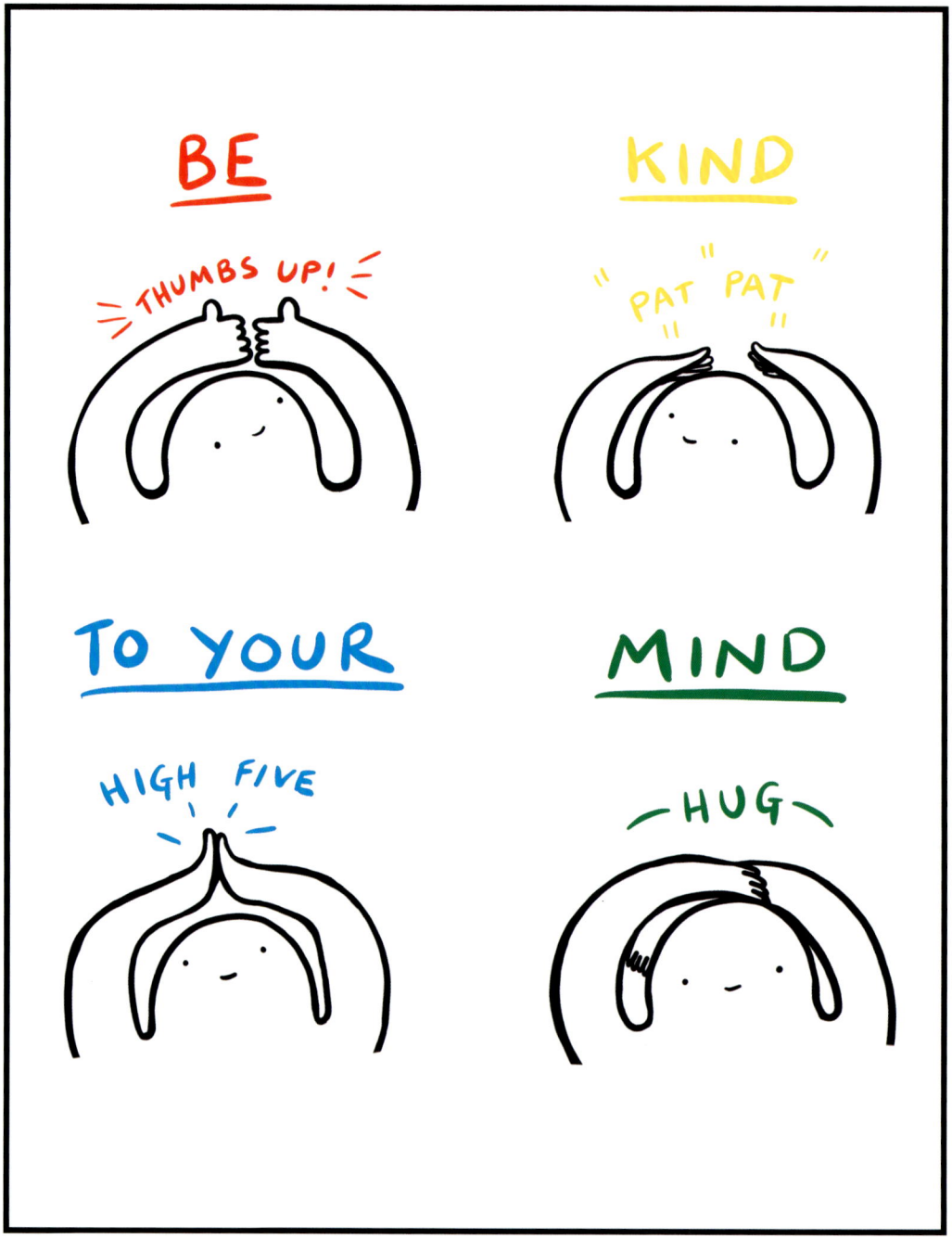

GREAT MINDS.

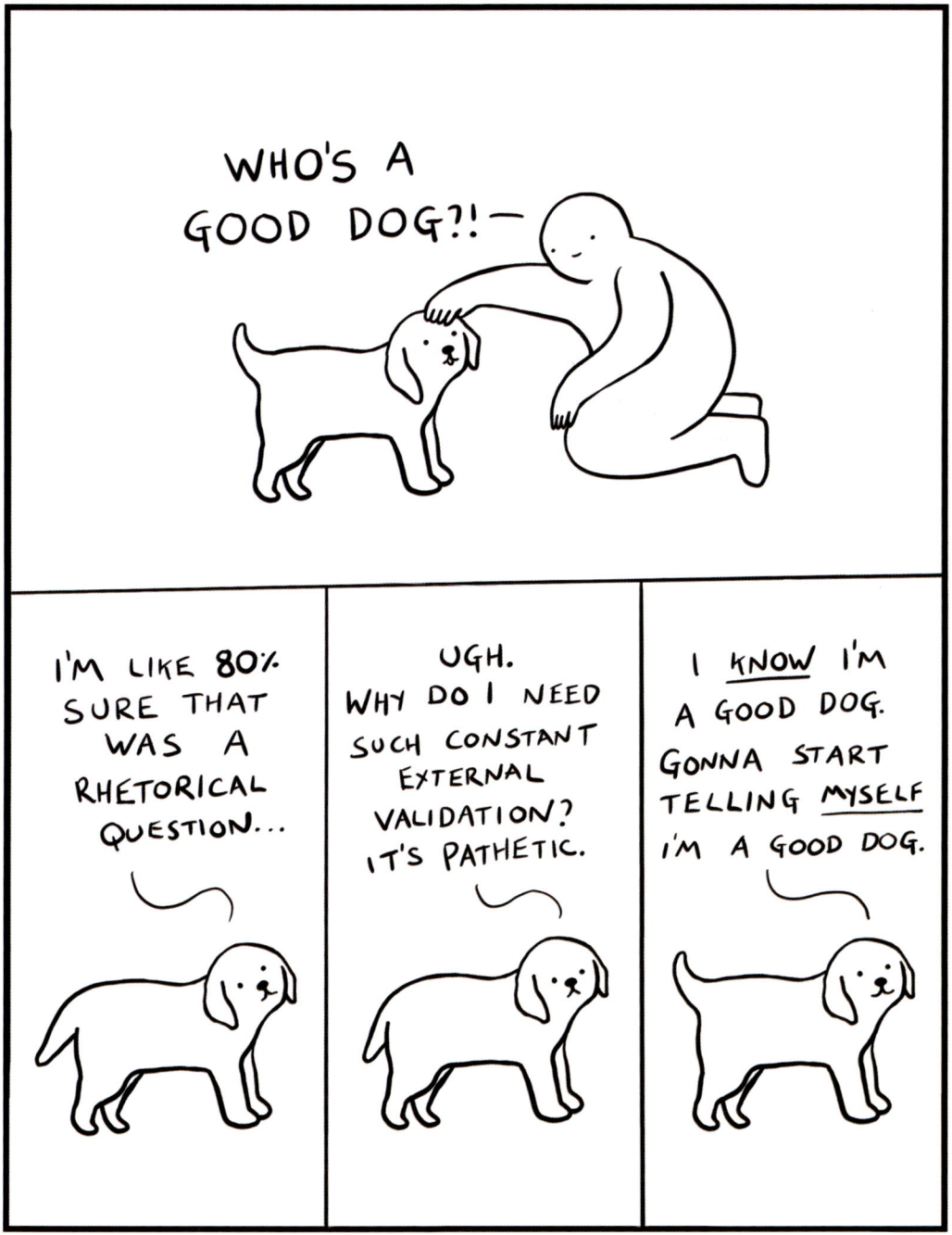

TIME TO GO DIG UP THE GARDEN.

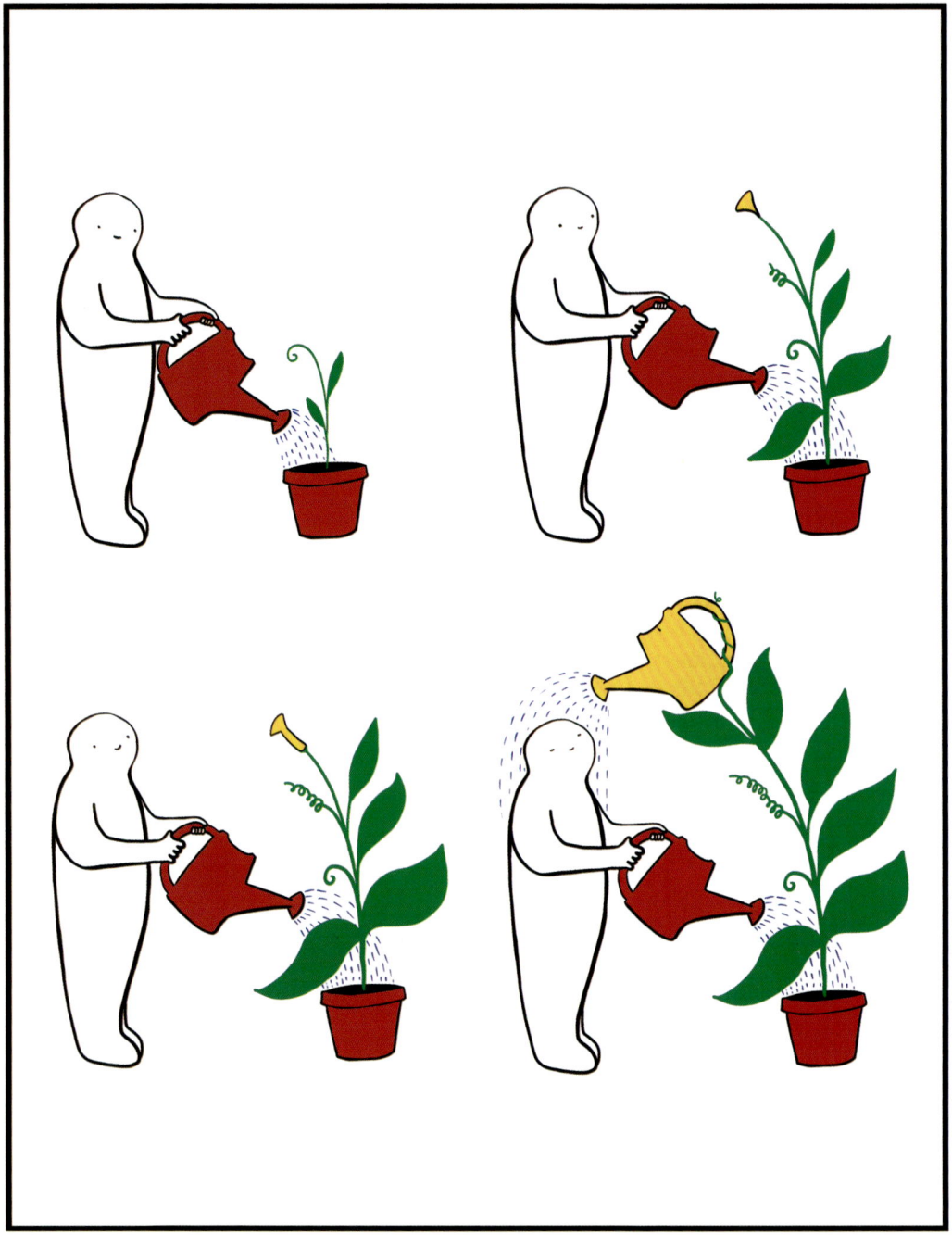

SYMBIOSIS.

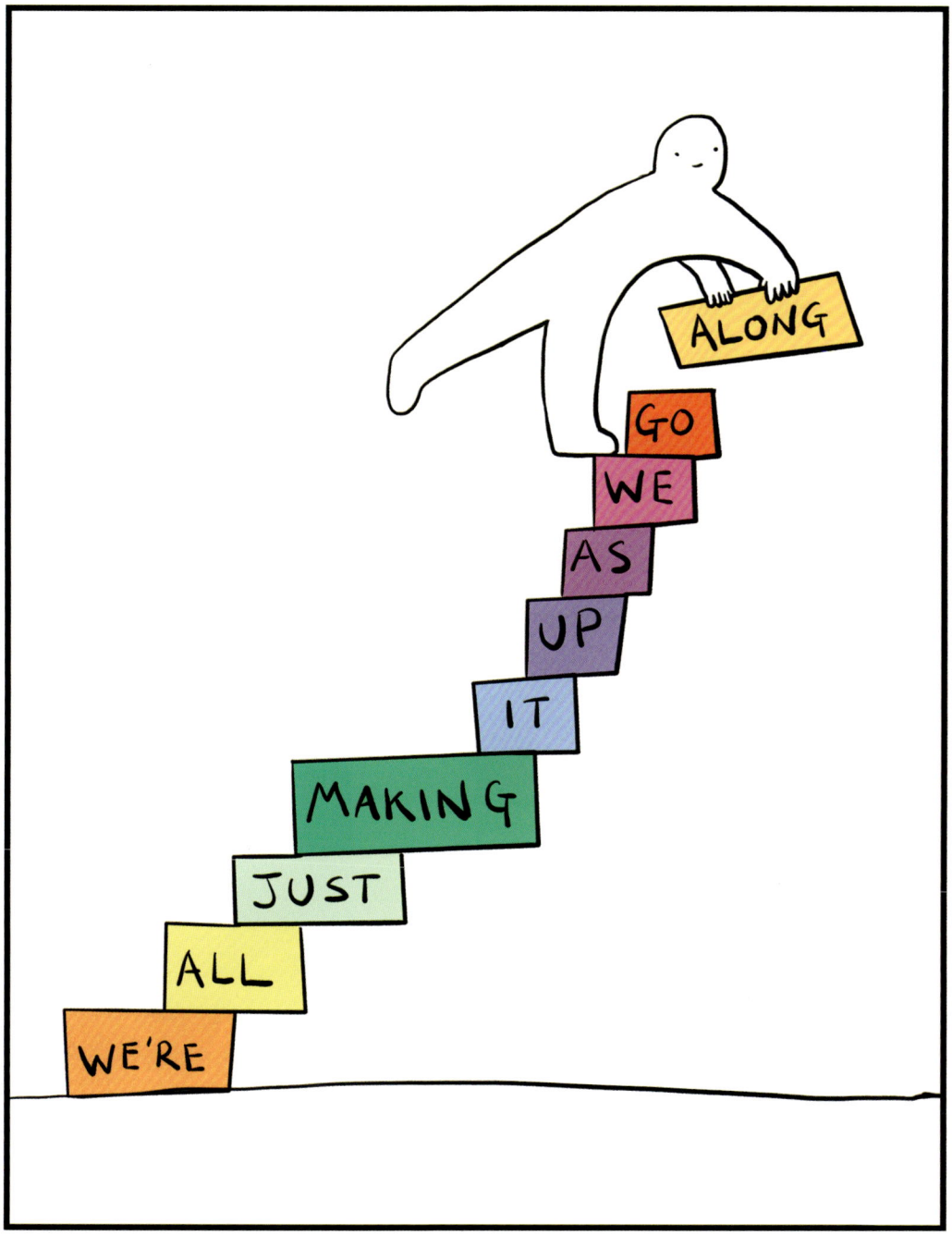

ONWARD AND UPWARD.

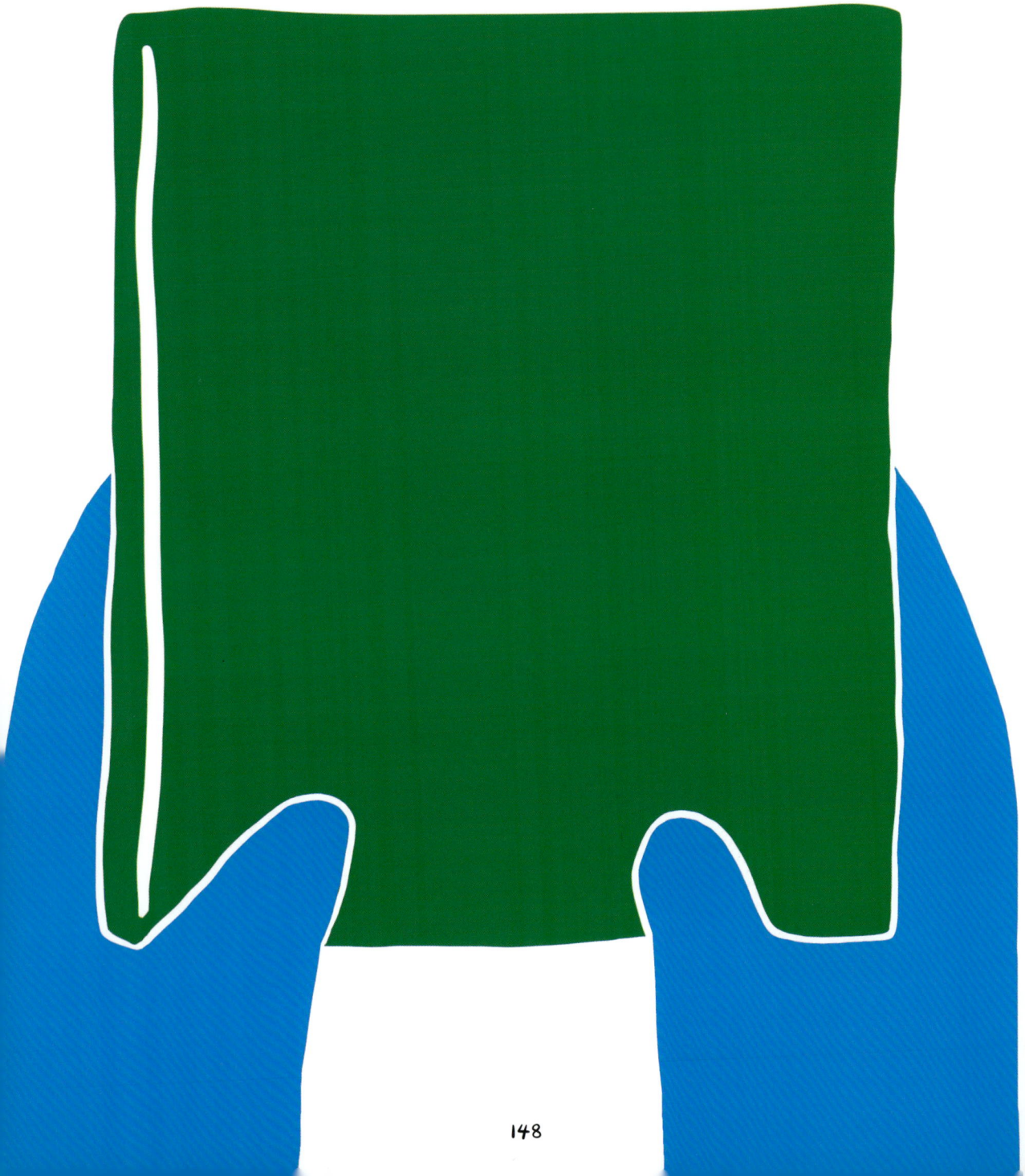

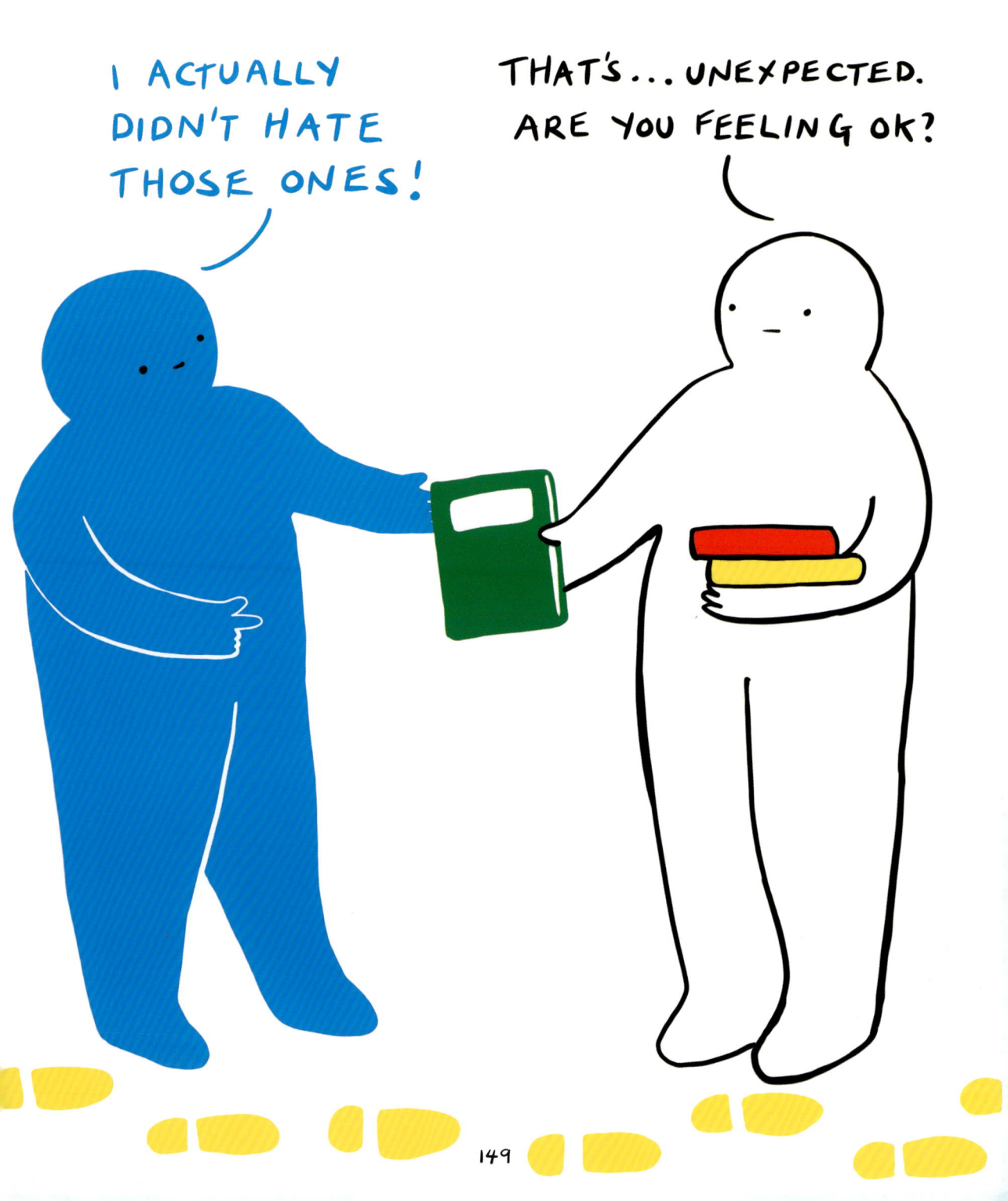
I ACTUALLY DIDN'T HATE THOSE ONES!
THAT'S... UNEXPECTED. ARE YOU FEELING OK?

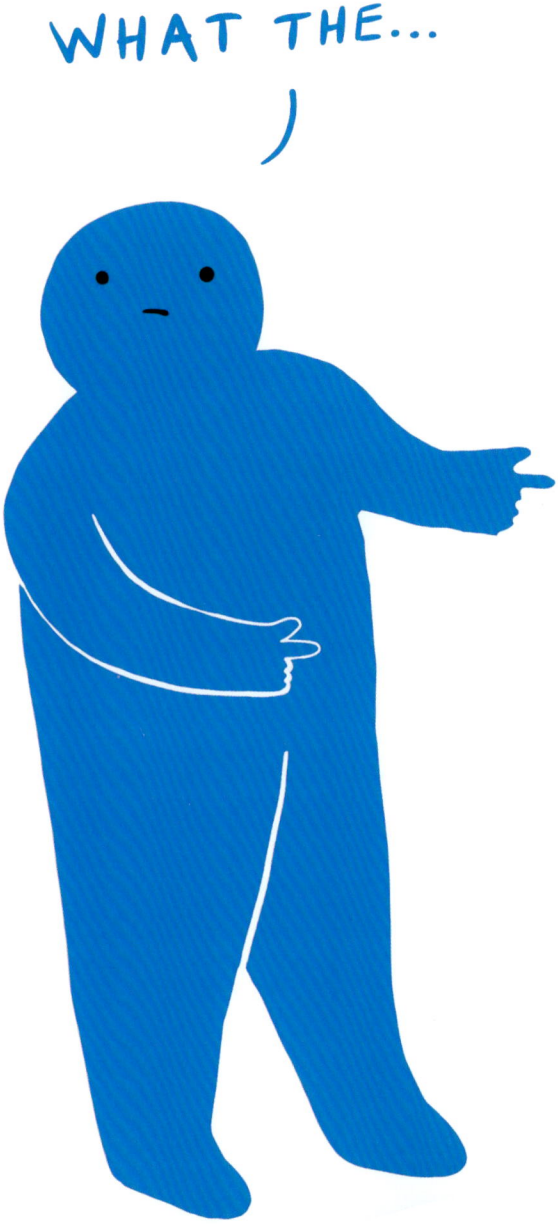
WHAT THE...

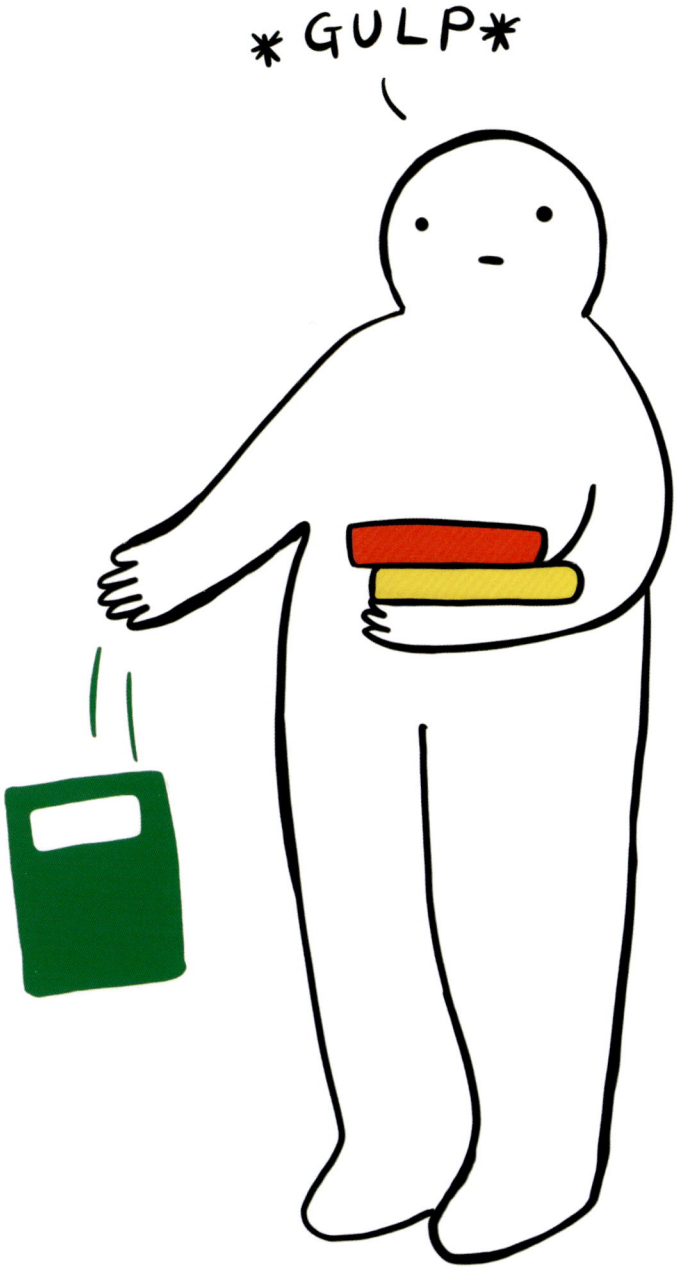
GULP

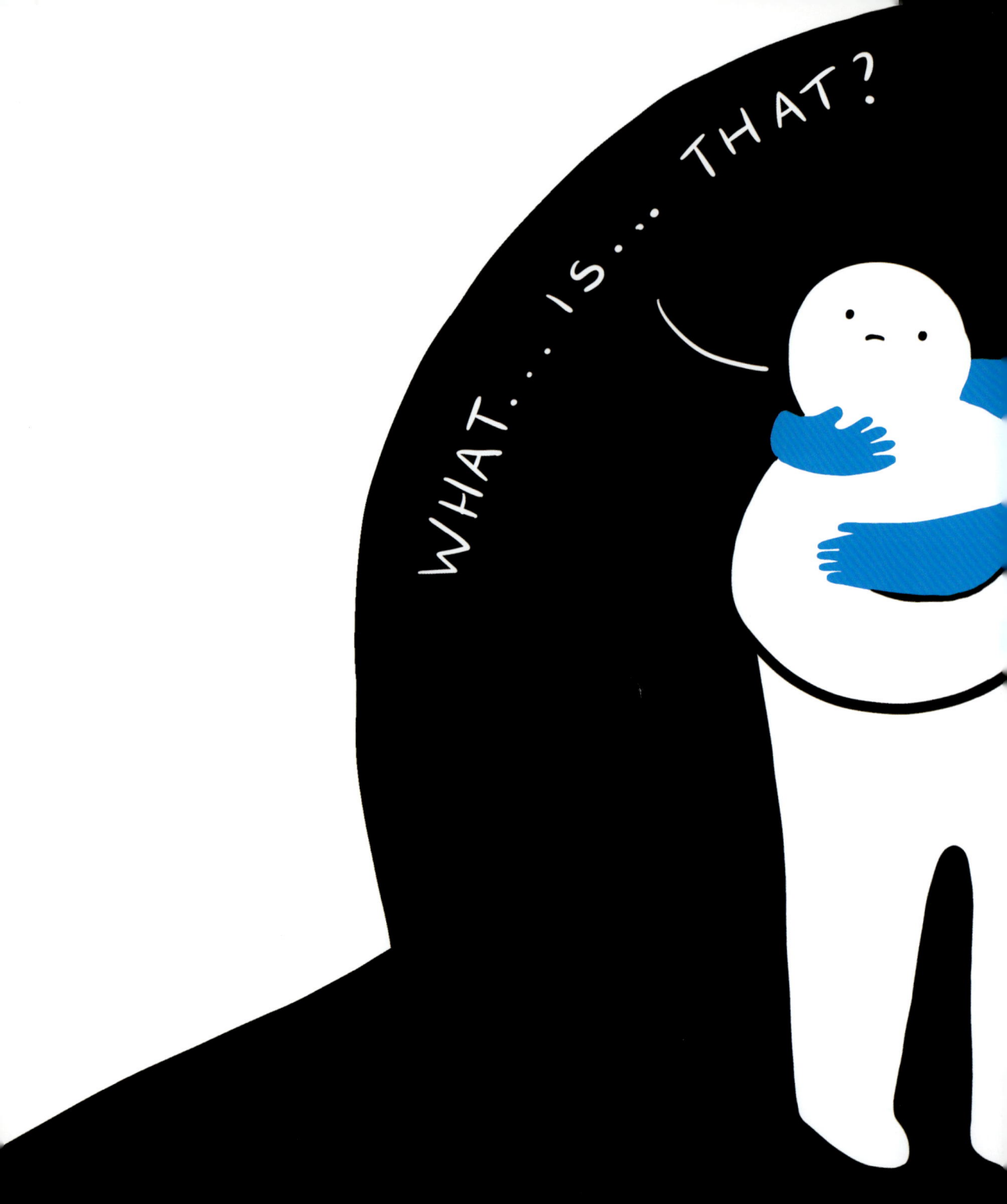
WHAT.... IS.... THAT?

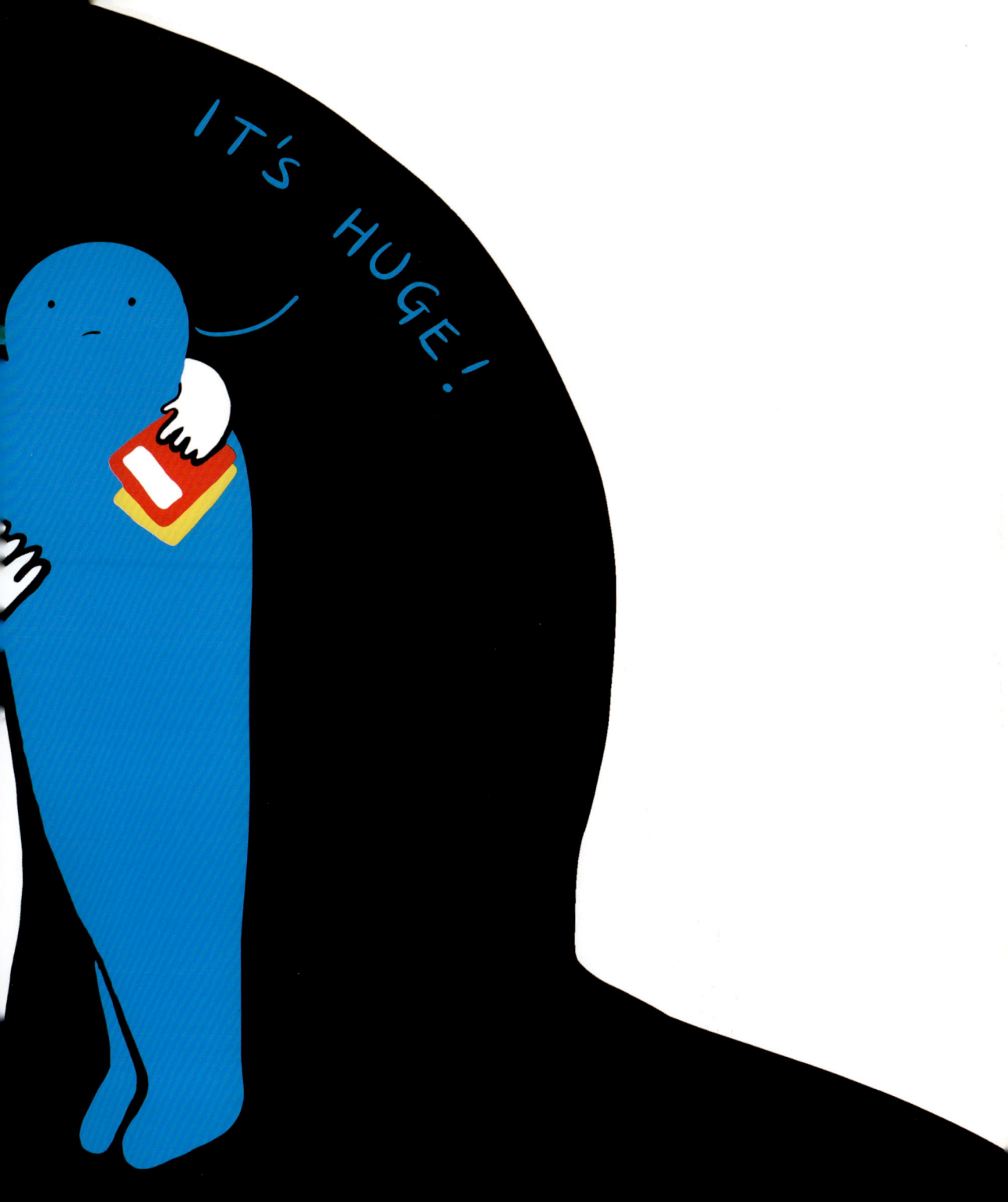
IT'S HUGE!

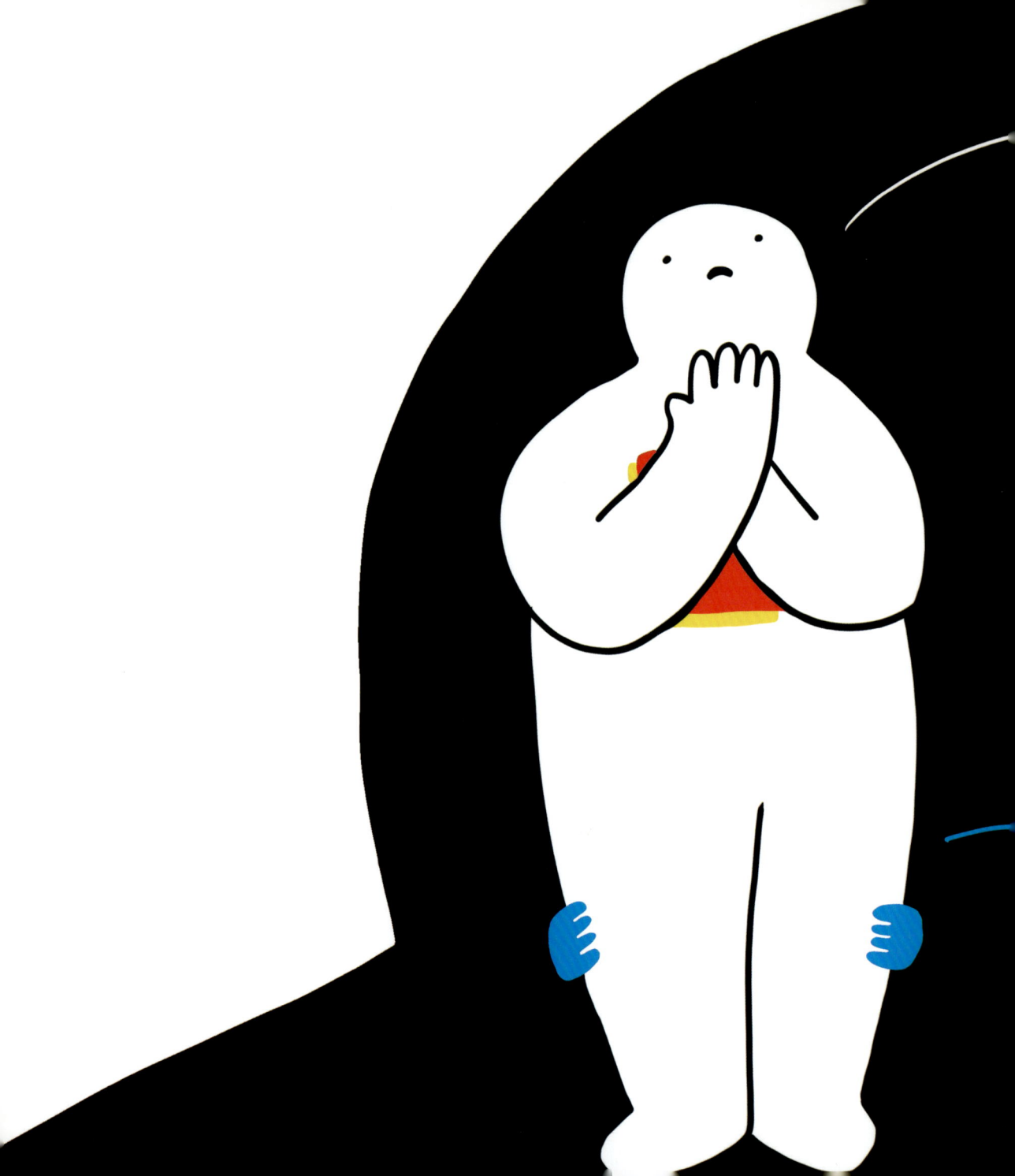

OK.

DON'T PANIC...

JUST—

WHIMPER?

PASS OUT?

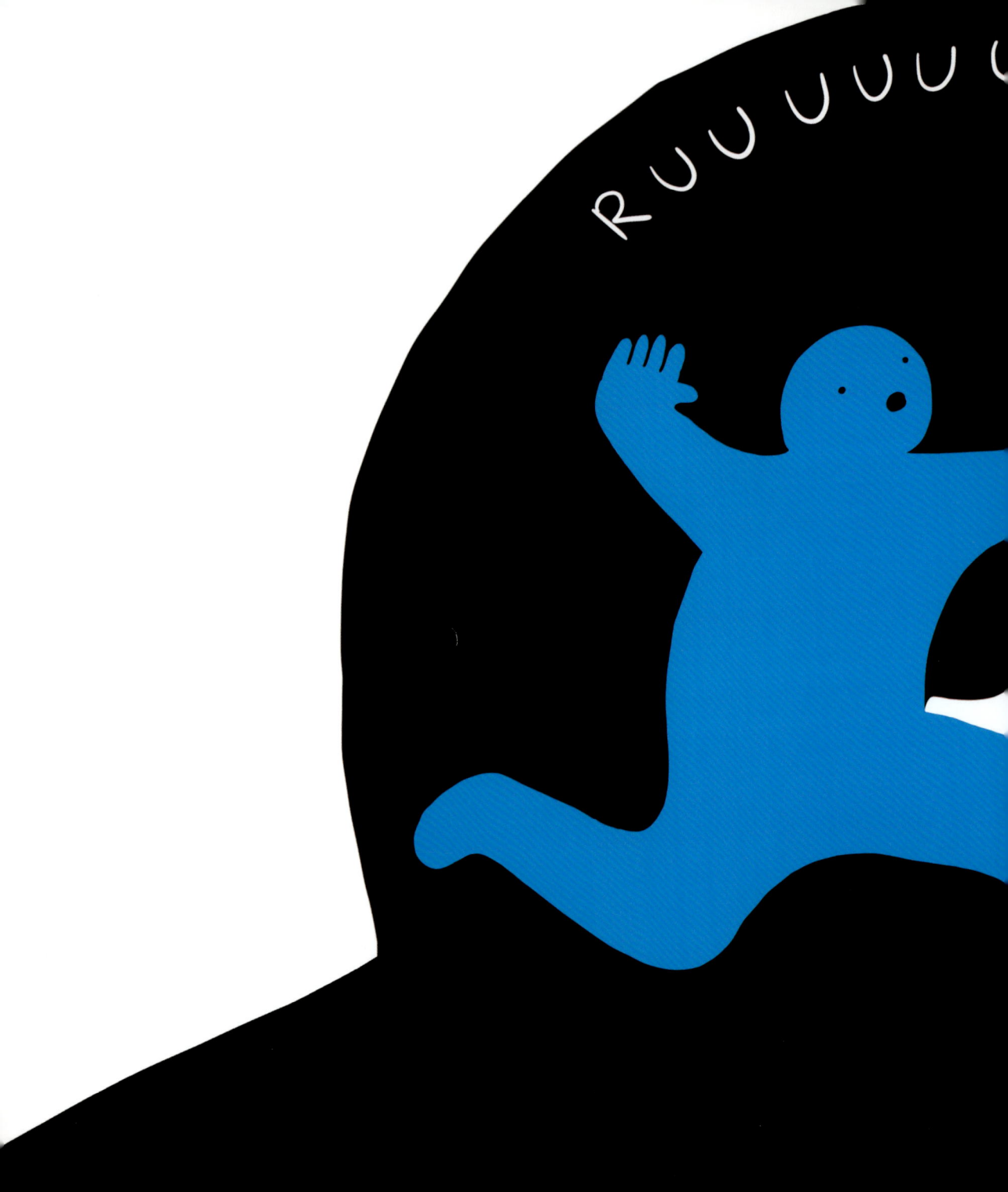
RUUUUUU

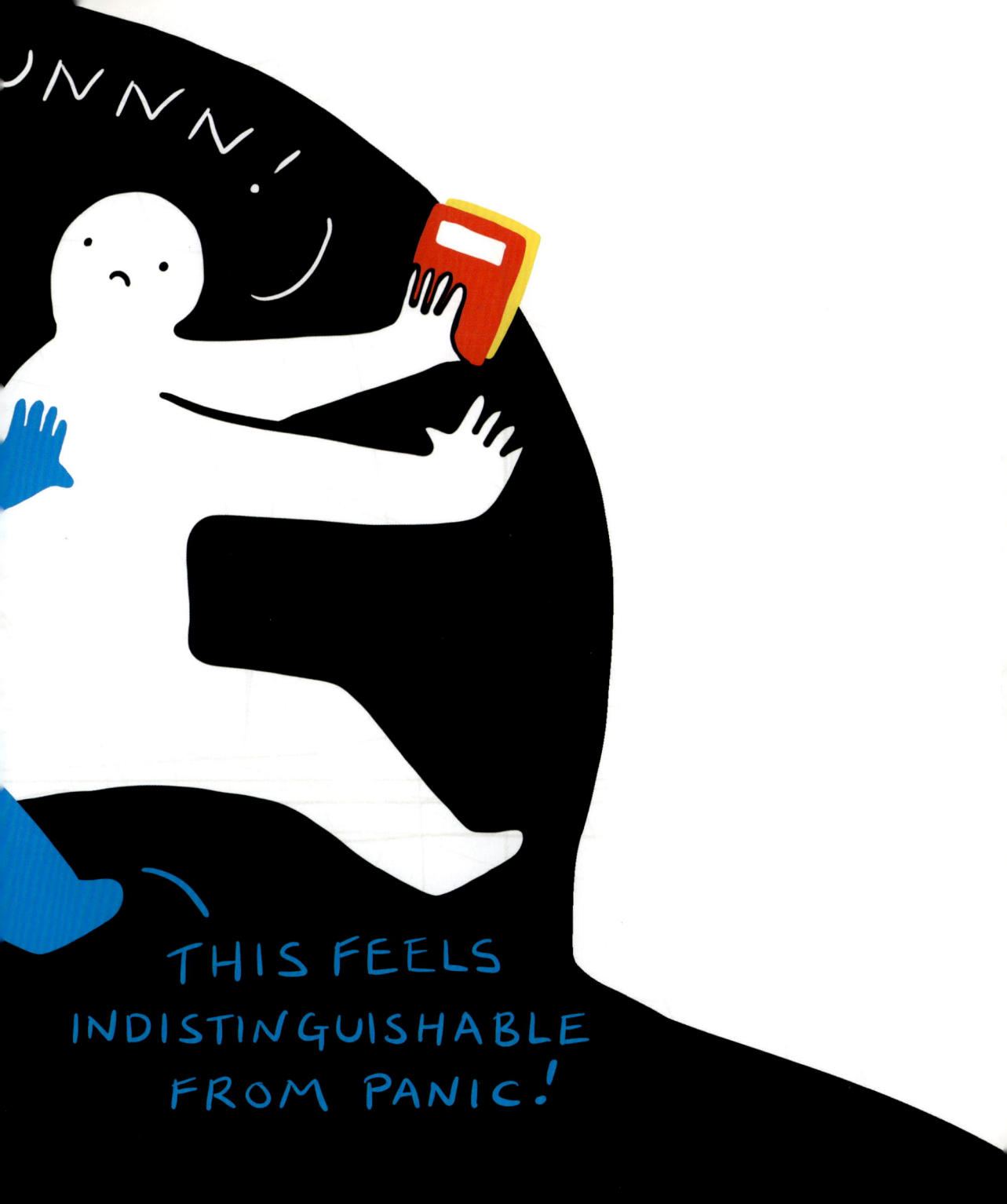
UNNN!
THIS FEELS INDISTINGUISHABLE FROM PANIC!

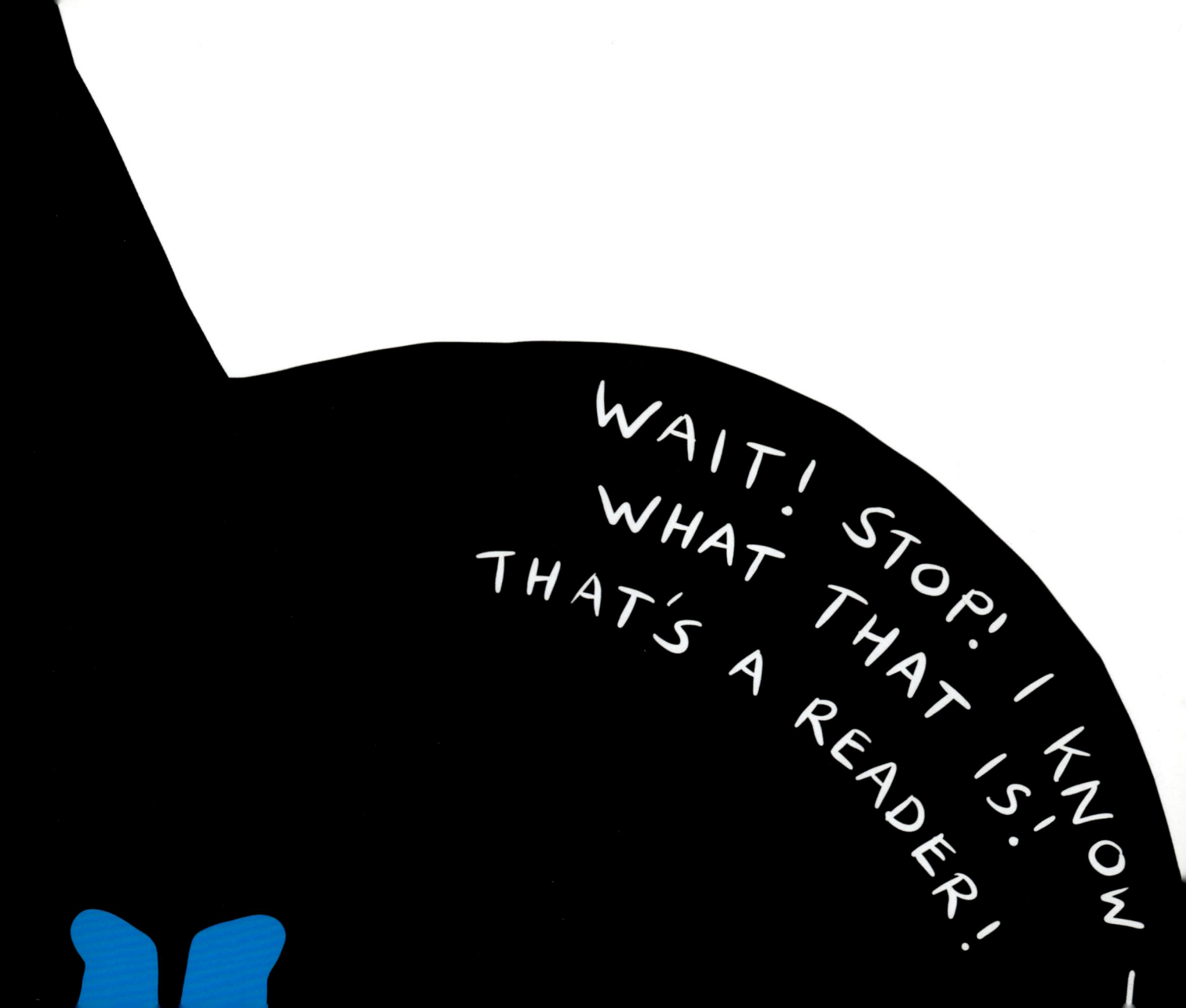
WAIT! STOP! I KNOW
WHAT THAT IS!
THAT'S A READER!

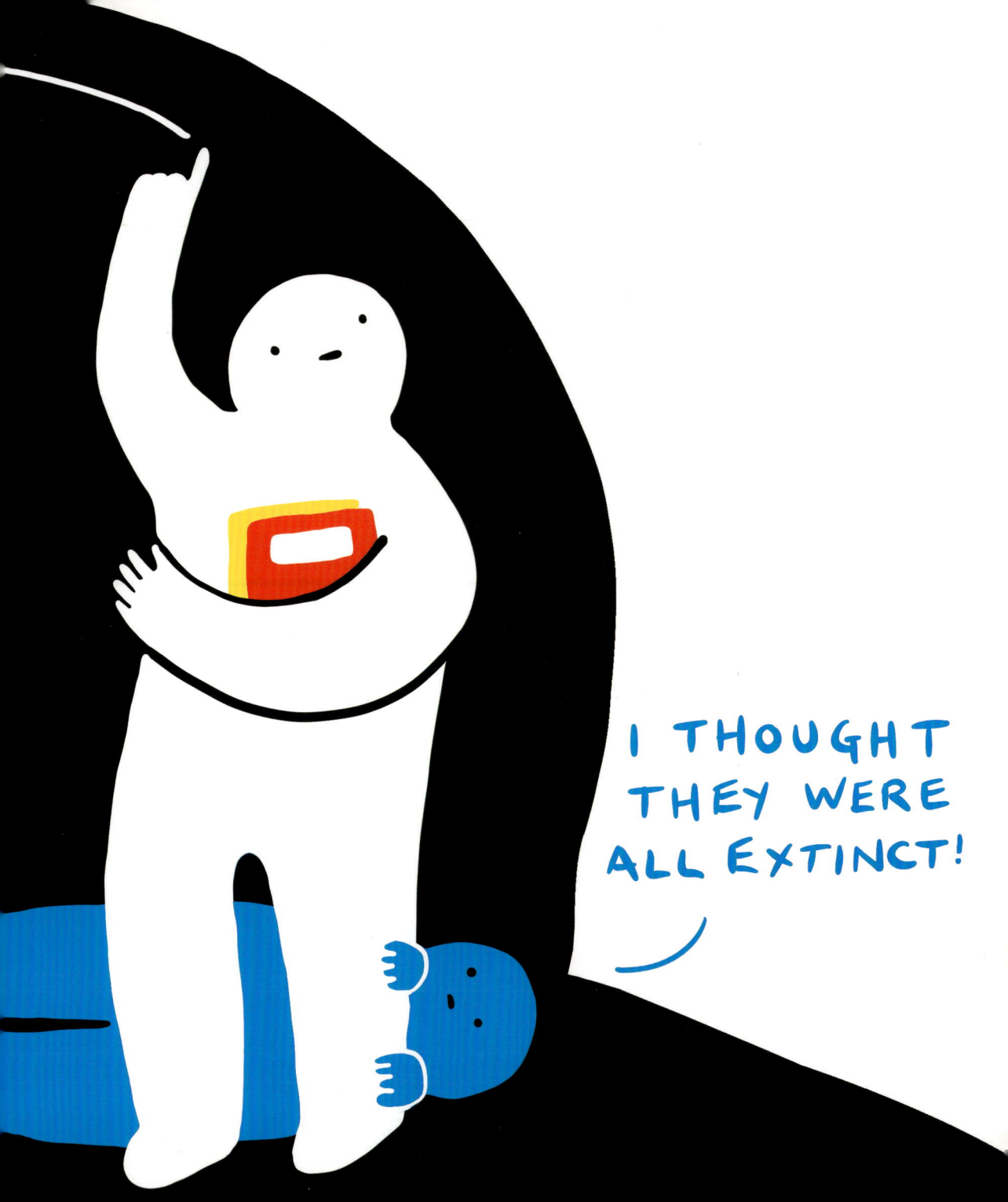
I THOUGHT THEY WERE ALL EXTINCT!

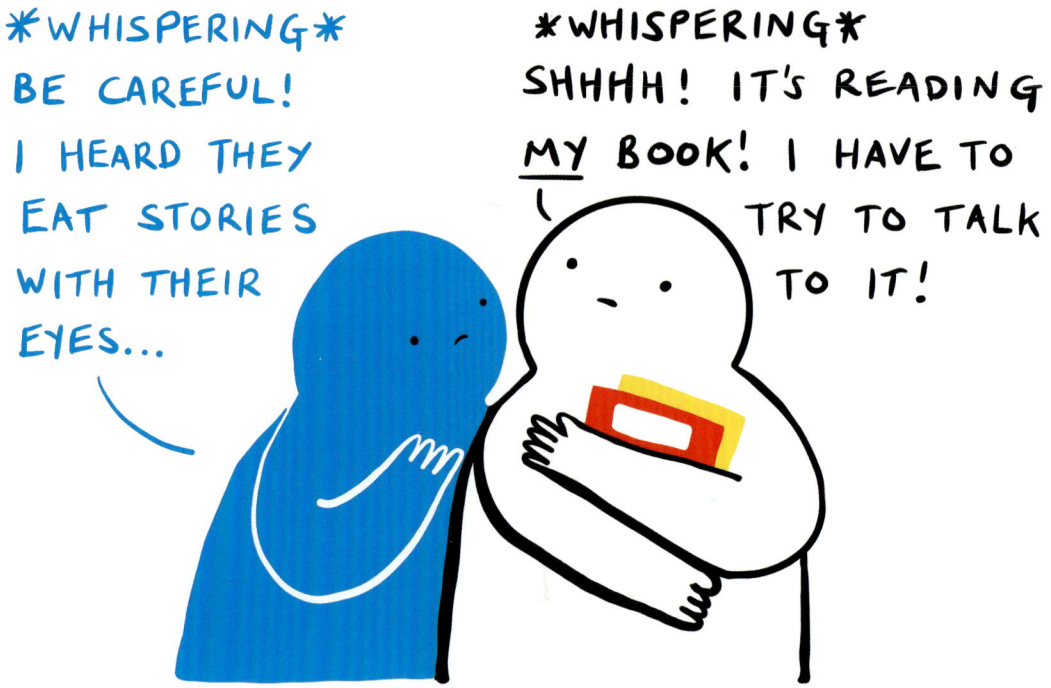
WHISPERING BE CAREFUL! I HEARD THEY EAT STORIES WITH THEIR EYES...
WHISPERING SHHHH! IT'S READING MY BOOK! I HAVE TO TRY TO TALK TO IT!

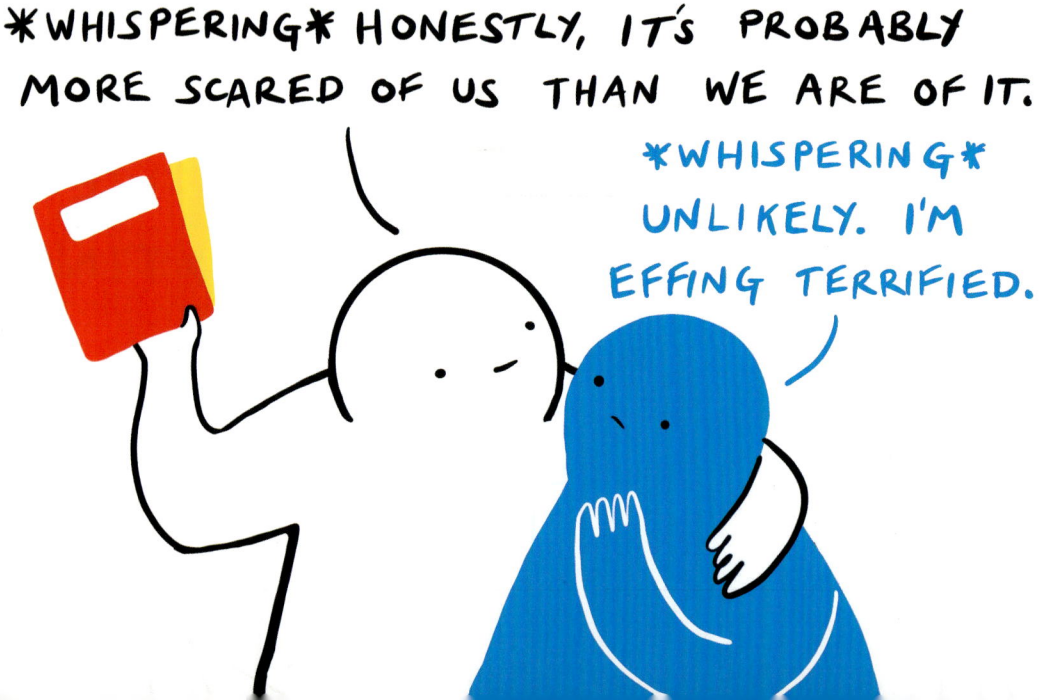
WHISPERING HONESTLY, IT'S PROBABLY MORE SCARED OF US THAN WE ARE OF IT.
WHISPERING UNLIKELY. I'M EFFING TERRIFIED.

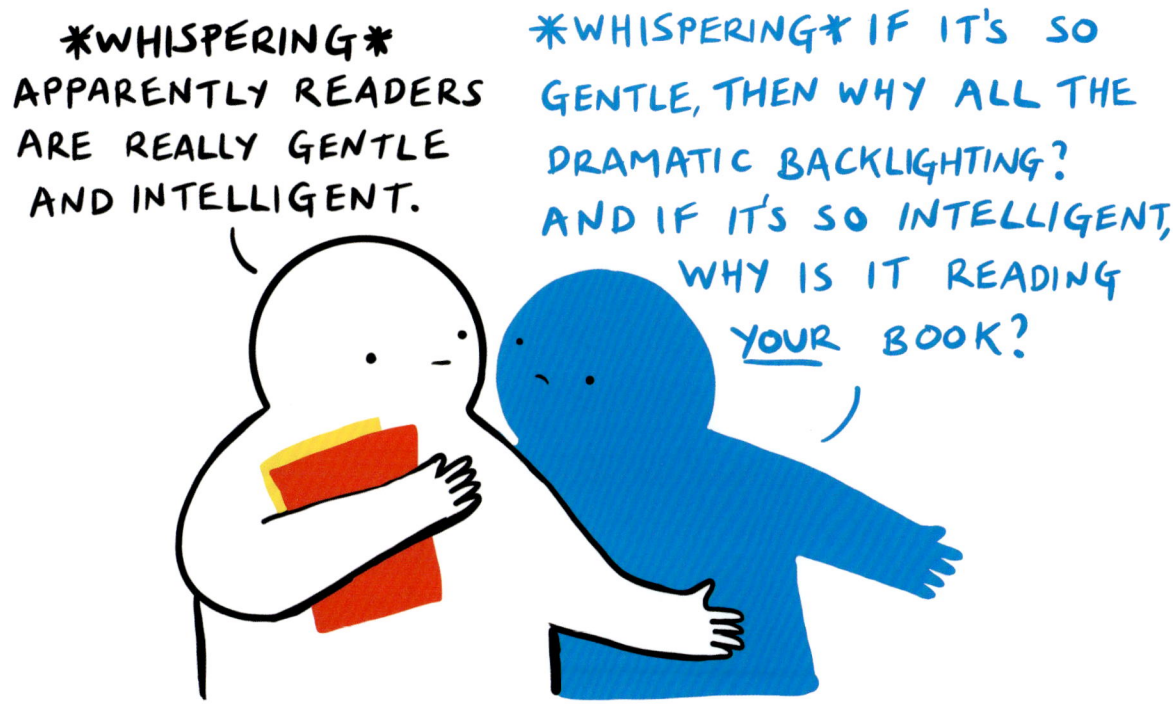
WHISPERING APPARENTLY READERS ARE REALLY GENTLE AND INTELLIGENT.
WHISPERING IF IT'S SO GENTLE, THEN WHY ALL THE DRAMATIC BACKLIGHTING? AND IF IT'S SO INTELLIGENT, WHY IS IT READING YOUR BOOK?

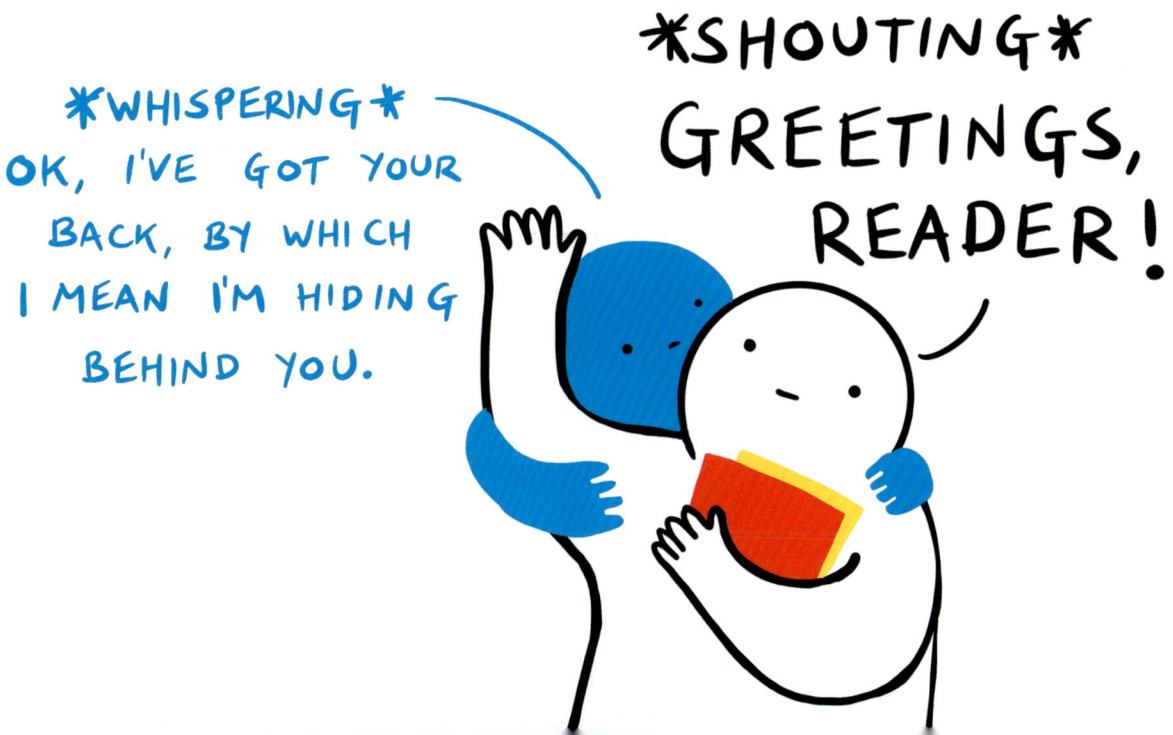
WHISPERING OK, I'VE GOT YOUR BACK, BY WHICH I MEAN I'M HIDING BEHIND YOU.
SHOUTING GREETINGS, READER!

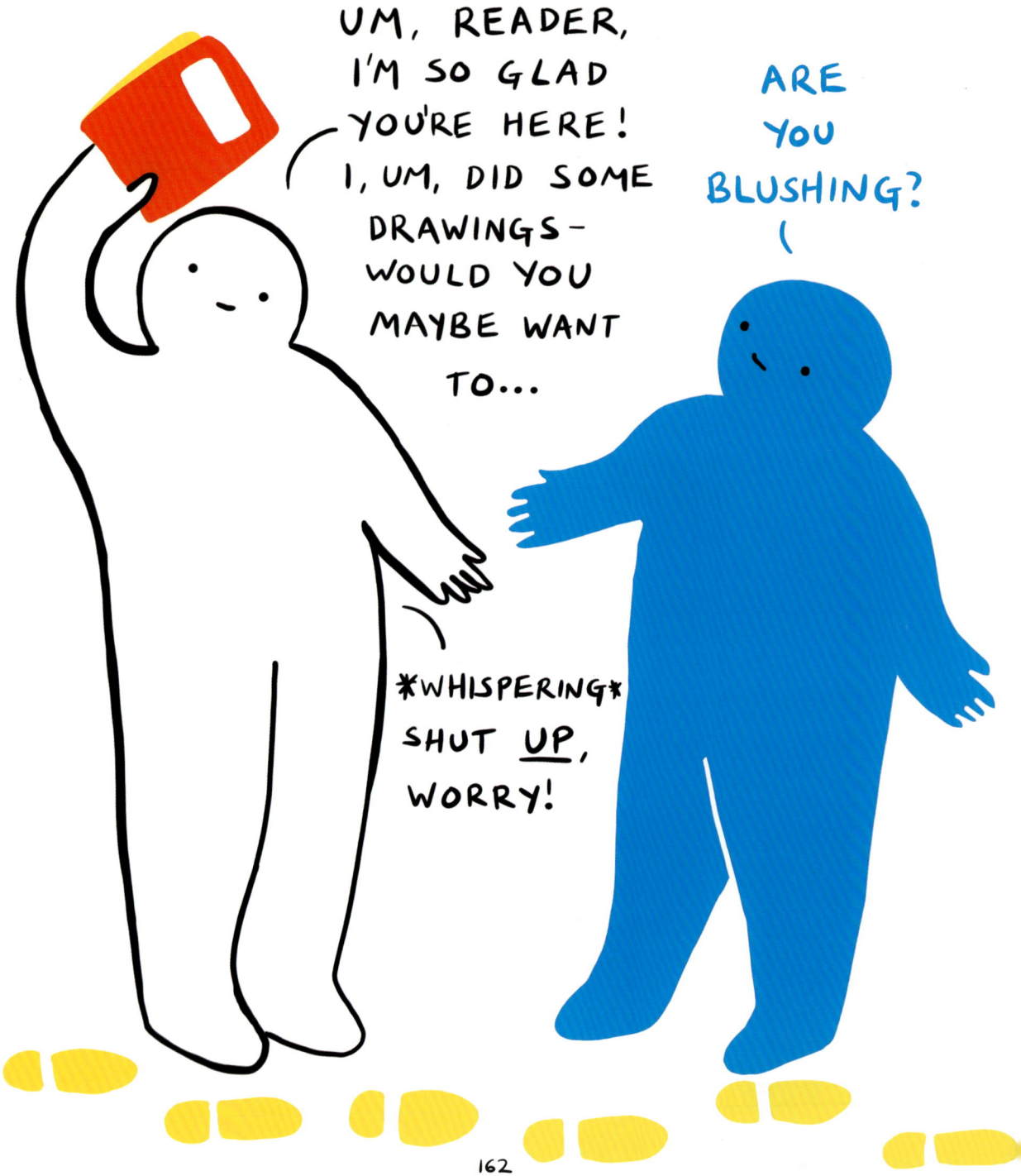
UM, READER, I'M SO GLAD YOU'RE HERE! I, UM, DID SOME DRAWINGS - WOULD YOU MAYBE WANT TO...
ARE YOU BLUSHING?
WHISPERING SHUT UP, WORRY!

DRAWINGS ABOUT
LOVE

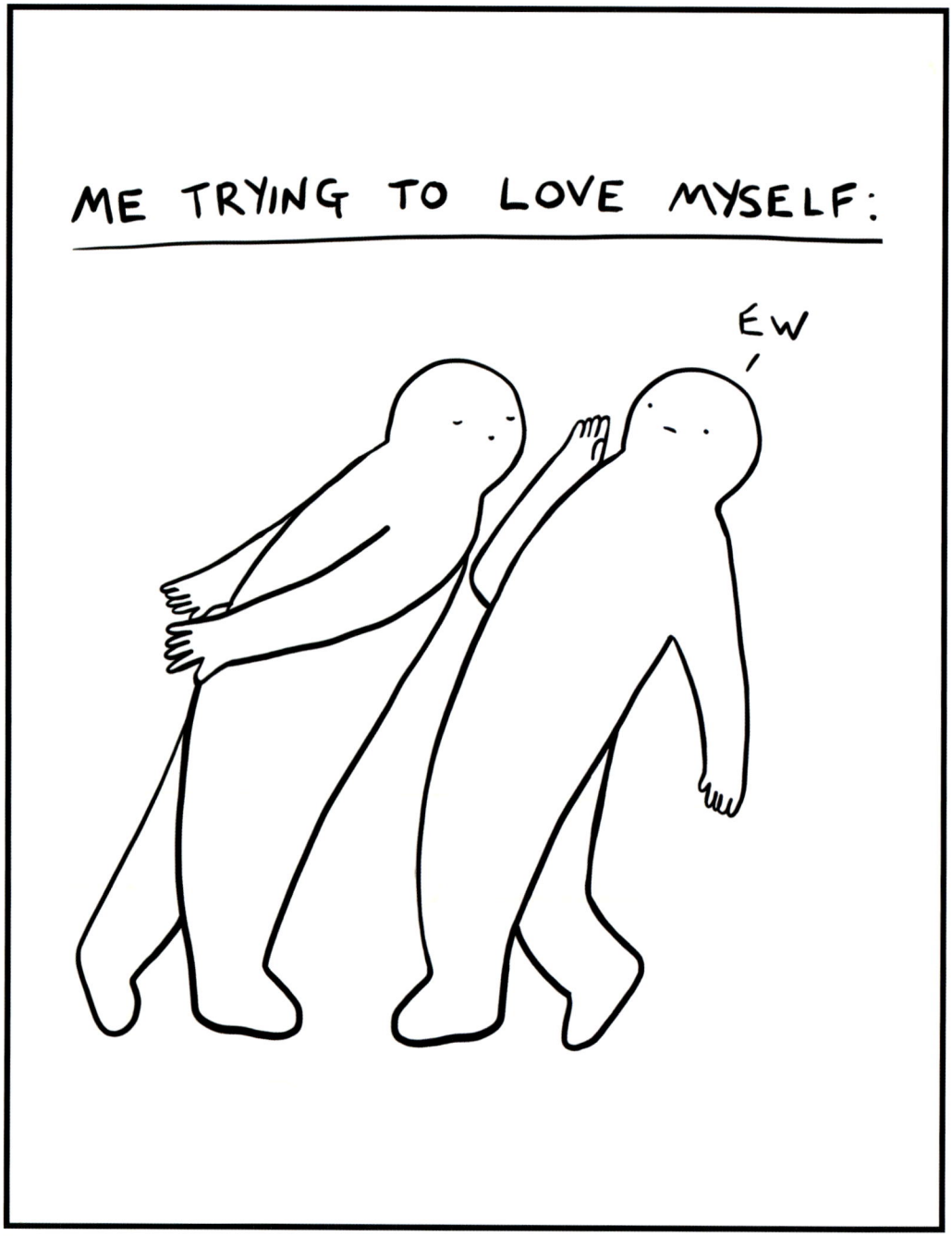

LEAN IN.

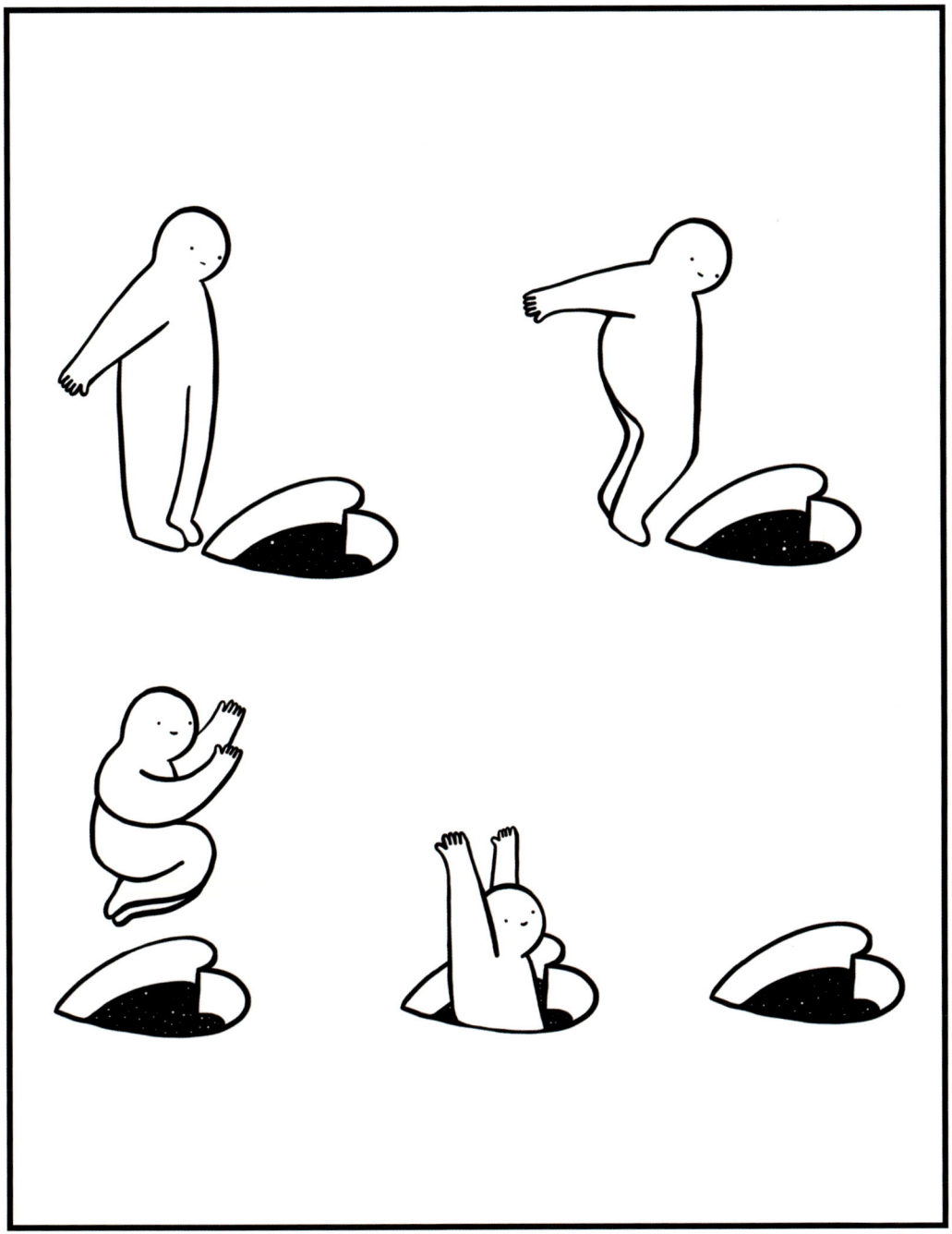

IN DEEP.

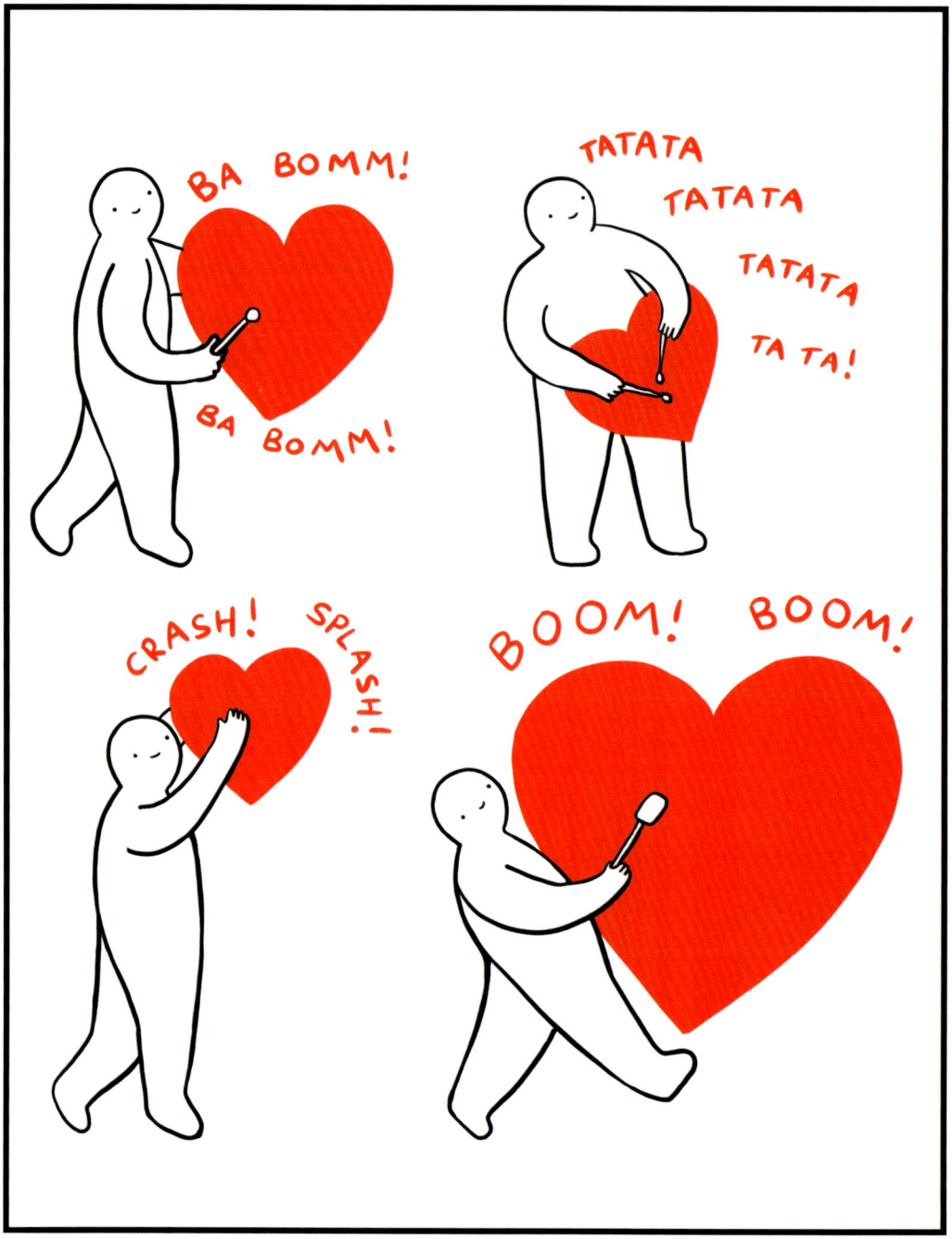
BA BOMM!
BA BOMM!
TATATA
TATATA
TATATA
TA TA!
CRASH!
SPLASH!
BOOM!
BOOM!

HEARTBEATS.

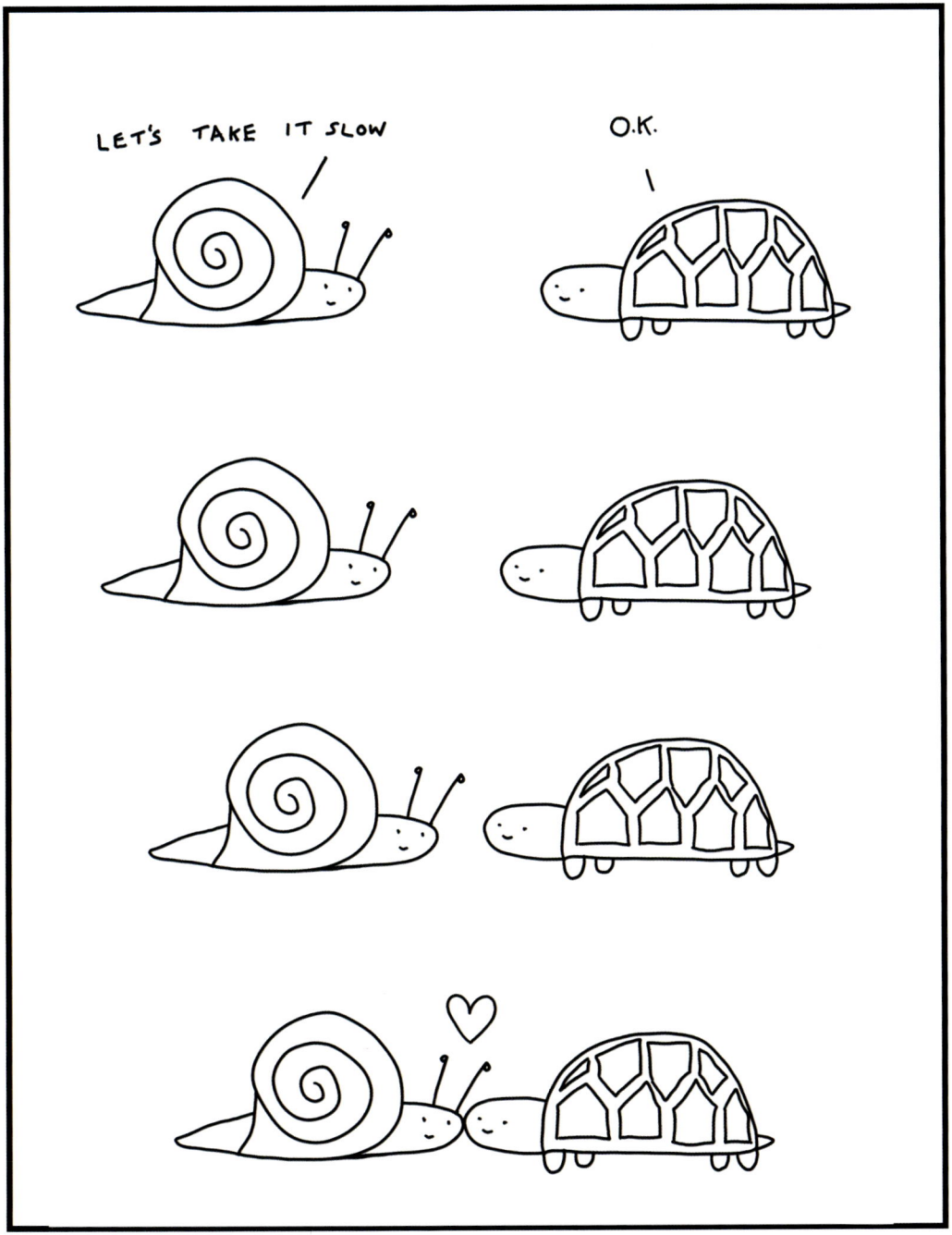

SNAIL'S PACE.

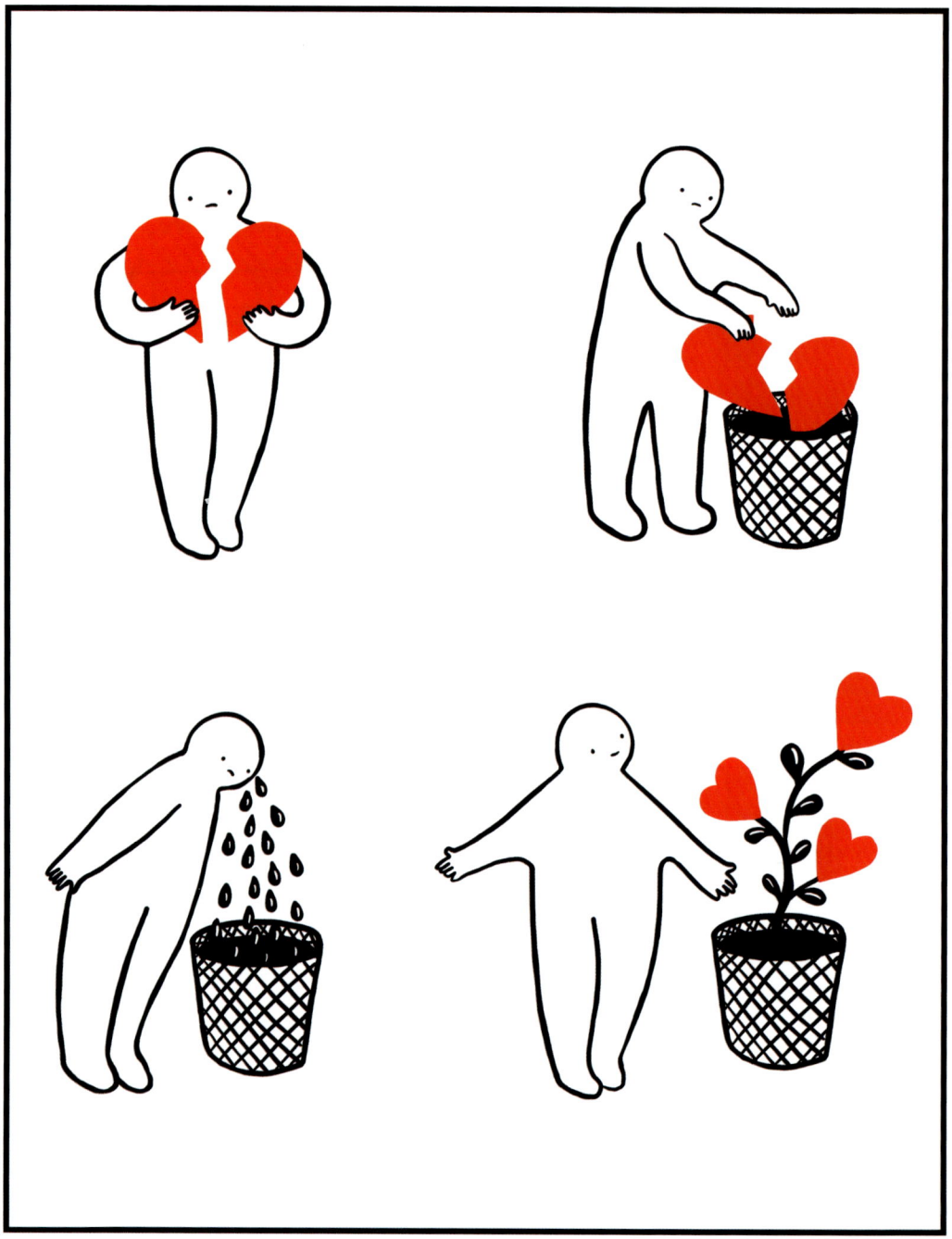

A LOVE STORY.

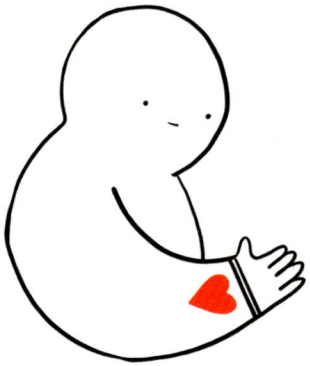

I USED TO WEAR MY HEART ON MY SLEEVE

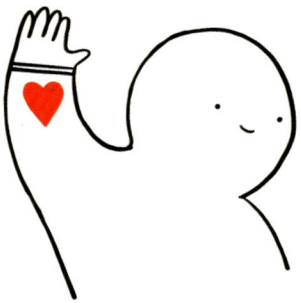

WHERE EVERYONE COULD SEE IT

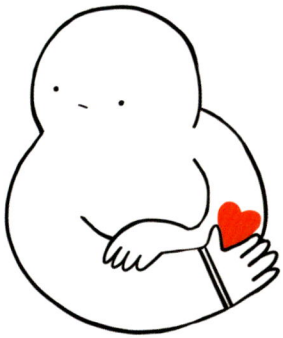

BUT THEN I CHOSE TO MOVE IT

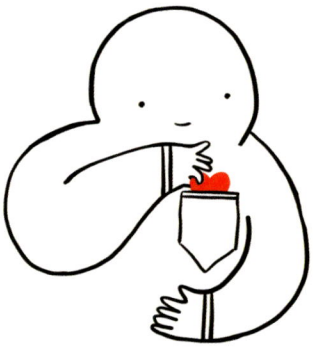

AFTER SOMEONE TRIED TO STEAL IT

ALSO, I KEPT ACCIDENTALLY DIPPING IT IN SOUP.

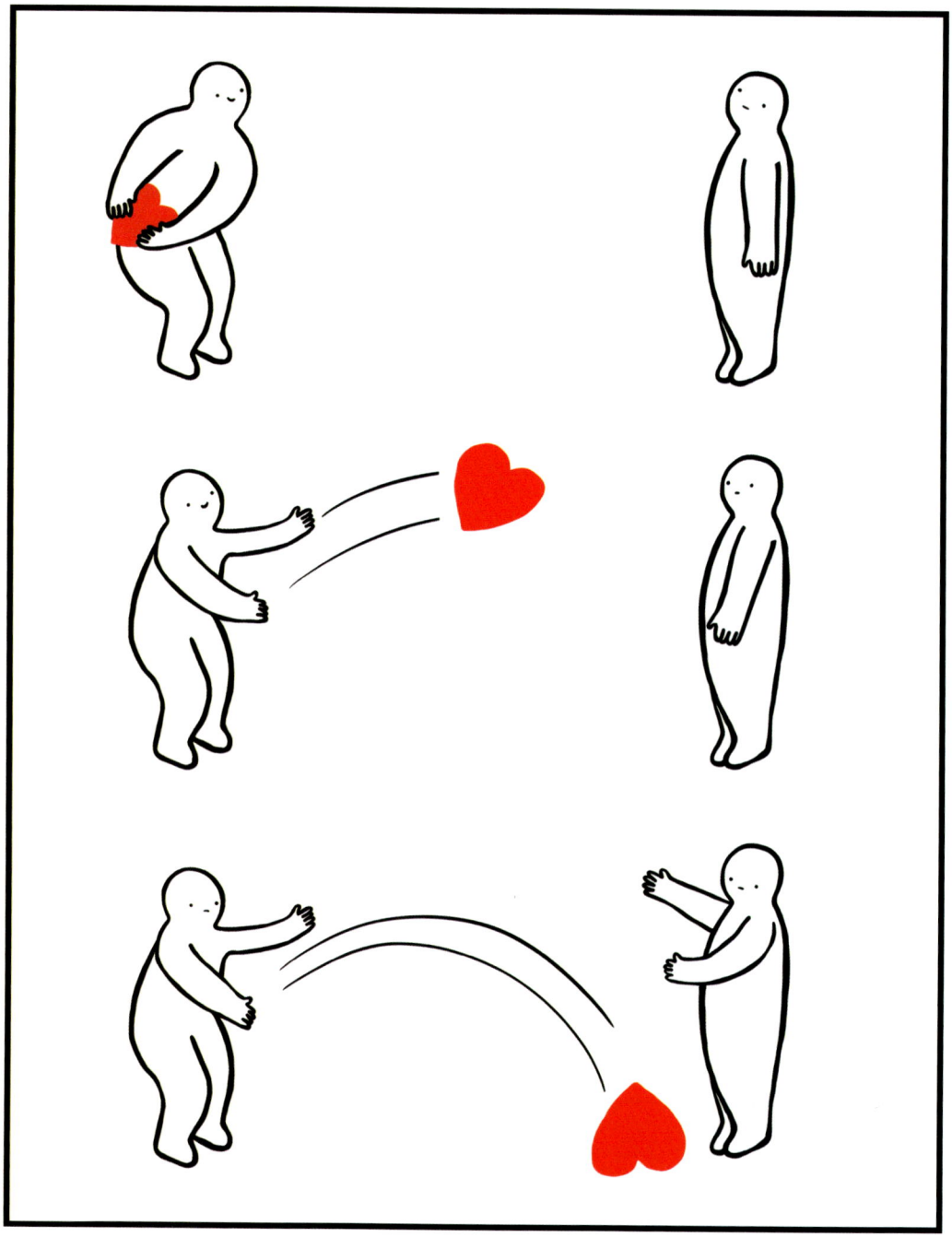

TOO SLOW.

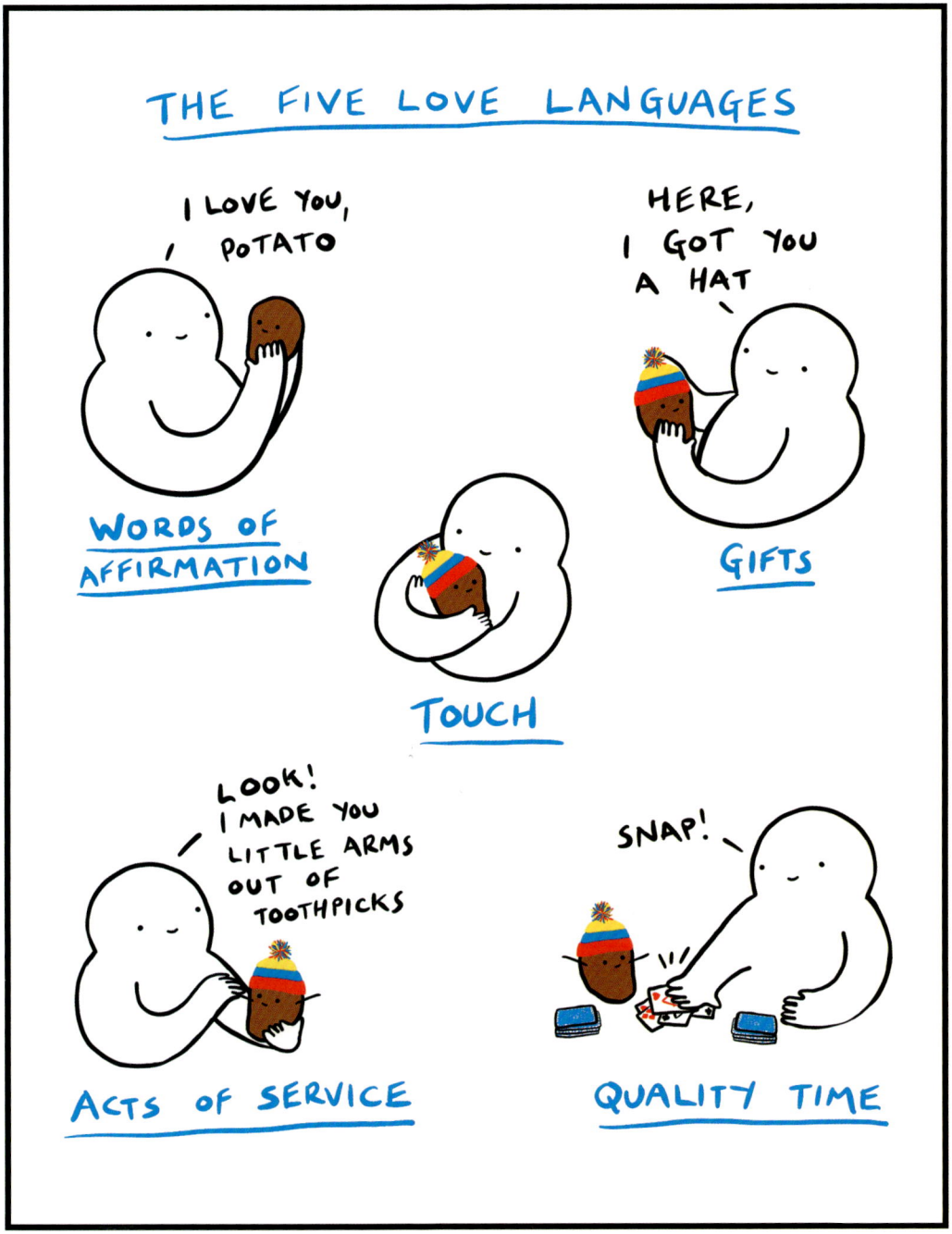

I ONLY HAVE EYES FOR YOU.

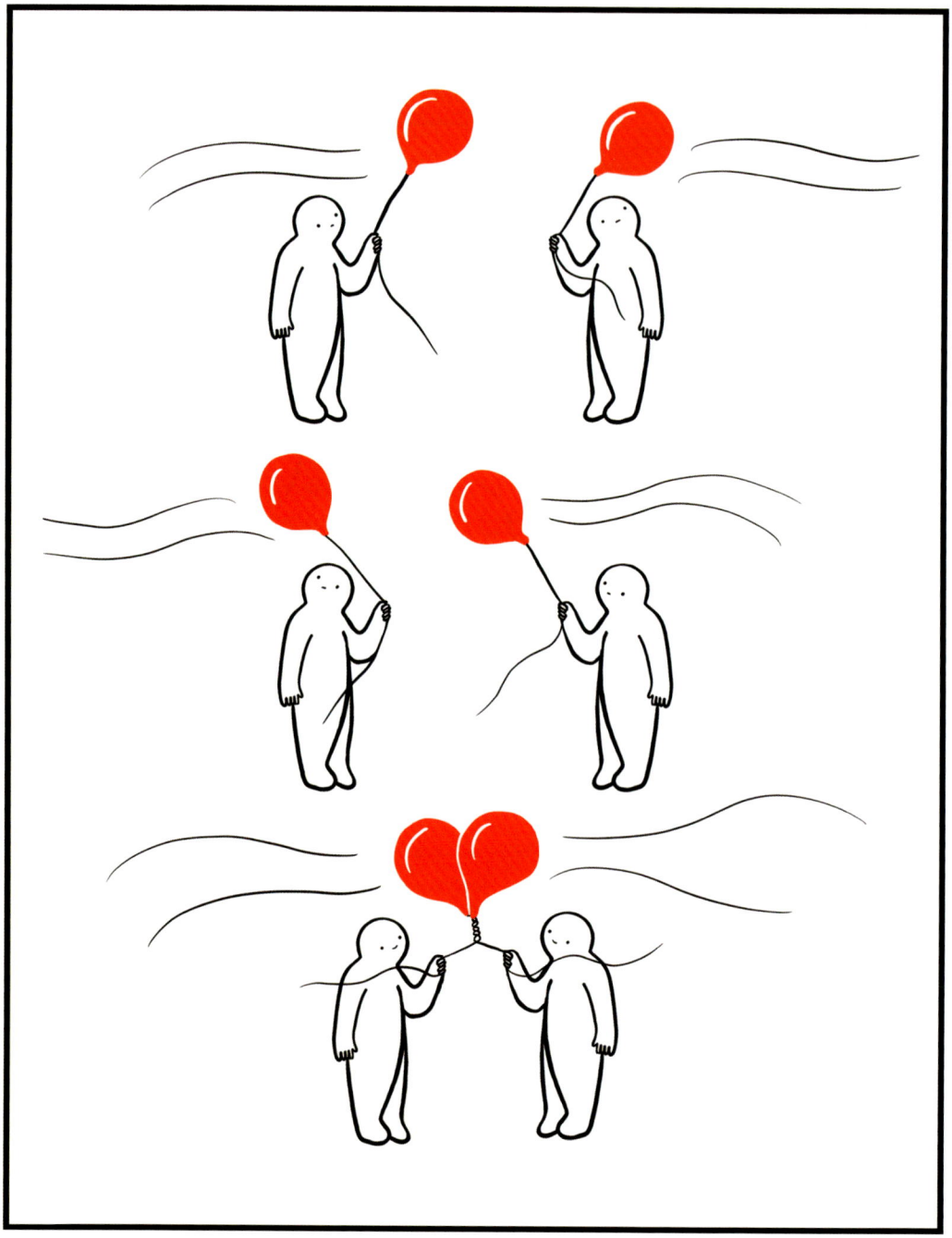

FIT TO BURST.

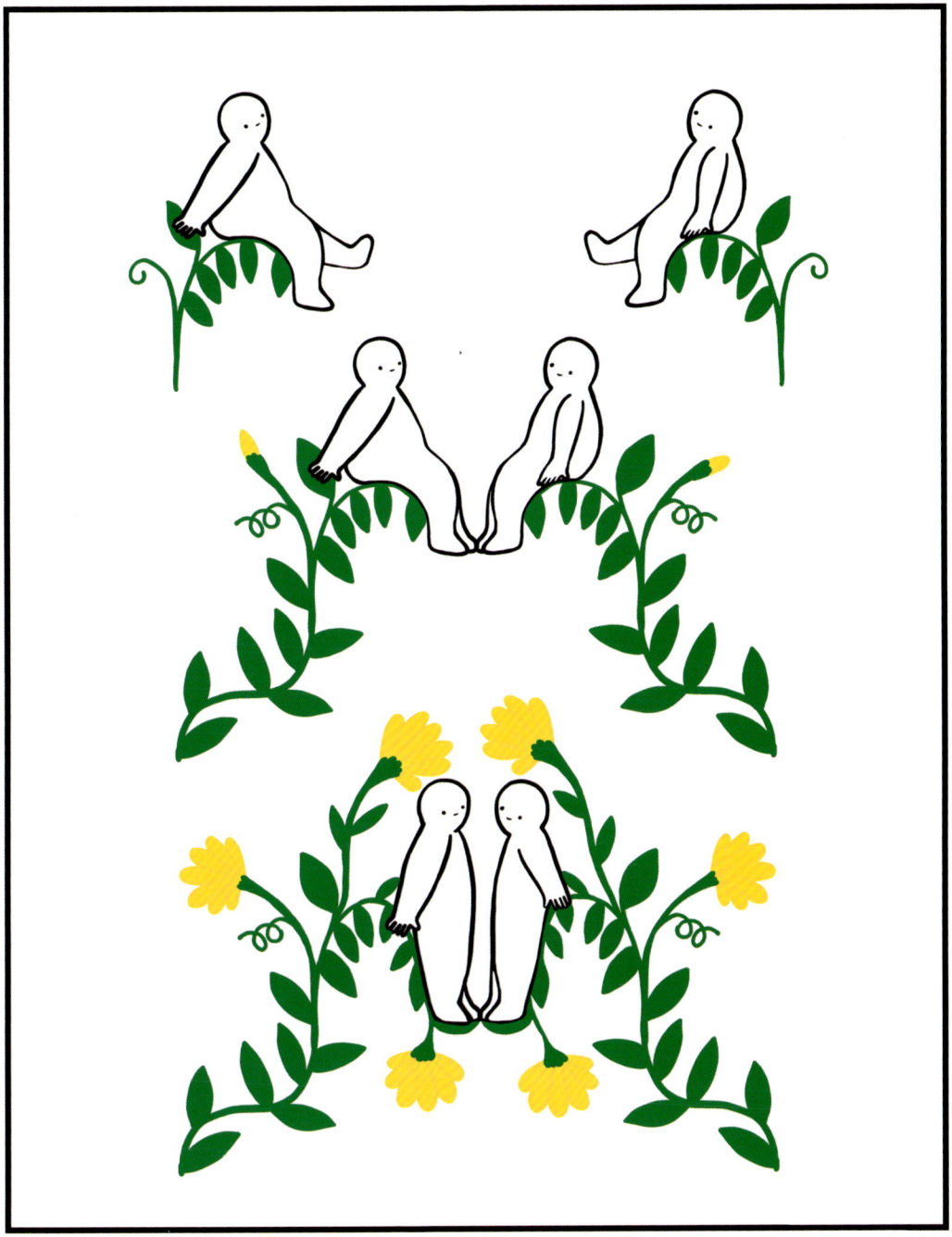

GROW CLOSE.

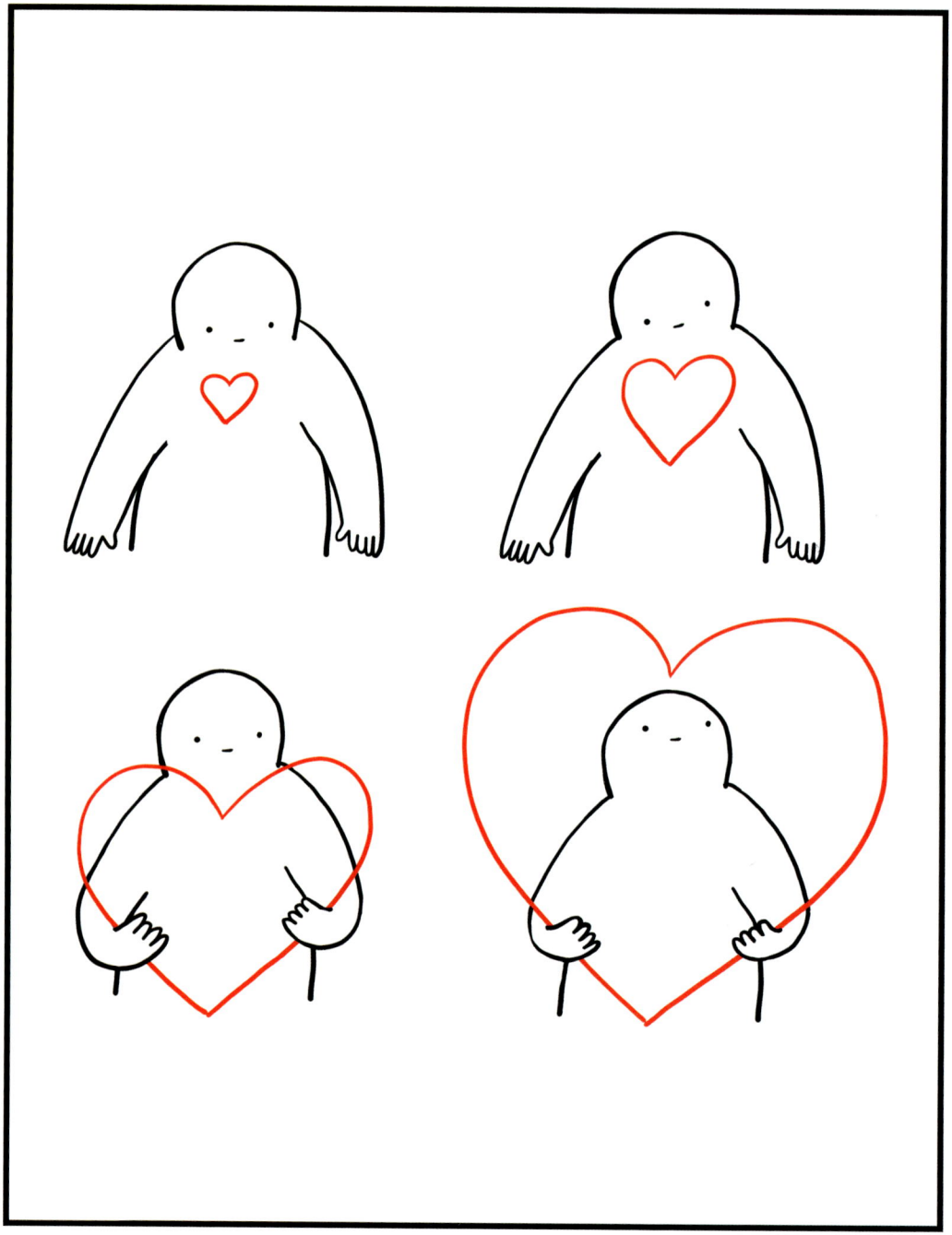

CHANGE OF HEART.

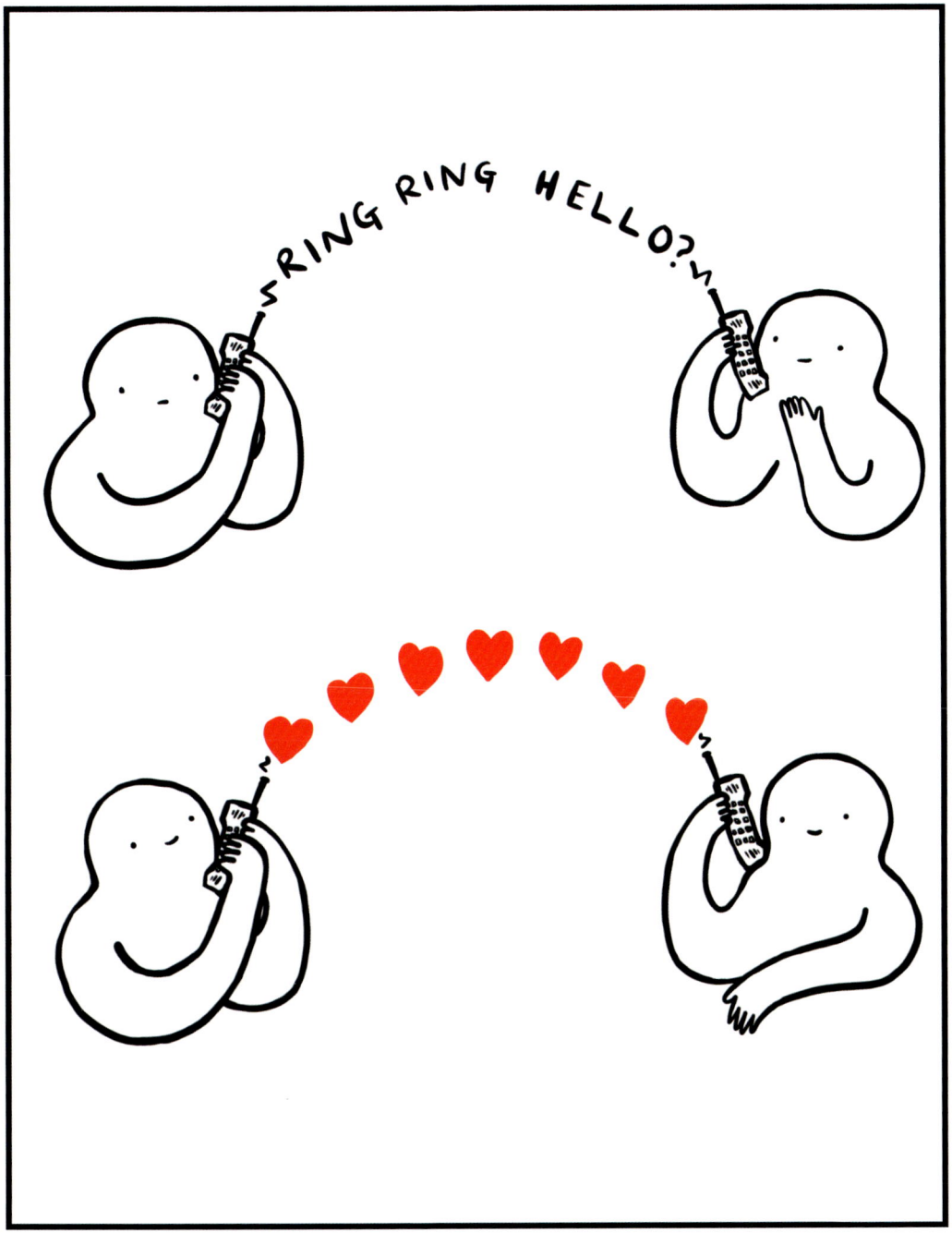

PHONE A FRIEND.

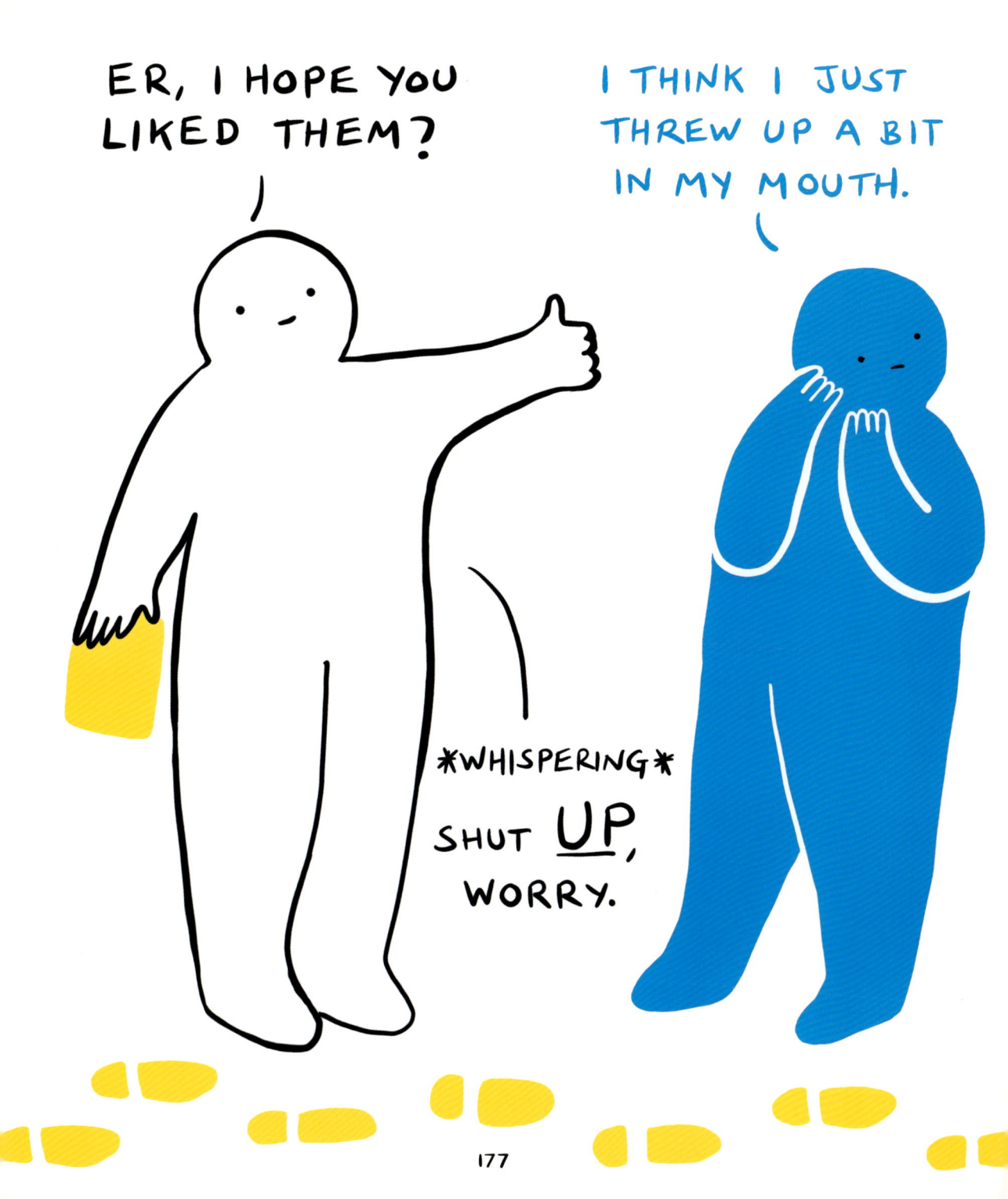
ER, I HOPE YOU LIKED THEM?
I THINK I JUST THREW UP A BIT IN MY MOUTH.
WHISPERING
SHUT UP, WORRY.

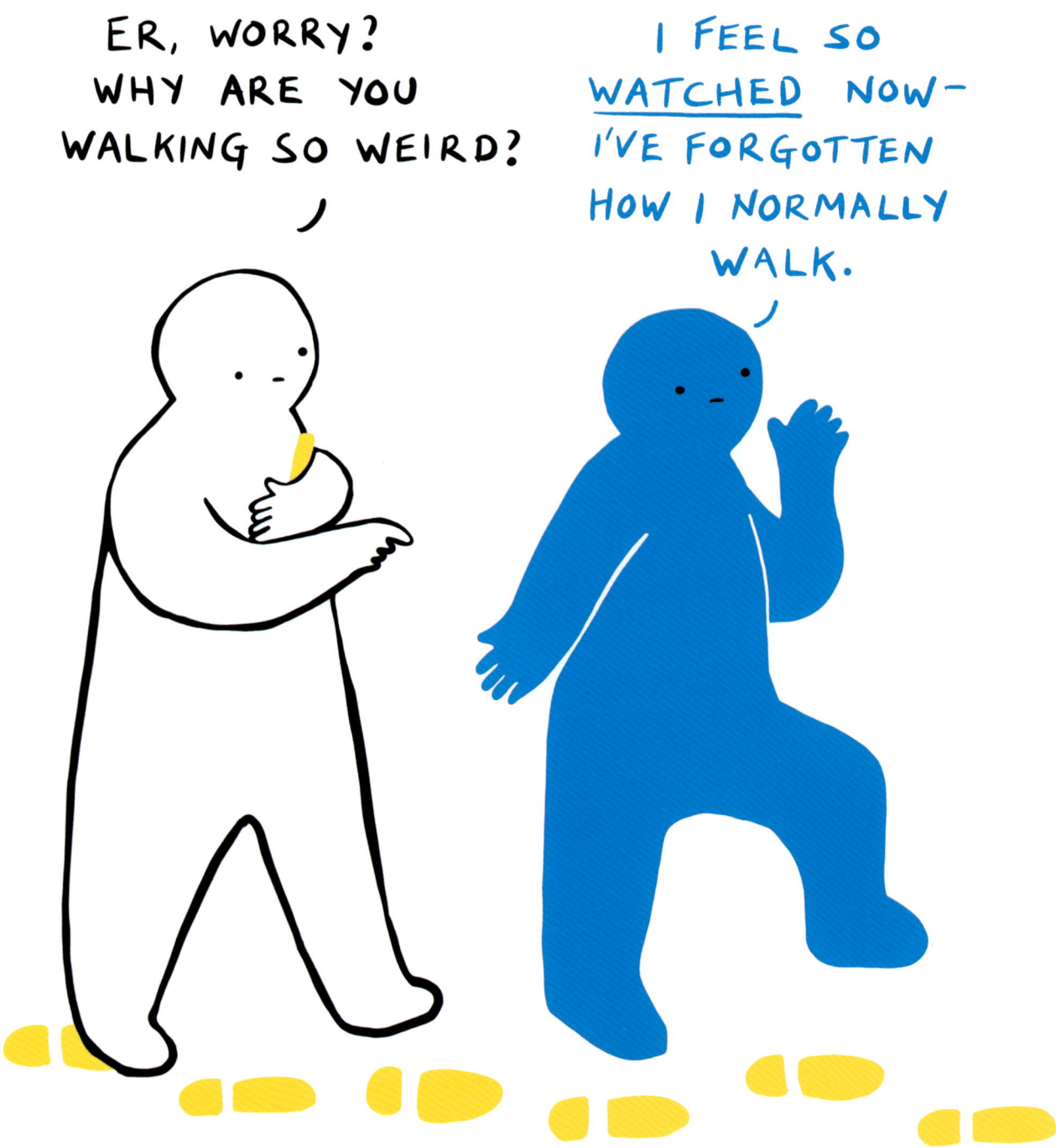
ER, WORRY? WHY ARE YOU WALKING SO WEIRD?
I FEEL SO WATCHED NOW– I'VE FORGOTTEN HOW I NORMALLY WALK.

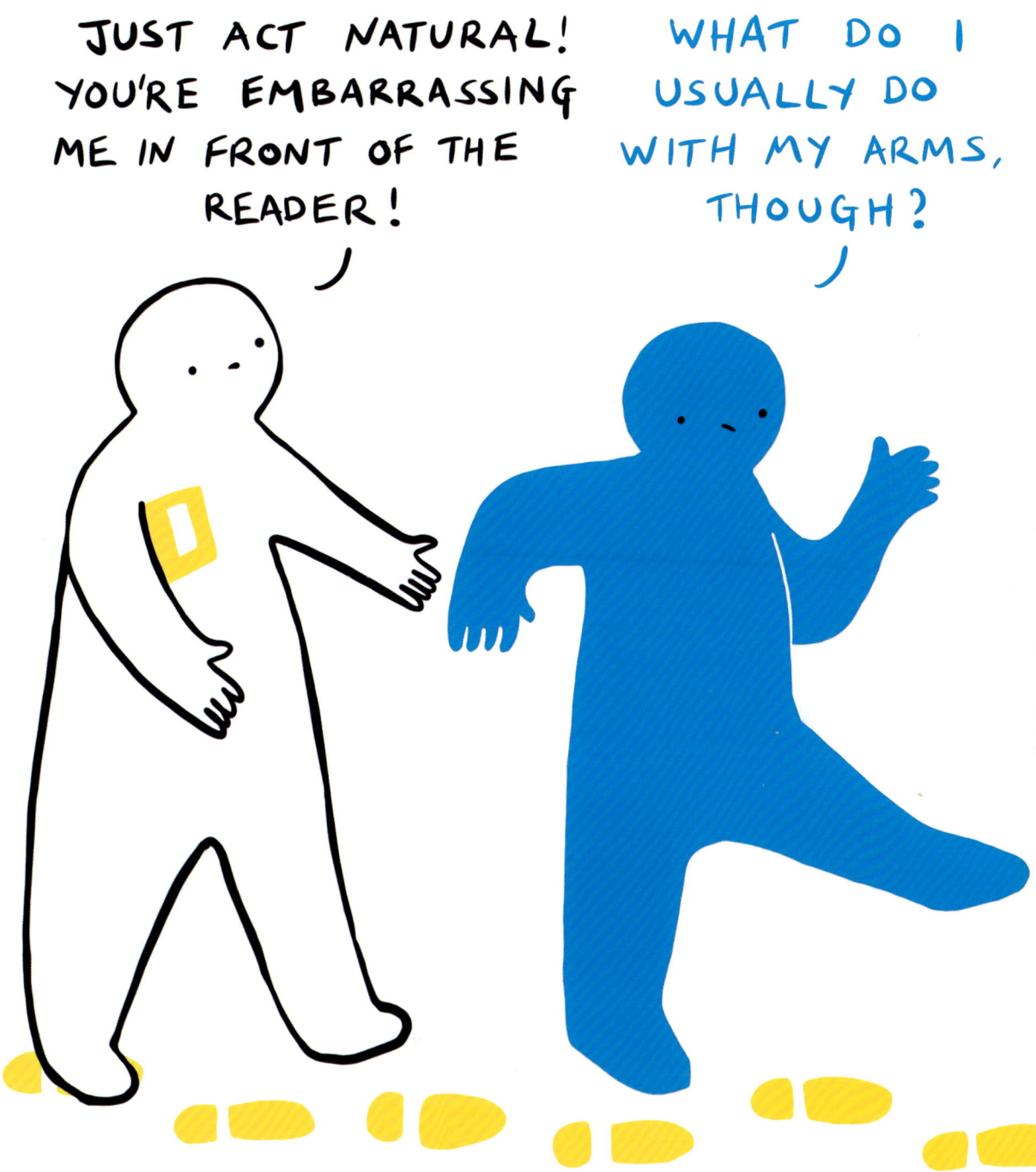
JUST ACT NATURAL! YOU'RE EMBARRASSING ME IN FRONT OF THE READER!
WHAT DO I USUALLY DO WITH MY ARMS, THOUGH?

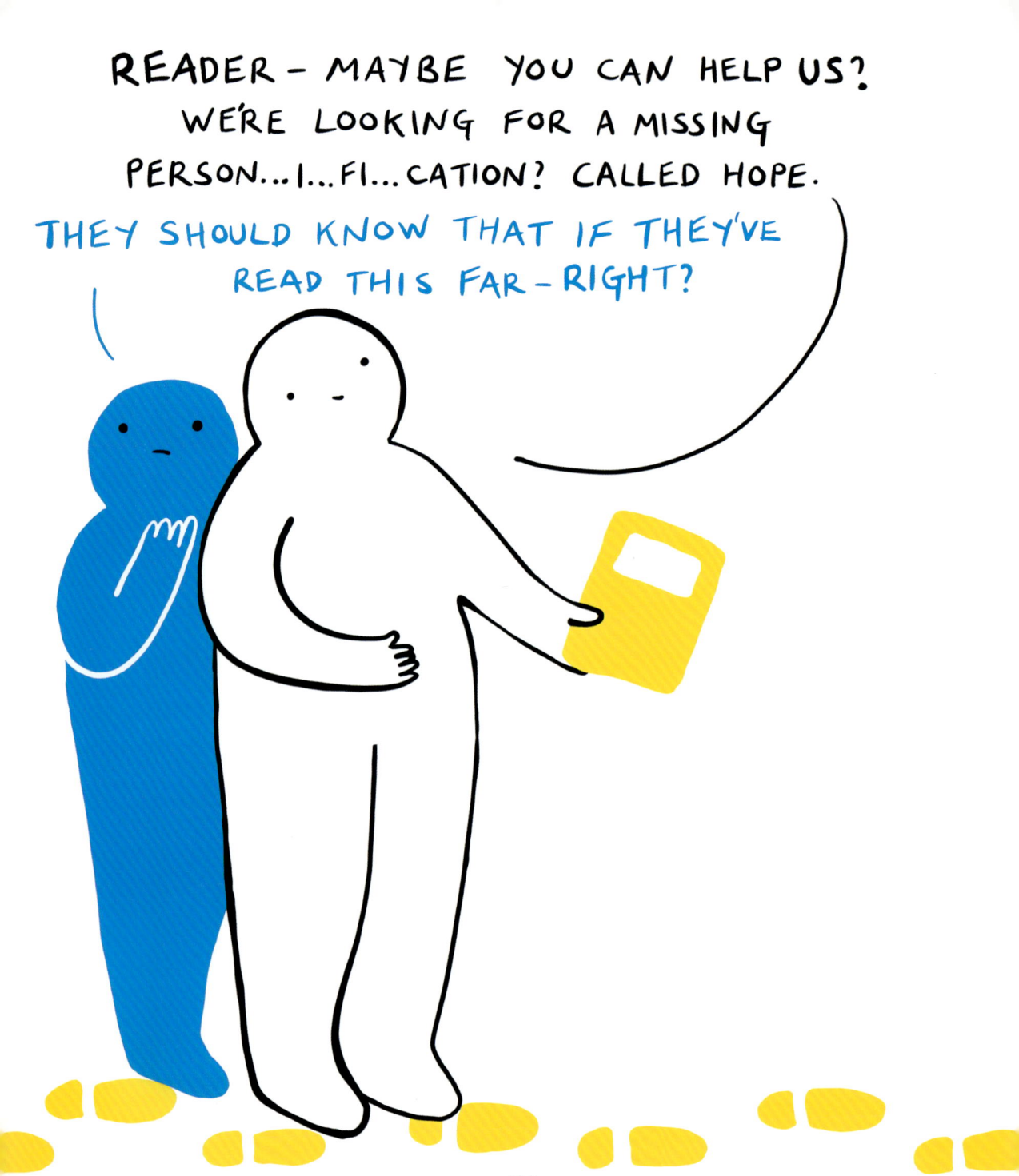
READER - MAYBE YOU CAN HELP US? WE'RE LOOKING FOR A MISSING PERSON...I...FI...CATION? CALLED HOPE.
THEY SHOULD KNOW THAT IF THEY'VE READ THIS FAR - RIGHT?

DRAWINGS ABOUT HOPE

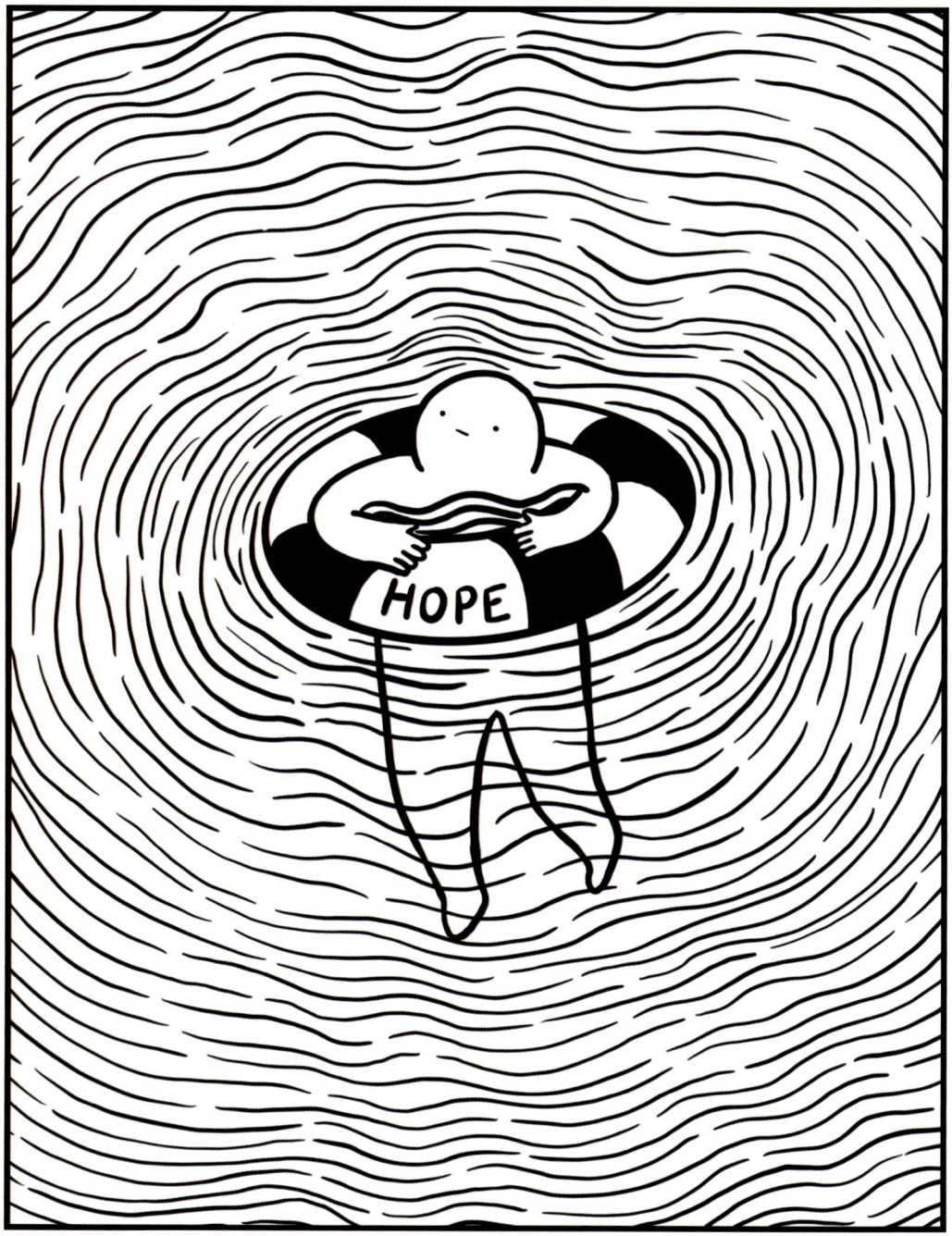

HOLDING ON FOR DEAR LIFE.

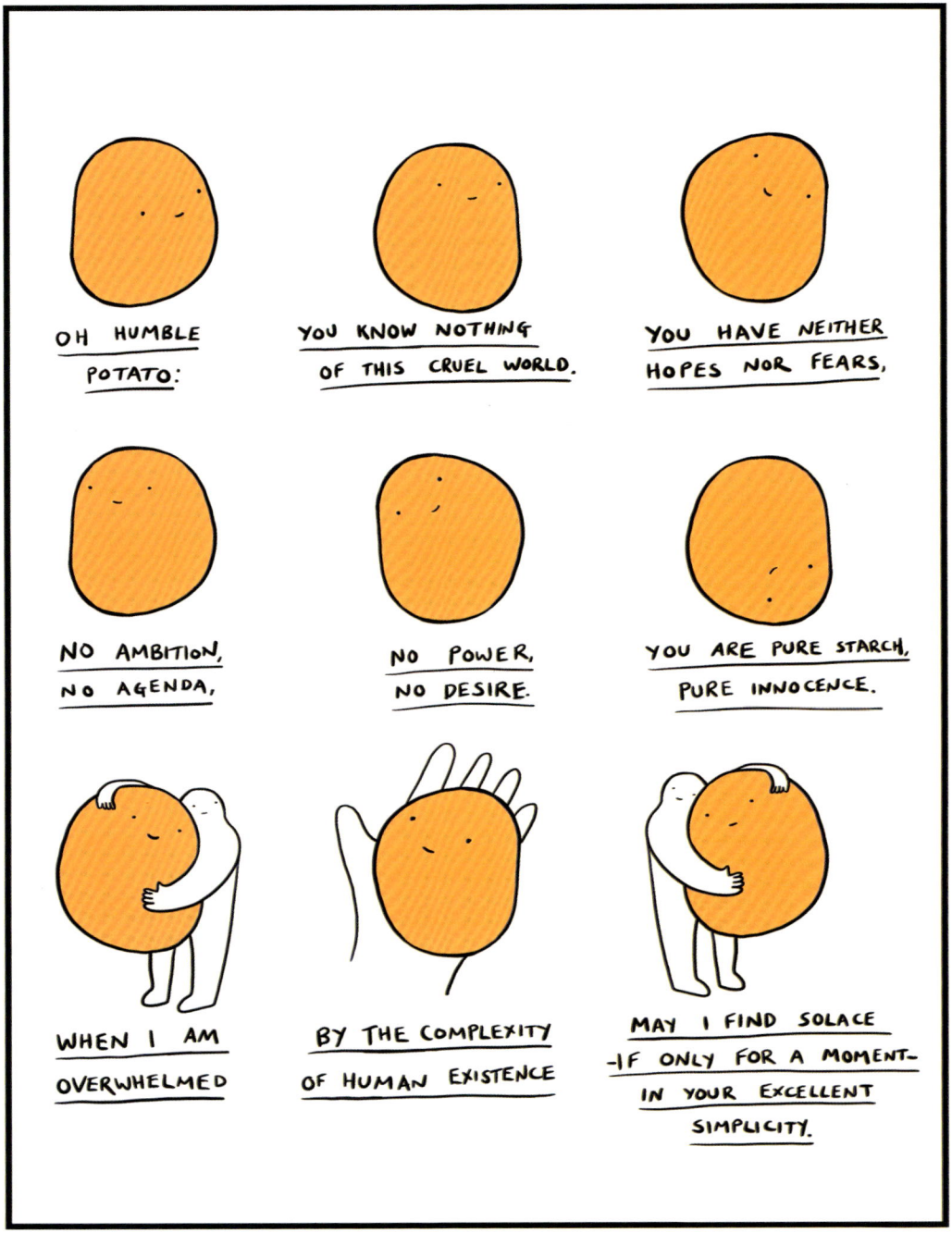

SWEET POTATO.

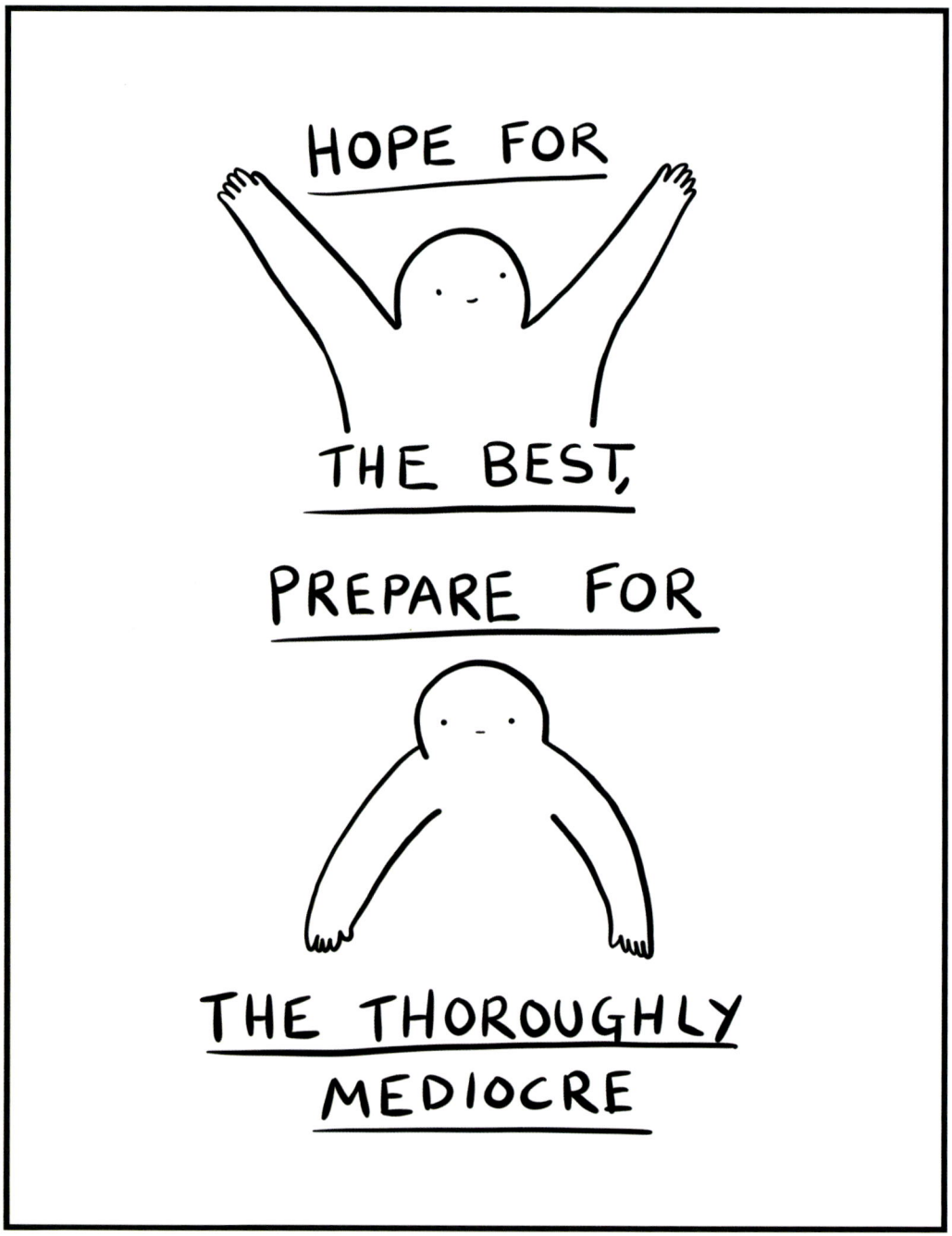

IF YOU STAY READY, YOU DON'T NEED TO GET READY.

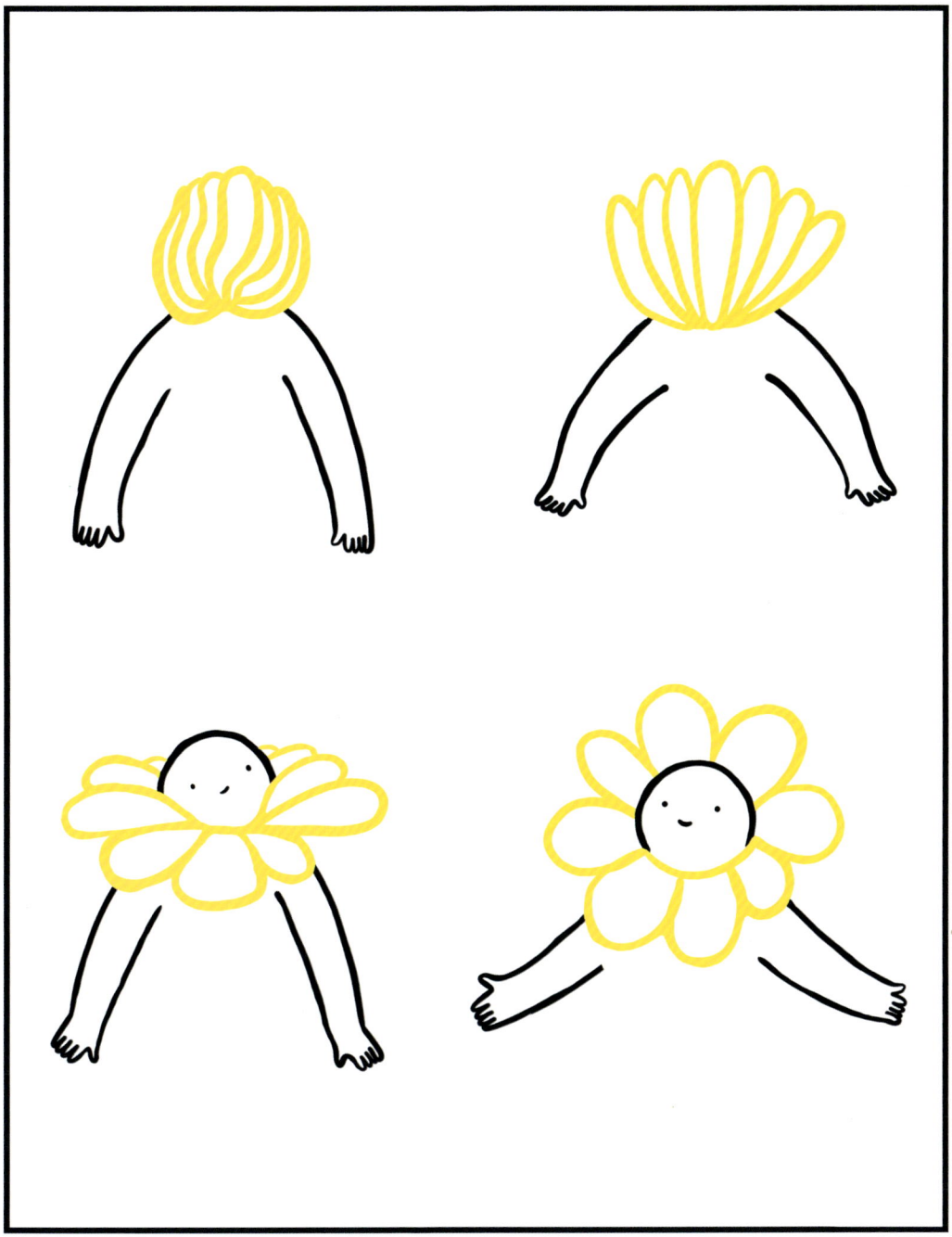

KABLOOM.

AFFIRMATIONS

I AM BRAVE

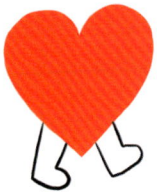

I AM LOVE

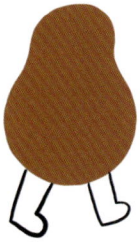

I AM POTATO

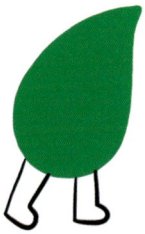

I AM GROWTH

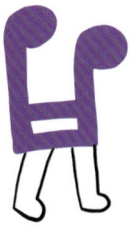

I AM GREAT SONG

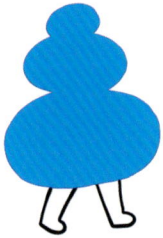

I AM SEA BREEZE

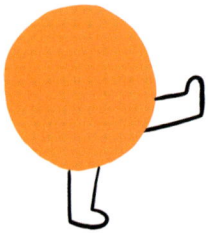

I AM HIGH KICK

I AM HOPE

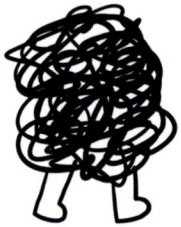

I AM BEAUTIFUL MESS

SAY IT WITH ME NOW.

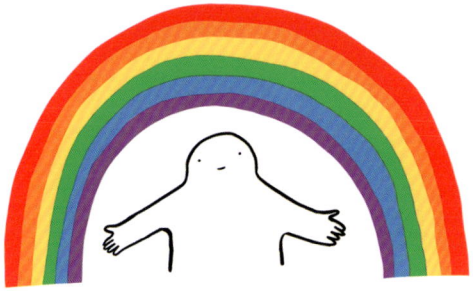

YOU ARE WELCOME

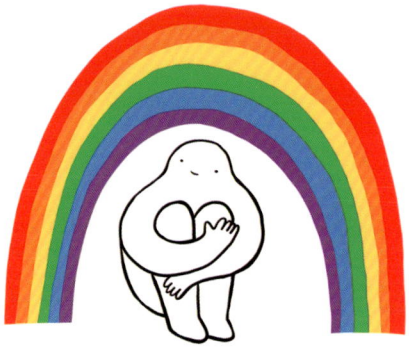

YOU ARE SAFE

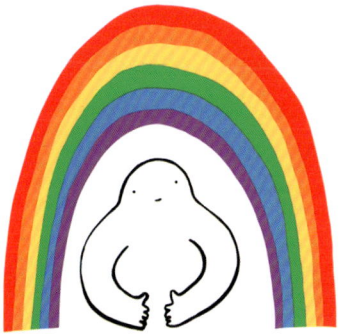

YOU MATTER

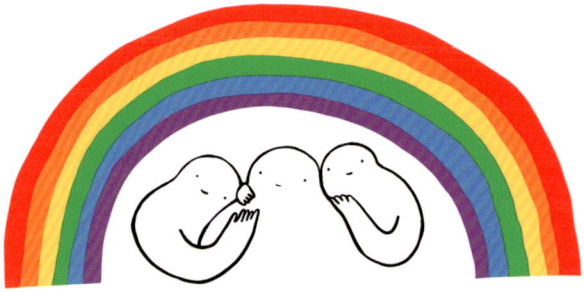

YOU BELONG

HAPPY PRIDE.

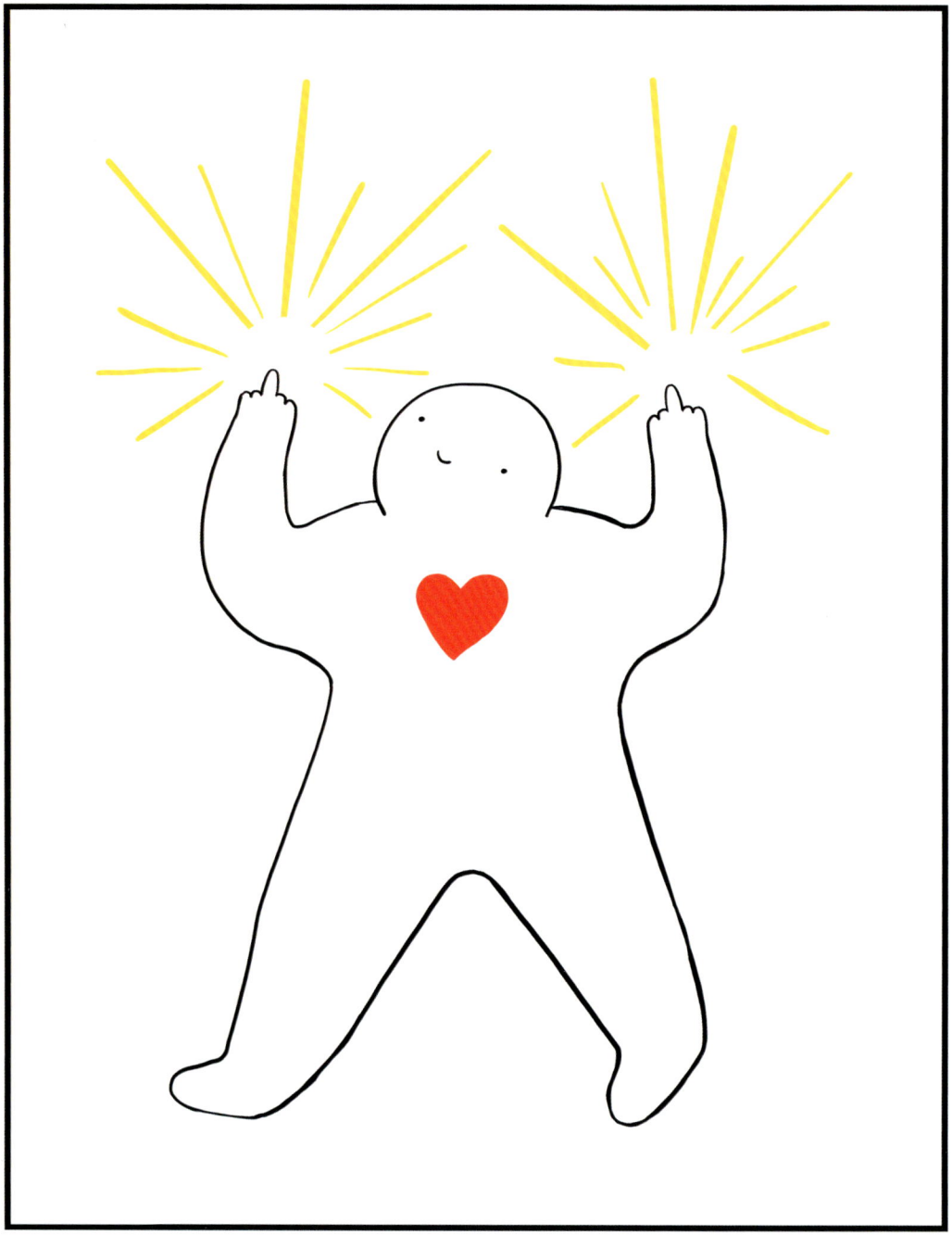

MOVING ON.

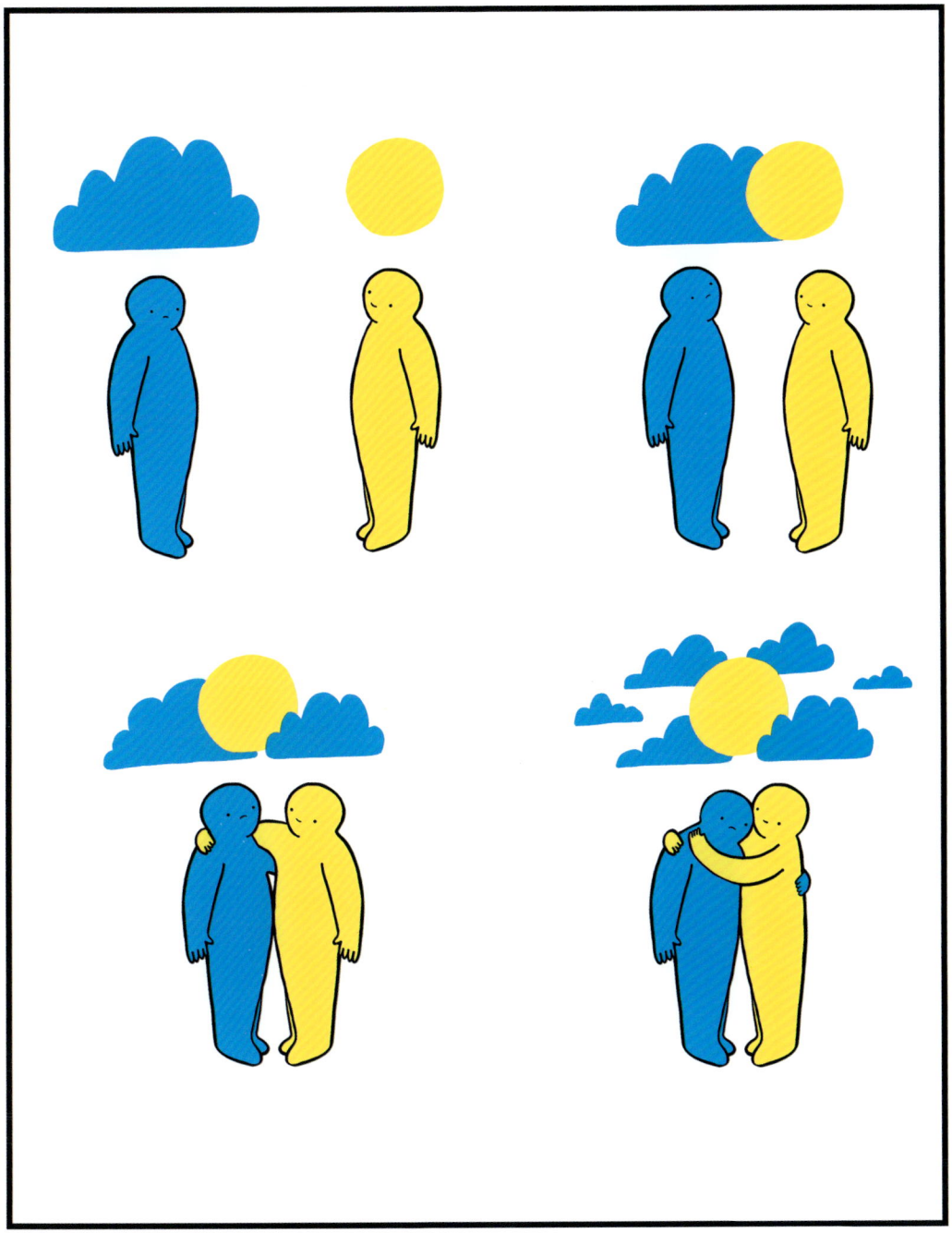

YOUR CLOUDS ARE WELCOME HERE.

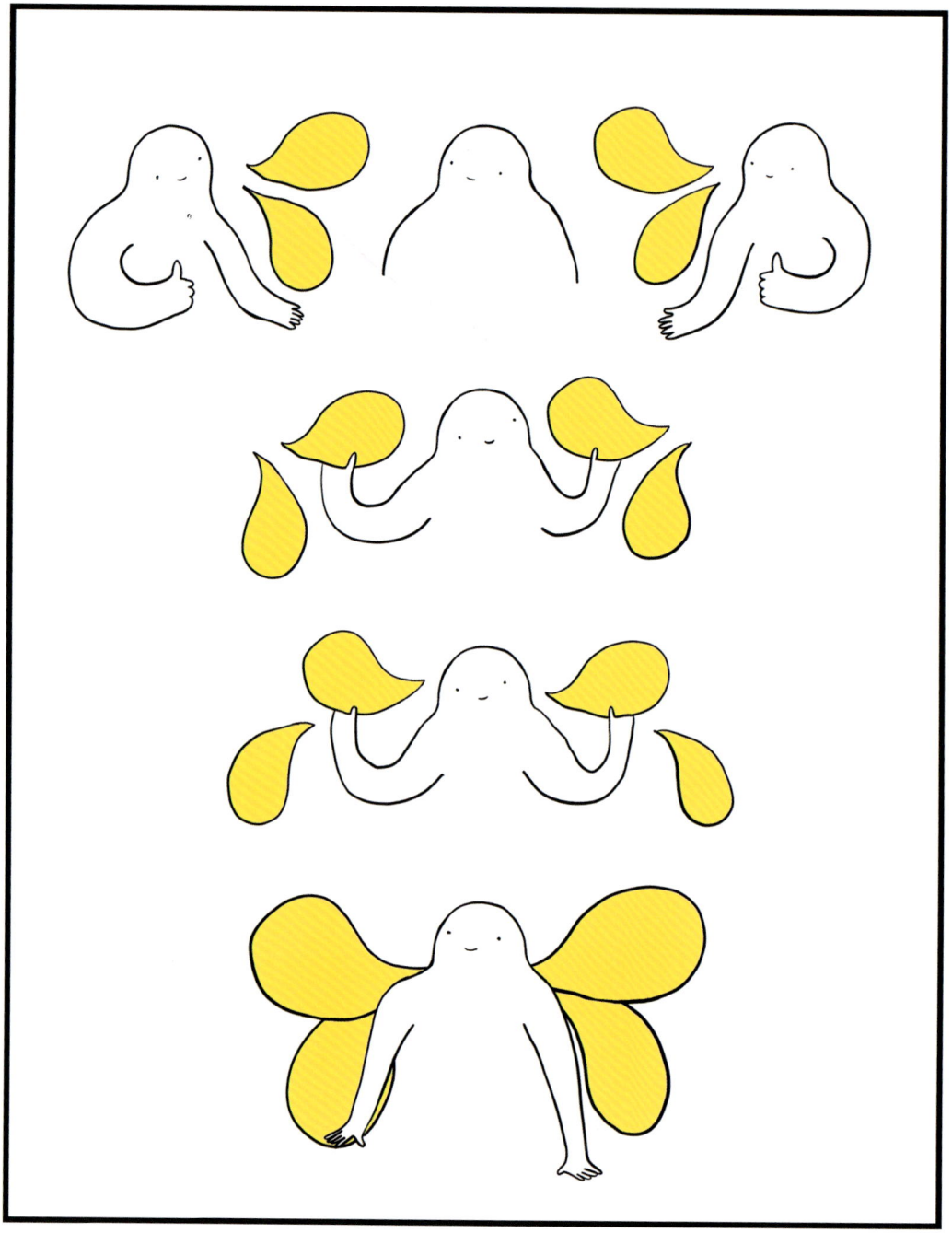

WORDS OF ENCOURAGEMENT.

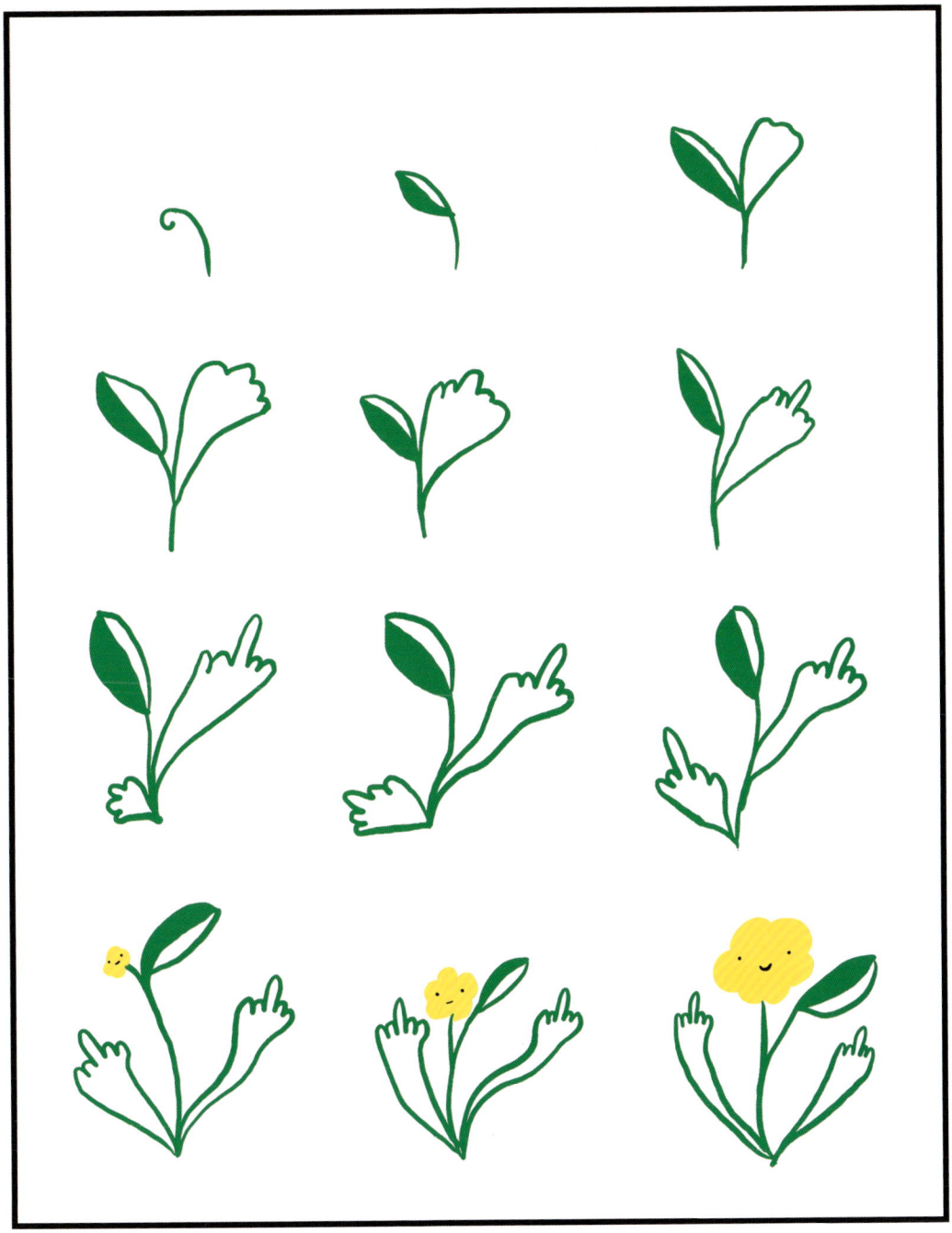

IN FULL BLOOM.

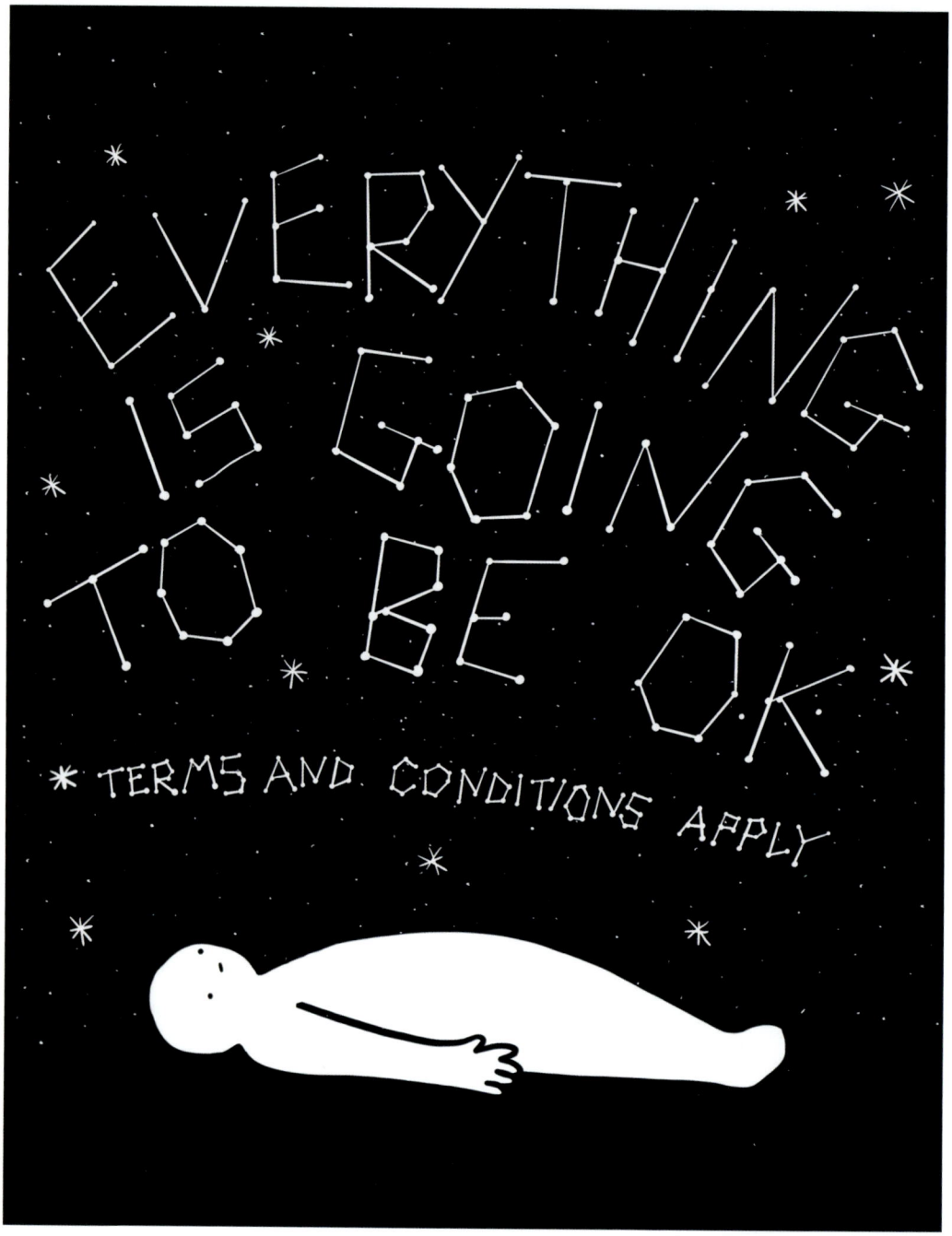

ALWAYS READ THE FINE PRINT.

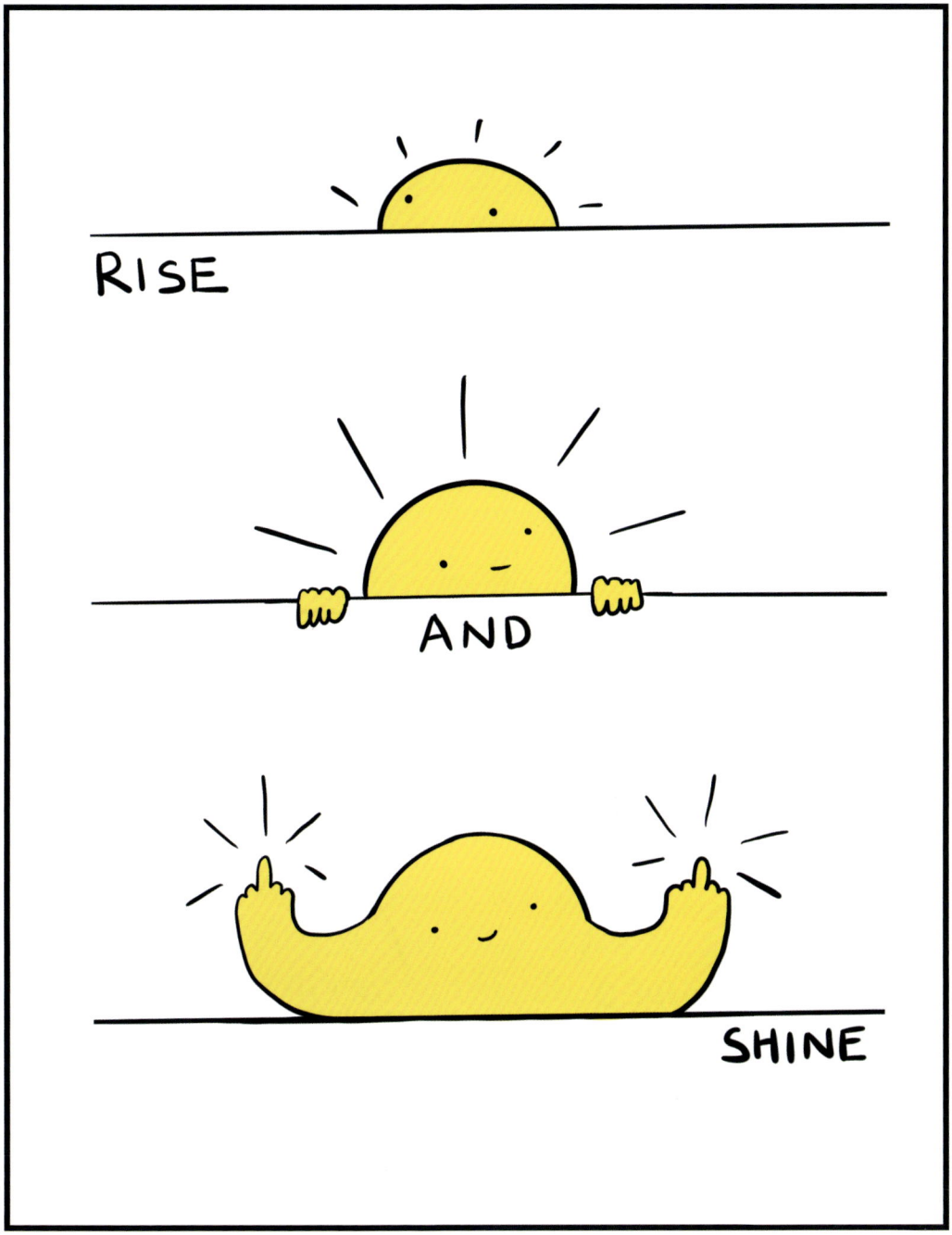

MORNING!

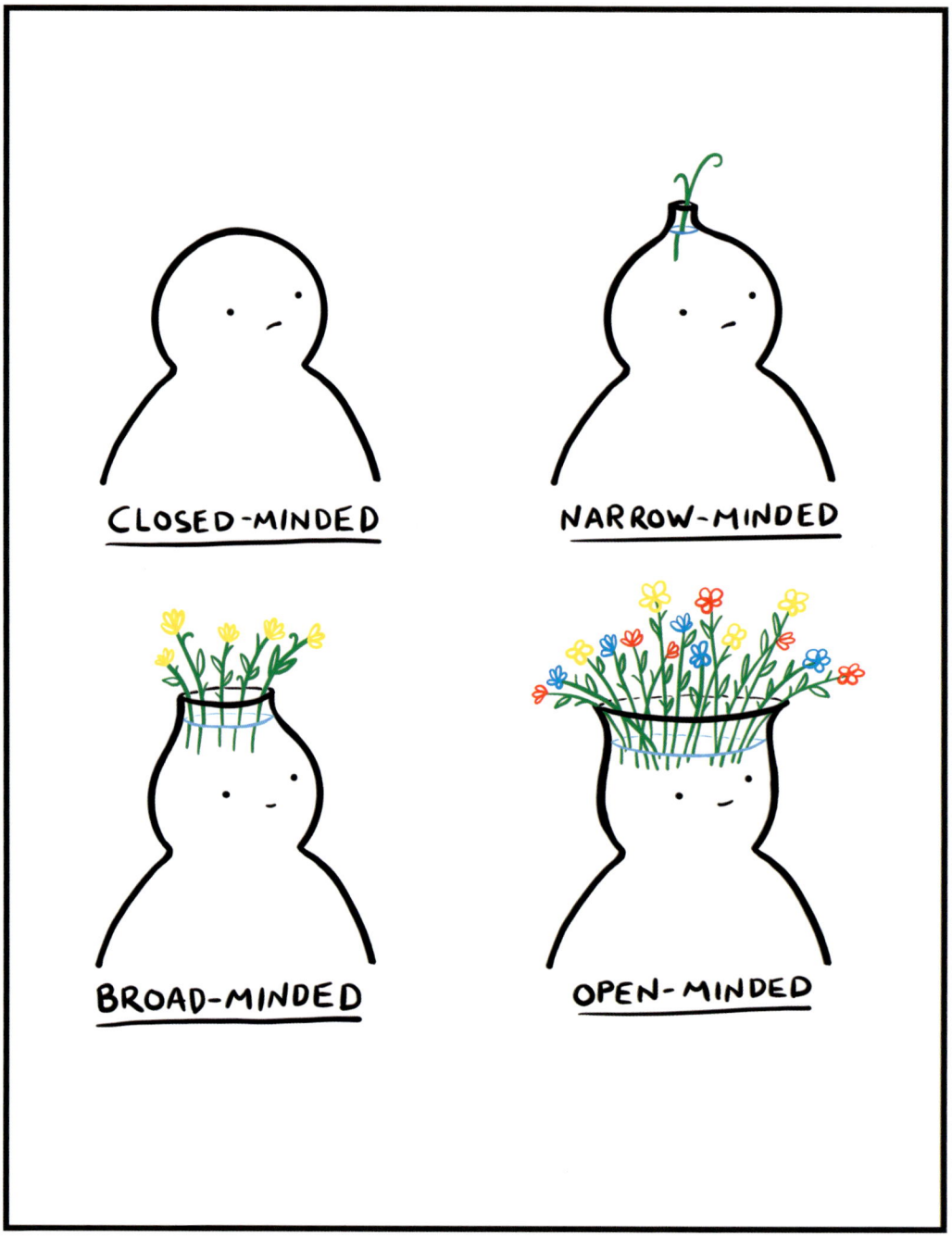

MIND FULL BLOOM.

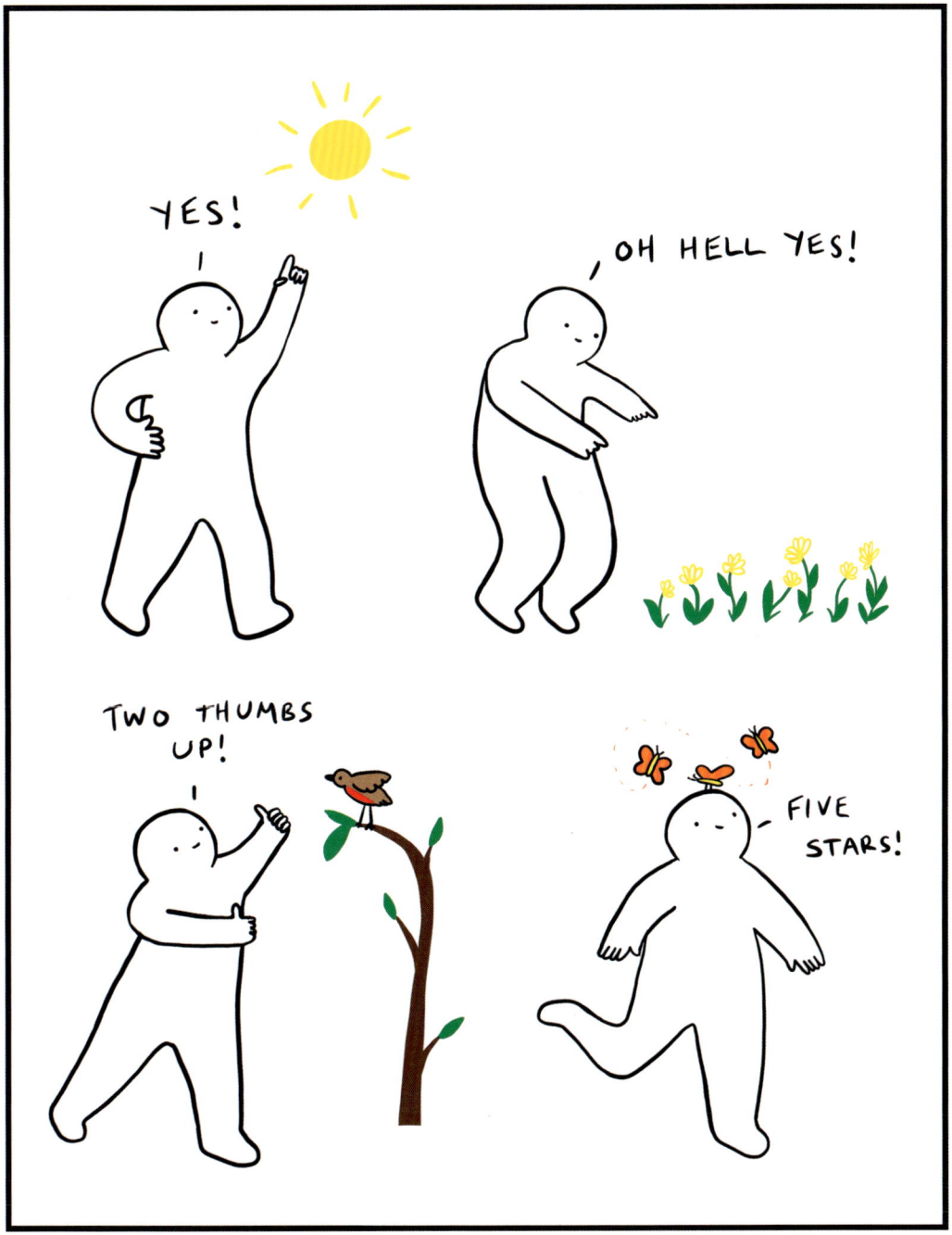

EARTH.

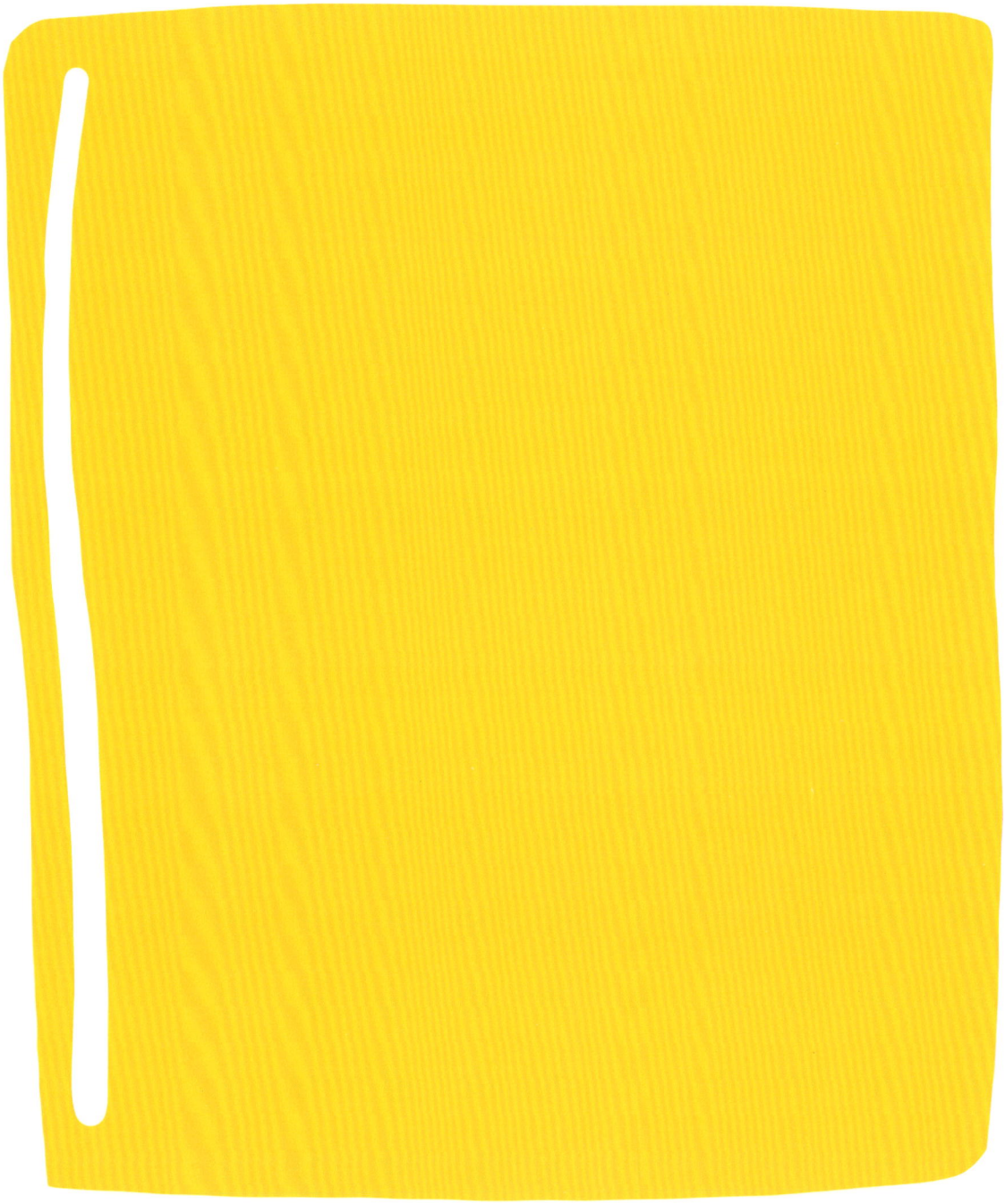

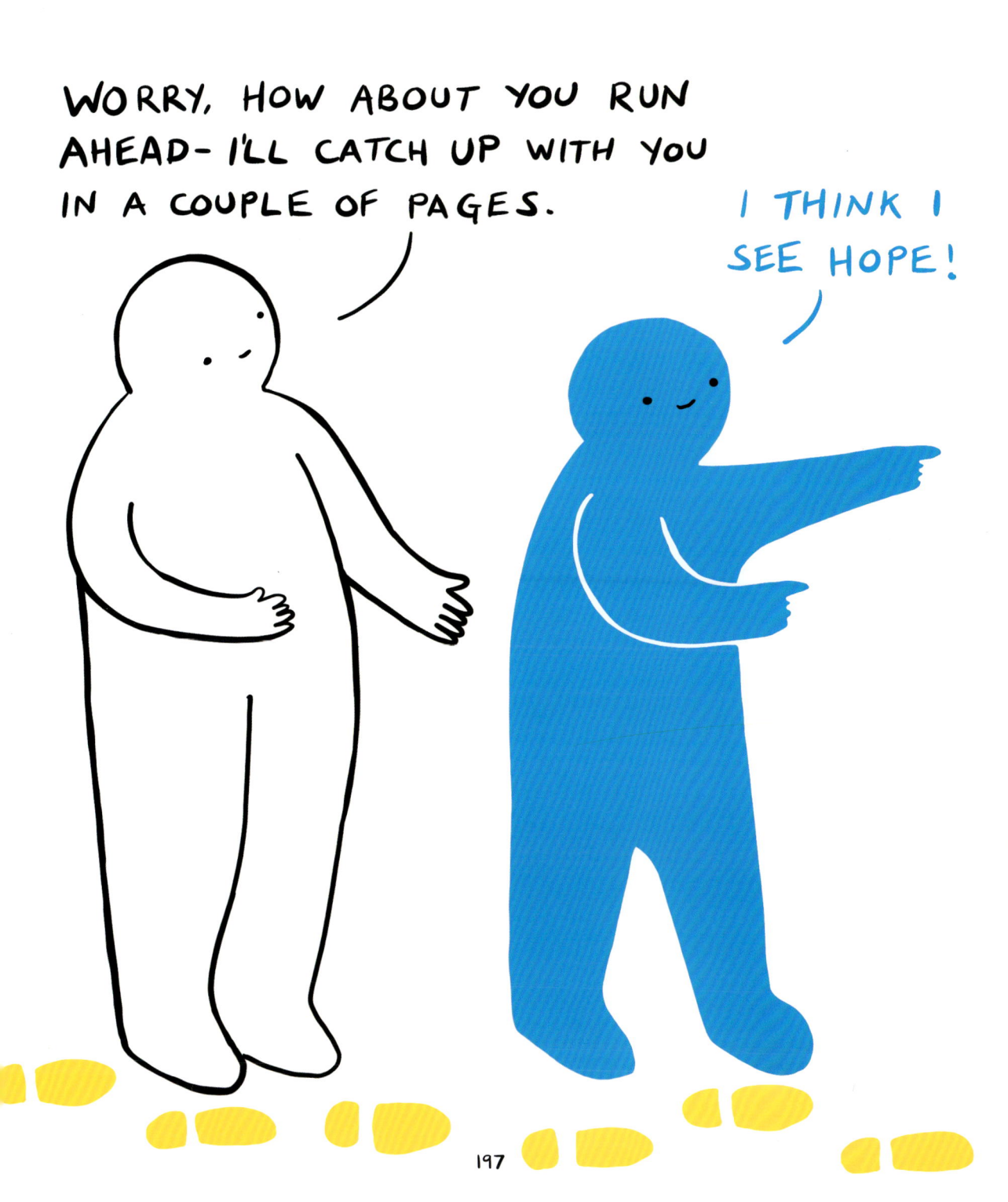
WORRY, HOW ABOUT YOU RUN AHEAD- I'LL CATCH UP WITH YOU IN A COUPLE OF PAGES.
I THINK I SEE HOPE!

READER... I HAVE TO TELL YOU SOMETHING BEFORE WE GET TO THE END OF THE BOOK. ALSO - SPOILER ALERT - THE END IS JUST OVER THERE.

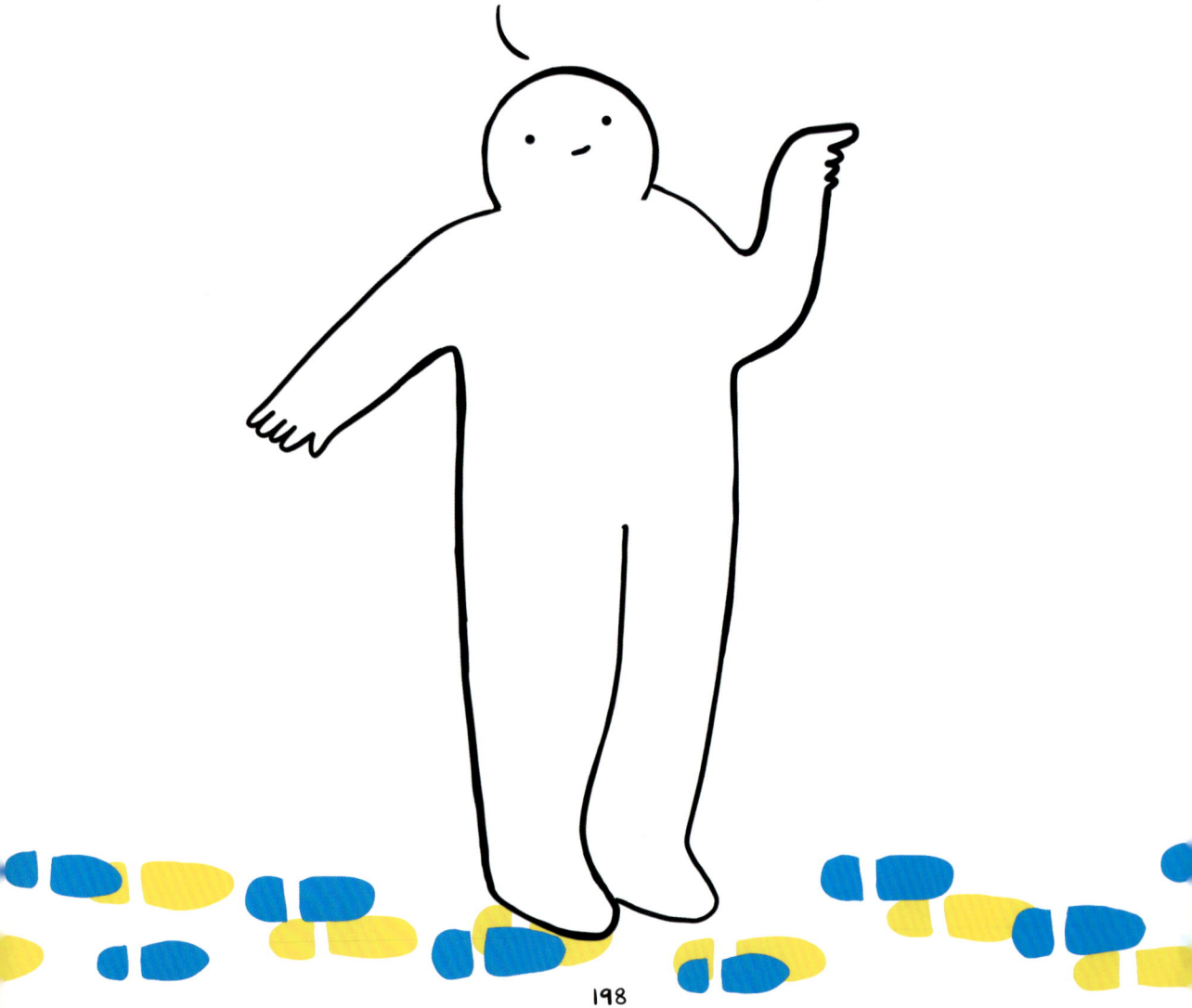

OOF. IT FEELS WEIRDLY VULNERABLE TO TALK DIRECTLY TO YOU LIKE THIS, BUT I NEED YOU TO KNOW THAT I AM HONESTLY, GENUINELY SO GLAD YOU'RE HERE, READING THIS BOOK.

AND WHEN I THINK ABOUT YOU, WELL...

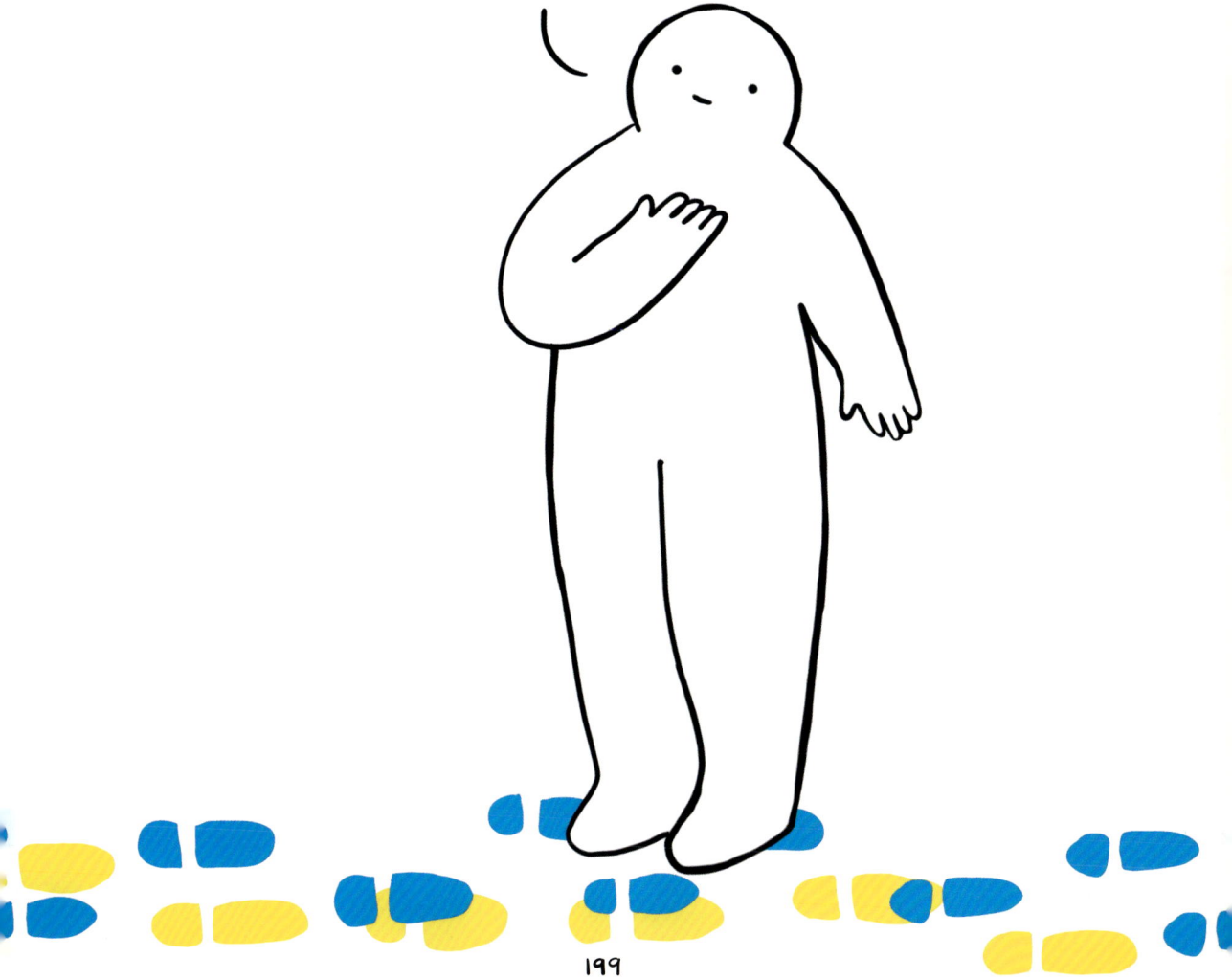

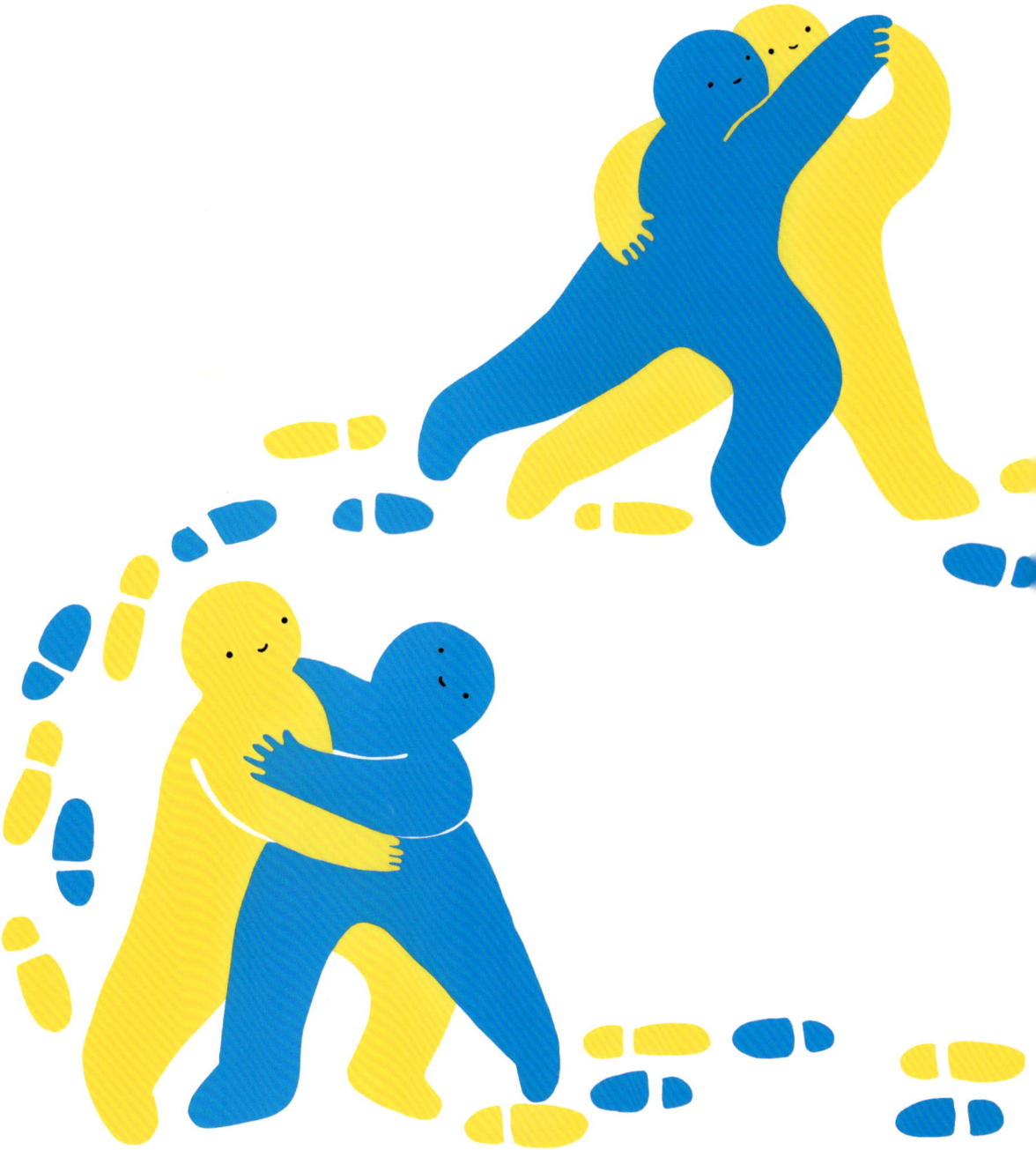

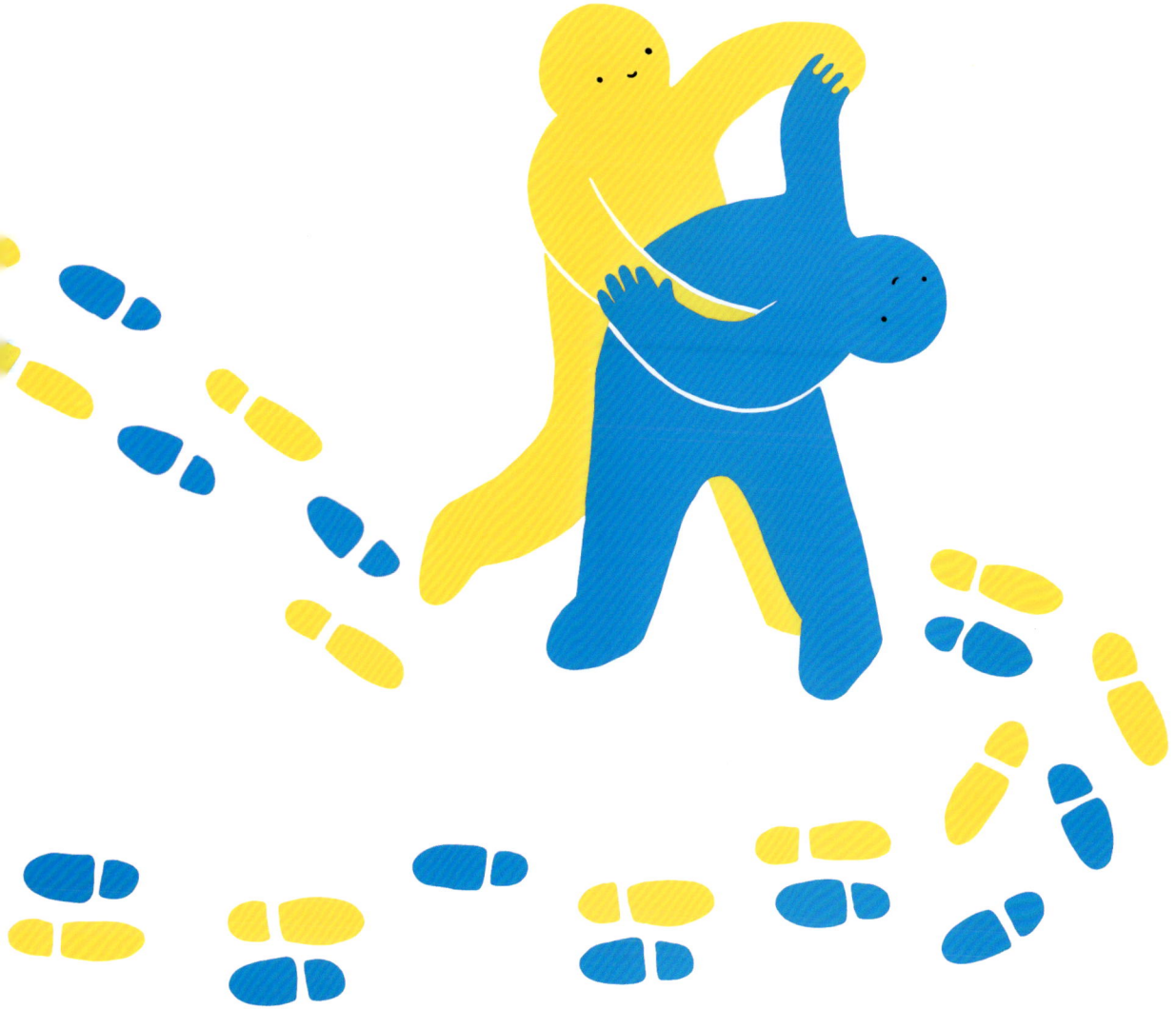

I HOPE THAT ME TALKING ABOUT MY WORRY MIGHT MAKE IT EASIER FOR YOU TO TALK ABOUT YOURS. I MEAN - IF YOU WANT TO.

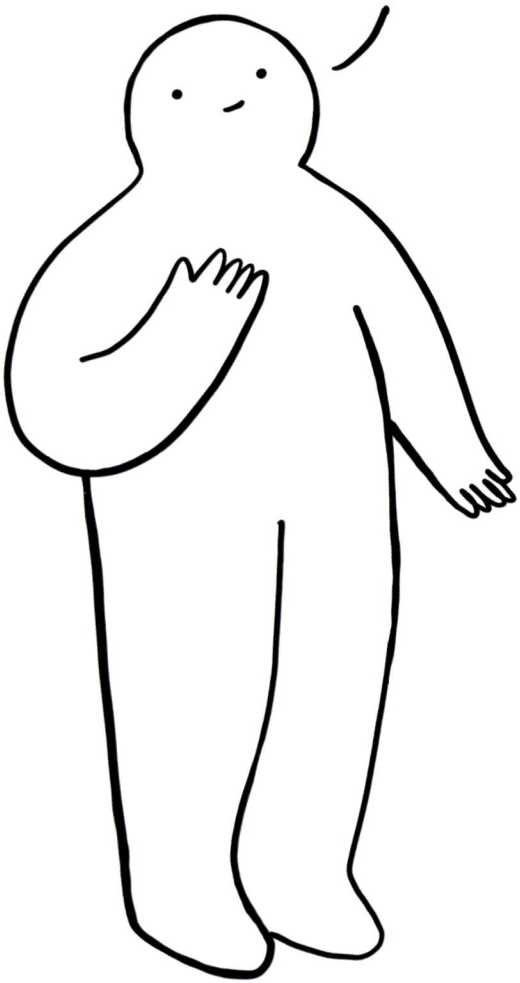

AND IF YOU, LIKE ME, EVER FEEL LIKE HOPE IS LOST, REMEMBER THAT PERHAPS IT'S JUST A FEW PAGES AHEAD.

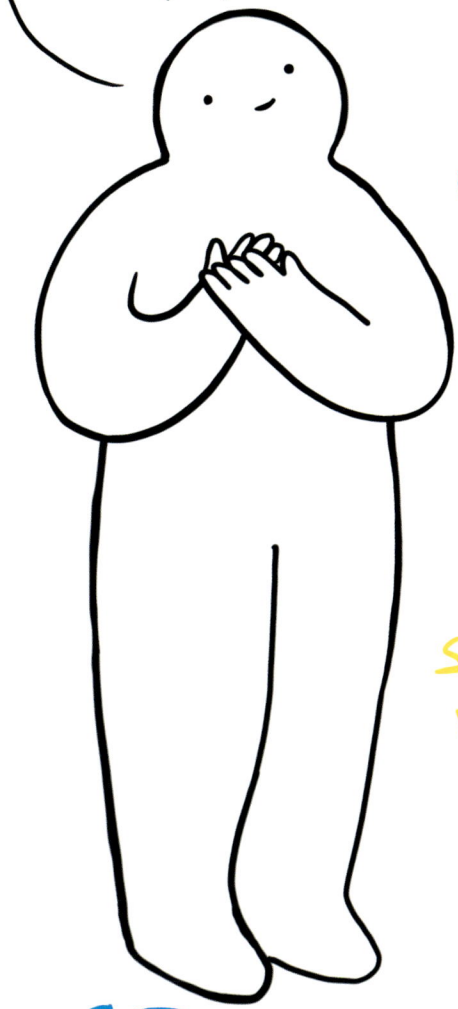

UGH, I THINK I JUST THREW UP IN MY MOUTH AGAIN.

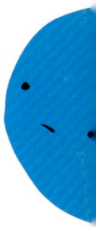

AW, SHUT UP WORRY!

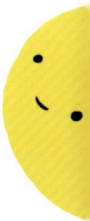

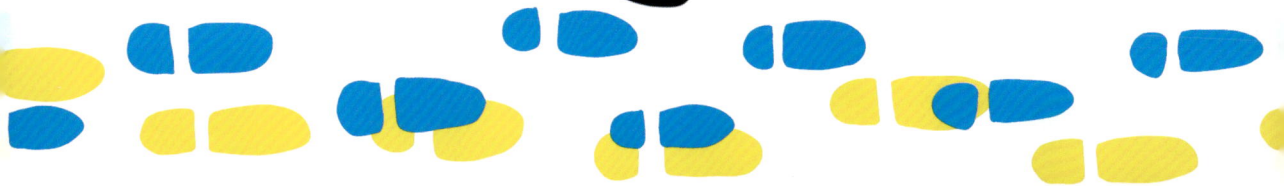

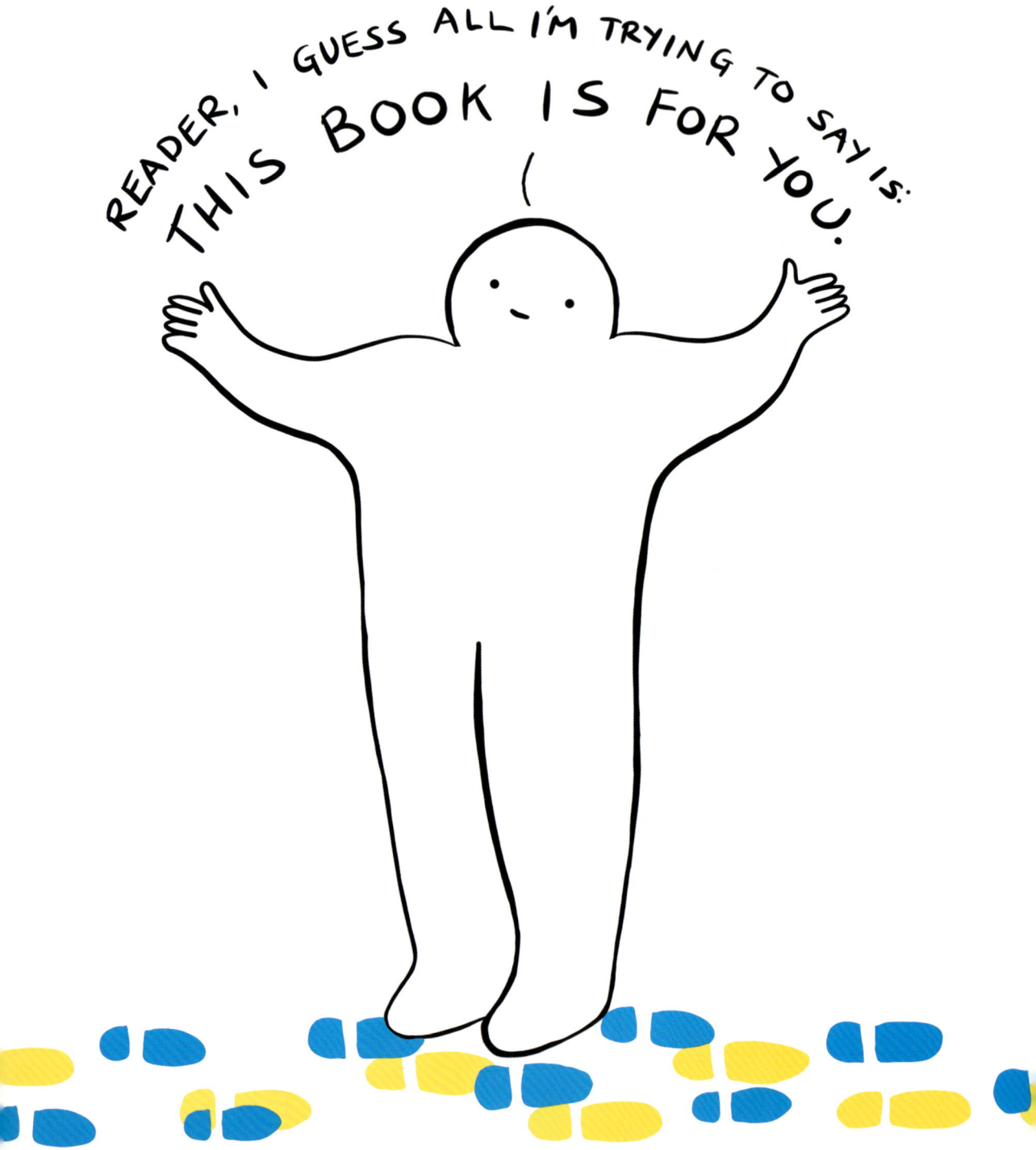
READER, I GUESS ALL I'M TRYING TO SAY IS:
THIS BOOK IS FOR YOU.

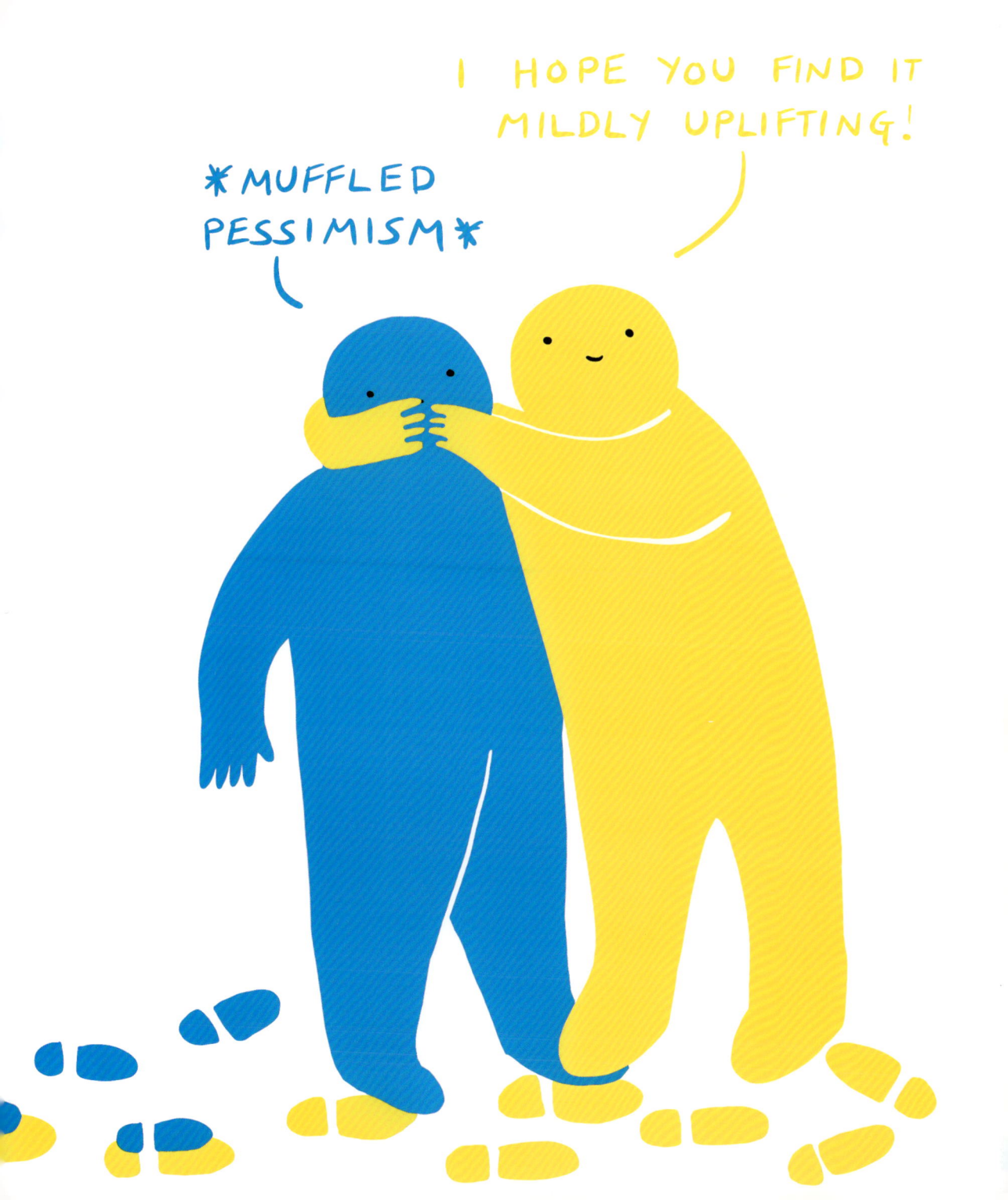
I HOPE YOU FIND IT MILDLY UPLIFTING!
MUFFLED PESSIMISM

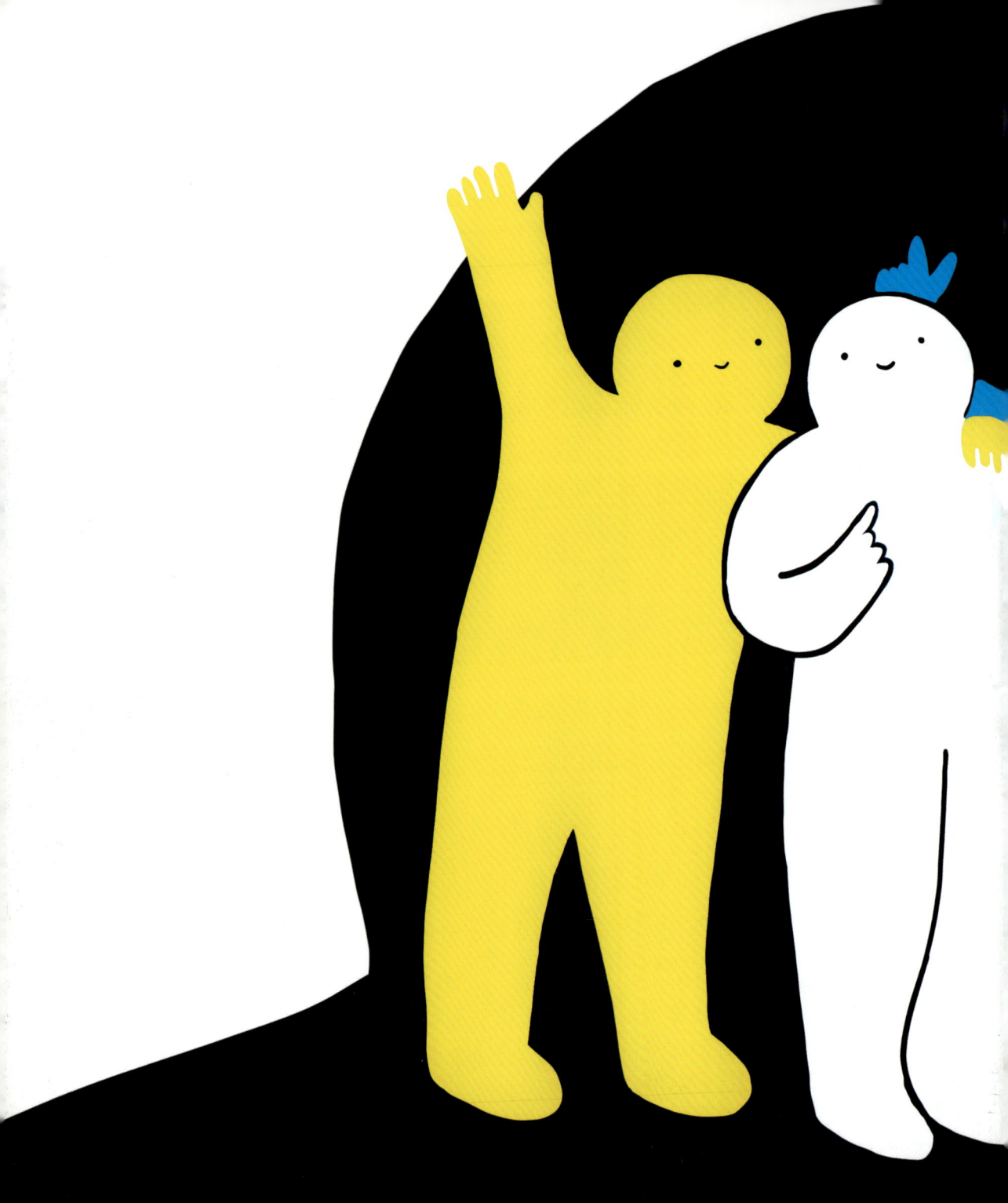

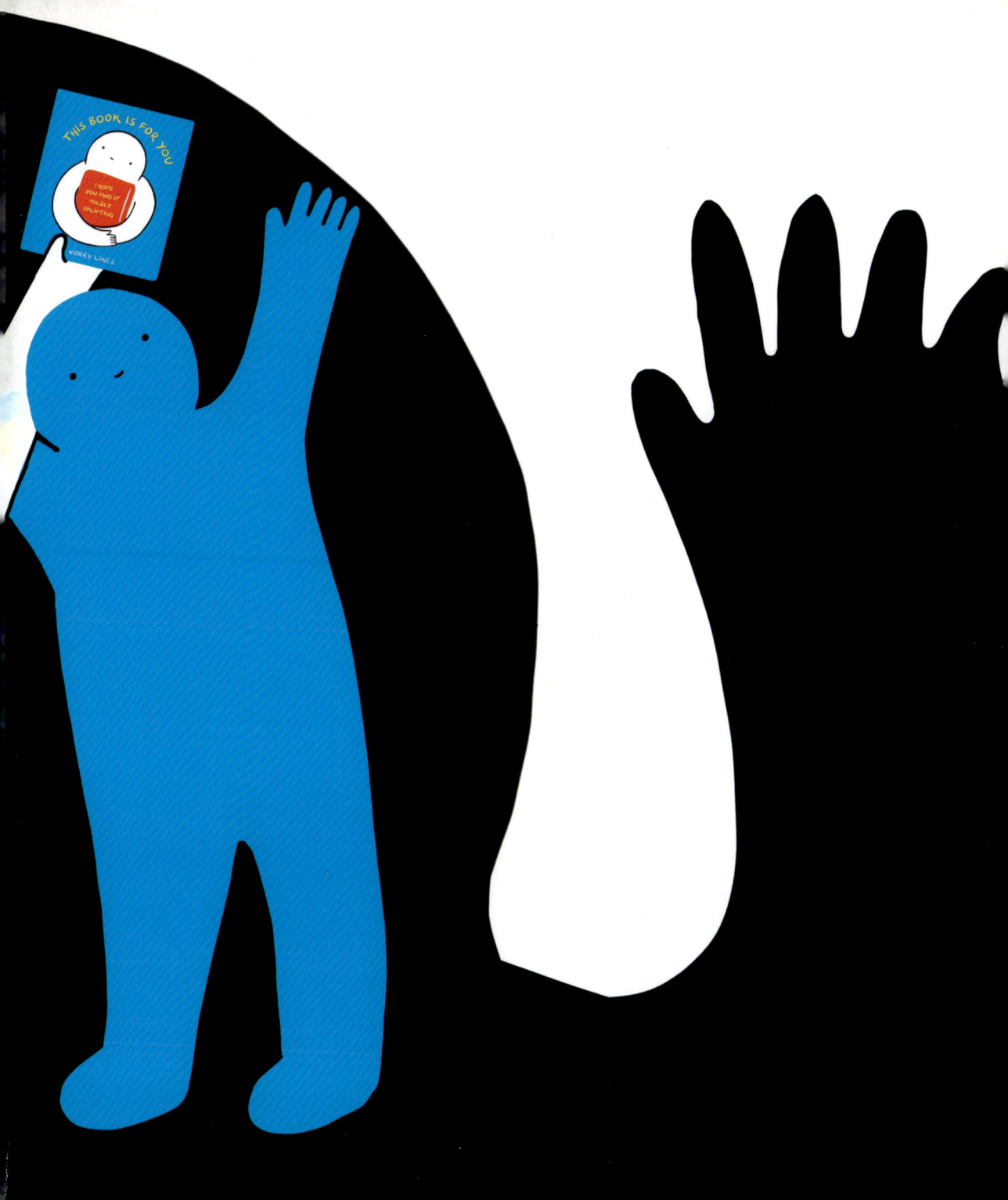
THIS BOOK IS FOR YOU
I HOPE YOU FIND IT MILDLY UPLIFTING
WORRY LINES

COPYRIGHT © 2021 BY WORRY LINES.

ALL RIGHTS RESERVED.
PUBLISHED IN THE UNITED STATES BY
TEN SPEED PRESS, AN IMPRINT OF
RANDOM HOUSE, A DIVISION OF PENGUIN
RANDOM HOUSE LLC, NEW YORK.
WWW.TENSPEED.COM

TEN SPEED PRESS AND THE TEN SPEED PRESS
COLOPHON ARE REGISTERED TRADEMARKS
OF PENGUIN RANDOM HOUSE LLC.

SOME OF THE ILLUSTRATIONS IN THIS
WORK WERE ORIGINALLY PUBLISHED
ON THE AUTHOR'S INSTAGRAM PAGE.

LIBRARY OF CONGRESS CONTROL NUMBER:
2021932480

HARDCOVER ISBN: 978-1-9848-6026-2
EBOOK ISBN: 978-1-9848-6027-9

PRINTED IN CHINA

EDITOR: SARAH MALARKEY
PRODUCTION EDITOR: KIMMY TEJASINDHU
DESIGNER/ART DIRECTOR: CHLOE RAWLINS
PRODUCTION MANAGER: DAN MYERS
COPYEDITOR: CAROL BURRELL
PROOFREADER: KAREN LEVY
PUBLICIST: LAUREN KRETZSCHMAR
MARKETERS: DANIEL WIKEY, MONICA STANTON
AUTHOR'S AGENT: KATE WOODROW

10 9 8 7 6 5 4 3 2 1

FIRST EDITION

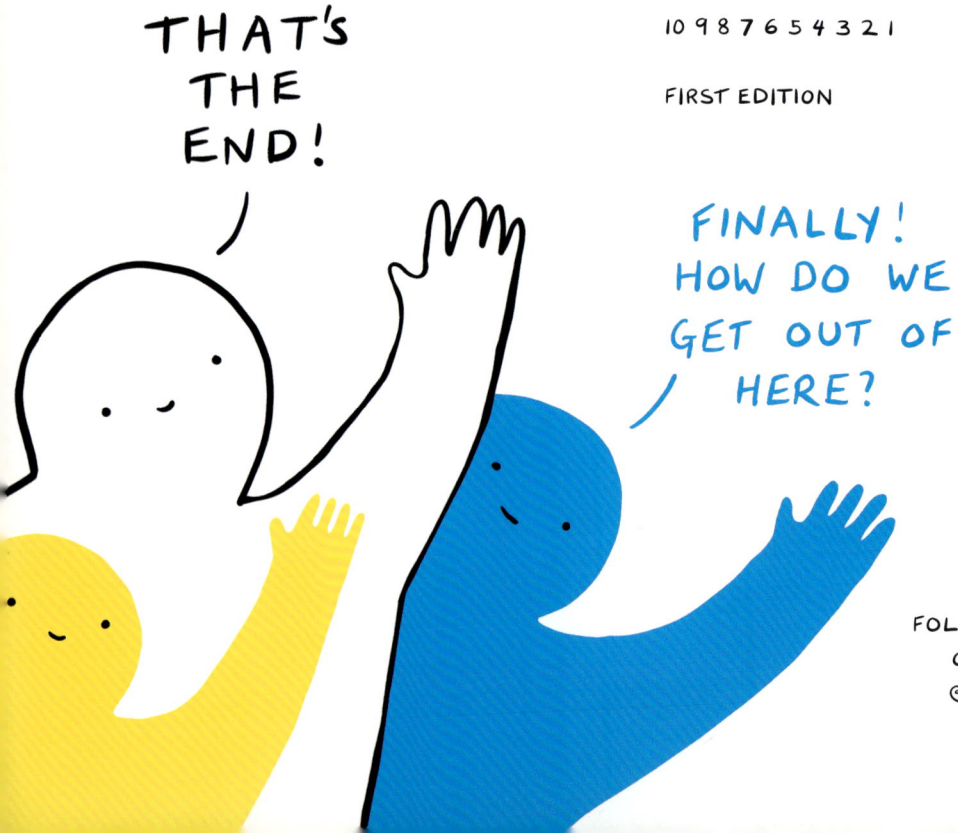

FOLLOW WORRY LINES
ON INSTAGRAM:
@WORRY__LINES

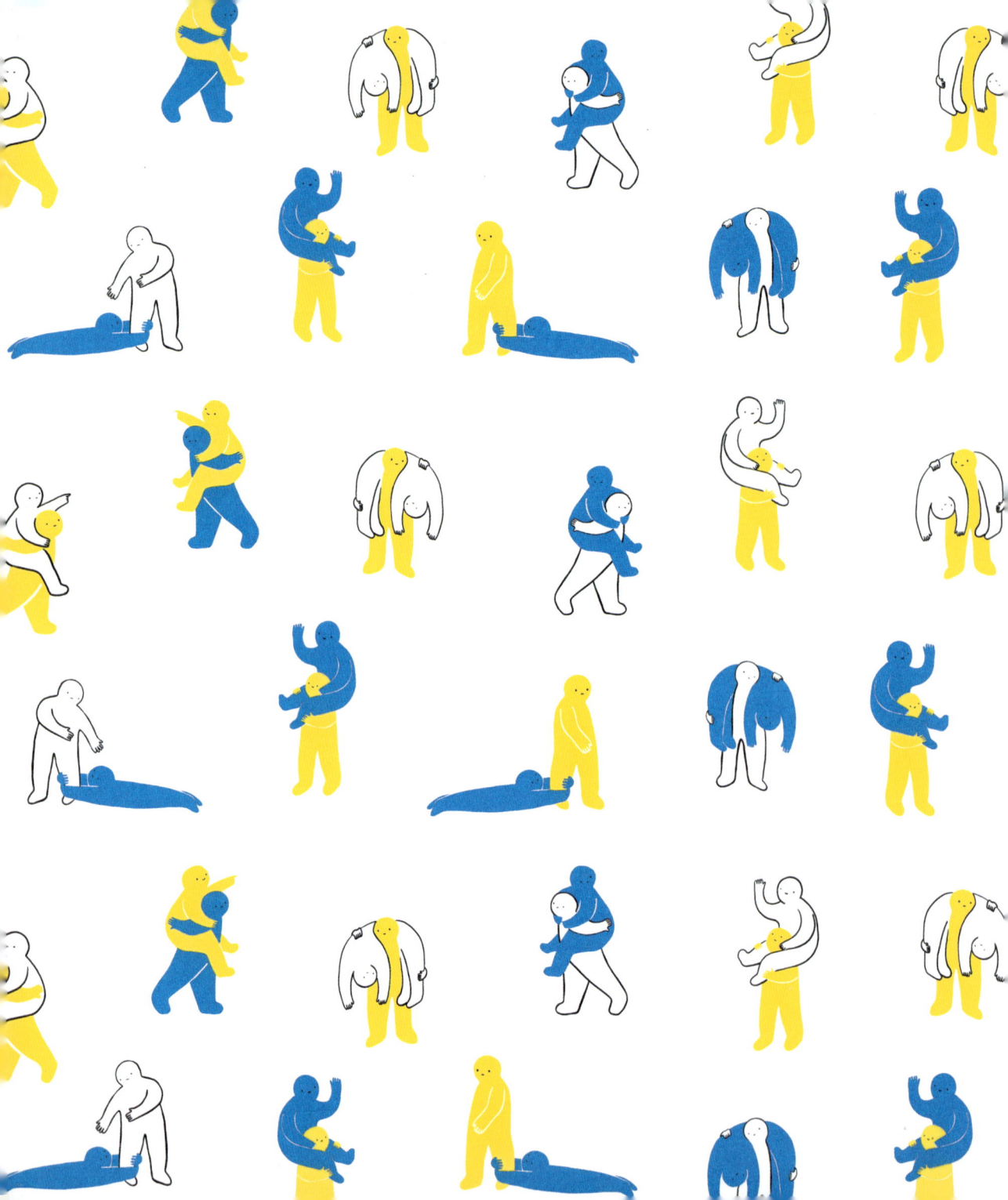